UNSETTLING UTOPIA

*Columbia Studies in International and Global History*

COLUMBIA STUDIES IN INTERNATIONAL AND GLOBAL HISTORY
*Cemil Aydin, Timothy Nunan, and Dominic Sachsenmaier, Series Editors*

This series presents some of the finest and most innovative work coming out of the current landscapes of international and global historical scholarship. Grounded in empirical research, these titles transcend the usual area boundaries and address how history can help us understand contemporary problems, including poverty, inequality, power, political violence, and accountability beyond the nation-state. The series covers processes of flows, exchanges, and entanglements—and moments of blockage, friction, and fracture—not only between "the West" and "the Rest" but also among parts of what has variously been dubbed the "Third World" or the "Global South." Scholarship in international and global history remains indispensable for a better sense of current complex regional and global economic transformations. Such approaches are vital in understanding the making of our present world.

For a complete list of titles, see page 303.

# Unsettling Utopia

THE MAKING AND UNMAKING
OF FRENCH INDIA

Jessica Namakkal

Columbia University Press
*New York*

Columbia University Press
*Publishers Since 1893*
New York   Chichester, West Sussex
cup.columbia.edu
Copyright © 2021 Columbia University Press
All rights reserved

Library of Congress Cataloging-in-Publication Data
Names: Namakkal, Jessica, author.
Title: Unsettling utopia : the making and unmaking of French India / Jessica Namakkal.
Description: New York : Columbia University Press, 2021. | Series: Columbia studies in international and global history | Includes bibliographical references and index.
Identifiers: LCCN 2020049323 (print) | LCCN 2020049324 (ebook) | ISBN 9780231197687 (hardback) | ISBN 9780231197694 (trade paperback) | ISBN 9780231552295 (ebook)
Subjects: LCSH: French India—History. | French India—Politics and government. | Decolonization—India—History. | Utopias—India—History. | India—Foreign relations—France. | France—Foreign relations—India.
Classification: LCC DS485.P66 N36 2021 (print) | LCC DS485.P66 (ebook) | DDC 954.02/9—dc23
LC record available at https://lccn.loc.gov/2020049323
LC ebook record available at https://lccn.loc.gov/2020049324

Cover image: A French-Indian police officer stands at the border between French India and India, demarcated by a line of rocks, 1953. FR ANOM. Aix-en-Provence (COL 1AFF-POL 2273) – All Rights Reserved
Cover design: Chang Jae Lee

*To my parents*

# Contents

Acknowledgments ix
Chronology xv

INTRODUCTION: ON MINOR BORDERS AND COLONIAL TIME    1

PART I  Making

1  Carceral Borders: Exile, Surveillance, and Subversion   33

2  The Future of French India: Decolonization and Settlement at the Borders   67

3  Making the Postcolonial Subject: Goondas, Refugees, and Citizens   108

PART II  Unmaking

4  Decolonial Crossings: Settlers, Migrants, Tourists   141

5  From the Ashram to Auroville: Utopia as Settlement   173

CONCLUSION: THE MESSINESS OF COLONIALISM   201

Appendix 209
Notes 223
Bibliography 265
Index 287

# Acknowledgments

I am grateful to all my teachers both within and outside of classrooms. I went to the University of Southern California to become a *very serious* filmmaker, but ended up pivoting to history after taking classes with Paul Lerner my first semester. I am glad to have the chance now to publicly thank him for his support over the years. At the University of Minnesota, I had the great pleasure to work under the guidance of Patricia M. E. Lorcin, who is not only a phenomenal historian, writer, and painter, but also a true mentor and friend who modeled what an outstanding dissertation advisor should be like. I also benefited tremendously from studying with Jigna Desai, Donna Gabaccia, Mary Jo Maynes, and Ajay Skaria, all of whom comprised a truly enviable dissertation committee. At the University of Minnesota, I was also lucky to study alongside an impressive cohort of cross-disciplinary scholars, many of whom helped me in the initial formation of this project. Thanks to Justin Biel, Emily Bruce, Fernando Calderón, Charmaine Chua, Jesse Fields, Nick Fox, George Hoagland, Mark Hoffman, Melanie Huska, Elliot James, Isaac Kamola, Garrett Karrberg, Matt Konieczny, Christine Manganaro, Christopher Moore, Nichole Neuman, Kevin Riordan, Emily Rook-Koepsel, Eric Roubinek, Tiffany Vann Sprecher, Elizabeth Venditto, Elizabeth Williams, and Ann Zimo for asking great questions, making connections across disciplines, times, and spaces, and being supportive comrades.

Although I did not have the chance to work with him while I was a graduate student, Kevin Murphy has greatly expanded my intellectual and political horizons by introducing me to radical public history and inviting me to join the *Radical History Review* editorial collective. My work is better because of the relationships developed and deepened through our collective work on the *RHR*. Special thanks to Steve Fabian, Monica Kim, Marissa Moorman, A. Naomi Paik, Jason Ruiz, Sandhya Shukla, and Evan Taparata, along with the entire *RHR* team, for doing the work to make radical history visible and accessible both within the academy and broader audiences.

At Duke University I have had the great fortune of working alongside, and learning from, many wonderful and generous colleagues. Sumathi Ramaswamy has been an untiring role model, mentor, and friend. I thank both her and Rich Freeman for their gracious hospitality, intellectual engagement, and all-around good humor. The esteemed feminist scholar Frances Hasso is largely responsible for me coming to Duke, and I am incredibly grateful to her for this, as well as her continued mentorship, intellectual engagement, and support. Leo Ching is a brilliant, patient, and kind mentor and colleague. Without his encouragement and support this book may never have made it off my desk. Harris Solomon, my favorite academic auntie, has read parts of this book multiple times, and I thank him for his generous feedback and his ability to respond to frantic text messages with the appropriate Bollywood gif. I am very grateful to have had the opportunity to share work and learn from so many other colleagues at both Duke and the University of North Carolina, including Nicole Barnes, Maya Berry, Emily Burrill, James Chappel, Eileen Chow, Samuel Fury Childs Daly, Mark Driscoll, Prasenjit Duara, Michael Hardt, Nayoung Aimee Kwon, Ralph Litzinger, Wahneema Lubiano, Anne-Marie Makhulu, John Mathew, Ellen McClarney, Diane Nelson, Jocelyn Olcott, Giulia Riccò, Carlos Rojas, Gabriel Rosenberg, Tamar Shirinian, Phil Stern, Aarthi Vadde, Priscilla Wald, Kena Wani, Kathi Weeks, and Matt Whitt. Ben Trott, Marisol LeBrón, Monica Huerta, Ashley Farmer, and Jenny Kelly all spent time in Durham on their way to other nodes in the academic diaspora and have been bedrocks of support even from afar, always willing to give feedback at a moment's notice or help out with teaching, writing, and eating nachos.

The number of people doing work on French India is small, yet powerful! I am especially lucky to have the intellectual companionship of Danna Agmon, Jyoti Mohan, Blake Smith, and Akhila Yechury. Kate Marsh, who passed away in 2019, was a true visionary in working to expand scholarship on connections between France and India. I had the privilege of meeting with her in Paris while I was conducting research and have been both inspired and motivated by her brilliant work and generous spirit. Her passing is a tremendous loss to all those working in and on French India.

I am grateful to the Pondichérian novelist Ari Gautier for taking an interest in my work, and for sharing pictures and stories about Pondicherry with me. Likewise, the documentarian Pankaj Kumar has been making truly fascinating films on French India that is bringing attention to the history of this understudied region. I owe many thanks to people in Puducherry and in Auroville for sharing documents, stories, and hospitality while I pursued this project. Krishna Tewari, who was at the time of my research the director of the Auroville Archives, allowed me complete access to the archives, a gesture that was both kind and generous. Kripa Borg at the Sharnga Guest House in Auroville also shared her experiences and personal ephemera with me. I am grateful for the friendship of Kannan Dasan and Iyyappan Jayamurthy, who helped me navigate Auroville and understand its place in and out of local economies and cultures. In Puducherry, Sivakumar Elambooranan shared his perspective as a native Pondichérian who has become a follower of Integral Yoga in recent years. Douglas Gressieux at the Association les Comptoirs de l'Inde in Paris graciously shared his personal stories and documents with me while I was doing research in France. I also thank the archivists and workers at the Institut Français de Pondichéry, the Puducherry State Archives, the Centre de Archives diplomatique du ministère de Affaires étrangères in la Courneuve, the Archives nationales d'outre-mer in Aix-en-Provence, the Archives nationales in Paris, the Bibliothèque nationale de France, and the British Library in London.

One of the most exciting developments I have witnessed and participated in over the course of this project has been the expansion of work in what I will unofficially call global South Asian studies, a space that I have found both exciting and welcoming to new approaches to studying the place of South Asia in the world. Thanks to Jesús Cháirez-Garza, Swati Chala, Mabel Gergan, Sneha Krishnan, Durba Mitra, Kalyani Ramnath, Malini Ranganathan, Sara Smith, Saiba Varma, Pavithra Vasudevan, and Lydia Walker for initiating so many of these necessary conversations and for inviting me to the table.

Although this is a technically a solo-authored book, many people have helped me get it into shape through close reading, editing, transcribing, translating, and offering feedback and comments on various parts. I thank my editor at Columbia University Press, Caelyn Cobb, along with Monique Briones and Emily Shelton for their support of this project, and for all the work they did to get it published, especially in the midst of a global pandemic. Thanks as well to the two anonymous reviewers for providing generous, thoughtful, and incisive feedback on the manuscript, which has made the book immeasurably better. Cemil Ayden has been supportive of this work since we first met and is responsible for bringing the book to Columbia. He has read drafts, provided feedback, and made space for me to present this work in various venues. I am deeply indebted to him for his support and encouragement. I am also grateful to the Franklin Humanities Institute at Duke University, in particular Deborah Jensen, Ranjana Khanna, and Sarah Rogers, for all the work put into the inclusion of my manuscript in the Faculty Book Manuscript Workshop Program in 2017. Maia Ramnath and Todd Sheperd graciously served as outside commentators, and I thank them for all their sharp critiques and suggestions for revisions. Parts of chapters 3 and 5 have appeared in earlier forms in *Interventions: International Journal of Postcolonial Studies* and the *Journal for the Study of Radicalism*. I thank the anonymous reviewers and editors of these journals for feedback and support.

Parts of this book have been presented at numerous workshops and conferences, but special thanks are due to Yesenia Barragan for the invitation to speak about the book at Dartmouth as I was completing the manuscript, an experience that helped me cross the finish line, so to speak. Thanks also to the participants of the "Connected Histories: Decolonization in the 20th Century" workshop at Yale University, the "Archives Matter: Queer, Feminist, Decolonial Encounters" workshop at Goldsmiths' Centre for Feminist Research, the Carolina Seminar on Global and Transnational History, Pondicherry University (especially the Department of History), and the "Toward a Non-Eurocentric Academia: Border Thinking and Decoloniality" workshop (especially Sandeep Bakshi, Israel Durham, Amal Eqeiq, Julianne Hammer, Anastasia Karklina, Priscilla Layne, Caleb Moreno, and Imani Wadud) for engaging with the work and providing energizing feedback as well as radical friendship. Thanks also to the American Institute for Indian Studies, especially Mytheli Sreenivas and Geraldine Forbes, for providing feedback on an early iteration of this book through the American Institute of Indian Studies Dissertation to Book workshop at the South Asian Studies conference. Many thanks are due to Patricia Bass and Clare Doyle, who assisted in transcription and translation of some materials from French, and Anusha Harihan, who assisted in transcription and translation of some materials from Tamil. Tim Stallmann is not only an outstanding friend, but also a fierce radical cartographer. My thanks to him for preparing maps for this book.

My work could not be done without support and encouragement from a wide variety of people I am proud to be in solidarity with—in struggles large and small. Thanks to Neel Ahuja, Zac Aliotta, Neda Atanasoski, Mike Blank, Mark Bray, Chris Buck, Emile Chabal, Nick Doyle, Elaine Dunbar, Steph Gans, Regina Kunzel, Lisa Lloyd, Meghan McDowell, Grania McKiernan, Andrew Meeker, China Medel, Randy and Ramona Meyerhoff, Annie Segrest, Nick Thalhuber, David Theurer, Vijay and Rajani Raghavan, Dylan Rodríguez, Nitasha Sharma, Chuck Wheeler, and Rosa Williams. Liz Ault—neighbor, fellow nacho and fizzy-water enthusiast, and whip-smart editor—has been an unwavering cheerleader and source of support. Siobhán McKiernan has not only been my best friend since high school; she is also an extremely talented copyeditor and indexer, and I am incredibly grateful for her work on this book. Sheela Namakkal, my big sister, has put up with decades of academic shop talk and yet still seems to like me (even though I used to steal all her toys, especially the Cabbage Patch Kids). Many thanks to her for her enduring love and support.

My partner, Eli Meyerhoff, has been with me since the very beginning of this project (and even before it began!). He is always ready to join me on an archive trip and has spent many days in different parts of the world reading big books, looking for anarchist free spaces, and getting our daily baguette or paratha. He has suffered through long-haul sleeper bus trips and been treated to the joys of street food in at least three countries. Throughout archive trips in India, France, and England, we had the extreme fortune to have been welcomed into the homes of friends and family, which sustained this work in countless ways. In Bombay, I thank my cousins Harsha Raghavan, Lulu Raghavan, Nikhil Raghavan, and Maithili Raut for all the hospitality, local food recommendations, and jet-lagged gin and tonics. In Bangalore, my aunt and uncle Kamala and Ramabadran Raghavan always provide a much-needed respite after months of travel and research. In London, Jessamy Dipper (alongside a changing array of housemates), Nellie McKay, and Mara Ferreri all opened their homes to us while I made my way to the British Library. I am grateful for this network of friends and family, and even more so to Eli, for always encouraging me to research, write, and ask critical questions. He reads everything I write and is really good at finding unmarked Indian archives that no one else can seem to find. His love and curiosity make all of this possible.

Ever since I was a young child, my mother encouraged me to write, often telling me to "go write a book" when she caught me wandering aimlessly around the house. My daughter, Usha June, was born during the final stages of writing this one. People like to compare the birth of child to publishing a book, and now that I have experienced both, I must say, childbirth took a lot less time! My mother passed away in 2016, and although she is not here now to share in the excitement, I hope to pass this accomplishment on to my daughter. I now eagerly await her first publication.

I dedicate this book both to my mother, Carol June Sarraillon, and to my father, Srinivasan Namakkal, for having the courage to travel through the world with decolonial intentions, and for teaching me to do the same. I owe everything to the care and love they so freely shared with not only me and my sister, but with the many people they have encountered on their journeys.

# Chronology

1667—10 December: French East India Company (Compagnie des Indes Orientales) lands in Surat, marking the beginning of the official involvement of French interests in India.

1673—French East India Company arrives for the first time in Chandernagore and purchases land from Ibrahim Khan.

1674—French establish the first *loge* (factory) in Pondicherry.

1699—First French governor-general of Pondicherry, François Martin, installed in Pondicherry.

1731—Joseph Francois Dupleix appointed governor of French Indian territories.

1740–48—First Carnatic War, which included the British and French fighting for more control in India.

1756–1763—Seven Years' War, during which France lost Pondicherry during the British Seige of Pondicherry in 1760–61.

1763—10 February: First Treaty of Paris, which reduces French holding to the five *comptoirs* (trading posts).

1790–1792—During the French Revolution era, *topas* (mixed-heritage/-race) men in Pondicherry write to France demanding enrollment as French *citoyens* (citizens) in the burgeoning French Republic.

1793—Pondicherry falls to the British.

1793–1816—Pondicherry under British occupation until the enactment of the 1814 Treaty of Paris. The Second Treaty of Paris (1814) restored all the settlements and factories that France had possessed in India on 1 January 1792 to France; no military presence was to be allowed except for policing. The restoration of the territories took effect in 1816.

1872—15 August: Birth of Aurobindo Ghose in Calcutta.

1878—21 February: Birth of Mira Alfassa in Paris.

1881—21 September: Decree Relative to the Personal Status, allowing men domiciled in French India to acquire French citizenship through "renunciation of personal law," a formal declaration made in the presence of a magistrate to adopt the French civil code in lieu of "native" laws and customs. While only men were eligible to make this declaration, it was applicable to his spouse and children as well.

1910—4 April: Sri Aurobindo arrives in Pondicherry, via Chandernagore, on the French-owned steamship *Dupleix* (he had been in hiding in Chandernagore since February). Aurobindo spends the remainder of his life in Pondicherry.

1914— Mira Alfassa and Paul Richard arrive in Pondicherry.

1915—Alfassa and Richard leave India due to the war.

1920—April: Mira Alfassa returns to Pondicherry with Paul Richard, who leaves shortly after their arrival. Mira remains in Pondicherry until her death.

1926—Ashram founded.

1947—15 August: Indian independence/partition and the creation of Pakistan.

1949—19 June: Referendum in Chandernagore results in a landslide to merge with the Indian Union and end French rule.

1950—26 January: Indian constitution promulgated.

1950—5 December: Death of Aurobindo.

1954—13 March–7 May: French defeat at Dien Bien Phu, signaling the end of French rule in Indochina.

1954—July: Geneva Agreements signed.

1954—2 October: Chandernagore merged with West Bengal, four years following the referendum.

1954—18 October: Kíjéour convention held, 170 out of 187 representatives from the Municipal Councils and Representative Assembly vote to merge the French territories into the Indian Union.

1954—1 November: De facto transfer of French territories of Pondicherry, Karaikal, Mahé, and Yanam to the Indian Union takes effect, dependent on ratification by both France and India in their respective legislative assemblies.

1956—28 May: Treaty of Cession. Treaty of Cession signed by Prime Minister of India Jawaharlal Nehru and French Amabassador to India Stanislas Ostroróg, marking the de jure transfer of the French territories in India to India.

1962—Evian Accords signed, signaling the end of the French occupation of Algeria. The accords also ratified the 1956 Treaty of Cession.

1968—28 February: Auroville founded.

1973—17 November: Death of the Mother.

*Map 00.1* Map of French Indian Territories. Map prepared by Tim Stallmann.

UNSETTLING UTOPIA

# Introduction

*On Minor Borders and Colonial Time*

The year was 1964, the place, Pondicherry, a seaport town in the south of India, which only two years earlier had been under French colonial rule.¹ The French television news program *Cinq colonnes à la une* (Five columns into one) had sent its crew to Pondicherry to explore what remained of French life, culture, and politics in the aftermath of decolonization. The twenty-four-minute black-and-white documentary titled "Les trois mondes de Pondichéry" (The three worlds of Pondicherry) suggests that life in Pondicherry in 1964 was split into three distinctive worlds that were spatially and culturally segregated.² According to the documentary, the first world is that of the "cultivated," or *French* French-Indian, a person who was ethnically Indian but culturally French, often held French citizenship, probably spoke Tamil and French fluently, read French literature, and was remorseful that Pondicherry had been severed from its direct relationship with France.³ This population primarily lived in the historic *ville blanche* (white town) near the sea, an area that the documentary depicts as quiet, clean, and orderly, with straight, grid-like streets, largely devoid of people. The camera moves swiftly to the second world, comprised of the *Indian* French-Indian, a population that was ethnically Indian (almost certainly Tamil), possibly Catholic, and included some French citizens. In contrast to the first world, these French-Indians were domiciled in the *ville noire* (black town), which the narrator describes as "an Indian town," as images of crowded streets and close-ups of young children and older men and women fill the screen. This world was crowded, chaotic, and loud, in tune with popular images of India that circulated globally at the time through film, literature, and journalism.[4] The narrator slyly suggests that even though many of the Tamil French-Indians were Catholics who attended church, they "never ceased the rites of the Hindu gods." These first two worlds represent the Manichean framework of the colonial era, illustrating the divisions imagined by the colonial mind—between civilized and barbaric, rational and superstitious.

The third world presented in the documentary, however, disrupts the well-worn colonial binary by moving to engage with the inhabitants of the Sri Aurobindo Ashram.[5] If the ville blanche of Pondicherry was a quaint and curious remainder of the colonial past, and the ville noire a fully (dys)functional Indian city, the documentary elevates the Ashram to a space so modern that it resembles a developed Western city. As the narrator muses while sitting in the "ultramodern" Ashram hostel, "You need to make a considerable effort to persuade yourself that you are still in Pondicherry and that just on the other side of this oasis an Indian woman is removing lice from the head of her child"—a statement that is accompanied by footage of this very act in progress. The filmmakers marvel at the Olympic-sized swimming pool, the paper factory, and the "quasi-California décor"; the Ashram was, through their lens, truly the world most out of place and time, not only because it was physically located in India, but because of its temporal resemblance to the so-called developed world.

The Ashram inmates (the word used by those living in the Ashram to describe themselves) lived at the time under the guidance of Mira Alfassa, the Mother, often called *la mère*, a Frenchwoman by birth.[6] At the time that this documentary was made, there were over two thousand Ashram residents, a mix of Europeans and Indians (although the Indians present were mostly from other parts of India, not local Tamils). Despite the documentary's argument that the Ashram encompassed its own world outside of the space and time of its surroundings, the Ashram was a major presence in Pondicherry and had been since its founding in 1926. The Ashram owned many of the buildings in Pondicherry as well as a fleet of cars; oversaw multiple small industries, including printing presses and papermaking; ran a school; and even had its own post office.[7] As I will show throughout this book, it was common for French colonial officials who governed in Pondicherry to have close ties to the Ashram. These relationships were in tension with the Ashram's insistence that it was an apolitical entity.

Although Sri Aurobindo had passed away in 1950, the Mother successfully oversaw the operations until her own death in 1973. Before his death, Aurobindo and the Mother had discussed a new project separate from the Ashram: the founding of a city that would be a space to bring the future into being.[8] Four years later, in 1968, the Ashram launched the project: the intentional community called Auroville. Unlike the Ashram, which is an ascetic space devoted fully to the study of Aurobindo and the Mother's philosophies, Auroville was envisioned as the "first city of the future," a "city of universal culture."[9] Designed to resemble a galaxy, Auroville was meant to be a launching pad for the postcolonial future, a break from the colonial past (see fig. 0.1). While imbued with the spiritual presence of the Mother and Aurobindo, Auroville is otherwise devoted to the projects of the people who live there that range from architectural experiments to organic farming, fashion houses, and schools. Recognized from its inception by the United Nations Educational, Scientific, and Cultural Organization (UNESCO), Auroville began with global aspirations and has been quite successful in achieving international recognition.[10] Unlike the residents of the Ashram, the original inhabitants of Auroville came largely from Europe (France, Germany, Italy, and the UK) and Australia, making it truly a project guided by European interests, a way for the privileges of colonial mobility and wealth to continue into the postcolonial world in a movement I call "settler utopianism."[11]

Auroville is proof that the French colonial mission in India transcends both the bounded territory of the French Indian possessions and the formal time of colonialism. Although Auroville resides officially on land in Tamil Nadu, not the Union Territory of Pondicherry, it is almost always associated with Pondicherry—in newspaper articles, in popular tourist guides such as the *Lonely Planet*, and even with the residents, many whom either came from France or arrived first in Pondicherry before seeking out Auroville. In 2018, Buzzfeed India released a seventeen-minute documentary on Netflix called *India's Utopia*, which follows Indian journalist Rega Jha's journey to Auroville. The thesis of the documentary is that greater India could learn a lot from Auroville, which Jha portrays as the opposite of India's large, polluted, overcrowded cities, an argument that mirrors the description in "Les trois mondes de Pondichéry" of the ville blanche/ville noire.[12] Auroville is in many ways a thriving project today that continues to shine a positive light on the colonial memory of French rule in India, a space that invokes a relationship with the colonial past

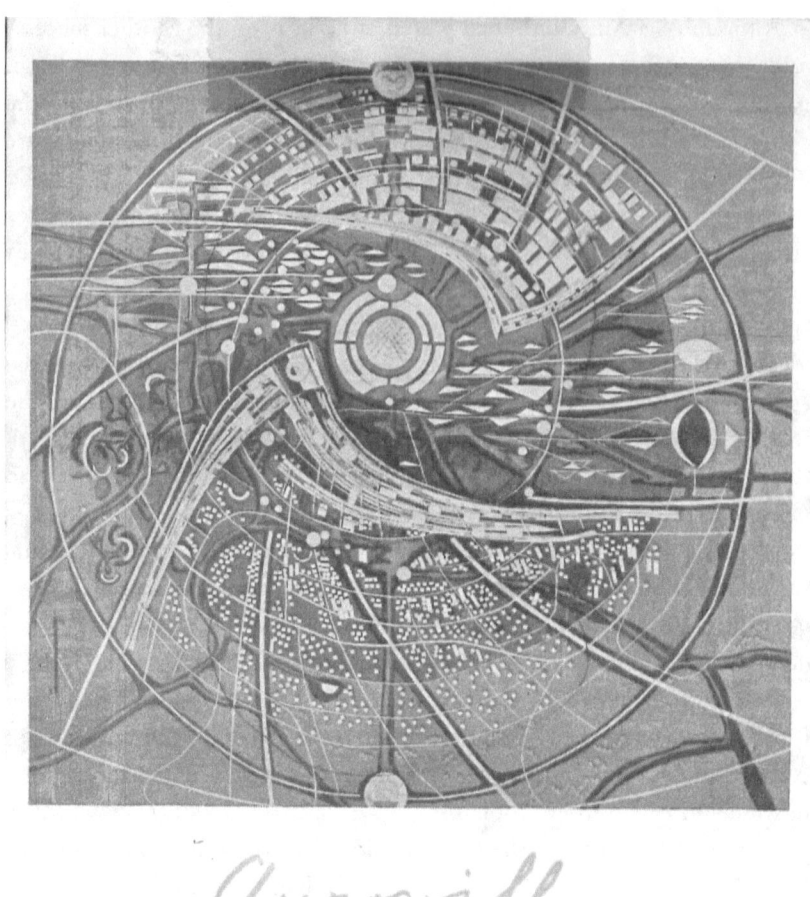

*Figure 0.1* Postcard featuring the model of Auroville, 1968. From the author's collection.

while also emerging as a global site for spiritual tourism, green capitalism, and settler utopianism. It is also a continuation of the projects of colonial and carceral border-making, which I explore in chapter 1, in the ways that Auroville segregates spaces for use by Aurovilians and non-Aurovilians that almost always keep dark-skinned Tamil villagers separated from lighter-skinned Aurovilians who have settled on the land from a variety of origin points.

The historiography of the French Indian territories is small in comparison to the enormous bodies of work on British colonialism in South Asia, yet it has been growing in both size and significance as scholars work to deepen histories of colonial South Asia.[13] However, my argument that Auroville is a part—or at least an extension—of the French colonial project runs contrary to the historiography of Pondicherry. Histories of Pondicherry, and of French India more broadly, tend to treat the Ashram as existing outside the scope of French colonial concerns, thus excluding it from histories of the territories. Some of this has to do with temporality: the Ashram was formally founded in 1926, and Auroville did not begin construction until 1968, well after both the British and French had given up their territorial holdings in the region, situating Auroville outside the era of study. In addition, the memory of French colonialism in South Asia is often very positive, in no small part due to a deliberate move on the part of the French state to continue to promote a positive history of colonial influence in India. According to these histories, the violence of decolonization in India and Pakistan, specifically, was only a result of British rule, and the modern Indian state is a postcolonial state founded on an ethos of anticolonial nationalism. This narrative leaves no space to question the colonial infrastructures that continue to define the Indian state, nor to allow for an understanding of the complicated relationship many people throughout the subcontinent had (and continue to have) toward developing an Indian national identity centered on anything outside of an upper-caste Hindu norm.

This book is a direct response to this tendency by historians, academic and popular, to want to understand decolonization as a completed event that took place in very specific times and places, a narrative that has overlooked the impossible messiness of colonial rule. According to historians Nicolas Bancel and Pascal Blanchard, "Memory is not history," as memory is based not on archival sources but instead on the cumulative socialization that interprets history through shared experiences and memories.[14]

The colonial memory of French India becomes intertwined with the Ashram and Auroville, because the Ashram and Auroville exist in the present moment in a way that French India does not. The way that the colonial past is remembered may or may not be based on historical evidence, often leading to colonial nostalgia, which, Bancel and Blanchard argue, often legitimizes colonial projects as successful in retrospect—a sentiment that swirls around discussions of French India in popular media and culture (in France, India, and the United States).[15] This book takes the colonial memory of France as a "good" colonizer and turns it on its head in an effort to deepen historical and popular understanding of the limits, struggles, and failures of decolonization to do away with colonialism in ways significant to people on the ground.

The overlapping yet distinct "worlds" of Pondicherry explored in "Les trois mondes de Pondichéry" elucidate the complexities of decolonization for a territory that faced a steep uphill battle toward achieving sovereign independence, due to its size, relative to its surroundings and its minor position in the French, British, and Indian imperial and state projects. French India was much more than Pondicherry, although colonial memory tends to favor just this one site. "French India" was in fact an umbrella term used to refer to five territories (Pondicherry, Karaikal, Mahé, Chandernagore, and Yanam) that France governed for centuries, as well as a smattering of small territorial holdings (called *loges*) that housed factories. Pondicherry, though today autonomous as a union territory, is embedded in Tamil Nadu, a state in South India that had a much greater cultural affiliation with the local linguistic culture—in this case, Tamil—than with the hegemonic Hindi- and English-speaking central government headquartered in New Delhi.[16] Karaikal is just south of Pondicherry, also within Tamil Nadu; Mahé, in the neighboring state of Kerala; and Yanam, north in Andra Pradesh. Chandernagore, which voted to join the Indian Union in 1949 and is thus not a part of the Union Territory of Pondicherry, is located in West Bengal, basically a suburb of Kolkota. French India was always a scattered collection of territories, often considered minor to France, England, and, after 1947, India. Yet French India is an important and dynamic site for thinking about global histories of decolonization, mobility, and border-making in the twentieth century.

This book is about French India in the twentieth century. Consequently, it is also about France, India, and England, as well as Indochina/Vietnam, Algeria, and the United States. It challenges the widespread

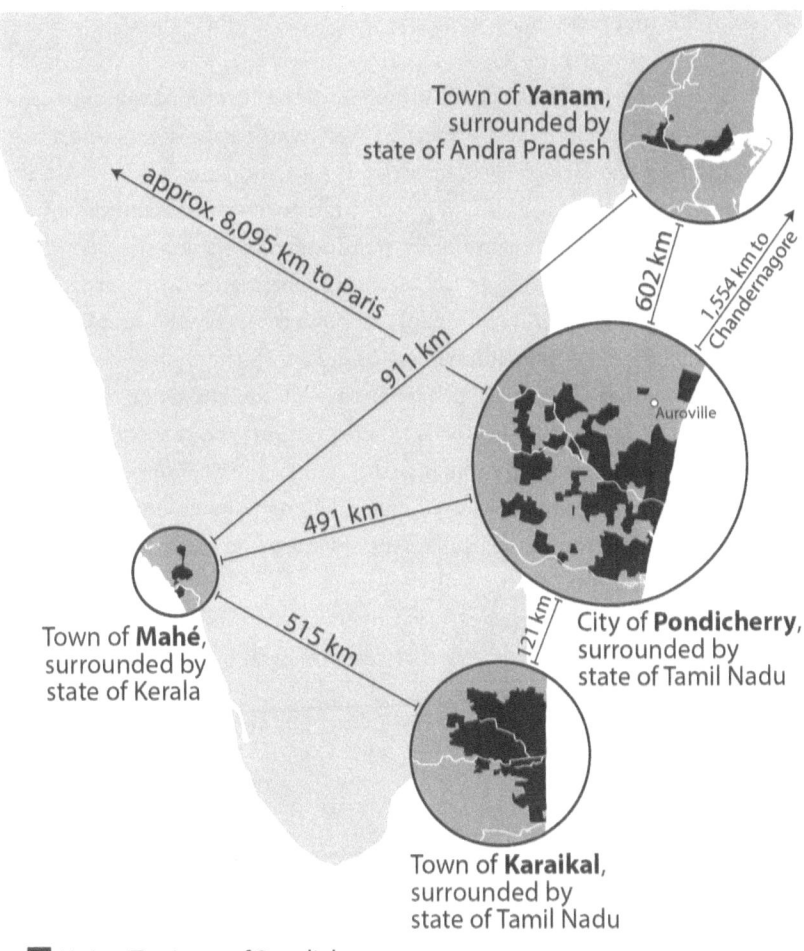

*Map 0.1* Map showing the distances between the French Indian territories. Map prepared by Tim Stallmann.

scholarly consensus about the time and space of decolonization. The people whose lives, movements, and ideas are discussed in this book lived and continue to live between colonial and postcolonial sites and cities, from Pondicherry to Paris, on borders and in borderlands barely visible to people outside of the immediate area. The decolonization of French India, which I roughly categorize as occurring between 1947 and 1962, occurred within an era of global anticolonial struggles but also postcolonial independence in South Asia, the "glory days" of Indian nation-making, when the victory against the British was still fresh in the air. French India, which was established amid the tumult of the expansion of European trade routes and imperial proxy wars in the seventeenth century, outlasted the British Raj, stretching into the foundational years of independent India, yet it hardly registers in histories of colonial or postcolonial India. Though the future of French India was on the minds of many different people as the struggle for Indian independence from British rule moved toward liberation, most people in power—in France, the UK, and India— bracketed the question of how to deal with these minor territories for after the "major" event had happened. Yet the existence and persistence of French India into the 1960s raises questions about the many active meanings of decolonization during this time; how imperial forms of nationalism were consumed, altered, and challenged by colonized subjects; and how national identity and allegiance were to be understood in what people began to define as the postcolonial era. I argue that decolonization in the space of French India was not a liberatory act, but instead an opening for reformulated acts of colonial settlement and disenfranchisement and dispossession of local populations.

## On Decolonization

Decolonization has become, in the first decades of the twenty-first century, a term associated with radical leftist struggles for liberation, independence, and the dismantling and abolition of colonial epistemologies, ontologies, and institutions, as well as the movement to return land to Indigenous nations and peoples. Social movements, from South Africa to England to the First Nations of Turtle Island, have taken up the rallying cry of decolonization to address the ways in which the supposed colonial past continues to rule the present.[17] Student movements such as Rhodes Must Fall, which started in South Africa in 2015 as a call to remove a statue of Cecil Rhodes from the University of Cape Town campus, transformed into multiple movements to abolish university fees (Fees Must Fall), and to "decolonize the curriculum," not only in the former colonies but throughout institutions of higher education, questioning the system of knowledge production that continues to center European epistemologies.[18] Student-led movement-building around questions of decolonization are not new;

the Third World Liberation Front, founded at San Francisco State College in the late 1960s, actively worked to center global movements for decolonization in the building of third world studies curricula.[19] While the third world studies movement was successful in creating space for new academic departments devoted to ethnic studies in its various forms, by the early 1980s most disciplines had accepted that decolonization was a completed event, that the world had been "globalized."[20] It is only recently that people, within the university and beyond, have started to widely question the assertion that decolonization was successful, which has opened up important new spaces for conversations about the historic meaning of decolonization as well as ongoing struggles to decolonize, especially in regard to giving land back to Indigenous peoples who continue to experience massive dispossession through ongoing settler colonialism.[21]

Recent works that employ the language of decolonization in major analytical ways fall into three overlapping categories: epistemological, ontological, and territorial. The school of decolonial studies, or decoloniality, which mostly comes from Latin American scholars—notably Aníbal Quijano, María Lugones, and Walter Mignolo—argues that to understand the power of colonialism it is necessary to understand that modernity and coloniality are opposite sides of the same coin.[22] In other words, modernity is not possible without coloniality. Mignolo in particular has argued for the need to engage in epistemic decolonization—that is, to decolonize knowledge itself, in part by acknowledging where and how knowledge is and has been produced. Mignolo calls for people to "delink" from Eurocentric epistemologies in order to understand histories prior to and independent of European conquest.

While decolonizing knowledge and the ways we understand our being in the world is an ongoing and critically important project, it is also a project that is generally isolated in certain spaces, often academic in nature. For those working to address the violence of continued settler colonialism, seeking to decolonize knowledge without centering the physical and immediate need to return land to Indigenous nations and peoples continues the colonial project. In their influential article "Decolonization Is Not a Metaphor," Eve Tuck and K. Wayne Yang warn that "the language of decolonization has been superficially adopted into education and other social sciences," which has the effect of "center[ing] settler perspectives."[23] Tuck and Yang argue that decolonization needs to always center Indigenous struggle, particularly the issue of territory, and refer to an *active* political struggle to return land. In order to act in accordance with this line of argument means to accept one's own role in ongoing structures of settler colonialism, to unsettle what Tuck and Yang call "settler innocence," a process I discuss throughout this book.

Contemporary debates about the use of "decolonization" as an action and/or a field of analysis are rather distant from the historical origins of the word, which lay within the milieu of the European intellectual elite. Decolonization (*decolonisation*) was first used by a French journalist Henry Fonfrède, in his 1836 article "De la décolonisation d'Alger" (On the decolonization of Algeria), published in a now-defunct newspaper based in Bourdeaux, Le Mémorial borderlais.[24] In the first decade of the French colonial occupation of Algeria, Fonfrède wrote in opposition to the French occupation of Algeria. However, over the following century, the term "decolonization" was not deployed very often, and, when it was, it was often in the interest of maintaining European supremacy once the age of European colonial domination came to an end. According to historian Stuart Ward, it was not until Frantz Fanon's last work, *The Wretched of the Earth* (1961), that decolonization became a radical idea. Despite a lack of engagement with it in his previous works, precisely because of its use in diplomatic circles, Fanon worked to transform the concept from a diplomatic process of friendly transfer of power to a call to arms to abolish colonialism in every form that it takes.[25] The form of radical decolonization espoused by Fanon has been deeply influential around the world and is especially noteworthy for the attention Fanon paid to both political action and epistemic revolution.

Decolonization in South Asia is not typically read along the lines of Fanon's radical thinking of decolonization's potential, largely due to the way the postcolonial Indian state has operated since independence. Taking just independent India (and leaving aside other parts of post-1947 South Asia), we can see that struggles for sovereignty and autonomy in India—including the Princely States, Pondicherry, Portuguese-held Goa, and the still-contested Kashmir and Jammu—have never ceased. Decolonization, at its most conservative, was a call for self-determination and sovereignty, which scholars have interpreted as a call for sovereign nation-states. While this was often true, there were other forms of being in the world formulated by people involved in movements for decolonization.[26] It is thus important to look at the outliers and minor holdings to get a sense of the complexities of working oneself out of the imperial web.

This book works across a timeline that spans before, during, and after the "official" period of decolonization in French India to show how state-sponsored decolonization—the bureaucratic process of transferring governance from an imperial state to a postcolonial state—rarely aligned with local visions for decolonization, whether originating from the colonized or colonial settlers. Despite the calls for liberation often inherent in movements for decolonization, including in French India, I show that state-led decolonization often meant the building and securitization of borders, increased policing and criminalization of marginal communities, and the reimagining of space as nationally, and often racially, homogenous. The need to securitize the postcolonial state, to create and protect claims to postcolonial sovereignty, exists in tension, but also in cooperation, with utopian projects that projected a vision of global unity that could be experienced within a certain (settler) space. While movements committed to decolonial liberation were all but obliterated by the needs of the state by the time French India was integrated into India in 1962, two utopian projects continue to thrive in and near Puducherry today, both rooted in histories of colonial settlement: the Aurobindo Ashram, and Auroville. The continued success of these two distinct global sites of settlement shows how decolonization, a project that is thought to have succeeded with independence from colonial rule and ended the age of empire, actually opened new spaces of settlement, perpetuating colonial power into the time of independent postcolonial states, an example of the settler ignorance theorized by Tuck and Yang. The history of decolonization in French India thus offers a challenge to the idea that India has been decolonized, from 1947 to the present day.

## Mobility, Settlement, and Utopia

India was not a settler colony. In fact, the most prominent European colonizing force in South Asia—England—though very powerful, was never really able to control vast amounts of continuous territory in South Asia due to negotiations with local rulers that resulted in a series of Princely States, as well as the continuous presence of other European powers, most prominently Portugal and France, during the high period of British imperial rule. However, imperial settlements were common throughout South Asia, from the forts built by competing European trading companies to small, experimental communities founded by various local and global actors for the purpose of spiritual exploration, missionary projects, political organizing, intellectual pursuits, or a host of other autonomous projects. By the early nineteenth century, when the British and French empires were both gaining more power and territory, the sheer vastness of imperial holdings that needed to be understood, mapped out, disciplined, and controlled meant that minor holdings such as the French territories in India were often dismissed as unimportant backwaters. Yet places like Pondicherry, because of their status as minor holdings, became sites of global experimentation, of trying a wide range of alternative modes of world-making.

A positive aspect of existing on the border can be the chance to experiment with different ways of living and being, an opportunity for a forced exile (from the state, from the mainstream, from normative society) to become an experiment in "heterotopia," Michel Foucault's formulation of a non-normative society.[27] In his work on settler colonialism, the anthropologist Patrick Wolfe has argued that "settler colonizers come to stay," an act that should be considered structural, not a singular event that occurred by chance.[28] In fact, many of the utopian settlement experiments of the nineteenth and twentieth centuries throughout the world occurred during the height of imperial expansion and were made possible by colonial occupation, leading to the questions: What are the connections, overlaps, and imbrications of utopian thinking and colonial settlement? If, as Wolfe has argued, settler colonialism is a structure and not an event, what structures of settler colonialism are present in utopian settlement experiments rooted, quite literally, in the land of colonized space?

In other words, though not a settler colony, India has certainly been the site of settlements. The modern usage of the word "utopia" originates with Thomas More's 1516 work of the same name, in which "Utopia" is an imaginary island that has perfect legal, political, and social systems.[29] The important ideas here are that it is *imagined*, and that it is imagined as perfect. If one is working toward a utopian society, it is often easiest to work toward building it someplace else, free of whatever constraints were causing unhappiness or discord in the place of origin. Throughout modern history, discord and unhappiness have often been caused by systems of government and societal norms that have sought to exclude or persecute certain groups of people, often because of an identity marker such as religious belief, skin color, sexuality, or class status. Sometimes that has meant moving internally (the Mormon church, or Church of Jesus Christ of Latter-Day Saints, in the United States, who moved from east to west in the nineteenth century, is a good example of internal movement), or fighting to establish a utopia by overthrowing the people in power (for example, the Russian Revolution of 1917).[30] Other times this has meant leaving one's place of origin to establish utopia in a "new place." Constructing a utopian society requires a stretch of "vacant" land, uninhabited by people who possess distinct cultures, languages, and ways of living. History shows that, to achieve this, populations have been displaced and decimated. The pilgrims who left England because of religious persecution to settle in the United States are an important example of this: while the settlers often portrayed North America as an empty, barren land, inhabited only by "savages," there were of course established Indigenous nations living on the land that was settled, who were consequently murdered, conquered, and colonized to facilitate the settlers' utopian beliefs.

The experiments of socialist utopianists in the nineteenth century, such as the Saint-Simonians, who moved throughout the French Empire advocating colonial reforms under the guise of the *mission civilisatrice* (civilizing mission), sought to use land under military occupation such as in Algeria, as an "experimental lab," often to the detriment—or at least the exclusion—of Indigenous cultures and peoples.[31] The Theosophists, an occult/spiritualist movement established in the mid-nineteenth century in New York City by American Henry Olcott and Russian émigré Helena Blavatsky, relocated permanently to India in 1875, citing the importance of "Eastern thought" as an impetus. Theosophists, perhaps most notably the Irishwoman Annie Besant, became important players in the Indian independence movement by the late 1920s. The aforementioned Sri Aurobindo Ghose came to Pondicherry in exile, wanted both on charges of sedition for the printing of anticolonial material and in connection with an assassination of a British official. His ashram, the biggest attraction in Pondicherry today, was settled there because it was on French territory and thus spatially protected from the British.

While the organizing principles of socialist utopianism often set it apart from the capitalist drive of imperialist expansion, both colonialism and utopianism imagined many non-Western lands as empty and available for their experiments. Political theorist Lucy Sargisson has argued that the process of estrangement has a "profoundly positive relationship with utopianism," as it permits the members of an intentional community to create a critical distance between the reality of the present time and the future "good place" of the utopia.[32] Imagined utopias take place far from home, often in unimaginable places, in order to provide enough distance from contemporary forms of living to construct a community critical of the present time. This distancing has far different consequences in practice, the history of which I explore in this book in order to bring together important conversations about settlement, colonization, postcolonial sovereignty, liberation, and utopian thinking.

The divide between the Westernized global citizen and the third world subject is visually evident in present-day Pondicherry, in and around the Ashram and Auroville. Pondicherry and Auroville are both global sites that attract tourists and residents from many parts of the world. They are also both products of colonialism, in different but related ways, and continue to rely on and profit from colonial labor relations that depend on local labor to serve global interests. Although France officially handed over control of the French Indian enclaves in 1962, decolonization in French India did not put an end to colonialism, but instead shifted the sites of power from the imperial state to many fractured institutions, including, in the case of French India, forms of settlement sustained largely though spiritual tourism. In addition to Westerners who come to visit the Aurobindo Ashram and Auroville, the "French history" of Pondicherry makes it a prime tourist destination, not just for French travelers, but also for Indians from throughout the subcontinent who are seeking bits of little-known history that they can feel good about because of its distance from British colonial history—a "utopic" vision of "positive decolonization." Interpretations of the decolonization of French India as peaceful and friendly serve to distance people from the histories of the horrors of Partition or the brutal violence France enacted upon colonized populations in North Africa, Indochina, and Madagascar during the high period of anticolonial movements and decolonization between 1945 and 1962. Puducherry, the minor French possession on the Coromandel Coast, has become in this way a sort of crossroads of modernity/coloniality, a series of paths that cross the French Indian past; the Indian present; and the evolutionist, utopic future projected by the intentional community of Auroville.

## Scattered Geographies: Territory, Colony, Borderlands

How does a small port village in South India become "a little piece of France"? Was it the people, the architecture, the city planning, or the tricolor flying from the hôtel de ville that transformed Pondicherry into a French space? Can we actually say this space was Indian before it was French?[33] The history of French India begins neatly, with the arrival of the French in India: a simple enough narrative that tells a somewhat benign story of exploration, adventure, and global trade. Histories of colonies often begin this way, with the arrival of the eventual colonizers, reproducing a narrative structure that accepts the premise of imperialists imagining territories into cartographic existence, which became material reality with the conquest of land and people. French India was made through imperial expansion, but it was also imagined into being through writing about French India as a place, in, for instance, the historical diaries of the first governor-general of French India, François Martin, and Ananda Ranga Pillai, the Tamil dubash to the Marquis Joseph Dupleix, as well as the histories of French India itself. Many of the works in French about the origins of French India were written between the two world wars, by Pondichérian men and women associated with the Société de l'histoire de l'Inde française (SHIF), including Yvonne Gaebelé, Edmond Gaudart, Margueritte V. Labernadie, and Alfred Martineau, former governor-general of French India (1910–1911, 1913–1918).[34] More recently, Jacques Weber, a historian based in France with roots in Pondicherry, has offered the most comprehensive and academic histories of French India to date.[35] Unsurprisingly, given the French focus of the great majority of writers on French India, a wide consensus exists among histories of French India that, before the French took control, the area that is today Pondicherry was not a space unified under a common identity.

Despite the great diversity of people and religions present in pre-French Pondicherry, there are two French figures, François Martin (1634–1706) and the Marquis Joseph François Dupleix (1697–1764), and one Indian, the Islamic ruler of Mysore Tipu Sultan (1750–1799), who remain synonymous with the history of the French territories in India. Scholars often credit these three men with transforming Pondicherry into what it is today: a non-British, European enclave separate from the surrounding land and people. As the first governor-general, Martin consolidated

French trade interests in India and centered them in the new French possession of Pondicherry.[36] Martin was an expansionist, and he spent a great amount of his time in Pondicherry trying to acquire more territory for the French in India, although he ran into strong opposition from the Dutch. While Martin lost control of Pondicherry to the Dutch for six years between 1693 and 1699, by 1702 he had begun the process of building fortifications around the French territory, in the interest of attracting merchants and weavers to settle there.[37] Martin also supervised the construction of one hundred new houses, transforming a town of transient soldiers and traders into a space where families could settle.[38] Following Martin's death in 1704, orders were sent from France to future governors "to maintain the alignment of the streets and ensure the beauty of the town," in order to preserve the attachment to France via architecture and city planning.[39] The attention to aesthetic detail and the construction of residential houses indicate that the French were interested in grooming Pondicherry as a possible settlement, although the majority of these early houses would be destroyed by the British in 1761.

Throughout the eighteenth century, Pondicherry became the main trading post of the French East India Company in the Indian Ocean.[40] While it was Martin who transformed Pondicherry from a transnational trading post into a French enclave by building infrastructures that included colonial administrations, it was the Marquis Joseph Dupleix who, on becoming the governor-general in 1742, began the campaign for French control of South Asia.[41] Dupleix was successful for a time, which has led many people—in the past as well as the present—to suggest that France had the ability and the opportunity to conquer much larger segments of South Asia, while simultaneously proving its superiority to British forces.[42] Dupleix began his career in India in 1731, in Chandernagore, where he remained until 1742, when he was appointed the governor of French India and left for Pondicherry. Historians credit Dupleix with transforming the small French enclave of Chandernagore into a "great commercial centre."[43]

The eighteenth century was an important era of struggle between French and British imperialisms, not only in South Asia but in the Americas as well. Just as Dupleix arrived in Pondicherry in 1742, the Austrian War of Succession, a battle fought primarily in Europe, had reached the subcontinent, creating tensions between the French in Pondicherry and the British in nearby Madras. Madras fell to the French in 1746, causing Dupleix to try frantically to retain the territory by forming alliances with local Indian leaders.[44] Unfortunately for the French—and especially for Dupleix, who was removed from his post and recalled to Paris as a fallen hero—Madras was returned to the British in the Treaty of Aix-la-Chapelle in 1749. For the next few decades, France and England continued to fight for control of territory in South Asia. At one point during the Seven Years' War (1756–1763), France lost all five territories to the British: Chandernagore was captured in 1757 and Pondicherry surrendered in 1761. Following the war, the 1763 Treaty of Paris returned the five possessions to France but forbade any fortifications or a military presence. Chandernagore, which had been surrounded by a trench, was forced to hire a British engineer to fill it in—a bitter moment of capitulation for the French in India.[45]

Despite France's numerous losses in India over this period, local Indian leaders who wanted to resist British expansion looked to France for assistance. In the late eighteenth century, Tipu Sultan, the ruler of the southern Mysore State, was eager to collaborate with the French in defeating the British East India Company. Tipu Sultan, known popularly as the "tiger of Mysore," followed in the footsteps of his father Haidar (Hyder) Ali, who had built up military strength in Mysore and sought an alliance with France in order to oppose the British forces.[46] Tipu sent three ambassadors, Mahomet Dervich Khan, Akbar Ali Khan, and Mahomet Ousman Khan, from Pondicherry to France in 1787 in an effort to strengthen the alliance.[47] King Louis XVI was preoccupied with the economic instability of the late 1780s and thus did not provide much assistance to Tipu Sultan. However, following the events of the revolution and the downfall of the monarchy in 1789, and after experiencing defeat in the third Anglo-Mysore War (1790–1791), Tipu began a correspondence with Napoleon Bonaparte, in the hope that Napoleon would consider expanding his battle against Britain to South India. The French chose not to send help, and Tipu was killed by the British in 1799 during the Battle of Seringapatam, thus ending the possibility of a military alliance. The death of Tipu Sultan became another node in a list of French failures in India in the eighteenth century. As the wars between France and England raged in the first decade of the nineteenth century, the French possessions changed hands several times. Eventually, Pondicherry was returned to France in 1815 under the Second Treaty of Paris, and the other four territories followed suit in 1816 (Chandernagore) and 1817 (Karaikal, Mahé, Yanam).[48]

It was the arrival of the French that provided future historians and citizens with a foundation for an identity separate from the surrounding territories. Historian Prasenjit Durara writes that nations "prefer to *misrecognize* their origins, seeing or presenting only the part of the story in which they emerged as the expression of the will and culture of their citizens."⁴⁹ In histories of French India that circulate among French-Indians as well as in France, the French-Indian nation—if indeed there is such an entity—was imagined into being through the circulation of knowledge about France, France's relationship to England, and the place of France in the larger context of India. Imperial histories have led many to believe that the people who inhabit territories come into historical being only once they enter the civilizational story of Europe and are incorporated into the major narrative, often with the arrival of Europeans. French India became French with the arrival of French people, beginning with François Martin. Without the arrival of the French, there is no French India. François Martin and the Marquis Joseph Dupleix set the stage for what would become French India, and in the twentieth century it was the arrival of Sri Aurobindo Ghose and Mira Alfassa (one from Bengal in north India, the other from France) that continued the narrative of Pondicherry as an exceptional space marked by the French presence. It should be noted that none of these major figures is indigenous to the French-Indian land.

The term "French-Indian" is itself a contemporary designation, based on an identification with two separate nation-states. Throughout the late eighteenth and nineteenth centuries, when the people who lived in and around the geopolitical borders of French India spoke and wrote of themselves, they used identifying markers such as religion (Hindu, Catholic, Muslim), caste, and race—European, métis (mixed-race), or *indigène* (Indigenous or native). These categories were not specific to French India, but spanned the subcontinent, with regional variations, and were used by both French and British officials in descriptions of local populations. However, by the late nineteenth century, the local populations in British and French territories were becoming distinct. This distinction, argues Adrian Carton, was because "concepts of hybridity" and "race-mixing" were common in the French Indian territories and were not seen as threatening, a practice that allowed for a new class in the French Indian territories: that of the créole, or the métis.⁵⁰

The messiness of defining a French-Indian community is consistent with the blurry boundaries of colonial categorization, a tension between exclusion and inclusion that anthropologist Ann Laura Stoler has described in her work on French Indochina and the Dutch Indies.[51] After the French had lost the majority of India to the English in the eighteenth century, they were faced with the question of how to establish a significant and important French space in South Asia without extensive military and economic conquest. French officials never thought there would be a large French settler/European society in India, but it was still important to make Pondicherry as European as possible in order to mark the French presence, especially against the British.

The few works of historical scholarship devoted to decolonization in French India assume that it has never mattered much to the various states that have ruled it—to the French, to the British, or to India. One of the more recent books about French India suggests that the five French settlements were "cut off from the political upheavals of the places that surrounded them," and that "these isolated pockets were, in fact, more of a weakness than a strength to France."[52] Instead of determining whether or not French India provided benefits to states and empires, I aim to treat the French Indian territories here on their own terms, as borderlands. I argue that French India, or *l'Inde française*, as a hyphenated space (*trait d'union*), is a borderland, neither purely French nor Indian, but somewhere in between, an approach that I hope will prove useful for scholars looking at other marginalized areas of the subcontinent and beyond. Cultural theorist Rajagopalan Radhakrishnan equates the idea of diaspora with the "space of the hyphen that tries to coordinate, within an evolving relationship, the identity politics of one's place of origin with that of one's present home."[53] The people of French India, as in other colonial societies, often dwelled in this "space of the hyphen" without ever leaving home, living their lives on the edge, well before decolonization appeared as a possible future.

Constructing strong nationalist narratives was an important project for creating postcolonial national unity in both the metropole and the former colonies.[54] After Indian independence in 1947, historians of India largely took to writing the history of independence as a teleological becoming of the secular Indian nation-state, a drama that required the British as an imperial foil for liberation to be possible. Likewise, in post-1962 France, the decolonization of the empire became an integral part of the telling of French history, the rising tide of French progress.[55] While the British were not the only game in town, they were clearly the victors for a significant amount of time. The adage that "historians write the history of victors" is apropos here: the wealth of scholarly materials produced on the British rule of India have eclipsed lesser-known histories about the 562 Princely States, which existed throughout South Asia in various forms of indirect rule, as well as the Portuguese colonies and the French territories, all areas that persisted past independence in 1947.[56] Although the Portuguese colonies and French territories were minor in comparison with the areas of British control, as imperial states France and Portugal were of major importance to Britain as foes in the maintenance and expansion of its empire.

Recent scholarship by geographers and historians examining what the anthropologist of South Asia Vazira Zamindar has called "the long partition" illustrates that the occurrence of discontinuous borders was more common in late colonial South Asia than nationalist imagining of postcolonial unity has led people to see.[57] For example, geographer Jason Cons's work on the enclaves that lay on the border of India and Bangladesh shows how anxiety around issues of territory and citizenship on the borders reveals the unstable nature of both borders and national subjects.[58] Although Cons argues that the real anxiety occurred after independence as India and Pakistan entered into heated battles over territory, a similar struggle pre-dates, and in some ways anticipates, this conflict in and around the French Indian territories.

Part of this project, then, is to understand not how French India fits into the national story of India's becoming per se, but instead to understand French India as a formation that challenged and challenges the closed borders of nationalist history. As the sociologist Radhika Moniga has written, "Since European nation-states developed simultaneously as empires, then we must reconsider both the received history of the concept of the nation-state as a territorially circumscribed entity and the received understanding of the notion of sovereignty that accrues to the state via the nation."[59] Destabilizing nationalist narratives is an important part of a project of decolonization because it challenges both bounded territories and nationalist epistemologies. I direct attention to French India to suggest that there are important histories that defy the dominant narratives of an independent India based in Sanskrit/Hindu culture and the British rule of India. During debates about the future of French India in the late 1940s, French-Indians proposed many alternative futures to absorption into India, but they never called for an independent French-Indian nation-state. Across the five territories there is not a shared common Indian language, or even ethnic identity. Unlike resistance movements in South Asia that centered ethnic identity, local proponents of the continuation of French India saw their common history of French rule, primarily their French citizenship, as the foundation for community.

## Conceptualizing Minor Borders, Unsettling History

Decolonization in India was in many ways an attempt to erase the in-between spaces carved out by the subjects of empire—not only in French India, but in Portuguese India, and in some of the former Princely States, particularly Hyderabad and Jammu and Kashmir. Nationalist narratives, often disguised as anticolonial histories, have swallowed centuries of opposition fomented by subaltern subjects, as well as hybrid identities. One reason that conservative nationalist narratives continue to engage colonial logic is because histories of colonialism are uneven and disjointed. A certain story has been told that reaffirms the desire of the nation-state, or, in the case of work devoted to the history of the subaltern, justifies the banishment to the margins. The academy, much like the state, desires a certain type of narrative that fits into specific molds of "normal" life, with everything else as an outlier, relegated to marginal histories and small cramped basement offices in university buildings.

It is unclear where the archive of French India is located. Records pertaining to French India are scattered throughout India, France, England, and the United States, but, even when collected and compiled, as I have done in this book, it is unclear whether the documents, memoirs, newspaper clippings, photos, and interviews brought together here present a unified story of French India—as a scattered yet bounded territory; as a nation, a people, a community; or even as an archival event. French India is a product of empire and also of modernity/coloniality, constructed through tools of imperial governmentality including enumeration through the census, the implementation of borders and border security, the issuing of identity papers, and movements by the people for sovereignty in the face of continued colonial rule in the post-1947 era.

Margins, much like centers, are not organic, but constructed through discourse, geography and mapping, geopolitical movements, and the politics of remembering. Widely remembered and celebrated historical events often serve a political purpose that is in the service of whoever is doing the remembering: memorialization is a powerful tool in the maintenance of nations and states. Scholarship of and at the margins is marginalized often because it threatens the center of power. This includes histories of colonies that disrupt the predominant narratives of decolonization dedicated to teleological narratives of national liberation. Among discussions about the ways the collecting practices and geographies of archives shape histories, minor borders are often erased because they do not fit narratives of institutions interested in the promotion and memory of either nation or state.[60]

Dwelling in the margins is often quite frustrating. Scholars of colonial history, especially those committed to addressing the histories of the colonized, often feel the weight of impossibility in their projects, as the structures of colonial power continue to govern the colonial archive. As Ann Laura Stoler notes in the opening to her 2009 book *Along the Archival Grain*, "Colonial administrations were prolific producers of social categories," and these categories have traditionally shaped our understandings of colonial histories and postcolonial spaces.[61] Organizing knowledge, imagining new boundaries and divisions, and building borders were the bread and butter, the mango and chili, of systems of colonial surveillance and control. Access to knowledge under empire signified the holding of individual power, much like producers of knowledge, or "experts," possess capital—social, political, and economic—in our contemporary world. There is a value attached to certain types of knowledge, produced by certain bodies that reside in specific locations. This has been well established by thinkers of the postcolonial and decolonial, including Stoler, Jacques Derrida, Frantz Fanon, and Michel Foucault. Whether French, British, Dutch, German, Italian, Portuguese, or Spanish, European knowledge production and systems of archiving have shaped not only the histories of Europe, but also, by extension, the histories of the rest of the world told through European conquest. This colonial logic has shaped much of our collective understanding of the colonial past, even for those whose politics are geared toward a decolonial future.

While many historians have felt trapped by the coloniality of the archive, there is now a chance for a decolonial shift, an unlinking from what decolonial theorist Walter Mignolo has called the "matrix of power," in the focus on colonial categories through a transformation of the writing of the history of the margins to a writing of minor history.[62] Stoler defines minor history as a "critical space" that "attends to structures of feeling and force that in 'major' history might otherwise be displaced."[63] Building on Stoler's work, I believe that minor history necessitates an approach that transforms the margins not merely as an off-part of the center, but as a destabilizing force that seeks to destroy the center of power from within. Instead of the center, or the major, appropriating or colonizing the histories of the oppressed to benefit their own interests (often in a false sense of diversity or inclusion), the margins become the minor, a force set to destroy the foundation the major rests upon. In addition to destruction, minor history also has the potential to bring to light alternative world-making projects. I draw here on the work of feminist scholar Cindi Katz, who argues in her 1996 article "Towards Minor Theory" that minor theory "tears at the confines of major theory, pushing its limits to provoke a 'line of escape,' a rupture—a tension out of which something else might happen."[64] Thus, this text engages with the idea of "minor theory" in order to disturb the closed sphere of the major.

The margins, in minor theory, are distinct from the major. To be on the margins is to be outside of the scope of history, a position the colonized experienced throughout their subjugation through the denial of the existence of history outside of Europe.[65] In order for minor histories and minor archives to realize their potential, it is important that they resist marginalization from or incorporation into the major, which here is the realm of the nation-state.[66] This is a daunting undertaking: the major is sustained by laws and regulations enforced by regimes of carcerality, of military and police, a powerful force that demands obedience from all, but also depends on the creation of marginal spaces and bodies. There is not a major without a minor, no belonging without exclusion, no empire without colonies. The minor archive can be many things, but at root it must be a part of the major, not marginal to it. As Katz writes, "The minor is so much a part of the major that its deployment completely reworks the major *from within*. One cannot 'translate' it into the major, so to speak, without destroying it."[67]

Reading the colonial archive through a minor lens, I argue that historians and thinkers committed to decolonial work must take a more holistic approach to archival work, actively engaging with the geographies of archival diaspora (the scattering of colonial-era documents and ephemera), the role that archives play in the postcolonial spaces they inhabit, and the archival labor of the thinker of minor history. Engaging the minor will encourage us to work outside of the frameworks we've been given, the borders that have been drawn, for even the practice of dwelling in the borders reinforces their strength. While decolonization narratives give nation-states a convenient temporal break from the era of empire, employing minor histories in order to decenter and destabilize the major (the dominant narrative of the triumph, and sometimes failures, of the modern nation-state) will provide the opportunity to rupture the major, moving the "history of the margins" into a site of active resistance and productive construction.

Historians, of course, find their livelihoods in archives, but scholars interested in bringing the minor into the major have a hard time accessing the records they need, often lacking the funds and time necessary to look at the whole story. For example, the vast majority of records pertaining to life in the French colonies in India are housed at the Archives Nationales d'Outre Mer in Aix-en-Provence, France, over seven thousand kilometers from former French India. The colonial records were packed up by "special European officers" even before the French signed over Pondicherry to India in 1954, in an act that sent all colonial records "home" to the metropole, out of the reach of the colonial subjects who may desire to see them.[68] The records in Aix, though, are only one piece of the puzzle. In order to research French India, I have bounced between Aix, Puducherry, London, and Paris; and back to homes in Minneapolis, Minnesota (during graduate school), and Durham, North Carolina (where I now live and work). Writing transnational history is in itself a transnational journey, marked by dead ends, surprising turns, and documents that are thousands of miles away when you need them. It takes more time to write these histories, and requires greater resources, which are often hard to come by when major funding bodies are not interested in the stories that lie within them. For a Pondichérian to read archival documents about the French rule in India, they need to be able to travel to France, to the colonial archive in Aix-en-Provence. This is a common roadblock for people of the former colonies who are distanced from their history. It also defines who is able to write the history of the colonized. Recognizing and identifying spatial inequalities, the great distances that keep French-Indians from writing their own histories, is a necessary part of doing decolonial work.

Certain research subjects are of course also privileged. Young scholars are encouraged to pick topics and areas of research that will make them competitive on the job market, which feeds into a certain logic of what knowledge is important. This is reflected in the physical experience of working in the archives. In Aix, I was always one researcher out of dozens, mostly Americans, researching France's colonial past. It seemed I was the only researcher working on French India, surrounded by scholars reading government memos from Algiers, Dakar, Saigon, and other sites that have become important nodes in understanding the history of the French Empire. In contrast, the Puducherry State Archive, located about eight kilometers from the ville blanche of Pondicherry, is tucked away at the end of a residential road. Rickshaw drivers don't know where it is. There are no signs leading researchers to the doors. Unlike in Aix, I was the only researcher in the reading room for days at a time, the materials guarded by one archivist, who chose what to share with me—primarily records that showed the desire of the people of Pondicherry to be free of French rule. All records deemed pertinent were rolled out on a cart into a dusty pink room and left with me to discover alone, as the guard lingered nearby, bored and often looking for conversation.

When I left the Puducherry archives each day, I turned onto streets named for French-Indian "freedom fighters," memorialized by the Indian state but often unknown or unimportant to local residents. The most widely memorialized French Indian in contemporary Puducherry is a man named Edouard Goubert, a mixed-race politician who was once a French senator and eventually the mayor of Pondicherry (July 1963–September 1964), a man seen as a flip-flopper, a slippery being, hell-bent on obtaining power no matter the consequences. The major road bordering the heavily trafficked beach in Puducherry is named for Goubert, as is the large city market. Yet no one I've met in Puducherry refers to these landmarks by name (they are widely known as Beach Road and Nehru market, respectively). At the time of decolonization, Goubert stayed in India, changing his name to the more Indian E. G. Pillai. His statue stands proudly in the White Town in Puducherry, near the statues of Nehru and Gandhi, and he is recognized as an official "freedom fighter" by the Indian government.

The streets of Puducherry told me much more about Goubert than the documents in the Puducherry archives. The contrast between the well-memorialized man and the general dislike for him in the city is difficult to navigate, but an important indicator of the disconnect between state and popular memory. It is hard to know what Goubert was thinking when he transformed his identity from French to Indian. Some think he kept a diary, but his family won't release it, presumably because its content may cause the Indian government to retract his status as a freedom fighter (which comes with a pension). As a mixed-race man, Goubert walked a fine line between social categories that, with the coming of decolonization, ceased to be compatible in bureaucratic terms. Goubert's family migrated to France, leaving E. G. Pillai to himself in India. His name is remembered in official ways, while in reality most local residents have chosen to refer to the same streets and markets by different names, showing how the official record often falls into obscurity. Goubert's legacy may take up physical space in today's Pondicherry, but his memory is mostly absent from the minds of the people in those spaces.

## Against the Imperial Binary, Seeing the Imperial Present

Amid a political landscape that has revealed the many people who remain colonized, scholars who have previously contributed to the periodization of the colonial/postcolonial temporal formulation wherein decolonization rests quite comfortably in the space of the hyphen have begun to see that decolonization did not end empire. Even if we were to accept the idea that decolonization was an event that has ended, when can one say that a state went from colonial to postcolonial? The answers to this question have been varied. Historian of France Eric T. Jennings sees the Vichy period (1940–1944) "at the very crossroads of colonialism and postcolonialism."[69] Political scientist Partha Chatterjee has recently written that "just as we continue to live in the age of nation-states, so have we not transcended the age of empire."[70] And, as Todd Shepard has argued, decolonization had to be invented in order to reconcile the future relationship between France and Algeria.[71] The diplomats in France and India were keenly aware of the need to remain friendly while they struggled over the future of French India. In her work on partition, Vazira Zamindar asks readers to "stretch our very understanding of 'Partition violence' to include the bureaucratic violence of drawing political boundaries and nationalizing identities that became, in some lives, interminable."[72] Building on this argument, I aim to expand our understanding of the space-time of decolonization to include current struggles against colonization, especially in contemporary borderlands—a move to unsettle the idea that decolonization was achieved, and, if it was, that it was in any way a liberatory project.

Drawing on recent scholarship that calls to decolonize academia, this book is a history of the decolonization of French India, as well as a call for the decolonization of history itself. It proposes that decolonizing requires a deep engagement with the people and spaces on the margins of the major, whether that major is the state, empire, or academic disciplines. The history of decolonization in French India shows that underneath the diplomatic debates of states and the actions of military and police forces, people knew that the choice between France and India did not spell out the end of empire. For French-Indians, like many populations who live on the margins and make up the minor, nationalism (both Indian and French) seemed like a distant object, unrelated to local life. Thus, there were discussions among French-Indians about the possibilities of imperial citizenship through the French Union and what shared sovereignty might look like, conversations that were also happening in other parts of the French Empire.[73]

## French India, French-Indian, the French in India

Categories are important for understanding and analyzing historical events; they are often necessary to identify who believes in one thing, and who may believe in an opposite thing, to clarify the importance of one ideology over another. Still, static categories can be dangerous. As Gary Wilder has written, by making links between France and its colonies, historians of colonialism risk "reenact[ing] that which they are supposed to explore: the incorporation of overseas territories into a republican metanarrative."[74] The alternate danger is taking for granted the opposite— that, for instance, a person in French India, if not French, must be Indian. Throughout this book, you will encounter references to "French-Indians," "the French in India," "créoles," and "Pondichérians." These categories will sometimes, by necessity, overlap, simply because the person or people in question changed their location, their nationality, or their self-identification. In every instance of categorization, I have done my best to take my cues from the subjects themselves; their fluid nature will show how categories of national belonging are often limited and narrow and suggest ways that we can destabilize these categories.

The period under investigation in this book begins in the early twentieth century and ends in the early 1970s, starting with the exile of Aurobindo Ghose that led him to Pondicherry in 1910 and ending with the early history of Auroville, which was established in 1968. The chapters are more thematic than chronological, with overlapping time periods that work to give depth to a political history that has already been written. I strive, thus, not to provide a detailed history of the day-to-day events of the time period in French India, but instead to contemplate the ways in which various forms of space-making and settlement operated within a framework of tension between different empires and subsequent movements for decolonization.[75] In chapter 1, "Carceral Borders: Exile, Surveillance, and Subversion," I turn to the period between the 1910s and 1940s to look at how the physical borders that enclosed the territories of French India came to be carceral borders as well as spaces of refuge for various people who had differing relationships to the imperial states of France and England. Colonial subjects became targets of surveillance through the introduction of passports and customs checkpoints, as the imperial states focused on making colonial borders more securitized. The chapter also looks at the Sri Aurobindo Ashram as a supposed site of exile and contrasts the Ashram with the political exile of those targeted by the French state in other parts of the Empire.

In chapter 2, "The Future of French India: Decolonization and Settlement at the Borders," and chapter 3, "Making the Postcolonial Subject: Goondas, Refugees, and Citizens," we move to 1947 and the liberation of British India, exploring the ways in which independence, liberation, and sovereignty were received and addressed in the French Indian context. These chapters cover the years 1947–1954, detailing the politics of liberation and decolonization in French India. Histories of decolonization in South Asia broadly, and French India specifically, all dismiss the violence that occurred on the many borders of French India, placing the blame on "goondas," claiming that it was ultimately unrelated to decolonization. These two chapters work against this trend, arguing that the violence that occurred between 1947 and 1954 on the French Indian borders is dismissed because both India and France worked to promote the idea that decolonization could be purely diplomatic, that it was simply a matter of two rational states coming to terms with each other. In contrast to this, in chapter 3 I look to the ways that the Indian government continued many of the policies of the British Raj in French India in terms of border enforcement and the criminalization of political opponents, creating new populations of refugees, citizens, and goondas, a method of population control similar to the refugeeization of those affected by Partition.[76]

In chapter 4, "Decolonial Crossings: Settlers, Migrants, Tourists," I look specifically at the question of citizenship in French India and for

French-Indians during the 1950s and early 1960s and contrast it with the mass arrival of Europeans in Pondicherry *after* France had agreed to leave India. There are today tens of thousands of "French-Indians," although this moniker is employed to describe a range of people: those of Indian origin who chose to retain French citizenship at the moment of transfer (1962); those of mixed French and Indian heritage, almost all of whom migrated to France at the moment of transfer; and those of French origin who have migrated to former French India since 1962. This chapter asks questions about race, settlement, nationalism, and citizenship during the period of transfer.

Finally, in chapter 5, "From the Ashram to Auroville: Utopia as Settlement," I think through the implications of building a utopian community during a period of decolonization, seeing the existence of Auroville as a key site for understanding how colonialism, including white settlement, has continued well past decolonization. "French India" as a geographic space is a place that once existed—and still does, to the extent that nostalgia for the colonies continues to circulate—through the promotion of tourism in the former colonies. I argue that the *structure* of colonial settlement in French India in the form of utopian projects was framed as anticolonial while contributing to the construction of institutions that would outlive the colonial empires under the guise of working toward a "global vision." Despite the proclamation of being anticolonial (or, more accurately, against the imperialists), these projects opened space for new settlement projects, instead of working to abolish imperial structures.

The documentary "Les trois mondes de Pondichéry" serves as an illuminating example of how the history of Pondicherry has been widely understood as three separate stories: that of French French India, Tamil French India, and the Aurobindo Ashram—three histories that may have some overlap but are overall distinct. On the contrary, this book works on the margins of these histories to show how all three are intertwined. French India is, and has been since its founding in the seventeenth century, a global site of exchange and experimentation, a hot spot for debates about imperial sovereignty, religious conversion, settlement, border-making, decolonization, and colonial and postcolonial citizenship.[77] The minor status of the territories allowed people to work outside of mainstream movements often well remembered in state-based historical scholarship. Building on current trends in the field of global history that use the construction of nationalism and national borders to destabilize the centrality of states to contemporary understandings of the world system, this book looks to French India in the twentieth century to explore the ways that colonized peoples, as well as those from the imperial centers of England and France, utilized imperial networks to experiment with utopian projects—an often misaligned assortment of settlement, socialism, liberation, evolutionary transformation, and liberalism, some of which reinforced colonial institutions while others sought to destroy them.[78]

# PART ONE
# Making

CHAPTER I

## Carceral Borders

*Exile, Surveillance, and Subversion*

> The nationalities are hopelessly mixed up, and many persons do not know, and cannot prove, whether they are French or British subjects.
> —REGINALD SCHOMBERG, HM CONSUL GENERAL
> IN THE FRENCH ESTABLISHMENTS, 1937

During the summer of 1939, the British authorities in India began construction on a barbed wire fence that would enforce the boundaries between British and French India. The fence, which was built in two out of the five French Indian territories, Pondicherry and Karaikal, cost approximately Rs. 3.21 lakhs (321,000 rupees), a toll incurred by the British government in India.[1] As the fence was erected, British consul in Pondicherry Reginald Schomberg reported that "although only a dozen odd miles have been put up . . . good results have already been noted."[2] The fence had a double barrier, and the posts were sealed in concrete to "prevent the earth being dug away."[3] Schomberg estimated that it would take a "smuggler" forty minutes to cut away both fences, so the fence was patrolled every forty minutes to ensure no one passed through unnoticed.[4] Before the fence was built, customs agents were forced to "pursue smugglers over rice fields and swamps," a chase that rarely favored the customs agent. Schomberg ended his report by praising the construction of the barbed wire fence but offering a note of caution: "No fence, however, will by itself stop smuggling, just as no prison without a guard will confine its inmates."[5]

Officially, the fences around Pondicherry and Karaikal were built to stop the smuggling of goods between British and French India, as the British were concerned they were losing out on millions of rupees of revenue in import and export tariffs. However, Schomberg's use of a prison

[ 33 ]

as an analogy for the customs barriers captures the sentiment of local responses to the fence. A prison, of course, is not built to contain material goods, but to control bodies that are considered dangerous to those outside the prison walls. The people who lived both within and around these territorial fences were left confused about their relationship to them, and, essentially, to the land itself. The dual-language French-Tamil newspaper *Dessobagari* ran an editorial questioning the purpose of the fence, asking, "Why the plan of barbed-wire fencing around French territory? Will the fence enclose the British enclaves or will they surround only the French territory?"[6] In this context, it is unclear whether French or British India was the interior of the prison, but what is clear is that the two areas, divided by borders drawn by imperial powers concerned primarily with the politics of expansion, had become important markers of identity, dictating the movements and livelihoods of the local populations.

## Colonial Border-Making

The five French Indian territories of Pondicherry, Karaikal, Mahé, Yanam, and Chandernagore were scattered throughout India, rooted in the trade interests and routes of the seventeenth-century European trading companies. In 1763, France, England, and Spain signed the Treaty of Paris in order to bring the Seven Years' War to an end. The treaty formally recognized the competing imperial powers' territorial gains and losses throughout the world, including in the Americas, the Caribbean, Europe, South Asia, parts of the African continent, and areas of the Indian Ocean. The treaty marked an important moment of territorial division between three of these imperial powers, including setting the foundation for British dominance in South Asia. Article 11 of the treaty addresses the struggle between France and England in India, granting France control over the five *comptoirs* (trading posts) while also forbidding it from erecting any fortifications in South Asia or keeping a military in Bengal.[7] Though there was some territorial movement and exchange after 1763, the Second Treaty of Paris, which came at the end of the Napoleonic Wars in 1814, once again granted France control over the five comptoirs while continuing the ban on a military, noting that the only troops allowed on French territory would be those "necessary for the maintenance of the police."[8] This statute stood in place until 1962, when India took over control of the territories from France.

The demilitarization of the French Indian territories established in the treaties meant that maintaining the borders between French and British India fell primarily to customs agents and local police. This was complicated for spatial reasons: Pondicherry was a fractured territory, split into enclaves (which the French called communes) that were surrounded by British territory on at least two sides (see map 1.1).[9] The physical appearance of a border marking territories, along with the accompanying security regime to maintain the integrity of the border, instigates a regime of fear of being watched, tracked, and identified. Territory is essential to the maintenance of power in states as well as empires, where territory is utilized as a political technology of rule.[10] Geographer Stuart Elden argues that controlling people within a territory with "terror" or fear is a tool for governments to maintain sovereignty. This was certainly the case in Pondicherry and Chandernagore, the two French Indian territories that experienced intensive border securitization, both before and after 1947.

The borders enacted by colonial agents were often incredibly porous, especially when no physical barrier marked separate, supposedly sovereign, territories. Geographers Willem van Schendel and Erik de Maaker have argued that the colonial borders of Asia were frequently ignored by people native to the areas, who are often united by "languages and ethnic identities" as well as "trade, agriculture, religious practice, and marriage." Colonial border-making was a common practice throughout Asia, where "even the borders of states that were never formally colonized, such as China, Thailand, and Nepal, were the outcome of interaction" with colonial desires.[11] While some areas of Asia, such as the region of the Southeast Asian highlands that political scientist James C. Scott has identified as "Zomia," were somewhat impervious to the imperial proxy wars being fought out through colonial border-making because of their geographic remoteness (among other reasons), Pondicherry was subject to highly visible border-making that included the construction and securitization of physical borders.[12] In other words, the porous colonial borders became securitized carceral borders. Pondicherry was certainly not the only area of South Asia that was subject to the haphazard cartography of empire, yet it stands out as a unique example of a bordering that created deep divides among a population that was otherwise united by language, ethnicity, and often religious and cultural practices.

Before the physical border between French and British India was put into place, the territory of each imperial power was both marked on maps

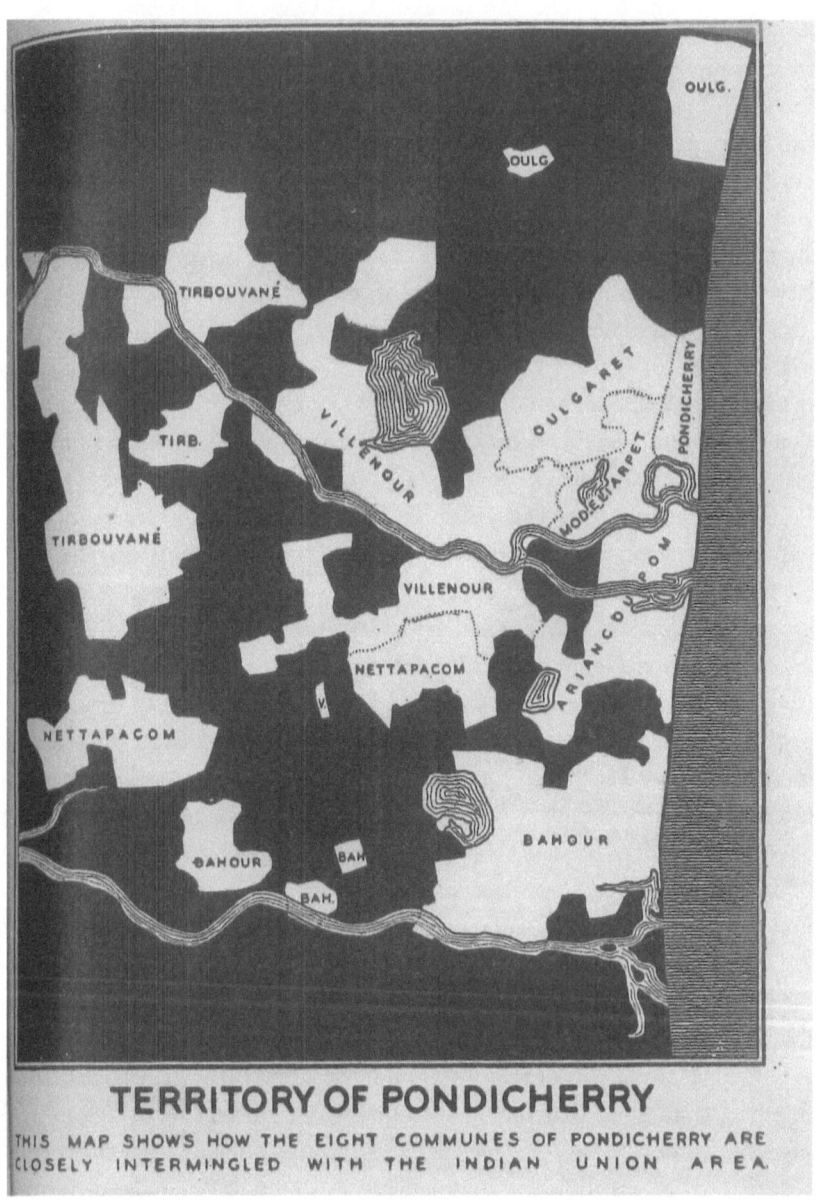

*Map 1.1* Map of Pondicherry that highlights the space between the communes. From N. V. Rajkumar, *The Problem of French India* (1953).

and also visible to the local population through policing and access to education, transportation, rights of citizenship, and differing tax rates. While chapter 2 will delve into the citizenship question, in this chapter I look at the physical space of French India itself and the arrival of revolutionaries and exiles in French India to argue that, during the twentieth century, both French and British colonial bureaucracies worked to establish, control, and make visible their territories in India by carceralizing the border, transforming a previously imagined boundary into an oft-violent site of divided nationalisms. Central to the carceralizing process was transforming the territories into spaces of surveillance and instituting a regime of identification through passports and identification cards that would signify to officials who legitimately belonged where and who the (British) government of India labeled as anarchists, dacoits, or goondas, terms that in this time and space served as code words for "purveyor of meaningless violence": not necessarily a signal of a political ideology, but instead a way for the colonial powers to criminalize those who opposed the colonial order.[13]

Pondicherry and the other French territories in India were already global sites by the late nineteenth century, due to their importance to both France and Britain in the struggle for imperial dominance, as well as the territories' status as trade centers. However, in the twentieth century, the global importance of the French territories in India transformed as the settlements became spaces of exile and refuge for anticolonial thinkers and fighters. The presence of exiles, primarily in Pondicherry and Chandernagore, transformed these "sleepy towns" into "hotbeds" of revolutionary activity linked to Paris, Berlin, London, and other parts of India through the import and export of seditious literature and arms for use against the British in India.[14] This required active surveillance and policing that placed everyone in these border zones at risk of being tracked. In part, this chapter looks to the anticolonial exiles who settled in Pondicherry and Chandernagore, as well as in France, to examine how anti-British, anticolonial organizing took place in French territory and subverted the carceral system of terror and territory. As Reginald Schomberg was fond of noting, "Many persons [did] not know, and [could not] prove, whether they [were] French or British subjects," and this instability gave anticolonial agitators a great advantage against the two imperial rulers who could not manage to tell them apart.[15]

## From Colonial to Carceral Borders

The territories of French India were useful to France in the early twentieth century for a few key reasons. First, they were symbolic of France's global position: without the French Indian territories, there would be no reminder to Britain that it had once made an effort to rule in South Asia.[16] Second, building on the affective symbolism was the desire to show to the world that the French were better, more civilized, more humane colonizers than the British. This was often achieved through the admiration that Indian freedom fighters who visited French India such as M. K. Gandhi voiced for France and the ideals of the French revolution. Third, the territories were geographically strategic in relation to the French colonial holdings in Indochina, which were becoming active nodes in the French imperial world by the late nineteenth century.[17] Lastly, the continued French presence in British India was a headache for the British that could possibly be leveraged to gain more territory for France in other parts of the world, although the French never did agree to cede any of the territories. With British interests focused in other areas of South Asia, and French interests concentrated in Indochina and North and West Africa, the French possessions in India were, in the words of one British administrator, "an administrative inconvenience," until they became a space for anticolonial organizing after 1905.[18]

Britain had made gestures toward rectifying the "inconvenience" of the colonial borders throughout the nineteenth century. According to records at the British India Office and the archives of the French Ministère des Affaires Étrangers, the British and French governments had engaged in discussions about reducing and/or consolidating the French Indian territories in 1857, between 1883 and 1885, and with increasing frequency following the end of World War I in 1918.[19] While an agreement was not reached at any point in these negotiations, in 1857 the two governments discussed the French relinquishing all territory except for Pondicherry and Karaikal, and in 1883–1885 had debated the "extinction of all French rights in the *loges* in return for territorial compensation in the Pondicherry region."[20] The *loges*—small sovereign spaces that usually housed French-owned factories—were scattered throughout India and often caused trouble for British administrators. The hope was that France would be willing to give up the loges in exchange for consolidating some of the British territory that broke up Pondicherry. As the India Office wrote immediately following

World War I, in 1918, Pondicherry "is very irregular in shape, dovetailing in and out of British territory: it also contains a British enclave approximately at its centre."[21] Consulate memos make it clear that Britain knew France was unlikely to relinquish Pondicherry, citing the importance France placed on having some sort of presence in India to the image of France as an imperial power, as well as the need to maintain strategic posts near French Indochina. However, the British government in India made continued efforts to trade more territory in Pondicherry for a cessation of the other territories and loges, including an offer to swap the French Indian territories for British-held land in West Africa.[22]

If French India represented a mere inconvenience to the British Raj, why were the British set on regaining control of these territories? In his work on the numerous enclaves that exist today on the India-Bangladesh border, geographer Jason Cons shows how borders mark zones for policing and surveillance. "The enclaves are presented as territorial accidents," he writes. "These spaces accumulate criminality because they are holes in the territorial net of the border."[23] The numerous "holes in the territorial net" between French and British India did indeed become "hotspots" for people seeking refuge who were in exile because of their critical stance toward British colonial rule.

Chandernagore, the only French territory in India that was located outside of Madras Presidency, covered four square miles, and in 1933 its population was counted at twenty-seven thousand people. Chandernagore was located on the River Hooghly, just twenty miles north of the city of Calcutta, an area that following the partition of Bengal in 1905 became an important space for organizing against the British.[24] In 1905, when the partition occurred, Bengal was home to over eighty-five million people, including significant Hindu and Muslim populations, both of which primarily spoke Bengali. The partition, which occurred on 16 October 1905, split the province into two: one Hindu-dominated and the other Muslim-dominated. The Indian Congress Party decried the move as an attempt to divide and rule, while tens of thousands of Bengalis protested the partition, signing petitions and enacting boycotts against British goods. The partition inspired many previously uninvolved Indians to take up the mantle of British anticolonialism. Chandernagore, situated on the outskirts of Calcutta, the intellectual center of the rapidly growing anticolonial nationalist movement, became an important space for anticolonialists to escape direct British persecution. After 1905, the government of India escalated the targeting of Bengali political groups classified by the British as anarchist and/or terrorist organizations. Indeed, both Chandernagore and Pondicherry were spaces for the production and distribution of seditious (anti-British) material, and for the import of arms from abroad. Because the French police in Chandernagore failed to stop this activity, British officials in Bengal began to blame the increase in violent attacks against the British—mostly bombings and assassinations, with some acts of arson as well—on French administrators in India for allowing the formation of these groups.[25] Terror accompanied the making of new territory with the partition of Bengal.

As early as 1906, Bengali revolutionaries saw the possible advantage of appealing to the French against the British, much as Tipu Sultan had appealed to King Louis IV against British rule over a century before. A letter written by a group of Bengali swadeshis (a term used by those who identified with the new Indian independence movement fomented by the partition of Bengal) to Joseph François in the French Ministry of Colonies in April 1906 praised the French for granting the French territories the power of representation in the French Chamber of Deputies.[26] The idea that life was better and more fair under French rule was an early and persistent notion associated with the freedom struggle against the British. Memos written by British officials concerned with the situation in Chandernagore make it clear that the British believed that the French were weak and unable to stop the terrorists: the French space of exception was, in the minds of the British, crawling with violent criminals, terrorists, and dacoits. Chandernagore had joined Paris in the British geography of "anarchist centres." Descriptions of Chandernagore written by British officials paint a picture of a lawless border town filled with terrorists making bombs behind every door, hoisting their rifles and shooting haphazardly in the streets with no regard for human life. According to an intelligence report of July 1907, "Every middle-class Bengali home at this little settlement has each got at least a gun and a revolver."[27] Within this imagined geography of armed anti-British revolutionaries, Chandernagore transformed from a sleepy curiosity into a direct target of British surveillance.

By 1918, the panic in the India Office about anti-British organizing in Chandernagore had reached new levels. An India Office memo states that Chandernagore had become "a veritable hotbed of revolutionary conspiracy directed against the British Government," directly due to the "weakness of the French administration." A telegram written from a British official in Calcutta some time later, in 1933, stated the primary problems of controlling Chandernagore as "a) the inefficiency of the French police b) the rigidity of the French legal procedures governing police actions and c) the stupidity of the local authorities."[28] Officials hoped to impress upon the imperial center in London that quashing the anticolonial movement depended, in large part, on France ceding Chandernagore to the government of India.[29]

Border towns and zones are often seen as illegitimate spaces that quickly fill with outlaws, smugglers, and criminals of all sorts. What exactly defines a space as a border zone is extremely malleable, as we see in the conversion of Chandernagore, Pondicherry, and even Paris, into incubators of anti-British organizing, made possible by a geographic proximity to England, both on the European continent and the South Asian subcontinent. Chandernagore was just one of many places throughout India, Europe, and North America where anti-British and anticolonial revolutionaries gathered to organize actions against the British and to collect and make weapons, from bombs to rifles and handguns. As a French territory, Chandernagore did not fall under the jurisdiction of the British Indian Arms Act of 1878 that "made it illegal for natives . . . of India to possess swords, firearms and most other weapons."[30] The lack of any laws prohibiting Indians from owning weapons meant that Chandernagore became an important meeting place for Bengali arms trafficking, a development the British attributed once again to the weakness of the French to police the population. In a note written by Charles Tegart, deputy general of police, Intelligence Branch, Criminal Investigation Division, Bengal, in March 1917, he refers to Chandernagore as "an Alsatia for revolutionary fugitives," an "active centre of plots directed towards the subversion of British Rule in India."[31] Tegart, in calling Chandernagore "an Alsatia," made an important link between the French territory in India and disputed territory in Europe, ushering French India into the global imagining of borderlands as spaces of illegality. In popular usage, "Alsatia" refers both to Alsace, a region between France and Germany that had been fought over and traded back and forth since the Franco-Prussian War in 1870, and to an area just outside the city of London called Alsatia that existed in the seventeenth century and was famed for being a sanctuary for outlaws, debtors, and murderers.[32]

Whether in Chandernagore, Alsatia, Pondicherry, or Alsace, the borders put in place to carve out spaces of legitimacy have always created a counterspace of illegality. Drawing on recent work in carceral studies and carceral geographies, I term these borders that mark French India "carceral borders" to signal their importance in making new regimes of policing, surveillance, and identity tracking in spaces that were formerly fairly autonomous, with the porous colonial borders common to many parts of Asia during this time. Unlike "incarceration," which refers generally to legal, state-sanctioned imprisonment, "carceral" has a wider meaning that points to the ways in which technologies of policing and "mass supervision" penetrate the lives of people who have not committed crimes, but are marked by the state as likely to commit a crime, an expansion of the criminal justice system into the everyday lives of citizens.[33] Immigration detention, wherein refugees, asylum seekers, and other types of migrants are often held for extended periods of time, has roots in the many minor borders created by colonial powers. In later years, after India became independent in 1947, these same borders between British and French India would be used to determine who was a refugee and who was a criminal—a delineation as fragile and unstable as the borders between French and British India itself.

The groups forming in Chandernagore, and before long in Pondicherry and in the other French territories and loges, were almost exclusively focused on anti-British activity in the service of Indian independence. They used French territory, in India and in continental France, strategically against the British. Anti-British agitators in India saw French India as territory that was safe from British persecution, where they could seek refuge from British charges of sedition, theft, murder, libel, and a litany of other crimes levied against anticolonial revolutionaries that did carry over into French territory. Indian revolutionaries not only sought refuge in French India, but also, prior to World War II, fled London for the relative safety of Paris. During this period, French India *and* France were spaces that were at once colonial and anticolonial, offering refuge from the British Empire and British India for those willing to respect the power and ideology of the French Republic, itself an imperial nation-state.[34]

What role, then, did the border between British and French territory play in revolutionary struggles for independence, and how did it affect the everyday lives of people in the French territories? While France did consistently assert its sovereignty over the French Indian territories, it also, at various points, either agreed to allow British CID (Criminal Investigation Division) officers onto French territory to surveil the anticolonial exiles, or placed French police on surveillance duty, most actively in Chandernagore and Pondicherry, from 1911 until the 1930s.[35] The border between French and British India may have provided some degree of comfort and safety to those seeking refuge from the British government, but the border also became an active site of policing and tracking. Concerns over the "illegal" activities of anticolonial people in a space that appeared impossible to contain led to the development of regimes of identification and control that continue to operate today. As surveillance of anticolonial agitators ramped up in the 1910s, the borders between the territories transformed from colonial to carceral.

In the following section, I look at how various non-European populations in the region split by French and British interests responded to attempts at colonial control, paying specific attention to the malleability of colonial subject formation, as well as how the European presence shaped lives in the French territory. While the imperial nation-state (both France and Britain) needed to create borders to exercise power over the land and the population, anticolonial agents appropriated the same borders for their own uses, directed against not only imperial boundaries but national ones as well. Indian anticolonialists took advantage of long-standing tensions between England and France to evade colonial controls, carving spaces of refuge for themselves and their ideas in both French India and France.[36] The ease with which "French" and "British" Indians switched their identities and crossed borders, identifying with whichever colonial power afforded them the most benefits, led colonial authorities to tighten borders, erect fences, levy taxes against "foreign" subjects, and begin in earnest to require colonial subjects to carry passports (British) and/or *cartes d'identités* (French)—all measures that influenced the paths of postcolonial migrations and have remained in place. Examining this period of transition reveals the many ways in which contemporary systems of global border security and national identity are rooted in colonial systems of control.

## Revolutionary Hotspots and Migrating Subjects

Sri Aurobindo Ghose is arguably the most famed individual to have ever resided in Pondicherry. Much like the French governors-general François Martin and Joseph Dupleix, who are widely remembered as the founders of French India, Aurobindo was not native to the area, but he has become a marker for it. Aurobindo was born in Calcutta on 15 August 1872, the third son to Krishna Dhun Ghose and Swarnalata Devi, both of whom had strong ties to the Brahmo Samaj, a Bengali Hindu reformist group popular in the late nineteenth century. Raised in an Anglophile home, Aurobindo studied in England, where he lived from the age of seven until he finished his schooling and returned to India in 1893 at the age of twenty-one.[37] Aurobindo excelled at his studies in England, mastering French, Greek, and Latin and earning a scholarship to Cambridge University. Aurobindo's father planned for him to finish at Cambridge, take the Indian Civil Service (ICS) exam, return to India, and join the colonial administration in the highest position allowed for Indians. In this way, Aurobindo's English education and engagement with Western thought and language shares commonalities with the other major players of South Asian nationalist politicians and leaders, including M. K. Gandhi, M. A. Jinnah, and Jawaharlal Nehru.

Although Aurobindo is still celebrated by the Indian government as a freedom fighter, his withdrawal from politics around 1910 marks him as separate from other celebrated figures. There are hundreds of biographies of Aurobindo, the majority of which are easily discerned as hagiographies written by Aurobindo devotees. A great deal of these works are in line with a teleological narrative invested in both the godliness of Aurobindo and his commitment to Indian independence. The 2008 biography *The Lives of Sri Aurobindo*, written by historian and longtime Aurobindo Ashram archivist Peter Heehs, is easily the most thorough and objective work on Aurobindo to date.[38] Unlike authors of hagiographies or nationalist narratives, Heehs treats his subject as a human, one who was simultaneously exceptional and flawed.

Heehs writes that as the ICS exam became imminent, and despite his father's insistence on the superiority of Western culture, Aurobindo realized that he would never be respected in England, because he was a racialized subject who could not achieve posts reserved for white men. This realization led Aurobindo to recognize that his focus on Western philosophy and languages had shielded him from his own culture, a culture that everyone around him in the West associated with him due to his skin color, but that he himself knew nothing about.[39] This was a turning point for Aurobindo, and "his own belief that Asian and particularly Indian culture was superior to anything in Europe grew in tandem with his conviction that India had to throw off the British yoke."[40] Aurobindo purposefully failed the ICS exam by tanking the equestrian test, and he returned to India determined to join the struggle for Indian independence.[41]

Aurobindo's return to India from England in 1893 is an important thread of the Indian independence narrative. Having faced directly the "superiority" of the metropole, Aurobindo returned to Bombay on 6 February 1893 and two days later arrived in nearby Baroda, a city that, to his British eyes, seemed to be a "thoroughly Indian city," with "no trace of the British Raj."[42] Baroda was one of the major Princely States that operated under, but was independent of, the British Crown, ruled by the Gaekwad family that had also ruled much of Gujarat since the early eighteenth century. Heehs suggests that because Baroda was one of the Princely States it was, through the European-conditioned eyes of Aurobindo, *more Indian* than the parts of India that fell directly under the British Raj. Aurobindo used his time there to begin to learn Indian languages and learn about the everyday life of the local populations, a gesture that he shared with many colonial administrators who had come before him, though perhaps with a different intent.

As if making up for lost time, Aurobindo returned from England prepared to fight against British rule with all possible tools, from words to weapons. Aurobindo held a series of jobs after his return to India, including school principal, professor, and civil servant, although his engagement with politics was his primary interest.[43] By 1906, when he moved to Calcutta, he was actively looking for ways "to popularise the idea of violent revolt."[44] Although he did become involved with some groups in Maharashtra that were dedicated to martial arts and other types of physical training, Aurobindo became most known for the seditious writing in his journal, *Bande Mataram*, for which he served as the editor in chief.

The Indian Penal Code (IPC) was introduced in 1860, three years after the first Indian uprising for independence in 1857, but sedition (section 124A of the IPC) was not included until 1870, as the British government began to feel the pressure against it mounting, articulated and disseminated widely through vernacular presses. Article 124A states, "Whoever by words, either spoken or written, or by signs, or by visible representation, or otherwise, brings or attempts to bring into hatred or contempt, or excites or attempts to excite disaffection towards the Government established by law in India, shall be punished with imprisonment for life, to which fine may be added, or with imprisonment which may extend to three years, to which fine may be added, or with fine." The sedition act focused on the written word and worked to shut down any newspaper, publisher, or printer that produced material critical of the British government of India.[45] The British colonial state used the law to control and instill fear into the colonized, effectively equating criticism of the government with treason.[46] While effective in imprisoning many anticolonial nationalists, the attempt by the British in India to vanquish dissent through various sedition laws often had the opposite of the desired effect, and dissidents worked to print seditious literature abroad—or, as was the case in French India, to work around the British laws.

Linking dissent to violence was an important tool for the British colonial administration. In 1908, the police commissioner of Bengal accused Aurobindo of instigating a bombing that killed two European women. Aurobindo was dangerous to the government of India because his nationalist agenda was popular with the "student class," the group of young, educated Indians that could potentially overthrow the British government.[47] Adding to his direct contact with students through his jobs as professor and principal, Aurobindo was Bengali, which contributed to his appeal for the many Bengalis who had been radicalized by the 1905 partition of Bengal.

Aurobindo was a bit surprised to learn that he was such a controversial figure. He wrote that he learned of his role in the alleged bombing while sitting in the *Bande Mataram* office in Calcutta, although at the time he "had no idea that I happened to be the main target of suspicion and that according to the police I was the chief killer, the instigator and secret leader of the young terrorists and revolutionaries."[48] Aurobindo was soon arrested, and although he was eventually acquitted, he spent the year of 1909 in jail awaiting trial at the Alipore Prison, along with several other accused revolutionaries, including his youngest brother, Barindra Kumar Ghose (1880–1959). Like many anticolonial revolutionaries, including M. K. Gandhi, Jawaharlal Nehru, and Bhagat Singh, Aurobindo published essays while imprisoned. In his *Tales of Prison Life*, he writes that his imprisonment led him on a spiritual journey, that "the only result of the wrath of the British Government was that I found God," which foreshadowed his eventual transformation from political revolutionary to yogi.[49] Yet, even as Aurobindo began his journey toward living an ascetic life, Viceroy Lord Minto wrote in 1910 that Aurobindo Ghose was "the most dangerous man [the British government] have to deal with at present."[50] The British government of India was deeply invested in promoting a discourse linking Indian nationalism to violent terrorism.

There were some elements of truth in the British assertion that a number of anticolonial nationalists who belonged to the extremist wing of the Indian National Congress—those who were amenable to the use of violence to achieve independence—spent time in French Indian territories.[51] Chandernagore was, as predicted by British authorities, an important gathering spot for Indian nationalists seeking refuge from British police and sedition laws. After completing his prison sentence, Aurobindo took advantage of the French territory and its proximity to Calcutta, departing from Chandernagore and sailing to Pondicherry on a French-owned steamship named *Dupleix*, amid rumors that he would be arrested, or deported to a prison colony, for writing and publishing the seditious essay "To My Countrymen" in the journal *Karmayogin*. While *Karmayogin*'s publisher, Monmohan Ghose, was arrested and sentenced to six months in prison for his role in publishing the allegedly seditious essay, British officials were unable to arrest Aurobindo; he had left for Pondicherry as soon as he heard there was a warrant for his arrest, in February 1910. An August 1910 telegram from the commissioner of police in Calcutta to the secretary of the government of India noted that Aurobindo was out of their reach in Pondicherry but was "being watched by the Madras Police. Should he attempt to escape by way of Colombo he will be arrested under the Fugitive Offenders Act."[52] Knowing that they could not arrest him in French India, the British authorities canceled the warrant by the end of November 1910. Hoping to stem the tide of wanted revolutionaries from "absconding" to French India, C. R. Cleveland of the Home Department issued a statement claiming that Aurobindo was free to "return to British India without fear of molestation from Government whenever he likes."[53] After his arrival in Pondicherry, however, Aurobindo remained there for the rest of his life.

While Aurobindo's exile did attract a number of visitors when he first arrived in Pondicherry in April 1910, he spent several months out of the public eye, despite his growing prominence as a fighter for independence. In November 1910, Aurobindo wrote a letter to the editor of the *Hindu* addressing the question of his whereabouts and his intentions, beginning by stating that he planned to remain in Pondicherry and not "step foot on British territory even for a single moment" until he could return publicly.

In addition to making public his location, he noted that since reaching Pondicherry he had lived as a "religious recluse" and planned to remain withdrawn from politics; he intended to stay where he was, in retirement from political life, in order to pursue his "Yogic sadhana undisturbed by political action."[54] His letter demonstrates that Aurobindo was well aware of the attention his arrival in Pondicherry had placed on the town, and of the police that were positioned to watch him. The lines between British and French India were clear to Aurobindo: in British India, he would be arrested and placed in prison, whereas in French India he would be left alone to study yoga and live the life of a "religious recluse."

By the time Aurobindo arrived in Pondicherry, he was a well-known member of the freedom movement. Aurobindo sought refuge not only in Pondicherry, but within his own dwelling. During the first years he spent in Pondicherry he was relatively social, meeting with people, attending the occasional baptism or wedding.[55] But he seldom left his home, choosing to communicate only with his close associates and devotees, making his own space in the ville blanche of Pondicherry. His position, however, did not sit well with many local Pondichérians who saw the Ashram as a colonial presence, particularly because of the great interest the French government had in protecting it.

Yet, although Aurobindo was safe in exile, his presence in Pondicherry brought a new and enhanced level of surveillance down upon the territory. The British police were quite busy trying to surveil the constantly changing group of anticolonial revolutionaries who came through Pondicherry. The Tamil poet and revolutionary V. V. S. Aiyer (1881–1925) arrived in Pondicherry about seven months after Aurobindo, on 4 December 1910, after a journey through Europe, according to British police records, "disguised as a Muhammadan."[56] Aiyer was connected to the high-profile assassination of Robert William D'Escourt Ashe, collector of Tinnevely District, who was fatally shot on 17 June 1911. The actual assassin, R. Vanchi Aiyer of nearby Senkottai, Travancore State, killed himself minutes after taking Ashe's life.[57] Aiyer, along with several other Tamil anticolonialists who sought refuge in Pondicherry, including the esteemed Tamil nationalist poet C. Subramanya Bharathi, were accused of planning the murder and were harassed by the police for years following the incident. The Tamil scholar and revolutionary V. Ramaswamy Iyengar was also in residence at the time. The British, frustrated with their inability to extradite their targets from French territory, began to post British India police on the Pondicherry border in 1910 with the mandate that if one of the subjects they suspected of a number of seditious crimes crossed into British India, the police could arrest them.[58] In this way, the borders separating French and British India transformed from a colonial to a carceral border years before the physical fence was erected.

## Exiled in an Enclave

In 1984, the Palestinian-in-exile and postcolonial theorist Edward Said wrote, "Exile is strangely compelling to think about but terrible to experience. It is the unhealable rift forced between a human being and a native place, between the self and its true home: its essential sadness can never be surmounted."[59] The act of exile is often thought to be rooted in rupture, movement, displacement, and loss of home.[60] Yet, as geographer Andrew Davies has recently argued, the dichotomy between home and exile often gives the false impression that home is inherently stable while exile is "unsettled," whereas, in actuality, defining the spatial reality of a "homeland" can be just as fraught as the space of exile itself.[61] For Aurobindo, this question of exile is indeed complicated, as it seems clear that outside of a belief that India was his homeland, and the fact that at one point he engaged deeply with the politics of its liberation, he did not have an attachment to a homeland as defined by traditional narratives. What could "India" mean as a homeland to a child such as Aurobindo? Raised in an Anglophile house and shipped to England at a young age, Aurobindo is a prime example of a colonial subject who had to, in the words of social theorist Ashish Nandy, "own up his Indianness to become his version of the authentic Indian."[62] Settling in the ville blanche with its French street planning and European objects surely brought Aurobindo some comfort, while his positioning in India—albeit French India—allowed him to remain true to his cause of living an Indian life. Pondicherry was a hybrid space partially because of its design and governance, but also because of its declared otherness to British India.

Aurobindo possessed the skills to thrive in a space like Pondicherry: he had a world-class English education, was a known anti-British agitator, and had begun to study seriously Indian (mostly Sanskrit and Hindu) literature, mythology, and languages, which he continued in earnest once in Pondicherry. It can be said that his exile transformed him into his most revered self—Pondicherry was truly a refuge for him, and for many of his devotees, as we will see in following chapters. However, not everyone had the social and cultural capital that allowed Aurobindo to flourish in exile. Aurobindo's younger brother, Barindra Kumar Ghose (1880–1959), followed in his elder brother's footsteps in revolutionary ferment, but, unlike Aurobindo, who was able to escape persecution and set the terms of his own exile in Pondicherry, Barindra was imprisoned in the cellular jail in Port Blair (popularly known as Kala Pani, or "black water") on the Andaman Islands in the Bay of Bengal.[63]

Originally sentenced to death for the same crime for which Aurobindo was released, Barindra suffered in ways not experienced by his brother.[64] He was unable to escape to foreign territory, and he did not leave his political life behind. In his memoir *The Tale of My Exile*, published in 1922, Barindra speaks of the anguish of both imprisonment and exile. He details the dimensions of his cell, the bolts that kept the inmates imprisoned, and the location of the guards in the watchtower who could look directly into his cell. He provides descriptions of the wardens, and the punishments they enjoyed inflicting on the prisoners, such as being forced to wear bells around their necks like bulls. He writes of the loss of identity that came with being a prisoner: "In all the prisons, here as elsewhere, the convicts immediately on their entrance lose their names and are given numbers instead. Each has to carry a wooden piece, 3 inches long, 2 inches broad, and 1 inch thick on which his number, the section under which he is convicted, the date of conviction and the term of sentence are written."[65] The "neck ticket" hung around the inmates' necks to identify them to the security guards, replacing the sense of identity that comes with a name with both the anonymity of a number and the specificity of a conviction. Barindra lost his identity in exile, while Aurobindo found his, highlighting the vast differences between a carceral space and a prison.

## Life in Spiritual Exile

Exile can be an experience fraught with pain and loss, marked by the erasure of one's home and personal identity, as we see in the case of Barindra Ghose. However, if the circumstances of the exile are amenable, it can also be a useful tool to create new homes and identities, start new projects, and leave the past behind. Although Aurobindo was celebrated throughout

India for his work in the freedom movement, soon after his arrival in Pondicherry he detached himself from politics to concentrate on his spiritual journey and the development of a philosophy called "integral yoga." While Aurobindo himself was not French-Indian, his eventual spiritual companion was a Parisian-born French woman named Mira Alfassa (1878–1973). Before arriving in Pondicherry, Alfassa had been involved in the exploration of the occult and "Eastern" spiritual practices. She was a frequent participant in Parisian salons that engaged with the more Anglophone-centered theosophical movement and the esoteric teachings of the occult group Le Mouvement Cosmique (the Cosmic Movement), led by the husband-and-wife team of Max and Alma Théon, based in French-occupied Algeria.[66]

Colonial occupation opened spaces for people from the imperial centers to try out "alternative" spiritual practices, ways of living that may have been impossible to realize at home. The colonial occupation of Algeria, for example, cleared space for the Théons to experiment with esoteric communal living in a space outside of France, but easily accessible to French nationals, while the French possession of the comptoirs in India led Mira Alfassa to what she later considered her spiritual destiny in India. Mira came to Pondicherry for the first time in 1914 in the company of her husband, a French colonial administrator named Paul Richard. Paul and Mira quickly entwined themselves with the life of Aurobindo and his yoga. Mira's brother Matéo was also a colonial administrator, serving at the time as the lieutenant governor of French-held Congo.[67] In his memoir, Paul Richard recalls how he and Mira helped Aurobindo by using their connections with Matéo to "lose" the order of extradition sent by the British authorities to the French.[68] It is unclear whether this is actually true, since British records indicate that they had no intent in arresting Aurobindo if he stayed on French territory, but the Alfassas clearly believed that they were able to help Aurobindo in this regard.

In addition to making use of their political connections, Paul and Mira spent a significant amount of time discussing philosophy and yoga with Aurobindo, eventually creating a journal that was printed in French and English titled *Arya: A Philosophical Review*.[69] The increasing intensity of World War I caused the French government to order Paul and Mira to leave India and return to France.[70] Unhappy with their return, Paul requested a transfer to Japan for the remainder of the war. Eventually, in 1920, Mira returned to Pondicherry without Paul to join Aurobindo once again.[71] Aurobindo and Alfassa quickly became spiritual companions, spending their days together in meditation and discussion. By 1926, Aurobindo announced his "retirement" and christened Alfassa "the Mother."[72] Under the leadership of the Mother, the Ashram grew, attracting devoted followers from across South Asia, though mainly Bengal, as well as Europe (primarily France). While Aurobindo was a major figure in the Indian independence movement and thus attracted significant attention, the Mother's philosophical works were published throughout Europe and North America, in French and English. Bengalis, the ethnic brethren of Aurobindo, as well as French nationals familiar with the work of the Mother, were well represented at the Ashram by the mid-1920s.[73]

Aurobindo used his European education and connections to secure a place for himself in Pondicherry. Nolini Gupta, one of Aurobindo's devotees, noted that Aurobindo charmed the French police in Pondicherry with his knowledge of French, Latin, and Greek. In fact, Gupta suggested, "the French Government had not been against us.... They had helped us as far as they could."[74] Gupta believed that while the French sided with the Indian freedom struggle, they had to take into account their diplomatic relationship with England and thus collaborated in some amount of surveillance over Aurobindo and his devotees. Writing in 1969, Gupta looked back on the French as the superior civilization to the British, echoing the narrative promoted by the French. Considering the "asylum" that was unofficially granted to anticolonial Indians escaping British persecution, Gupta wrote that "we were looked upon as their guests and as political refugees; it was a matter of honour for them to give us their protection. And where it is a question of honour, the French as a race are willing to risk anything.... But at the same time, they had their friendship, the *entente cordiale,* with Britain to maintain, and it is this that got them into a dilemma."[75]

This type of glorification of France and of French people was typical of this time and place, particularly by *non*–French-Indians: because the identity of the "refugee" was dependent on their position as British exiles in French India, there was a political benefit to "siding" with the French. In this context, this often included ignoring the functions and consequences of French colonialism and focusing on the *idea* of France, which was portrayed in popular discourse as a republic that espoused fairness, equality, democracy, and freedom, all of which are also antithetical to colonial rule. The politics of exile in an enclave meant siding with one power over another in order to create a new life and way of living, to rise from the ashes of the past.

## From Pondicherry to Paris

The seemingly obvious contradiction of a colonial territory operating as a refuge from the neighboring colonial oppressor can be attributed in part to a particular construction of France as a space of freedom, a certain vision of utopia, in Indian nationalist discourses. I do not wish to suggest that there is or ever has been one homogenized idea of France in India, but it is clear that among Western-educated Indians in the late nineteenth and into the twentieth century, France was viewed as distinctly suited to freedom struggles, based most often on the history and, perhaps more important, the mythology surrounding the French Revolution. France appeared in French history, literature, and popular culture as a utopia for people in French India, a space geographically distinct from India that did not carry the oppression of caste, religion, or the British. This idea was reinforced with experience—at least in the early twentieth century—as Paris became the European headquarters for anticolonial Indian revolutionaries who found themselves forced to flee London.

In 1907, a Bombay-born Parsi woman known commonly as Madame (Bhikaji) Cama wrote a letter to the *Indian Sociologist*, an anticolonial newsletter published out of London, suggesting that British attempts to shut down presses and limit freedom of speech in India and England through the sedition laws meant the revolutionary movement should consider a move to Paris "beyond the reach of the tyrannical English, where we can publish all necessary circulars, etc. in different Indian vernaculars."[76] The *Indian Sociologist* was closely watched by British authorities. Publisher Shymaji Krishnavarma, much like Aurobindo, had been accused of writing and printing seditious material; he was singled out for writing, in the *Indian Sociologist*, that he was "not a British subject."[77] The English government thus declared he was "an undesirable alien endeavouring to debauch the loyal subjects" of India and banned the *Indian Sociologist* in India beginning in 1907.[78] That same year, Krishnavarma left London for Paris and joined the already growing movement of Indians in Paris as British authorities attempted to eliminate Indian nationalists on English soil.[79] Before the publication ever moved to France, the *Indian Sociologist* had already published "La Marseillaise," the French national anthem, in six different Indian languages.[80]

The move of the *Indian Sociologist* to Paris highlighted what many revolutionaries thought to be true about France: that it was a place where they could write what they needed to write and meet freely with Russian revolutionaries and French socialists, who were both sympathetic to the calls for the violent overthrow of the British espoused by this group of Indians. The Paris Indian Society began in 1905 as a continental branch of the London-based Home Rule Society, led by Sirdarsinghji Rewabhai Rana (S. R. Rana), along with Madame Cama and eventually Shyamji Krishnavarma.[81] The Sûreté Générale in Paris kept a file on this group, in compliance with a request from the British Embassy, although France would not agree to extradite Rana or Krishnavarma, or any of the other British Indian subjects, to London or India.[82] These records do, however, make it clear that French officials were aware that there were Indians (*hindous revolutionaires*) living in Paris, extorting money from wealthy Indians, learning how to assemble bombs, gathering weapons, printing seditious newsletters, and shipping all of these items to Pondicherry and Chandernagore.[83] According to one source, there were at least twenty-six Indians who were working for freedom against British rule living in Paris between 1905 and 1914.[84] A report prepared by the Sûreté Générale in 1909 at the request of the British Embassy in Paris reported that while they carried out "discreet surveillances" of Rana and Krishnavarma, their investigations did not yield any results that could lead to extradition.[85]

Krishnavarma and his compatriots knew they were being watched, and wrote about it regularly in the *Indian Sociologist*. They blamed the British authorities for spreading rumors that the Indians in Paris were planning a "terrorist attack," stating that "the existence of an Indian conspiracy in Paris is a myth." Further, Krishnavarma made it clear that he was *not* a British subject, as he was "born in India an Indian ... the natives of which, even according to the Imperial Gazetteer of India are 'foreigners in the eye of the law of British India.' "[86] This line of argument worked with a French public fascinated with Indian culture as well as with the perceived atrocities of British imperialism. A 1908 interview with Krishnavarma published in the leftist Parisian newspaper *l'Éclair* begins by stating, "It is well known in France what the true situation of India is."[87] This simple statement, that people in France were aware of the "true situation" in India, underlines the support the Indian revolutionaries felt in Paris.

Yet, nowhere in the *Indian Sociologist* or in the writings of Madame Cama or S. R. Rana is there an acknowledgment of France's treatment of its own colonial subjects, let alone the plight of their supposed Indian brethren in French India. The revolutionary Indians in Paris had support from French leftist parties as well as the popular press, which helped them avoid political persecution for their anticolonial views.[88] While a few Pondichérians were involved in the operation of the revolutionary network established in Paris, the movement stayed primarily an operation of British Indians, and the revolutionaries remained uncritical of France.

Similarly, in French India, Aurobindo was largely secluded from the French-Indian community at large. Both the residence Aurobindo initially occupied and the Ashram are located in the ville blanche, or the European part of Pondicherry. Unlike the majority of French-Indians who lived in the surrounding villages and in the ville noire, Aurobindo and his devotees did not face daily border crossings between French and British territory for work or constant inquiries about their nationality. Even though the French colonial authorities were spying on the refugees, the authorities also allowed them to project an image of Pondicherry as a refuge from British India, a colony within a colony.[89] However, this protection did not extend to French-Indians who spoke against the French.

## Inter/Anti/Nationalism

While Pondicherry, Chandernagore, and the other comptoirs appeared to many in British India and abroad to be a place of safety and asylum for Indian revolutionaries, this safety net did not extend to those French-Indians who defied the colonial project of the French. Varadarajulu Subbiah (sometimes spelled Soubaya by the French) was born in 1911 in the village of Kottaikuppam, a French territory about a mile and a half from Pondicherry town.[90] Kottaikuppam was one of the six original *chaukis*, or customs checkpoints, established in 1844 in order to enforce the Land Customs Act, right on one of the borders between the French and British territories.[91]

Subbiah was a communist and would become one of the most important leaders of the freedom movement in French India. Consequently, for the entire time that he was fighting for the independence of the comptoirs, his nationality was questioned by both British and French authorities. As the British Consulate wrote in a report on the political situation in Pondicherry in 1944, "The nationality of Subbiah is often in question, and changes with the political whims of the government, whether he is useful to them or not."[92] Whether he was actually French or British Indian, Subbiah was fighting the forces of colonialism, represented by the presence of both European powers.

Subbiah was born to parents of "British Indian parentage," but on French land, making him eligible for French citizenship. Subbiah attended the Petit Seminaire and the College Calve, both French schools in Pondicherry, although the French authorities would later accuse him of not being able to speak French, a critical criterion for proving one's Frenchness.[93] According to his own remembrances, he developed his political consciousness at the college when he organized a strike amongst the students in 1928.[94] After the strike he was "branded as an arch-agitator" and expelled from the school, attracting the attention of the French police, as well as the local government.[95] Unlike Aurobindo, who was revered by many French officials for his knowledge of European languages and philosophy, Subbiah was targeted by both states because his causes were in defense of students and workers against state oppression. French officials flocked to Aurobindo to engage with "Eastern philosophy," while Subbiah was always interpreted as a threat aligned with global communism.

Following his foray into student activism, Subbiah went to Madras and became involved with the Self-Respect Movement and eventually the freedom movement in British India. Returning to Pondicherry in 1930, he founded the French India Youth League, while continuing to build connections with anticolonial agitators in Madras. Subbiah soon allied himself with the Communist Party in Pondicherry, a group that had a growing presence and influence in French India, and began to agitate for labor reform in the three major mills in Pondicherry, which led to a series of labor strikes in the 1930s, drawing the attention of French and British imperial forces alike.[96] He was arrested multiple times, in both British and in French India, and was jailed for several years in various prisons, also in both British and French India. In 1946, he was elected to the French Senate as a representative for French India, and after independence he served as a member of the Legislative Assembly of Pondicherry.[97]

Subbiah's memoir illuminates the many contradictions he faced as he battled both French and British colonial institutions. The first chapter is devoted to highlighting the importance of Pondicherry for India's independence movement, as "Pondicherry served as a centre for political refugees and also for establishing communication with the Indian revolutionaries who stayed and operated, at that time, from Britain, Germany, and France."[98] He notes that Pondicherry became the refuge for Sri Subramanya Bharathi, "who roused the patriotic and revolutionary sentiments of the people through his writings against British imperialist rule in India," while Sri Aurobindo was "smuggled into Pondicherry through Chandernagore in April 1910," followed a few months later by V. V. S. Aiyer.[99] Yet, despite the importance of Pondicherry for the Indian independence movement, Subbiah himself spent many years hiding from the French authorities in an "underground shelter" in Madras because of his involvement with movements that challenged French rule.[100]

Subbiah represented the Communist Party and traveled between French and British India to make connections between workers who lived under both jurisdictions. Because of his association with anticolonial agitators in Madras as well as Pondicherry, the British police followed his movements; because he was agitating the workers in the mills of Pondicherry, the French police had him under surveillance as well. Still, the French officials in Pondicherry issued him a passport in 1937, allowing him to sail, via Colombo and Djibouti, to Marseilles and onward to Paris, carrying letters of introduction from Jawaharlal Nehru.[101] Subbiah spent much of his trip with Louise Morin, a French journalist whom he had met in Pondicherry in 1933, and who was also close friends with the nationalist leaders Nehru and Subhas Chandra Bose. He described her apartment as a space that "Indian friends used to frequent," as it had an "Indian atmosphere with portraits of Indian national leaders" and was decorated with "exhibits of Indian arts and handicrafts."[102] Subbiah spoke openly about the support he received in France, though it was mostly associated with his comrades from the Communist Party and others who sympathized with the anti-British independence movement. He does not mention any specific support shown toward his efforts to subvert French rule.

Neither the French nor the British wanted to claim responsibility for Subbiah. In 1938, the British Consulate in Pondicherry reported, "Subbiah, the refugee leader of the Mahajana party, has not yet been arrested in British India. The French who, if they had wished, could have seized this man a dozen times, are inclined to blame the British police for this failure to find Subbiah, and even go so far as to hint that this failure is deliberate."[103] In

1944, Subbiah was expelled from Pondicherry as an "undesirable alien," despite the fact that he was born in Pondicherry, attended French schools, and was involved in local French Indian politics.[104] A 1944 report from the British consulate in Pondicherry agonized over the fact that no one would take responsibility for him. The French authorities expelled him because he "was not a French Indian subject," and although "his father was a British Indian" and "he was born in Pondicherry," he "omitted to declare for French Indian nationality on attaining 21 years of age."[105] The fact that he was granted a French passport in 1937 and had all along been allowed to vote as a French-Indian was, in 1944, "declared now to have been allowed under a misconception of the true legal position."[106] French records make it clear that questioning Subbiah's nationality was simply a trick used to encourage his followers to question his legitimacy, although this eventually backfired, as a 1947 report from the French Indian government stated that his being hunted out of French India had made him a martyr, "une victime de l'imperialisme française" (a victim of French imperialism), which undermined French efforts to portray their own colonial rule in a positive light in comparison to the British.[107]

The arguments between British and French authorities on Subbiah's nationality continued into the 1940s.[108] While Subbiah was a major figure who had support locally and abroad, many other people straddled the borders between French and British India. The division between the political refugees from British India and the French-Indians who were forced to hide in British territory to escape prosecution from the French further defined the differences between French and British India. Specifying the particular characteristics of national identity is important to the construction of nationalism: in order for a French national to distinguish themselves from a British national, they looked at the time to certain key cultural traits and geographic boundaries. Of course, in the twenty-first century, we would now look also to an individual's passport for proof of national belonging, an act that will, coupled with certain widely held beliefs about race, ethnicity, religion, and language, pinpoint a person as an immigrant to or a "native" of the state that issued the passport. For the residents as well as the administrators of French India, and the surrounding areas of British control, the lines that separated one nationality from the other were rarely clear, even as the question of who was a French-Indian and who was a "foreigner" became increasingly important.

In addition to the movement of the revolutionaries themselves, seditious literature against the British colonial government as well as money and arms meant to support the overthrow of the British were shipped to Pondicherry, Chandernagore, and, to a lesser extent, the other comptoirs, for distribution throughout British India, often originating from factories and printing presses in France. While the French colonial police in Pondicherry did agree to the surveillance of those subjects considered dangerous by the British, they also insisted on exercising complete sovereignty over their territories, much to the dismay of the British authorities, who found it increasingly difficult to quiet the deafening calls for Indian independence.

## Passports and Fences: Tracking Subjects and Citizens

The restoration of Pondicherry to France from England in 1815 came with the stipulation that import and export duties were to be leveled on all goods coming in and out of British territory, making the French territories surrounded by British territory an economic boon. However, it quickly became clear that placing a tax on all goods was untenable for the French-Indians, and in 1817 an exception was made for the import and export of rice, on the condition that the French would not export rice by sea to foreign (that is, non-French) countries or territories. By 1882, the British agreed to abolish customs duties on all articles of merchandise *except* salt, alcohol, salted fish, and opium, although they reimposed some of these tariffs in 1894.[109] Because of the tight restrictions placed on these isolated French pockets, a significant amount of smuggling took place between British and French India, primarily, according to British records, of "cotton and silk, brass vessels, salted fish, groundnuts, seeds of sorts, jewellery, and kerosene oil."[110] In an area of less than 115 square miles, six customs stations, or chaukis, were established in 1844 to monitor the transfer of goods between the two areas.[111]

The building of fences and chaukis to separate French and British India was almost always discussed as a matter of tracking material goods. A report on the Pondicherry Frontier produced by the British in India in 1915 never explicitly mentions concerns with the smuggling of seditious materials, revolutionary contraband, or criminal peoples, but many other documents reveal that this was a very serious concern amongst British officials.[112] In 1908, seven years prior to the production of this report, a parliamentary notice appeared alerting the undersecretary of the state of India that "seditious literature habitually reaches India from France" and "prohibited newspapers and pamphlets are sent to French-Indian settlements, from which they are secretly distributed in British-India."[113] In other words, separating the material goods from the individuals and groups producing them was not a simple task.

While this may have been news in London, the authorities in India were well aware of the revolutionary activities gaining strength in Pondicherry. Earlier in 1908, the Tamil poet and anticolonial agitator C. Subramanya Bharathi had "fled to Pondicherry," bringing with him his nationalist newspaper *India*, which was printed in Pondicherry and smuggled into British India. The papers, which were sent by train, were often seized by one of the agents at chaukis on their way to Madras and subsequently destroyed by the Madras police.[114] Various British intelligence documents show that between 1906 and 1914 over two dozen Indian revolutionaries who were under surveillance by the British traveled to and from Pondicherry, often making trips between Pondicherry and Paris.[115] Despite the presence of what seems to be an unnecessary number of customs borders, the revolutionary movement could not be contained.

The arrival of the anticolonial revolutionaries in Pondicherry in 1910–1911 pre-dated the renewed interest among British interests in building up the border between British and French territory by just a few years. Once there were people present in French India whom the British saw as threats to their territory, and whom they could not properly track, they moved forward forcefully with plans to reinforce the border with customs patrols and police. The 1915 British report on the Pondicherry frontier acknowledges that despite the many customs checkpoints, on land and on the trains, the fact that British and French villages "intermingled" meant that it was impossible for stationary customs guards to stop the smuggling; the solution presented in this report was to "convert the more or less stationary out-gate staffs into a moving (patrolling) preventive force."[116] Pondicherry, which in 1912 extended sixteen miles north to south and about the same distance east to west and had a population of about 184,200 people, had a mobile border guard and at least six customs stations. In addition, a customs guard stopped all trains, for forty minutes during the day and fifty minutes at night, forcing passengers to exit the train, enter a shed (with a separate inspection area for women), and "register" any items they were taking into Pondicherry or planned to take out.[117]

The modern system of passport control, which has roots in the 19th century, began to be enforced in earnest at the start of World War I.[118] By November 1915, all British subjects leaving the UK were required to carry a passport. A year later, in 1916, India's secretary of state "suggested that the Government of India provide a passport for all European British subjects, Indian British subjects and subjects of native states setting out for British dominions and colonies," a proposal that was codified with the Indian Passport Act of 1920.[119] Throughout the decades preceding the implementation of a passport system for British subjects in India, the Indian government of India had opposed passport regulations for Indian laborers, thousands of whom regularly traveled to work in Ceylon (Sri Lanka), Malaya, Australia, and the British colonies in Africa.[120] As Radhika Singha has shown, colonial authorities had to weigh their desires to control the movement of "undesirable" individuals against the need to keep the borders within India—and within the empire—porous, to accommodate the need for labor on plantations and in mines, most of which required many poor workers to cross borders regularly.[121] For this reason, the Indian Passport Act of 1920 deals *only* with immigration into India, not emigration from India. The main purpose of the law was to stop foreign revolutionaries, specifically Bolsheviks, from spreading anticolonial material and ideas in India.[122] While the government discussed how it could prohibit "foreign revolutionaries" from entering India, the real problem was that the anticolonial revolutionaries were largely *Indian* and therefore could not be barred from living on Indian land under the existing laws. As I have shown, when threatened with prosecution for promoting seditious ideas and materials, Indians were able to seek refuge on French Indian land and in various European countries, again limiting the powers of the British to control the anticolonial movement.

The discontinuous borders that marked the areas of French rule in India were initially created in the eighteenth century to prevent any challenge to British power. This tactic of indirect rule, of dividing neighbors into distinct and separate communities based on colonial affiliations, was used throughout British territories to discourage the formation of resistance to colonial domination. In 1938, one year prior to the building of the fences in Pondicherry and Karaikal that would physically separate British and French India, Jewish subcontractors were hired to erect a barbed wire fence on the Palestine-Transjordan border in British-mandate Palestine. The fence became known as "Tegart's wall," after Charles Tegart, the British officer who built his career in Calcutta and spent a fair amount of time working to extradite wanted individuals from Chandernagore, before working in Palestine. Tegart's wall arbitrarily cut across Arab farmland and was violently contested by the local populations, who recognized that it was built to prevent the growth of Pan-Arabism.[123] Tegart had been instrumental in discussions about the need to track internal enemies of the empire in French India, particularly in Chandernagore, throughout the 1920s.[124] Like the one in Pondicherry, the fence in Palestine was accompanied by additional customs checkpoints and long debates about requiring people who crossed the fence to carry identity cards.[125] The two fences, in India and in Palestine, served the same purpose of control, the expansion of a global network of carceral borders. Reginald Schomberg, impressed with the fences in Pondicherry and Karaikal, wrote in 1939, "'Tegart's Line' in Palestine is a pale simulacrum of the barbed wire entanglement around both these French dependencies."[126] The global network of securitized borders had begun to take root, sinking deep into the soil of the occupied territories.

The French government in India attempted to stop the building of the fences in Pondicherry and Karaikal by proposing a poll tax on non-French subjects and citizens who lived in the comptoirs. On 22 November 1936, the government of the French settlements in India published a decree that called for the taxing of "foreigners" in French India.[127] The law, which was at the time still subject to the approval of Paris, would require non-French residents, those who were not "officers, civil or military agents, or their families," or citizens or subjects, to pay twenty rupees per person per year to live in French India, or even to travel to and from the French Indian territories.[128] The passing of the poll tax would not only tax the many non–French-Indians who worked in Pondicherry but would also require all people who crossed the borders between French and British India to carry some form of identification, which could, according to the proposed law, be in the form of a *livret de solde* (military paybook), *titre de voyage* (travel document), *carte d'identité* (identity card), or foreign-issued passport. After almost two years of discussion, the tax, as well as the regulations stipulating proof of identity, were announced on the streets of Pondicherry in early November 1938 "by the beat of a drum" accompanied by a call that all "British subjects must register at the police station by

25th November 1938."[129] This caused some amount of chaos and confusion among the people of Pondicherry, as many of the three hundred thousand residents had never had occasion to declare their nationality one way or the other.

The British consulate immediately protested the law, arguing that "to enforce [the poll tax] will be extraordinarily difficult, and must lead to endless disputes and irregularities. The nationalities are hopelessly mixed up, and many persons do not know, and cannot prove, whether they are French or British subjects."[130] British authorities saw the law as "discriminatory" toward "British subjects" and argued that it was a retaliatory measure in response to the increase in British customs patrols. The British consul Schomberg estimated that 99 percent of foreigners in Pondicherry were British Indians, and that British Indians made up 30 percent of the resident population.[131] As British opposition to the law moved up the chain of command, the focus of the protest against the French law narrowed to argue that the law would primarily negatively affect the "labouring classes," the group of people that the government of India believed needed the greatest freedom of mobility. Without the free movement of Indigenous labor, the colonial economy would cease to be profitable. A letter dated 21 December 1938 from the government of Madras to the secretary-general of external affairs for the government of India stated that "even this seemingly light tax will be a great hardship to the labouring classes." The memo refers to the borders between French and British India as "artificial political divisions imposed on a homogenous population," a claim that was rooted in truth but was no longer a reality for the people who had been forced to abide by these borders for decades.[132] While the memo argues that the movement between French and British India should not be treated like the "immigration of foreigners into France," it was too late, as this had already been made the norm.

The government of Madras later added that "the idea of 'foreigners'" was inapplicable in the case of Pondicherry and other small French areas situated in the Madras Presidency.[133] While the British government in India was intent on increasing the number of chaukis and collecting customs taxes from travelers from French India, it was appalled at the idea that an Indian would be asked to identify as either French or British. However, for many people in French India who had cultivated a French identity for generations, distinguishing between French and British Indian meant the difference between being a subject of the British Empire or a citizen of the French Republic, a topic that lies at the heart of the next chapter.

In response to the protests of the British government, the French Ministry of Foreign Affairs stated that French India was primarily for French citizens, including French-Indians, and British Indians were to be considered aliens on French soil. France would, however, be willing to negotiate if the British would consider removing the "British customs cordon to the outer limits of Pondicherry."[134] The British government responded that this would not be possible, "since such a removal would involve renunciation by them of the right to subject all the inhabitants of the intervening British Indian territory to the taxation imposed by the British Indian customs tariff, and would result in considerable loss of revenue and capital."[135] Discussions between France and England about the poll tax carried on into August 1939, when an agreement was finally reached that required British- *and* French-Indians to be able to produce a passport or an identity card on demand in either of the territories. Procuring these cards/passports would initially cost two rupees per person and would take the place of the proposed poll tax.[136] While this agreement resolved the issue of one group being subjected to more taxes than the other, the issue of who constituted a "foreigner" in British or French India only intensified with the imposition of a passport system that forced individuals to identify with one colonial power or the other, which became increasingly important as the move toward an independent India intensified.

The building of the fences between areas of French and British India in 1939 can be viewed as the physical result of a proxy war between French and British interests. The fences, and the corresponding taxes, border policing, and identity cards, are part of a much wider network of carceral border-making. While both France and England acknowledged the lack of cultural distinction between the *Indians* in the two areas, both countries insisted on marking their national territories—a project that began with claiming land and, by this period, included the need to claim people, as well. The French-Indian population in Pondicherry responded to the building of the fence with outrage. The newspaper *Dessobagari* ran a series of editorials decrying British customs officials for creating and enforcing customs fences, and for making it so difficult for both people and goods to cross these borders. While French subjects were allowed to carry goods from one French area to another, the British customs agents often doubted the veracity of their "birth certificates," the papers that were meant to guarantee their rights as French-Indians. The author writes that British customs agents "ask how they could believe that the holder of the certificate is the same genuine person" and if their name is the "one on their head or on their shirt."[137] Without the benefits of French subjecthood, which in this context amounted to being able to carry goods such as silk, alcohol, and fruit across borders without paying taxes, the author concludes by asking, "What difference is there between the British Indians who live like slaves under a foreign Government and us who live under a honourable Republic?"[138]

Borders and boundaries were important markers and tools of control in the colonies, just as they remain important tools for the functionality of postcolonial nation-states. Readjusting, erasing, and drawing new borders was often the first step toward "decolonization": colonial governments created colonial borders to reflect the attachment to the imperial ruler and the relationships between that ruling country and other imperial powers. Geographic borders separated British India from French India, just as internal borders throughout Pondicherry separated the Europeans from the indigenous population, the Europeans and the métis residing in the ville blanche and the local populations in the ville noire.[139] The borders between French and British India were uneven, dividing communities and villages along lines drawn by colonial administrators unfamiliar with the inhabitants and their land. French and British colonial powers used borders and boundaries, both geographic and social, to control goods, people, and land in the period leading up to decolonization.

By the end of the 1930s, there existed a legal distinction between a French and a British Indian that was enforced through the issuance of identity cards and passports, although these forms of identity were often flexible and could be changed, either by the individual or by the government. While the definitions of who belonged to which group were often unclear—particularly among the lower classes, who often lived in one territory and worked in another—the need to choose a nationality became imperative as it became evident that British India would achieve independence, while the future of French India was uncertain. The French Indian territories were not the only area of concern for Indian nationalists: in a 1939 pamphlet published by the All-India States' Peoples' Conference, Jawaharlal Nehru, then a strong figure in the Indian National Congress, wrote about the need to address the many fractured states within India.[140]

He begins by referring to the Princely States as a "problem," but "not only the problem of 584 political units in India but of scores of millions of people who inhabit these areas." Nehru paints a dark picture of the Princely States, writing that "politically and economically the States are very backward and many of them are still in a feudal age." Out of step with the modernizing vision of the pro-independence Indian National Congress, Nehru addresses the need to find out more about the States, asking, "What are they? Where are they? *What happens within their borders?*"[141]

Nehru's concern with the unknown that lurked within the 584 Indian states, which included the French territories, indicates the divides that colonial borders had created within a territory that many hoped to soon unite as one nation-state. The creation of more borders and fences and the growing enforcement of these borders, initially meant to control the movement of goods between French and British territory in India, had turned neighbors into strangers as India neared independence. While figures like Shyamji Krishnavarma, Aurobindo Ghose, and V. Subbiah attempted to unite all *Indians* in the struggle against colonial oppression, revolutionary figures depended on the territorial borders of European powers to provide them with a refuge. The designation of British Indians as "foreigners" in French India, as well as the reverse, set the stage for the crisis of belonging that would direct the relationships formed over the next two decades in this region, especially as British India gave way to independent India, instigating a new regime of power struggle in the French Indian territories.

CHAPTER II

## The Future of French India

*Decolonization and Settlement at the Borders*

On 15 March 1946, the newly appointed British prime minister Clement Attlee addressed the House of Commons about India's impending independence. A month previously, Attlee had announced that in the coming year India would be granted full independence from Britain. Attlee spoke of the importance of India's right to determine its future, while also congratulating his fellow countrymen for their work in India, since it was, after all, the British who gave to India a "sense of nationality which she so very largely lacked over the previous centuries."[1] Indeed, Attlee implied that the growth of Indian nationalism was the commonality between the distinct religious and ethnic communities—mainly the Hindus, the Muslims, and the Sikhs—who, according to the British, were poised to go to war as soon as Britain was gone. Attlee spoke of the need to encourage Indian leaders to unite all the people of India and to remain a member of the British Commonwealth. He noted that India was currently in a "state of great tension," and that it would be a "great mistake to stake out the claims of rival communities."[2] Attlee suggested that Indians remember the "principles of democracy and justice" that the British had delivered to them as a gift, to help guide them in overcoming the great many "minority problems" that faced independent India.[3] Attlee soon after created a commission to travel to India to set the stage for the imminent departure of the British.

The French government watched with great interest as the Attlee commission traveled to India in April 1946. The biggest concern about the events in British India was based on the idea that if the French ceded the French Indian territories to an independent India, France would be forced to grant independence to the other colonies that had been loudly demanding sovereignty following the end of World War II. While the decolonization of British India was at this point inevitable, metropolitan France was entrenched in discussions about how to maintain global power and remain implanted in the colonies and overseas territories, primarily through the creation of the French Union as a cornerstone of the emergent French Fourth Republic. To this end, the 1946 Constitution of the Fourth Republic contained a clause that required a referendum of the people in French territories and colonies before they could be granted independence or become members of the French Union. The question of the referendum in French India, which only ever took place in Chandernagore, became the center of concern in discussions on the future of French India between 1947 and 1954.

That the prospect of decolonization had different meanings for different imperial states as well as for different people tells us how complex and diverse our definitions of "decolonization" have been over time and how complex they remain today. Historians who have approached the decolonization of French India from the viewpoint of Indian independence tend to see it as an inevitable stage in India's national liberation. Take, for example, the historian Saroja Sundararajan, who writes in her 1995 book, *Pondicherry: A Profile*, that the freedom struggle in French India "dates only from the day the British left India."[4] She states that while those in French India were no less "heroic and patriotic than their counterparts in British India," the reason they did not rise up earlier against the French was because of the "immense faith the people of French India reposed in their white rulers. They sincerely believed that their colonial masters, having hailed from the nation which stood for liberty, reason and humanity would, on their own, leave their pockets in India emulating the example of England."[5] While there certainly were French-Indians who did not wish to sever the relationship with France because they believed France to be the bearer of democracy, the notion that it was a superior ruler was held not just by French-Indians, but, as previously discussed, by many anticolonial Indian nationalists as well.

Ajit Neogy's book *Decolonization of French India*—easily the most cited on the subject—reinforces the argument that anticolonialism in British India "spilled over to the French Indian territories," and that "[French-Indian] demand for fusion with India mounted when India gained her complete independence in August 1947."[6] The narrative at work here tells a story of a once-united India that had been divided by foreign powers (usually laying blame at the feet of Muslims, England, Portugal, and France, among a host of other "invaders"). The moment of independence from British rule is painted in national histories as a liberatory one, of a people being set free from the confines of an oppressor.

"Independence" is a tricky concept. Throughout history, actors have fought for independence from monarchical rule, from political tyranny and theocracy, from colonial powers and enslavers. Anticolonial revolutionaries often instrumentalized independence as the desired outcome of their struggle, while imperial rhetoric defined it as a privilege to be earned through civil action and discourse. The enormity of India winning independence from British rule in 1947 has dominated the popular imagination of twentieth-century Indian history, serving as a watershed moment for the establishment of the postcolonial Indian state. Yet this much-celebrated moment was more a performance of freedom than an actual practice. Historian Rohit De, writing on the period between 15 August 1947 and 26 January 1950 (the day that the Indian constitution was promulgated), reminds us that India was a British dominion for almost three years before it became a sovereign republic.[7] In addition, the Princely States were not automatically included, nor were the territories held by France or Portugal. Independence and decolonization were both slippery propositions that never happened immediately or conclusively, or in the way that people imagined that they would.

Working toward writing a non-nationalist history of the decolonization of French India contributes to decolonizing history, as it recognizes the complexities and heterogeneity of colonized people, especially when it comes to questions of liberation. We now turn to 1947 and India's achievement of independence from Britain to examine the consequences of "liberating" one territory while neighboring territories remained under foreign rule. Why did French India not immediately merge with India, and what arguments did people make for joining the French Union, for remaining autonomous, or for merging with India? The next two chapters are concerned with the transition of British Indian territory into Indian territory, and the way this transformation changed the dynamics on and around the border, part of the continual project of making French India. As India worked toward setting the terms of the Republic, the borders between French India and British India became borders separating French India from India, which meant that the borders stayed in place while their national character and surrounding territory changed. India, however, was much more committed to incorporating the French Indian territories than the British had ever been, and the borders became more policed—and more significant—after 1947.

## Postcolonial Networks: The British Commonwealth and the French Union

The last years of World War II made clear the waning of the European empires, at least in the form of colonization by direct rule. Much has been made of the way the war spelled out the end of British rule in India, as Britain realized how much it needed India's support to maintain any semblance of world power and began to come to terms with the fact that it no longer had the economic means to rule a vast land full of people who had no desire to be ruled. India had contributed to the war effort directly through the deployment of over 2.5 million soldiers, who fought with the Allied powers around the world, a contribution that nationalist leaders expected to be recognized with independence after the war.

Similarly, France recognized that it would have to address the growing resistance to its overseas empire. The Brazzaville Conference, held in the French Congo in January 1944, was an early site of discussions among high-ranking Free France officials about the future of the French Empire, and of France itself. The administrators attending the conference, according to historian Frederick Cooper, "wanted above all else to preserve the empire, and they accepted that in order to do so, they had to identify colonial rule with progress—for the colonized as well as the colonizers."[8] It was imperative, these men realized, for the colonized to have a voice in how they were governed; the French state would need to allow for more colonial subjects (limited, of course, to the "properly" educated, or the *évoluée*) to participate in local governance. The colonies, if given at least the idea or the prospect of autonomy, would allow the French state to continue to exercise sovereignty within the colonized spaces, while also promoting French culture and language, constructing a "French community."

The Brazzaville Conference gave birth not only to the idea of federalism among the people and lands ruled by France. It also, in the words of Cooper, introduced "a new name for empire": the French Union.[9] The argument for federating the empire was particularly important for the growing anti-French movement in Indochina, where the end of the Japanese occupation in 1945 led to the leader Ho Chi Minh declaring Vietnam independent on 1 September 1945. Presenting the option of federation—of increased autonomy within a union and the promise of unnamed privileges yet to come—was not what Ho Chi Minh was seeking, but the proposal did buy time for the French state. It became equally important as a signal that France was ready to change the parameters of their empire, as antinationalist demonstrations began to proliferate in Madagascar and in Algeria, and as it became clear that England would soon be leaving India.

The French Union was codified in the Constitution of the Fourth Republic, which was put into law on 27 October 1946. Article 27 guaranteed that the people domiciled in the French Union would have the democratic right to vote on whether or not they should remain within the French Union. The possibility of a referendum, through universal adult suffrage, on the future of the colonized people brought the language of republican democracy into the discourse of the postwar French colonies—an important move that worked to link the discourse of democratic freedoms of the metropole to the colonies.

Unlike France, Britain had a history of bringing its former colonies into a type of federation known as the British Commonwealth, beginning with the granting of dominion status to Canada in 1867.[10] The commonwealth was a network of self-governing nations that retained ties with the British Crown—they were, notably, no longer colonies, but dominions. By the end of the war in 1945, the commonwealth had become rhetorically much like a family, with the king at the paternal helm, and his white settler children—Canada, South Africa, Australia, New Zealand, and Ireland—united by "race, culture, and language."[11] While India did not join the commonwealth until after independence, the fact that all the major Indian leaders in the period, including Nehru, Jinnah, and Gandhi, had been educated in England, spoke English fluently, and participated in English cultural institutions made it clear that postcolonial India would not be able to completely break ties with the Crown.

After Attlee's declaration of Britain's intention to leave India in March of 1946, France needed to quickly assess the strategic importance of its territories in India and saw the importance of holding on to them as long as possible. In Pondicherry, François Baron, the newest governor-general of the French establishments in India, had been laying ground to promote the idea of the French Union. Many local leaders, including V. Subbiah, leader of the French India Communist Party and a longtime advocate for workers in the French-Indian textile mills, had been arguing for immediate merger with India as an anticolonial measure, a move he would eventually retract. Replying to these calls, Baron proclaimed to the people of French India that the creation of the French Union actually meant the death of colonialism, not the continuation. In a public address given on 6 April 1946, Baron declared,

> France proclaims that colonialism is dead, that all men and women of French land—be they from Paris, from Quimper, from Tananarive or from Pondicherry—are free and equal in rights. That all men and all women have the right and even the duty to freely elect, irrespective of caste, race, or color, representatives who must faithfully express the ideas and the wishes of their constituents. . . . There is no longer empire, there are no longer colonies. Henceforth there is only a great nation of 100 million perfectly equal and consenting souls, or, more precisely, a free association of original communities within the French Union, united willingly because they desire to be free, equal, and brotherly.[12]

Baron stressed the voluntary nature of inclusion in the French Union; he spoke of the end of colonialism, and the beginning of an era of free will and fraternity, a notion meant to light a fire of optimism among the people of the "former" French empire. The language of voluntary inclusion mirrored British rhetoric at the time that stressed the importance of self-determination for the people of India, while allowing the people in French India to remain distanced from the violent tensions surrounding the Partition. By basing the future of French India on a referendum to take place under universal adult suffrage, French colonial authorities hoped to avoid the development of any anticolonial movements in their Indian colonies, buying them time to figure out what to do about the more pressing issues in the other parts of the empire that were in open revolt against French rule.

Avoiding anti-French agitation in India was incredibly important to French officials, as the departure of the British from India marked a crucial point at which the French were forced to reckon with the possible decolonization of the French Empire. Much of this was uncharted territory for the French in terms of approaches to decolonization as well as negotiations with an independent nation that had overthrown their European rulers; in the lead-up to the departure of the British, French officials noted in a report that the strong position of independent India against foreign rule on Indian land was the "principal obstacle" facing the French colonies in India.[13]

Postwar France envisioned the transformation of the French Empire into a network of francophone localities that would not only maintain the many capitalist economic relationships that were developed during the colonial era, but also continue to promote French language and culture throughout the world. The French Union was walking a fine line between denouncing the colonial practices of the British and promoting the unity of its own colonies. Unfortunately for officials in Paris, the French administrators in Pondicherry were not always on the same page. In March 1947, Governor Baron announced that "the British decision to give to India her independence does not have any effect on the French possessions in India. The two questions are absolutely without connection. The French Possessions in India are an integral part of the French Union."[14] Baron had made this statement without the permission of the Foreign and Overseas Ministries in Paris.[15] The unauthorized proclamation greatly angered the office of the minister of colonies, which issued a reply that denouncing Governor Baron's attitude toward French India as "incompatible" with the views held in Paris.[16]

This incident is representative of the confusion surrounding the question of French India in the early months of 1947. Following Baron's statement, the Paris authorities rushed to put together a set of reports outlining the situation in French India, including the difficulties France might encounter in its attempts to retain the colonies, the reasons why the colonies needed to remain French, and the temper of the local population. They sent Tézenas du Montcel, the inspector general of the colonies, to travel to all five of the comptoirs and compile a report on his findings.

Issued on 24 June 1947, the "Report on the French Possessions in India" reveals that authorities considered attempting to hold colonies in India—what was to be the world's first postwar, postcolonial nation-state—to be their biggest challenge. Yet they also recognized that they had an important advantage in India, one that they had spent centuries cultivating. The mainstream nationalist freedom movement in India had cast the British as the true enemies of freedom and liberty, an idea that the French had supported by sheltering Indian freedom fighters in French India and in France. The 1947 report suggests that the friendship formed between France and India during the period of British rule should not be taken for granted.

While France worked to distance itself from the practices of the British, it also kept a close eye on how the Portuguese were approaching their own Indian colonies, primarily the state of Goa. On 23 July 1946, the Portuguese released a statement to the Indian press declaring that Portuguese India was integral to the Portuguese *mère-patrie*, and that they had absolutely no intention of leaving the fate of the territory in the hands of "millions of Hindus separated by irreducible differences"—a justification for continued colonial rule that mirrored British discourse about why India was not ready for sovereignty.[17]

The authoritarian approach of the Portuguese toward the question of Portuguese India led to many protests, riots, and calls for solidarity among the Indian nationalists. Gandhi encouraged those in Portuguese India to engage in passive resistance, and Nehru declared that the Portuguese would not be allowed to remain in India.[18] The French noted that the Portuguese approach was to be avoided at all costs; France would have to exercise diplomacy and stress the agency of the inhabitants of French India at all times in order to avoid being forced out of India. They also recognized that the Portuguese approach aided the French cause, as the Anglo-Indian press often compared the "liberal" attitude of the French to the authoritative-imperialist motives of the Portuguese.[19] However, du Montcel suggested, the moment also presented an opportunity for France to take advantage of any lingering ill-will the Indian government and people held toward the British, as well as toward the Portuguese.[20] The du Montcel report notes that the Portuguese approach, which had received a significant amount of negative attention from the Indian government and press, should be avoided. It was important to offer at least the façade of negotiation.

Unlike Portugal, which was at the time under the dictatorial rule of António de Oliveira Salazar, France was embarking on a new iteration as the Fourth Republic: committed to liberal democracy and self-determination, which could be achieved through participation in the French Union. If France could win the vote in the French Indian colonies, the other more volatile French territories might be swayed to join or remain in the Union. The du Montcel report recommended that France appeal to French-Indians by reminding them that, as French-Indians, they held a special position within India. In independent India, they would simply be incorporated into the whole: "In the mass of 400 million Indians, our 350,000 French-Indians would lose all their originality, all their importance—[they would become] a drop of water in an ocean."[21] It would be a loss for the French-Indians to integrate with their neighbors, while they possessed a tangible advantage by continuing to associate with a nation-state headquartered over a thousand miles away. While the position of minority communities in India, including religious and language minorities, as well those of low or no caste, were generally viewed as negative, French authorities knew that association with a European superpower could prove exceptional. However, the people must also be given a *choice*, because, as du Montcel wrote, "if one locks up a man, he will not rest until the doors are pressed open. Instead, open the doors wide and say to him: 'Think and choose.' "[22] If the majority chose to remain French, it would affirm the French argument that the imperial civilizing mission had been both successful and appreciated.

Once again functionaries employed a metaphor of imprisonment to illustrate the problem of French India and the desire for freedom. The liberation of India from British rule came about because, to follow du Montcel's metaphor, colonized subjects were locked up—they lacked autonomy and self-determination, much like a person imprisoned. The importance that du Montcel, as well as other advocates of the French Union, placed on *choice* implied that the people of French India—and by association, the French Union—would be autonomous, freely choosing *individuals*, the central figure in the liberal capitalist state, in both its colonial and postcolonial versions. France did not directly profit off of the scattered French Indian territories, but French political and social capital did rely on them, especially in direct market competition with England. Providing the formerly colonized population with the "freedom" to vote on the future of the French territories and thereby participate in democracy would supposedly emancipate the people of French India from the bonds of colonialism, liberating them from their chains without disrupting the capitalist-economic order of the imperial state.

The preservation of French-Indian culture and history was the most publicly visible concern of the French colonial administration.[23] Du Montcel stressed the importance of the French Union and the French family, reiterating to the French-Indians that their status as French residents *or* citizens made them members of France, a designation that gave them a unique status among their *Indian* neighbors and made them members of a much larger and diverse community that shared a common history. He also suggested highlighting the many links between France and India as two "grandes cultures" and making it clear to the inhabitants of French India that these connections would be lost if the comptoirs were swallowed by India; their unique history would be "annihilated."[24] The duty of both the French and Indian governments, du Montcel believed, was to preserve the "original personality, and political and cultural traditions" created by the synthesis of the two "grandes civilisations."[25] The argument for the preservation of cultural links between France and India underlined the social and cultural capital attached to French India and the French-Indian community, based on the *differences* between former British India and French India. The argument of du Montcel and the French Ministry of Colonies was that while French India was not wholly French, it was not wholly Indian, either. French India laid somewhere in between.

## Markers of French Identity in India: Revolution, Citizenship, Race

National identities are by nature exclusionary. For the colonized who desired a formal relationship to the imperial state, establishing a connection to the history of the nation was an essential element in developing a strong claim to national belonging. Because the French Indian territories were acquired prior to the French Revolution, they belonged to the *anciennes colonies* (distinct from the colonial expansion, primarily in North and West Africa and Indochina, that took place throughout the nineteenth century). The history of French India's involvement in French affairs, including the revolution, is an important signifier in French-Indian identity. For the people of French India, this took place in the form of writing letters to be logged in the *cahiers des doléances* during the time of the revolution.[26] In metropolitan France, the cahiers were in many ways the revolution's starting point, as they allowed people from all three estates to list their grievances and have them recorded for consideration in imagining the new French Republic.

The French in India, when writing to be included in the cahiers, argued that Pondicherry had been made French through the spilling of their own French blood on the Indian soil (referred to as "Carnatic," a geographic designation for the area in South India). "As Frenchmen," they wrote, "our rights have more than once been written in characters of blood on the plains of the Carnatic, and it is on the bones of our fathers and of our brothers, all deceased out of support of the Glory and Honor of the French name, upon which the ramparts of Pondicherry are raised."[27] The group of people who wrote this statement included both white and métis (mixed-race) men who considered themselves part of the essential fabric of both France and Pondicherry and were excited by the revolutionary language that was making its way to the colonies. Eager to assert their right to French citizenship under the new regime, they quickly moved to define who could and who could not be a French citizen. These free men of color in Pondicherry who felt it was their right, and destiny, to claim French citizenship were initially granted the status as "honorary European citizens," though this position was taken away within the same year, and mixed-race men were reclassified as "native."[28] This immediately excluded the many people who had previously been considered white and who were of Portuguese heritage. It also excluded the majority of the population, who were mostly Tamils. From 1790 until 1871, when universal male suffrage was introduced in the colonies, only white and métis men could be active in French civic life, excluding the majority of the population from French-Indian civil society. This created a deep divide between the French and Tamil populations, though the "French" population itself was largely comprised of mixed-race persons.

French colonial policy, especially in the century following the end of the Napoleonic years (1817) and the start of World War I (1914), used the ideology of the French Revolution to argue for the universal benefits of assimilating to French culture and "civilization."[29] Political clubs and associations devoted to *l'Inde française* and the connections between India and France provided a space for members of the intellectual and political elite to forge a relationship with the imperial center. Yet the majority of people who lived in Pondicherry were not members of the political or intellectual elite.[30] Educated Pondichérians had the opportunity to attend the French schools, the Collège Colonial and the lycée, and participate in the civic life of the colony by becoming members of the Société de l'Histoire de l'Inde Française and by reading and contributing to dual Tamil/French language publications such as *Le Progrès de l'Inde française* (1881), *Pontikseriyen* (1893), *Hindu nesan* (1893), *L'Hindou* (1895), *Djothy* (1929), *Dupleix* (1933), *Le Petit Pondichérien/Putuvei vaci* (1911), *Dessobagari* (1937), and the *Republique française* (1949). But most Pondichérians lived in small village communities and were generally unaware of the politics particular to the colonial administration.[31] Whether in French India or British India, the people in these villages spoke Tamil, and many celebrated the same holidays, attended the same temples and festivals, and, perhaps one of the most important markers of Hindu identity, practiced the same caste customs that separated these communities in ways that were largely uncontested by the French or the British, both of whom initially believed that it was important not to interfere with "local customs" in India.

Issues of caste have dominated discussions of India for centuries and remain central to the current social and political climate of the region. The need for the imperial powers to understand the "customs of the natives" drove colonial officials to try to understand caste and how it operated in Indian society, producing vast amounts of "expert knowledge" that could help enumerate the population.[32] One of the ways in which European interests sought to concretize their understanding was to promote the production of knowledge about the things they did not understand; in the case of caste, this fell on a French missionary, the Abbé Jean-Antoine Dubois.

Dubois originally travelled to Pondicherry in the service of the Mission Etrangères in 1792, fleeing the French Revolution and the threat of antireligious persecution. Unlike many of his fellow missionaries, Dubois learned Tamil and Sanskrit and dressed in local clothing. It was his interactions with the indigenous populations and his attempts to convert them that led him to write a book that became a cornerstone of imperial knowledge about caste. That book, *Mœurs, institutions, et cérémonies des peuples de l'Inde*, was purchased by the East India Company and published in English as the *Description of the Character, Manners, and Customs of the People of India, and of Their Institutions, Religious and Civil* in 1816.[33]

Dubois, as a missionary, traveled well outside French Indian territory to engage in his work of conversion; in addition to Pondicherry, Dubois worked in Mysore and surrounding areas in the south. Although he was a product of French education and society, his work in India, whether among French-Indians or British-Indians, led him to the same conclusion: that it would be impossible to convert any Indian, save for the untouchable or "pariah" caste that rested at the bottom of the hierarchy. According to Dubois, it would only be possible for the Catholics to have any degree of success in India if they could appeal to the "pariahs" (a derogatory term for people outside of caste), whom Dubois saw, in keeping with the morals of Indian society at the time, as dim-witted and incapable of progress or self-care.[34] Dubois observed that Brahmins, the highest and priestly caste, had too much power in society that they risked losing if they were to convert to Catholicism; breaking their caste would mean interacting with the pariahs—a measure almost all caste Indians were unwilling to take. Dubois's observations became a common point of discussion throughout French India as colonial administrators in both Paris and Pondicherry discussed the implementation of an assimilationist policy that would encourage colonial subjects to become French, in language, culture, and eventually, citizenship.[35]

Debates about assimilation in the colonies were important to the policies enacted by the Third Republic. Many French politicians saw universal suffrage in French India as a chance to show how the strength of republicanism could wipe out inequalities in "degenerate societies" such as those represented by caste hierarchies in India.[36] Universal suffrage in French India had been avoided up to this point, as upper-caste Indians protested that it would violate customs. It was not long before people who were considered pariahs recognized the opportunity French assimilation presented to improve their lives. Jacques Weber has suggested that those who were greatly oppressed by caste customs were the "most Francophile" of all the French-Indians, even though they were not the ones running and participating in French political clubs and speaking French, because they worked as domestic servants in the houses of Europeans and felt that they were treated much better by Europeans than by fellow Indians who practiced caste.[37] In this way, they had become French through their proximity to French spaces and consumption of French goods.

Beginning in September 1881 with the passing of the act of Renonciation au Statut Personnel, all men over the age of twenty-one in French India could "renounce" their Indigenous status and corresponding personal laws and opt to adhere to the French civil code, making them *renonçants*. Following French assimilationist policies, renonçants were required to choose a new, French name once they declared their status in front of a registrar, a judge, or the commissioner of police. While age and gender were factors in who was allowed to become a renonçant, caste and religion were not taken into account by the French. Thus, after 1881, French-Indians might be *topas* or métis, but they were also Tamils or Bengalis or Malayalis who had converted to Catholicism, or low-caste or noncaste Hindus looking to subvert caste structures (though this did not often work), or Muslims who lived in French villages on one of the many French–British Indian borders.[38] The combination of a political identity comprised of an ethnic marker with a national marker was unique to French India at this time.

The chance to overcome the disadvantages of caste oppression was an important reason for many in French India to choose to renounce their civil status and submit to the French civil code, an option that was available to "natives of French India" beginning in 1881.[39] Those who chose to affiliate with France were made to choose a French name, often as an addition to their Tamil name.[40] M. D. Moracchini, a one-time French colonial administrator in Karaikal and Chandernagore, suggested in 1883 that only outcaste people and Catholics would ever choose to renounce their civil status and become renonçants, a statement that echoed DuBois's earlier predictions.[41] It was commonly believed that for Indians of high caste, the idea of being treated as equals with pariahs was unthinkable and to be avoided at all costs.[42] By the turn of the twentieth century, low- and noncaste people, even those who had converted to Catholicism, were still excluded from schools, temples, and courtrooms, out of a fear that they would sully the "noble castes."[43] Eventually, in 1908, the French administration dealt with this divide by creating separate schools for low-caste French-Indians, preserving the social hierarchies assimilation was meant to erase.[44]

Even as caste oppression continued in French India well into the twentieth century, the *idea* that those in French-held territory were more able to free themselves from the constraints of caste had effectively spread throughout British India. When Gandhi came to Pondicherry on 17 February 1934, at the behest of the Harijana Seva Sangh of Pondicherry, he spoke of Pondichérians as being better able to understand the oppression that caste brought, better than those in the rest of India.[45] In his speech,

Gandhi told the people of French India that "equality and brotherhood were brought into France several hundred years before people began to realize that there was any such thing as brotherhood of man," and that, therefore, he had "every hope" that in Pondicherry there was no occurrence of "untouchability."[46] This was far from the truth, as many French-Indian anticaste advocates noted.

V. Subbiah looked on in dismay as the then-governor of Pondicherry, Georges Bourret, watched the speech and took pleasure in Gandhi's praise of French history and culture.[47] Gandhi's speech proved to be somewhat confusing to the French-Indian freedom fighters who organized the event, as they were hoping that he would advocate for their independence in addition to speaking of the plight of those harmed by caste. By endorsing the French ideas of brotherhood and equality and suggesting that they had been realized in French India, Gandhi seemed to imply that the struggle for freedom from colonial rule was limited to the British Raj, while French India had been the beneficiary of a positive relationship with its colonizer.

Race also figured prominently in the development of French India. Taken as two distinct terms, "French" and "Indian," half of this identity, Indian, was ultimately determined in the colonial context by notions of race and ethnicity (often a combination of the two), while the French half could be acquired, initially by racial identity but later by the act of renunciation. The métis was of concern to French imperialists and intellectuals as early at the eighteenth century.[48] Despite the language of universal equality promoted through the liberal rhetoric of the French Revolution, specifically the Declaration of the Rights of Man and Citizen (1789), French experts continued to keep a close watch on the métis populations throughout the empire. The question of race-mixing in the French Indian territories was a part of the late nineteenth-century push to understand the science of race. N. Huillet, a French physician who wrote an 1867 text titled *Hygiène des blancs, des mixtes, et des indiens à Pondichéry* (Hygiene of the whites, mixed, and Indians of Pondicherry) commented on the great heterogeneity he found in Pondicherry's 121,186 inhabitants and generally encouraged creolization in the colonies, particularly Pondicherry.[49]

Huillet observed four "distinct elements" within Pondicherry's population: Europeans; the descendants of Europeans, or créoles; the "mixtes," or *topas*; and the Hindus (and, he adds to this category, the Muslims who were naturalized after the conquest.)[50] Huillet counted 954 white, 1239 mixed, and 118, 993 in the "Indian population."[51] The French administration had made its first attempt at a systematic count of the residents of the Indian comptoirs in 1842, although, according to the *Gazetteer of India*, registration was not compulsory, and the survey therefore failed to provide a total count of those domiciled in French India.[52] This initial categorization of the population was divided into Europeans, métis, Indian, and Muslims.[53] While Huillet was happy to place Muslims and Hindus into the same category, under the title of Hindus (as his interest was biological, not social), the imperial government understood the social divisions between European, mixed-race, Hindu, and Muslim.

Despite the lack of a concrete and homogenous understanding of the category of French-Indian, the colonial systems that interacted in French India, of the French and the British, did construct certain internal boundaries that dictated, to varying degrees of success, how people were positioned in relation to one other and came to understand themselves in relation to the greater colonial society. While interracial relationships were tolerated and in some ways encouraged in the early years of French rule in India, the resulting population born of these unions was separated from the population at large, through both racial and spatial segregation. The mixed-race population in French India in the late eighteenth and nineteenth centuries, which self-identified as "métis," became part of the white class, as they mostly converted to Catholicism, purchased and sewed European clothes, imported French furniture, consumed French foods, and participated in the public life of the nonindigenous population.

There has been numerous debates about the use and meaning of the term "métis"—most commonly over the past three decades, it has been used to describe the coming together of two or more cultures, or as a linguistic term, referring to the merger of two or more languages.[54] In French India, and in many of the other colonies, "métis" referred to people of European origin who were born in the colonies, a definition that has fallen out of general use.[55] Most commonly employed today to describe cultures in the Caribbean, the West Indies, and Louisiana, the postcolonial framework of creolization does not transfer well to French India, partly because it has been used in French India primarily to describe race-mixing (*métissage*), not culture-mixing, since the mid-nineteenth century.[56] French-Indians, both those who were mixed-race and those who were not, became French in a way that was similar to but distinct from people in France.

Lourdes Tirouvanziam Louis, herself a self-identified Pondichérian créole, who was born in Vietnam to a French-Indian family, wrote a doctoral thesis on the créole of Pondicherry. According to Louis, in the first years of the nineteenth century, the term "créole" was used to describe *both* Europeans born in the colonies *and* those with mixed blood, or métis.[57] The word *topas* was also used in several areas of colonial India during the same period, to signify a person with Portuguese heritage, a designation that separated the French and British *colons* from the often lower-class descendants of Portuguese colonists, and the mixed Indian-Portuguese heritage population. During the late seventeenth century, there were very few European women in India, and the French soldiers in South India often married and/or had children with *topasine* women, who were preferable to *les femmes du pays* (local women), largely because they were often already Catholic and thus seen as more appropriate marriage partners than the local Hindu and Muslim women.[58]

In this way, we can see that, at this point, religious compatibility was a primary factor in choosing a partner, although it is difficult to ignore the direct association of religious identity and heritage or racial background in this particular time and place. From the very first days of European presence in India, there was a hierarchy in place, relative to the power of imperial and economic institutions that operated in this geopolitical space. While it is easy, in hindsight, to call this a racial hierarchy, eighteenth-century conceptions of race were not based in the same biological discourse that became popular in the mid- to late nineteenth century.[59] Indeed, religion played an important role in the earliest unions between European men and local women in India. Beginning with the Portuguese settlers in India in the sixteenth century, the Catholic Church encouraged interracial unions as a way to convert non-Catholics and create a larger Catholic presence in the colonies.[60] This led to the births of many mixed-race children, who, during this time, were more likely to have a higher class standing than the Indigenous populations, because of the one European parent and the likelihood they would own property or other capital.[61] The elevated class status of mixed-race persons made it probable that European men would consider a métis woman a good match. In this way, religious, economic, and racial identities became intimately connected.

The Portuguese presence in South Asia in the sixteenth century meant that when French and British sailors and merchants began to arrive in the eighteenth century, there was already a population of mixed-race men and women living throughout the Indian port cities. By this time, the métis population was increasing, and many French men of high class standing were marrying métis women.[62] Joseph Dupleix himself married a métis woman, Jeanne Dupleix (née Albert) (1706–1756), whom he met in Chandernagore. Mme Dupleix had been raised in Pondicherry, the daughter of a Frenchman, Jacques-Theodor Albert, and a métis mother, Rose de Castro, who was believed to be of Portuguese and Indian parentage.[63] While Dupleix and Jeanne did not have children of their own, Dupleix is to this day remembered as the father of Pondicherry; while he was not the founder of the colony, he was the man who gave the sleepy town life, and Mme Dupleix is revered as a key figure in her husband's success as governor, and in the building of Pondicherry as a rival to British power in India.

Mme Dupleix spoke Tamil, as well as French and English, a common trait amongst the métis population. She was one of many métis Catholics in Pondicherry. Métis individuals were not considered caste Hindus, because of firmly held beliefs that one must be born to two Hindu parents to be of pure caste—thus, the majority of the métis in French India were Catholics.[64] While her familiarity with the local landscape and population as well as European customs and languages made her a useful, and necessary, person for the European settlers, her reputation among the local people was largely negative. The tensions between Madame Dupleix, other métis in the area, and the local, mostly Tamil communities, is evident in the diaries kept by Ananda Ranga Pillai (1709–1761), the Tamil man who served as Governor Dupleix's dubash.[65] In this way, Mme Dupleix and Ananda Ranga Pillai, a métis woman and a Tamil man, served a similar function for Governor Dupleix, of translator and interpreter. In his diary, Pillai wrote extensively of his dislike of Mme Dupleix, especially concerning her involvement with politics, which he believed would be better left to the governor.[66] His writings also suggest that he resented her for what he saw as the persecution of Hindus through destruction of their religious practices.[67] While Pillai had respect for the power and authority of the governor, who came from France and had no knowledge of local customs, he saw Mme Dupleix as a traitor to the lives of the local people, by deriding Hindu and Muslim customs and suggesting the superiority of European ways. While Governor Dupleix could be excused, there is a sense in Pillai's writing that the métis community were passing as white Europeans when they were not.

Despite her inability, or lack of desire, to form friendships with non-European and non-métis people in Pondicherry, Mme Dupleix has become something of a local hero in Pondicherry, at least among the Francophile community. She has captured the attention and imagination of many Francophone authors who have written about her life in eighteenth-century French India.[68] Sometimes called Johanna Bégum or Jeanne Albert, Mme Dupleix has been mythologized in Francophile Pondicherry, portrayed as a strong woman who was actively involved in the political affairs of her husband and of French India. The two major French works that have attempted her biography have made her power over the dubash and her influence on Governor Dupleix a centerpiece of her life story.

These works have also noted the importance of her métis heritage: the 1934 work by Yvonne Robert Gaebelé, *Métis et Grande Dame: Johanna Bégum, Marquise Dupleix (1706–1756)*, carries a title that clearly implies that her métis heritage was her primary identity.[69] Gaebelé's book suggests that Dupleix depended on his wife's mixed background to help him negotiate with local princes, as well as local people, including the dubash Pillai. It was more logical, these books suggest, for the governor to trust his wife than his dubash: while Pillai may have been loyal to the governor, his true interests would lay with his Tamil-Hindu community, not with the values and goals of the Europeans. The divisions between Mme Dupleix and Ananda Ranga Pillai, two people separated by gender, race, and religion, are indicative of the boundaries formed as French colonialism came to Pondicherry. Despite the overlaps in their lives—they were born in the same location, spoke the same languages, and knew many of the same people—the arrival of Dupleix and the colonial system reordered local communities in such a way that, instead of working together, they could only compete to be the most useful to those with the most power, who were, in this case, the French officials, military officers, and settlers.

## Untying the Colonial Knot: The Ashram as a Space of In-Between

The diplomatic approach to maintaining the Indian comptoirs, and thus the hope of building the French Union, depended on the suppression of all anti-French opinions in the territories. While many in the Francophone community in French India began to look toward forming cultural and scholastic institutions to continue their relationship with France, both governments turned in the direction of the Aurobindo Ashram as the potential negotiator of the situation, the representative of the in-between—a significant shift from viewing the métis and French-Indian community as the potential mediators in the final stages of colonialism in French India. As members of the French-Indian communities began to speak out about the future of the territories, it became clear to the French colonial administration that the hybrid communities in the comptoirs were not guaranteed to support continued French rule. The 1947 du Montcel report suggests that the best route to maintaining power in India would be to gain the support of the occupants of the Sri Aurobindo Ashram. Du Montcel stressed the importance of the Ashram to French concerns, noting that it is on "French territory" and that "*la 'MERE' est française*," ("the MOTHER is French"); to ignore the Ashram would be, in the words of the author, "an error."[70] After all, the Ashram was the project of Sri Aurobindo, who had come to Pondicherry to take advantage of the protection of the French colonial state, and Mira Alfassa, who was indeed a French citizen.

Du Montcel believed that the key to maintaining the French colonies in India, or at the very least a French presence in India, was exactly the Ashram model: to blend what he saw as a specific Indian mysticism with Western education, culture, and civilization. The Ashram had always been located in the ville blanche, and while the inhabitants of the Ashram were a mixture of ethnicities, mostly Bengalis and Gujaratis from North India, with a small population of Europeans and Americans, there was a heavy emphasis in the Ashram on the practice of French language and culture.[71] Despite her dedication to Eastern religions and mysticism, the Mother strongly believed in the value of "classical" Western education and stressed Greek, Latin, and French texts in the Ashram school.[72] She believed that every nation possessed unique qualities, and that these qualities should be taught to children so that they could understand "the mission their nation had to fulfill in the world." For the Mother, France was defined by "generosity of sentiment, newness and boldness of ideas and chivalry in action." It was these attributes that led to France "command[ing] the respect and admiration of all: it is by these virtues that she dominated the world."[73] The persona of the Mother offered the colonial administration an opportunity to appeal to the greater Indian community and project an image of France as a gregarious and benevolent cultural friend to India.

While Pondicherry and the other French possessions loomed large in the French imagination, it was Aurobindo and his Ashram that came to define Pondicherry on a global scale. A 1949 *Life* magazine article noted that the Ashram "includes dozens of impressive buildings and covers a large part of the French-administered town," and that "it is no exaggeration to say that Sri Aurobindo's ashram is Pondicherry's leading industry, attracting thousands of pilgrims annually."[74] The arrival of Aurobindo and the growing fame of the Ashram began to eclipse the visibility of the colonial métis society in Pondicherry, as Western eyes turned to the Ashram as the primary representative for the future relationship between France and India. While race-mixing was in many ways an inevitable product of imperial conquest, mainstream anticolonial nationalisms tended to favor ideas of racial purity, often in the interest of building strong nation-states.[75] For India and France, the celibate relationship between Aurobindo and the Mother was a sign of what future friendship between nations and states should look like: friendly, but not too friendly. Decolonization was an opportunity to some, then, to untie the sexual knot created by imperial conquest and to separate national bodies in a manner that emphasized the national character of race and ethnicity. In other words, the actions of Aurobindo and the Mother, while encouraging alternative ways of thinking about sexuality and heteronormativity, also reinforced the idea that nationality was biologically determined, a notion that became increasingly popular following independence.

Aurobindo and the Mother portrayed their relationship as loving but nonsexual—they had both taken up the role of *brahmacharyans*, committed to a vow of celibacy.[76] Alfassa had decided to live a celibate life before she came to India; early on in her marriage to Paul Richard, she told him that "the animal mode of reproduction was a transitional one," and that until a new way of bearing children was discovered, her motherhood would be "spiritual."[77] It was with Sri Aurobindo that Mira found her spiritual motherhood. By 1926, Aurobindo had christened Mira as "the Mother," and placed her in charge of their Ashram and Ashram school, a position she would hold until her death in 1973. Both Alfassa and Aurobindo were married to others when they met—it is interesting to note that in the thousands of pages of hagiography that have been written about the pair by their followers, their spouses are rarely, if ever, mentioned.[78] In their own ways, Alfassa and Aurobindo had both already rejected marriage as a union that could be a useful marker of their relationship, encouraging others to break the norms of the heteronormative family structure and join the Ashram family.[79]

Although the Ashram had a major presence in Pondicherry, it claimed to be nonpolitical. A 1946 statement from the Mother reminded people, "I told you already—no politics can originate from the Ashram; it could bring a mountain of trouble."[80] The avowed apolitical stance of the Ashram did not sit well with local politicians and inhabitants who saw how the Ashram had dominated the ville blanche, as well as outside perceptions of Pondicherry. Nirodbaran, a devotee and physician who came to the Ashram in the 1930s, wrote in his memoir, *Twelve Years with Sri Aurobindo*, "Though we in the Ashram are not supposed to take part in politics, we are not at all indifferent to world affairs."[81] Many of the Ashram inhabitants wrote about the reasons they ended up living there, which often grew from dissatisfaction with the norms of the colonial, capitalist, heteronormative institutions throughout the West and the colonies. Walking away from the expectations and responsibilities of marriages, families, and wage labor, Ashram residents sought a new kind of life, impossible to achieve within their own communities.

In the lead-up to 1947, many local residents in Pondicherry accused the Ashram of hypocrisy. While it may have refrained from making public statements about political matters, the Ashram did hold a significant amount of power with the government of France, a decidedly political position. Antoine Mariadassou, the president of the Students' Congress of French India, recalled that when he tried to approach Governor Baron in 1947 to discuss the possibilities of decolonization, he was not allowed to speak to him, but was sent instead to the "secretary of propaganda," a young man named Bernard Enginger.[82] Enginger, who was Governor Baron's nephew, was also a devotee of the Mother and became one of her most important disciples, better known under the name of Satprem.[83] Mariadassou was not alone in his frustration with the power held by the Ashram. Internal documentation from the British consulate in Pondicherry in 1946–1947 indicates that the local population in French India did not trust the Ashram or, by proxy, Governor Baron; increasing quantities of anti-French propaganda were circulating in Pondicherry that stated that "Baron was a liar," and that he "took his instructions from the Mother in the local Ashram."[84] Locals accused the Ashram of having great wealth and hiding it; during a time when there were few cars in Pondicherry, the Ashram owned five of its own.[85] The local press often complained that the Ashram was buying too much property in the ville blanche, chasing Pondichériens out of the "good side" of town. A report from the British Consul in January 1946 notes that the Ashram had bought more than one hundred houses, which left a shortage of "suitable houses" in the ville blanche—a problem for both the French-Indians and the French residents of Pondicherry.[86]

Governor Baron would later write that on the day of Indian independence, 15 August 1947, that he traveled to Delhi not in his "official capacity as Governor-General of French India," but instead as "a representative of French Culture and Literature," and as "one who agreed with the vision of one of India's most luminous sons: Sri Aurobindo."[87] Baron envisioned a future where the integration of French India into India would be "of a cultural type" and would "bring into close rapport the great liberal traditions of France and the great spiritual traditions of India. . . . As a French patriot I would always fly the Tricolour over my residence in India but I would simultaneously raise over my residence the Indian flag. A double or multiple symbol of human culture would be my ideal."[88] Baron portrayed himself as a loyal member of two nations, an idea that did not sit well with the Indian nationalists or the Communists, particularly V. Subbiah, who accused Baron of manipulating the local populations by printing leaflets in Tamil claiming that Gandhi wished French India to remain French.[89] These leaflets, wrote Subbiah, were "an Independence day gift given by French Imperialism to people who demanded independence."[90] It was clear to many in French India, from Subbiah and the Communists to the métis community, that, despite discussions of belonging to the same family, the French colonial government was not listening to the concerns of the majority of the family members, as they looked to the Ashram for assistance.

Because the relationship between Aurobindo and the Mother was nonsexual, it did not disrupt the politics of race, religion, and nation, of who was responsible for the reproduction of the independent Indian nation. The partnership between Aurobindo and the Mother resembles contemporary models of multiculturalism: the coexistence of multiple, though distinct, cultures. It is in many ways a precursor to the cultural politics of postcolonial India, which sought to foster "unity in diversity." Aurobindo and the Mother believed strongly in the importance of national cultures.

They promoted national literatures and tended to attribute certain characteristics to particular cultures; the India that Aurobindo and the Mother presented in their work was a Hindu-centric space, steeped in spirituality. The Mother promoted post-Enlightenment French language and literature through the Ashram school curriculum, while simultaneously drawing on Orientalist tropes that imbued Indian land with spiritual power. They advocated for Indian sovereignty in the form of freedom from British rule while instrumentalizing the connections they enjoyed with the French imperial apparatus in order to continue their spiritual work on French-occupied land.

## From Multiculturalism to Internationalism: The Communist Party of French India

Unlike the multiculturalism espoused and practiced in the Ashram, the Communist Party of French India (CPFI) was an internationalist configuration. Aligning with the internationalist communist movement, Subbiah spoke not of the greatness of India as Aurobindo did, but instead of the fraternity of workers worldwide and the need to fight together to overthrow the colonial masters.[91] Beginning in the 1930s, Subbiah organized workers across the French India/British India borders in the three major textile mills. As a local configuration of an international organization, the CPFI adopted many ideas and tactics from comrades abroad, in an attempt to appeal to all workers in the area, most of whom crossed borders daily to reach their jobs.

The 1920s and 1930s were an especially trying time for the working-class populations of Pondicherry and Chandernagore. Many people who lived outside the juridical borders of French India were employed in the textile factories and jute mills in French territory and were subjected to "abnormally low wages" and twelve-hour working days "under inhuman conditions."[92] Subbiah and other party leaders had organized multiple strikes and protests in Pondicherry and Chandernagore throughout the 1930s, one of which led to the killing of twelve laborers by police in 1936.[93] While the strikes were eventually put down and new compromises made between the factory owners and workers, the CPFI had gained influence with a large segment of the French-Indian population through labor organizing. Subsequently, Subbiah, as a potent representative of communism as an international movement, was often persona non grata in both British India and French India and spent most of the 1940s and some of the early 1950s, after India's independence, in hiding from both governments.[94]

Subbiah made several trips to Europe, including extensive visits to France, in his capacity as representative of the CPFI. Upon his return from one trip to Paris in 1947, Subbiah denounced the "cultural connections" proposed by Governor Baron, citing his efforts to retain power in India through cultural institutions as "a mask for perpetuating French imperialism in India."[95] While Subbiah challenged the discourse of fraternity between nation-states, he continued to use the term "fraternity" in reference to the global connections between the working class in France and the working class in French India. In his memoir he acknowledges that "the fraternal link forged between the struggling toiling people of France and of Pondicherry through reports of the events in France roused tremendously the consciousness of the textile workers here."[96] The "support" of the "powerful working class organization of France" was helping the people in French India to direct their actions "against the European capitalist exploitation and simultaneously against the French Imperialism here."[97] While Subbiah and the CPFI did not endorse Nehru's Congress government and actively worked against the organization of the French India Congress Party to organize anti-French rallies and protests, they did advocate for the merger of French India into India in 1947, on the basis of the communist anti-imperialist platform.[98]

While there were many political parties in Pondicherry, such as the French India Socialist Party (FISP), Congress Party, and Social and Democratic Union, that advocated the merger of French India into India, the Communist Party of French India was the only group to actively denounce the proposal for a referendum on the future of French India.[99] Subbiah, in his memoir, described the proposals for a referendum as a "mockery of political reform" that "stood unmasked even at the early stage of its implementation as nothing short of a treacherous game of imperialism to perpetuate its colonial rule here."[100] Subbiah and his comrades argued that the presentation of a "choice" to be made by free individuals was an illusion, perpetuated by both colonialism and global capitalism. The communists of French India certainly believed in the importance of collectivity and comradeship, but expressed this through declarations of solidarity with the working people of France, Italy, England, Russia, and other countries with strong communist parties, as well as with their fellow colonial subjects in Indochina and Africa, relationships born of the common experiences of class struggle and colonial oppression. The refusal of the CPFI to work with the other political parties advocating merger isolated their efforts and made them vulnerable to attacks by both the national French and Indian governments, who often accused them of instigating physical violence against peaceful protestors and citizens who believed in the power of self-determination and the democratic equality of the liberal nation-state.

Historian B. Krishnamurthy, drawing on the Tamil-language newspapers *Sudandiram* (the CPFI newspaper) and *Dinamani*, shows how the CPFI came to be critical of both France and India as discussions of decolonization in French India dragged on.[101] He writes that "the Communists condemned that [the Indian Government] as the Government of Neo-Fascist exploiters and stooges of Anglo-American imperialism and announced that they would try to avoid the merger of the French Indian settlements with the Indian Union, as they doubted the very genuineness of the Indian independence."[102] Thus, the CPFI posed a threat to both the French and Indian governments, as well the maintenance of global economic relations.

Unlike the positive international attention that the Ashram brought to Pondicherry, the international mainstream Western press was critical of the presence of communists in French India, imagining the influence of communism in French India to be much greater in scale than it actually was, stretching far beyond the CPFI. The international press, especially the *New York Times*, applauded Nehru's decision to negotiate with the French government rather than allowing the communists to "capitalize on honest patriotic feelings, as they have so often done."[103] Despite the fact that the CPFI openly and consistently advocated for the merger of French India into India, the party's political ideology was viewed as incompatible with that of the capitalist democratic state, and its "patriotic feelings" were interpreted as insincere. Just as Subbiah was stateless throughout much of his life because of his political affiliation with communism, Indian and French nationalists portrayed members of the CPFI as extrastate actors, possible liabilities to the state and the nation. A *New York Times* article from 1952 on communists in French India concludes by suggesting that "France can afford the loss of the virtually worthless colonies far better than the loss of friendly relations with India and can better afford a generous gesture than giving an additional weapon to her Communist foes."[104]

The Cold War divisions that were starting to gain traction throughout the world were foundational to the debates about what decolonization would look like in French India.

## The Fluidity of Minor Identities

Membership in the Communist Party was a political act, and those who chose to join the party and speak on behalf of it are remembered and critiqued as political actors. Membership in the French Indian community at large was, in contrast, less voluntary, as most members of this group were subject to inclusion on the basis of their family and/or their place of birth and residence. As discussed earlier, some French-Indians had been French citizens since the French Revolution; others since 1881, when they were given the opportunity to renounce their civil status and claim French citizenship; and others since they fought for France in the world wars of the twentieth century. Many of the families that had chosen French citizenship in the nineteenth century had converted to Catholicism and thus were seen as practicing French, not Indian, culture. Still other French-Indians, particularly upper-caste Hindus, had never declared French citizenship, but were active members of a community that attended French schools, studied French history and politics, and considered themselves substantially different than their neighbors in British/independent India. Lastly, there was a significant French-Indian diaspora present in Indochina, where French-Indian migrants held on strongly to their French citizenship and the privileges it afforded in the context of a colony where far fewer people were allowed to become colonial citizens.[105] While political clubs, dual-language newspapers, French-Indian historical societies, and French cultural associations served as meeting places and media outlets for the construction of a French-Indian identity, there were always members, such as French-Indian Communists, who existed on the margins of this identity, many unable to communicate in French and unwilling to submit to an imperial identity.

The figure of the "French-Indian" was never stable, yet there *were* several overlapping groups that self-identified as French-Indian and viewed the potential decolonization of French India as a threat to their identities and livelihoods. While the pro-merger movement demanded that French India merge with India immediately and without referendum, there were also many people asking questions about what would happen to the people in French India if it did choose to join the French Union and reject India's claim to sovereign rights over the territories. In May 1947, R. L. Purushottam (Reddiar), president of the French India National Congress, wrote a letter to Jawaharlal Nehru, then vice president of the interim government of India, to express local concerns about the fate of French-Indians. In the letter, Reddiar worries that French-Indians will be considered as foreigners by the central government and will not be able to apply for positions with the government, as the jobs are reserved for "British subjects of Indian domicile or descent and subjects of Indian states." The letter makes the case that French-Indians are not actually foreigners because of their cultural, political, economic, and cultural relationships with India. Reddiar writes, "We hope that no distinction will be made between the subjects of French India and British subjects of Indian domicile or descent." He pleads with Nehru to do away with the "petty demarcations like French and British nationalities within India that is one and indivisible."[106] The closer the time came to Indian independence, the more the stability of imperial national identities weakened.

The development of Indian, British, and French nationalisms—ideologies formed over a period of imperial conquest and anticolonial struggle—pulled at these colonial subjects and citizens as they negotiated the political terrain of the twentieth century, leading many of them in different directions. Raphael Ramanyya Dadala was born in a village called Farompet outside of Yanam.[107] He grew up impoverished, and although his family lived in French Indian territory, they did not speak French or practice French cultural traditions. His "conversion" from peasant to French teacher and police officer occurred through the patronage of a Catholic missionary from France, Father Artic, who had him admitted to a French Catholic school, leading to his baptism in 1919.[108] Later, another priest, Father Gangloff of Alsace, helped Dadala travel to Pondicherry to continue his studies, encouraging him to fully immerse himself in French-Indian culture and the atmosphere of Pondicherry.

Dadala opens his autobiography by stating, "I am a Scheduled castes Catholic."[109] Like many other Dalit people domiciled in French Indian territory, Dadala chose to convert to Catholicism, though his description points to the lived reality that, even with religious conversion, one's caste status still remained an essential element of how they related to society at large. Following this statement is a list of identities he had practiced throughout his life, including farm boy, French teacher, "police officer in the Government of the French settlements in India," "leader of the French Indian liberation struggle," and, finally, "Superintendent of Excise and District Prohibition Officer in the Government of Andhra Pradesh."[110] While his autobiography is ostensibly devoted to retelling his role in the struggle against France for freedom, he devotes the entire preface and much of the small booklet itself to the importance of fighting for the rights of Dalits, an identity he finds much more powerful and unifying than either that of French citizen or Indian nationalist. While Dadala chose to fight for freedom from colonial rule, eschewing his position in the French police force and his favor with the French colonial authorities, he holds the Indian government accountable for "genocide against the scheduled castes community" claiming "caste Hindus" planned to "exterminate [the Scheduled Castes] as a race."[111]

During the era of anti-French demonstrations in French India (which will be examined in more detail in the next chapter), Dadala and his "gang" were seen by French authorities as the primary threat against the safety of French-Indian people, as they walked the streets shouting, "Down with the French!" and "Jai Hind!"[112] However, as he looked back, Dadala had changed his rallying cry to "Jai the All India Scheduled Castes and Tribes Liberation Organisation," while also suggesting that it may have been better for Dalits to remain under French colonial rule than submit themselves to the prejudices of the Indian government.

Dadala is an example of an individual whose French-Indian identity was a passing phase in his own lifetime. We now turn to Arthur Annasse, a man who lists his credentials as "Ancien Président des "Patriotes de l'Inde française," Chevalier de l'Ordre National du Mérite," and "Croix de la Fédération Nationale des Combattants Volontaires et de la Résistance." He served in the French military and was stationed in Indochina during World War II, becoming a well-respected lawyer in Indochina after the war's end. Annasse was a member of the French-Indian diaspora that had made its home in Indochina, while retaining French citizenship and arguing for a continued relationship with France.[113] Annasse published a book in 1975, highlighting what he saw as the glorious history of French India.[114] In it Annasse carefully describes the differences between Hindu families in French India, which he viewed as very traditional and rooted in old and "medieval" traditions, and the "very small" Muslim and Catholic populations, who had "adopted" more ways of Western living.[115]

His own Catholic grandfathers, on both the maternal and paternal sides, had worked with the "indignés" (natives) in the 1870s to lobby the French government in Paris for rights equal to those of French citizens. While men like Dadala and Subbiah spoke extensively of the need to combat the colonization of French India, Annasse believed that the people of French India had never been conquered or colonized, but instead had been *adopted* by France.[116] France, in the worldview of Annasse, and many of the other French-Indians resident in Indochina, had provided French-Indians with certain rights (*droits*) that separated them from Indians in the surrounding areas, and that these rights were worth defending and retaining within independent India.

Annasse worked closely with French authorities following India's independence to ensure the rights and needs of the French-Indian community were preserved. Annasse wrote that his primary goal in working with officials in Paris, including the then–Ministre de la France d'Outre-Mer François Mitterrand, in 1951, was "to work to maintain the rights and interests of the French nationals of India."[117] This objective led him to found, with the support of French officials, the Patriotes de l'Inde française, a political interest group dedicated to convincing the people of French India to support the referendum, in the interest of protecting the rights of French nationals (*ressortissants*). Beginning in 1949, the group produced materials in both French and Tamil outlining the importance of maintaining a unique identity as French-Indians, a mission Annasse considered successful until he "began to hear the speakers in the neighboring territories haranguing the people of Pondicherry and insulting France."[118] Throughout his book, Annasse makes it clear that he believed that the Indian state did not have the best interests of the French-Indians in mind when they asked for France to relinquish their territories— a stance consistent with many other groups in South Asia, including religious groups (Muslims), regional, cultural, and linguistic groups, (Tamils, Hyderabadis, Kashmiris), and other minoritarian groups, such as Dadala's All India Scheduled Castes and Tribes Liberation Organisation.

Dadala and Annasse represent two ends of the spectrum, as men who both considered themselves to be French-Indians in some capacity and chose to defend the interests of one nation-state over the other. There were, however, many people who fell in the middle of these two positions. One such individual was Edouard Goubert (1894–1979), the leader of the French India Socialist Party (FISP). Following the independence of

India in 1947, Goubert worked closely with the French colonial administration and was elected, as a representative of the FISP, to the French National Assembly. For years, he was the prime enemy of Subbiah and the Communist Party and viewed by many as a tool of the French colonial administration. However, in 1953, Goubert suddenly changed his position, resigned from the National Assembly, and demanded the immediate integration of French India into India. Goubert was a member of an important créole community in Pondicherry: his father was the son of a French family that had been rooted in Pondicherry for several decades while his mother was an "untouchable from the village of Arcot."[119] His compatriot Dadala noted that Goubert "had his own following in Pondicherry" and was eagerly embraced by them when he left the pro-French side, leading the pro-French factions "leaderless" the "moment he crossed to India."[120] After 1954, Goubert adopted the Indian name E. G. Pillai and began to wear the clothing associated with the Indian Congress Party. After his anti-French actions in March and April 1954, he wrote a letter to the president of the National Assembly defending his actions against "French despotism."[121] His letter echoed a sentiment that was voiced regularly among French-Indians: that of respect for the French but resentment for the empire. Goubert wrote, "I still like all the French people who have not left France, just as I see myself forced to hate the French who are located in the over-seas territories, except, of course, with a few rare exceptions."[122] As an anticolonial measure, Goubert had divorced himself from France and "returned" to India.

## Rethinking Liberation

The French Indian territories, once a home for exiled British-Indian freedom fighters, became a significant space for anti-imperial organizing against the French between 1946 and 1947. Several French-Indian groups that would become key players over the following years were formed in this period, including the French India National Congress (formed in May 1946) and the Congrés des étudiants, or French Indian Students' Congress (also formed in 1946, with a close relationship to the French India National Congress), as well as the Karaikal National Congress (September 1946) and the Karaikal Students Congress (January 1947). The French Indian Communist Party, which was already active, turned its attention more forcefully toward France and the global fight against French imperialism. While historians have suggested that political unrest in French India was simply an extension of British anticolonial organizing, the long decolonization of French India shows this to be untrue, as groups formed often in solidarity with British Indian organizations but with different causes, such as French aggression in Indochina and Algeria, and, importantly, with a different relationship to the emerging Indian state.

The months preceding 15 August 1947 were fraught for people throughout the subcontinent. While French India did not face the type of violence or displacement that erupted in the north around Partition, those associated with French India began to speak publicly about the question of French colonialism in new, less complimentary ways, making the French colonial administration notably uncomfortable. The imminent departure of the British began to tarnish the shine of France as a good colonial power. Several French-Indian politicians who had recently traveled to France called public meetings in the months leading up to India's independence, to describe the political situation to crowds of onlookers in several areas of French India. On 6 April 1947, Maurice Paquirissamypoulle, who had recently been elected as a senator, spoke at a public meeting in Mahé after his first diplomatic trip to France, reporting that "everything is perfect in France"; "we are very well liked"; "I was treated like a King"; and that French-Indians receive "3.000 francs a month for expenses." But, he continued, "if I spoke of the situation here, of unemployment, of the misery, no one listened to me. They make fun of us."[123]

Paquirissamypoulle, in this speech, began by retelling the vision of France that the French state projected onto the French Indian territories of a liberal utopia that provided mutual respect and significant access to wealth for all citizens. However, this utopian portrayal was quickly undercut, as he noted that the people he met "made fun of" French-Indians, ignoring his tales of colonial neglect and oppression. His message, directed at the people of French India who were wondering whether life would be better under French or Indian rule, sought to show them that France was not actually interested in French-Indians as French citizens, that the utopian dream was actually a façade for the hierarchical infrastructure of colonial rule.

Soon after this speech, Paquirissamypoulle traveled to Pondicherry, where he told the people, "French India will be independent when India is free of the British. France has done nothing here.... No need to fight against the French, they will disappear in a blink of the eye."[124] In other words, for those who were in direct contact with France, the notion of joining the French Union was a nonstarter, as it was clear that France did not have any desire to help the people suffering in the French Indian territories. The CPFI joined in these calls for independence, as the CPFI leader Soubramanien spoke in Pondicherry on the same day, 6 April 1947: "We must abolish the French dictatorship ... they are rabid dogs."[125] In his memoir, Subbiah recalls how the announcement that the British would leave India sparked "the patriotic sentiments of the people" who immediately began to organize marches to express "their determination to win complete freedom for Pondicherry from French imperialism."[126]

The prospect of French India being surrounded not by British India, but by *India*, shined a new light on the French Indian territories as a uniquely French space. As local French-Indian political leaders addressed crowds and spoke of the imperialist foundation of the French Union, students gathered in the French Indian territories to protest the continuation of imperialism. Groups from across India committed to anti-imperialism came together to protest not just continued French rule in India, but French aggression in Indochina as well. For example, on 2 February 1947, a march advocating the withdrawal of French troops from Indochina took place in Karaikal, organized by the French Indian National Congress (FINC), the Students Congress of French India, the CPFI, and the Dravida Kazhagam (Dravidian Party).[127] Of all the groups, the French India Students Congress was the most committed to systematically addressing French imperialism. Antoine Vallabh Mariadassou, one of the founding members of the Students Congress of French India and the president of the group from 1946 to 1947, remembers that, beginning with its inception, the group consistently organized rallies where hundreds of students would march in the streets, carrying signs that read "A bas le colonialisme française!"; "Jai Hind!"; and "France quittez l'Inde!" ("Down with French colonialism!"; "Long Live India!"; "France leave India!").[128]

While the CPFI, French India National Congress, and Students' Congress had common goals toward overthrowing French imperialism, there was also great friction between the groups. In a typewritten report filed by the French India National Congress and sent to Nehru and Gandhi in early 1947, the FINC accuses the CPFI of bringing violence to the other groups, accusing them of "mob hooliganism" and being "provocateurs."[129]

The primary goal of the Students' Congress in 1946 was to convince Governor Baron to declare publicly that France had the same intentions in India as the British: to leave as soon as possible.[130] A Students' Congress pamphlet printed in French and Tamil in 1947 calls on all *comrades étudiants* to recognize the regime of French imperialism that they were living under, referring to the French Union as "imperialist reform."[131] The students announced their intentions to hold a public meeting on 9 August 1947, and the French Indian government reacted by banning all public gatherings and processions, reiterating that it was illegal for foreigners (including British/Indian-Indians) from speaking at political functions in the French Indian territories.[132] Some French-Indian leaders sought to circumscribe these laws by having people speak from British India, where the audience listened while sitting on French Indian land.[133]

The internationalism of the CPFI was a problem for the FINC. Although both groups agreed that they wanted the French out of India, the CPFI were critical of the emerging Indian leadership and nationalist attitudes in general. This led to the FINC accusing the CPFI of having nefarious, unlawful, and unpatriotic intentions. According to a FINC report, the CPFI were "aiming to create disruption at any cost, while trying to maintain a grip over their fast sinking prestige." People in the press were paying attention to how many houses in the French territories were flying French flags, Indian flags, and Communist flags, and the FINC believed the CPFI were targeting people in houses with Indian flags. Ultimately, they blamed the French government for allowing the CPFI to loot houses, insult women, and damage personal property.

The accusations leveled by the FINC are a clear continuation of the criminalization that the borders surrounding the enclaves had begun in the early twentieth century. The French India National Congress went to great lengths to create a self-image as a group that was simultaneously French-Indian while also being Indian. It strongly advocated for a definition of national belonging based on ethnicity and race, using the language of blood ties in much of their literature. At the same time, it worked to paint a picture of the groups that advocated for a global revolution (CPFI) or for participation in the French Union (the French India Socialist Party) as outsiders. The FINC report sent to Nehru depicts the workers' strikes as communist plots, not sites of legitimate protest by French-Indians. The report states, "In the press the [mill strikes] were reported as merely a clash due to instigation by non-French India citizens, and that workers in the mills were sent out because there was trouble in their village, it was really a ruse to get all the Communist workers available, to launch their attack on the villages."[134] Were the communists, specifically members of the CPFI, part of French India or not? All the political groups, as well as the press, blamed the violence in the territories on what one might today call "outside agitators," identified here as "non-French India citizens." It stands to reason that without the colonial borders that separated French India and British India, the outside agitators would not be from the outside.

The violence and repression of speech that protestors faced came as a surprise to many in the days leading to independence. The French India Students' Congress leader Mariadassou, appalled by the repression of student voices in the days before independence, would write an editorial in the local French-Indian newspaper, *Le Trait-d'Union*, entitled "Démocratie?"[135] In it Mariadassou reports that Pondicherry had been saturated with police and military troops who "spread terror" in order to suppress any anti-imperial sentiment, treating students like prisoners and depriving them of their rights.[136] Mariadassou was explicitly concerned with the divisions that were being drawn between "Indian brothers": "Now that there is no longer a great family of Hindu citizens, it is difficult to accept the expulsions where our brothers are treated as foreigners."[137] He goes on to say that the will of the majority should not be subsumed by minority interests, calling for all the youth of French India to stand up for their rights as citizens and denounce the censorship and abuse of civil liberties they had recently witnessed in the days before independence.

The editor in chief of *Le Trait-d'Union*, Mohammad Houssaine, shared Mariadassou's uneasiness with the restrictions the French Indian government placed on the people of India. In a a front-page editorial titled "Atmosphère d'indépendance?," he notes that the coming independence in neighboring India occurred amid massive hardships, including famines, communal riots, and unemployment.[138] Houssaine reminds the readers of this French-language newspaper that their existence is fragile, adding that "slavery may have been abolished but servitude remains."[139] Independence was on the horizon, but liberation was a distant dream.

Tensions were high in the French territories as the day of independence approached. Despite the ban on public gatherings, various groups, including the French Indian National Congress, the Communist Party, and the French India Students' Congress, took to the streets to register their

*Figure 2.1* Front page of *Le Trait-d'Union*, August 1947.

displeasure with the way the French and Indian governments were addressing their many concerns.[140] On 15 August 1947, the French India National Congress spoke of the desired integration of French India into the Indian Union and declared that "August 15 which marks, for our neighbors, the beginning of an era of liberty, must be, at the same time for us the announcement of a real independence."[141] Several political groups banded together to demand the merger of French India into India, and stated that as of the 15th, they would consider themselves as citizens of India.[142] While Governor Baron faced hostility from many parties, including one demonstration of distrust in his leadership as a "mob" attempted to overturn his car on his return from Paris just before the day of independence, he marked independence day by hoisting the flags of both India and Pakistan on the town hall in Pondicherry.[143]

The division between the Aurobindo Ashram and the many different political formations in Pondicherry grew wider as independence approached. Governor Baron was widely seen as pro-Ashram: he went often to visit with Aurobindo and the Mother, and even considered himself at devotee to Aurobindo's philosophy. On his arrival in Pondicherry in February 1946, the British consul noted, "Baron is sympathetic towards the Ashram. The 'Mother' is the sister of a former French colonial governor, under whom he once served, and Madame Baron visited her at the Ashram soon after her arrival." The report goes on to state that "the Indian population and many of the French" would have preferred it if the French government had sent a governor "who was not popularly supposed to support the Ashram."[144] In addition to what many perceived as favoritism by the French authorities toward the Ashram, many local people were critical of all the land and houses that the Ashram had purchased.[145]

Altogether, these important details contributed to an overwhelming feeling in Pondicherry that the Ashram and Aurobindo himself may be anti-British but they were pro-French, an example of what I call "anticolonial colonialism." Despite the insistence by both Aurobindo and the Mother that the Ashram was "not political," Aurobindo would not issue a statement demanding that the French leave India. The local population, especially those involved with the French India National Congress and the Students' Congress, criticized the Ashram for this, seeing it as part of the French imperial project. In response, the Ashram sent a letter to appear in the Calcutta newspaper the *Statesman*. Although it is doubtful that the people of Pondicherry would ever task the Ashram with speaking for them, the statement begins by declaring that "everybody in Pondicherry without exception supports the right of self-determination for the people of French India and Sri Aurobindo always been a firm supporter of that right for all the peoples everywhere."[146] It goes on to defend the idea of the French Union, while also admitting that its promise was more utopian than what was actually on offer. Addressing critiques of Sri Aurobindo for staying silent on the issue of the future of French India, the statement notes that Sri Aurobindo "is not a citizen of French India" and thus has remained quiet, but privately he supports "the end of the colonial rule and a complete autonomy within the French Union accompanied by a dual citizenship and close association with the Indian Union which should control customs, communications and a common system of industry and commerce."[147]

The invocation of both Sri Aurobindo's citizenship (or, more accurately, that he did not have any legal attachment to French India), coupled with the suggestion of dual citizenship, reflects the Ashram's desire to work with whoever was in power to continue the Ashram project. The anticolonialism expressed by the Ashram at this moment of potential liberation and decolonization was bureaucratic and perfunctory, with no real critique of the institutions created through colonial rule.

Aurobindo and the Mother's adherence to a multicultural model of isolating distinct national cultures and treating them as separate entities, without consideration for the hybridity brought by the colonial world, allowed them to be anti-British while remaining pro-French, supporting the idea that one form of colonialism could be superior to another. The call for dual citizenship was an important element of the above statement, as the non-Indian residents in the Ashram—of which there were many—were concerned that they would not be able to continue living in India after independence. Unlike the internationalist vision of the communist, which envisioned a utopian society that did not have any national borders, the Ashram, and, eventually, Auroville would argue for being allowed to have multiple citizenships, a liberal utopianist projection that found unity not in common struggle but in the base idea of humanity as fundamentally equal. The deployment of anticolonial colonialism would become an important foundation for the establishment of Auroville.

On the day of independence, 15 August 1947, the devotees at the Aurobindo Ashram celebrated not only the independence of India from the British, but also Sri Aurobindo's seventy-fifth birthday. The Ashramite Nirodbaran noted that "the whole Ashram was vitally interested in India's fight for freedom," and when the day of independence came, the Mother "hoisted her flag over the terrace of Sri Aurobindo's room. The Mother called it the spiritual flag of India."[148] Later that afternoon, the Mother appeared on the terrace, where the devotees greeted her by singing "Bande Mataram," the Indian national anthem.[149] Sri Chinmoy, at the time a disciple of Aurobindo, wrote in his memoirs that, around the time of independence, the Ashramites "had to defend the Ashram from goondas," because "some Tamilians were displeased with us and threatened us. They were trying at random to kill some of the Ashramites."[150] As the British consulate in Pondicherry prepared to host a ceremony in honor of this historic day, an Ashramite named Mulshankar Jani was stabbed in the neck and killed outside the Ashram.[151] The perpetrators of the attack remained at large as the Ashram attributed the death to "paid hooligans" and "goondas," as Jani became a victim of the political violence in French India.

The French India National Congress blamed the violence surrounding independence on Communists, the Ashramites, "Tamilians," and on the French government. The local press looked for outside agitators, often alleged to be hooligans and goondas, to blame for the acts of looting, arson, and murder that accompanied independence. Much like in other areas of India that were experiencing the cataclysmic effects of Partition, the borders that demarcated the French Indian territories became geographic flash points for the reification of different identities, defined here as citizen and noncitizen, Indian or French-Indian, communist or nationalist.

The national and international press largely overlooked the violence of 15 August 1947 that engulfed many regions of India and the newly created nation-state of Pakistan. However, the beatings, harassment, and murders that occurred with increasing frequency weighed heavily on the minds of the French-Indian people. Emmanuelle Pouchepadass, a French-Indian who previously had moved to Paris and was involved there with the Association de l'Inde en France, wrote a letter to be published in *Le Trait-d'Union* entitled "A Letter to My Country: What Is It About?"[152] Pouchepadass was distraught by all the reports he heard from his "compatriots" about the brutality that was spreading throughout French India, about the violations of homes and the "terror" that had fallen on a city normally "calm and at peace." From his home in Paris, Pouchepadass laments the goondas who had been bribed by money and alcohol, outsiders who had agreed to descend upon French India for their personal gain and the benefit of politicians who were also more concerned with their own access to power than the people who dwelled upon French Indian land. Pouchepadass urges his fellow French-Indians to be patient as the details of "the inevitable fusion of French India with the Indian Union" were discussed by

France and India. He forecasts that despite the numerous official proclamations, the future of French India would not be decided by the people of French India, but by international accord. By predicting that French India would merge with India, not because of the will of the people, but because of the "friendship" between India and France, he asks his compatriots to consider what they *can* do to retain some elements of their unique culture and history as French-Indians. He ends his letter with these words, meant to provoke French-Indian readers to consider their bonds to both the French and the Indian nations: "Tomorrow, India will be entirely rid of the last vestiges of British imperialism; when it is ready to welcome French India in its heart, the latter will come not in the form of a poor relation, but as a son who, by his time spent far from home, has been matured before his time and endowed with a proud personality."[153]

Decolonization, envisioned by imperial powers as a diplomatic tool for maintaining international prominence, was meant to be a peaceful and friendly affair.[154] The language of referendum focused on democracy and the right to self-determination, highlighting the strong democratic traditions of the French Republic and the Indian government's commitment to democracy. However, the future actions of the French and Indian governments in regard to the referendum were far from democratic, as violence emanated from both sides, undermining the legitimacy of a vote. Both states were anxious about the repercussions of losing: France worried that a loss would set off a chain reaction in the other colonies, especially in Indochina and Algeria. For India, a new nation founded on the principles of anticolonial nationalism, losing a vote to France could discredit their claims to national unity and cause chaos in other regions of India that were seeking some amount of autonomy.

The reactions in French India to Indian independence from British rule were varied, and much more complex than the popular narrative that one was either pro-India or pro-French when it came to questions of liberation. The CPFI, who originally supported the immediate merger of French India into India in 1947, changed their position by early 1948, when both India and French India had issued warrants for Subbiah's arrest.[155] In a speech given in Pondicherry on 8 June 1948, Subbiah called the Nehru government "the puppet government of British Imperialism" and deduced that the new Indian consul general in Pondicherry, Ali Baig, was equally dedicated to the British. "Merger with the Indian Union will not be independence," Subbiah declared, suggesting that to merge would be "to tighten our manacles of slavery further."[156] Though the Communist Party did not hold a stable position on the question of merger in this period, Subbiah, who had been targeted now by three states—Britain, France, and India—did not view merger as a way to liberation for French India. After 1947, he advocated for merger with the French Union as a potential diplomatic tool toward global revolution, not as the patriotic-nationalist act that pro-French and pro-India propaganda suggested.

The next chapter looks to the period between 1947 and 1954, especially in regard to the violence that occurred on the borders between India and French India. While a referendum was held in Chandernagore, the smallest and most remote French colony in India, on 19 June 1949, the referendum would never take place in the other comptoirs.[157] It was surprising to many that the landslide in Chandernagore did not encourage the Indian government to hurry the referendum in the rest of the territories, but the vote was never allowed to happen. While the Indian observers of the elections claimed the French had hired goondas to win the vote, the French version was that the elections were held perfectly fairly. Commentators including the international press, local politicians, French senators, and Indian police chiefs placed the blame for the failure to hold the referendum on the problem of "goondas," though not only ones hired by the French. In the next chapter, I show that both states, fearful of a public loss, turned to nonstate actors, alternatively identified as goondas, hooligans, thugs, and terrorists, to manipulate public opinion, media coverage, and international attention into believing that a fair election to decide the future of French India could never occur.

CHAPTER III

# Making the Postcolonial Subject

*Goondas, Refugees, and Citizens*

The Partition of India into India and East and West Pakistan in 1947 was a time of territorial terror. The drawing and redrawing of borders that made the new India-Pakistan boundaries led not only to massive displacement and violence, but to the creation of hundreds of thousands of refugees who were forced to abandon their homes, property, livelihoods, and sometimes family members.[1] The changing borders and the reclassification of territory as marked by the increasingly important mixture of religious and national boundaries brought fear into the lives of millions of people. The geographer Stuart Elden writes that "sovereignty is an issue at the intersection of terror and territory; it operates as the crucial bridge between terror and the state and is integral to the state of territory."[2] In other words, the struggle between states for power through the right of sovereignty over bounded territory is an essential element of establishing state power. The borders that bound that territory become concrete through continued military or police power, an important tool in protecting the integrity of the state.

The carceral borders that were created in the French Indian territories in the early nineteenth century once again became sites of tension and violence after Indian independence in 1947. The French territories in India are not included in histories of the Partition, except as a footnote. With the notable exception of Chandernagore, which was in close geographic proximity to the new East Pakistan-India border as well as the city of Calcutta, the French Indian territories were located far from the major sites of Partition.³ However, the struggle over the territories occurred simultaneously with the Partition, and much of the discourse deployed by the Indian government around citizenship, belonging, and illegality originated in the Indian state's need to manage the refugee crisis that followed Partition.⁴ In this chapter, I work to draw connections between the border-making and territorial violence of Partition and the struggle over the future of French India by looking to the ways in which two states, France and India, used the existing colonial borders separating French India and India to classify the populations on either side of the border as citizens, refugees, or criminals (usually coded as goondas, terrorists, or rowdies). Historian Durba Mitra writes about the "excess" of the category of the prostitute in the colonial archives, arguing that the term was used to categorize almost all women "outside of monogamous Hindu upper-caste marriage."⁵ Mitra accounts for this excess by showing how female sexuality was foundational for social scientific understandings of modern India. Following Mitra's work, I argue in this chapter that the category of the goonda served a similar function, working as a tool for police and policy makers to identify, target, and exclude men who could potentially threaten the stability of the states, both colonial and postcolonial, through the subversion and stabilization of cartographic borders.

The cartographic violence of the Partition had deep roots in the many colonial borders erected over the preceding two centuries, and the post-1947 policing of colonial borders in French India increased after the British left. In French India, hundreds of incidents—which included acts of physical and sexual violence, arson, and property destruction, as well as claims of asylum and the creation of a significant refugee population, who usually sought refuge in Madras and other areas of Tamil Nadu—occurred on the numerous borders between French India and India between 1947 and 1954. Alongside these incidents came a discourse of terrorism and goondaism, enacted on both sides of the border, that allowed both France and India to displace the violence onto individual agents while preserving an image of the nation-state as invested in the interest of protecting its citizens. After 1947, the Indian government quickly blamed any trespass or assault at the border on goondas, terrorists, or rowdies—men who had been paid to enact violence and terror to destroy the Indian state. Simultaneously, the French government engaged in a similar discourse but directed it at different individuals, often accusing Indian agitators of being enemies of democracy who worked tirelessly to undermine the referendum on the future of French India.

The widespread circulation of stories about terrorism and goondaism on the French-Indian borders was symptomatic of larger anxieties, shared by governments and colonial subjects, about decolonization, national identity, and the future of the colonized subject. The goonda became the illegitimate other to the refugee and the citizen, two figures who deserved the protection of the Indian state, thus justifying the use of force and policing. Specifically, this moment in French India elucidates a crack in the popular understandings of postcolonial democracy, as this period of the "Goonda Raj" (the Indian state's term for the lawlessness of the French India territories) coincided directly with the struggle to hold the referendum on the future of French India. While the Indian state and the English-language Indian press attributed border violence to both the continued presence of colonialism on Indian land and the unknown criminal element, the importance to the Indian state of a positive diplomatic relationship with France—a stable and friendly road to decolonization—led to an overemphasis on the actions of the goonda. Ultimately, both France and India attributed the cancellation of the referendum on the goonda, the ultimate destroyer of democracy, displacing any responsibility the states may have had to their citizens.

Blaming the continued foreign rule of the French enclaves not on France per se, but the French colonial ideology in the form of the Goonda Raj, the Indian government drew a rhetorical distinction between the needs and desires of France, a European country it planned to do business with, and the French colonial government, which it portrayed as having an anachronistic attachment to colonial rule.[6] Drawing on police records, personal accounts, diplomatic records, and newspaper articles from India, France, and England, I will show here, first, that between 1947, the year of India's independence from British rule, and 1954, the year France agreed to withdraw from its Indian holdings, there was a significant amount of violence in and around the numerous borders separating French India from independent India. Secondly, I will analyze the language of terrorism and goondaism that was widely employed by figures in both the Indian and the French governments to explain the border violence that escalated between 1952 and 1953. Finally, I will look at a violent border incident in the French-Indian village of Suramangalam as a case study to illustrate how the categories of "terror" and "goonda" operated in the specific context of the decolonization of French India, and the complex relationship that colonized subjects had to the states in question.

## From Colonial to National Borders

The constructed nature of the often-intimate relationship between "nation" and "state" came into sharp focus as people began to call for self-determination and sovereignty, leading to a number of questions about the relationship between territory and nationality. Contemporary understandings of what makes a nation suggest that nations are sociocultural groups that have common identity markers, such as a common language, religion, history, and cultural practices. Alternately, a state is a legal entity that has fixed borders and a system of government that provides laws and governance within these borders. While nations often have a strong tie to certain geographic areas, including, primarily, the ownerships of land for agricultural and cultural uses (for example, schools and religious structures), it is possible, and not entirely uncommon, for a nation to be *stateless*, while the state must always be on some level geographically static. Very few people in French India made any claim to support French imperialism, yet not everyone was eager to immediately merge it with India. As the previous chapter showed, the departure of England from India brought new questions to French India about the future of the territories' relationship to France and to India.

In her book *The Long Partition and the Making of Modern South Asia: Refugees, Boundaries, Histories*, anthropologist Vazira Fazila-Yacoobali Zamindar argues for a broader temporal and geographic understanding of the Partition to include "the bureaucratic violence of drawing political boundaries and nationalizing identities that became, in some lives, interminable."[7] Building on Zamindar's call to expand our understanding of the geographic and temporal reach of the Partition, I argue that we must take into account actors beyond Britain, India, and Pakistan to understand how states dealt with the question of territory in the postwar moment. While India viewed the continued presence of France in India as an act of colonial aggression, the newly independent Indian government also used the language of national unity to justify its own movements to exercise sovereignty over territories and states that had strong movements against merging with India.

While the question of the future French India presented France and India with a new set of problems, neither state was a stranger to border disputes and corresponding questions of race, ethnicity, and nationality. France had spent the better part of the past century battling with Prussia and Germany over the eastern borderland regions of Alsace and Lorraine. The border regions between France and Germany held an important place in the construction of French national identity following the French defeat in the Franco-Prussian war in 1870.[8] Between 1870 and 1918, when the provinces were under the rule of the German state, French nationalist discourse cast Alsace and Lorraine as integral parts of the French *nation* that had been lost to the German *state*. While the borders had shifted to make these areas part of Germany, constructions of the French nation included the two provinces, depicted on maps and in schoolbooks during the period of German control as "lost provinces."[9] The French Indian territories, as symbols of France's "lost empire" in South Asia, were, like Alsace and Lorraine, depicted as integral to French national identity.

Are national identities determined by individuals, or are they bestowed upon people based on criteria determined by states? As discussed in chapter 1, in order to determine who was a British-Indian and who was a French-Indian, the French and British colonial bureaucracies instituted a complex system of borders, customs checkpoints, and passports to identify and track those who belonged and those who did not, which was at the time determined by the place of one's birth and the identity of their parents. India was at the time of Partition heavily entrenched in its own border disputes, particularly around the issue of the Princely States of Jammu and Kashmir in the northwestern region, Junagarh in the west, and Hyderabad in central India. At the time of independence and Partition, Jammu and Kashmir were caught between the two states of India and the newly created Pakistan—a conflict that continues to this day. People who live in these regions have been vilified by the Indian state as Muslim antinationals, a discourse that has become more criminalized into the twenty-first century.[10] The reintegration of Alsace and Lorraine into the French state following the end of World War II resulted in ethnic purges meant to weed out "bad" Alsatians and Lorrainers who posed a threat to France, either because of their allegiance to Germany (especially as the majority of people in Alsace were speakers of German and were also Protestant), or because they advocated for independence for the regions. Jammu amd Kashmir posed a similar ethnic problem for the newly independent India: while the majority of inhabitants of Kashmir were Muslims, India advocated a secular nationalism that did not, ideologically, preclude Muslims from being Indians. Thus, Sheik Abdullah, the prime minister of Jammu and Kashmir from 1948 to 1953, argued, along with a group of prominent Indian Muslims, that that ceding Jammu and Kashmir to Pakistan would jeopardize the safety of the substantial Muslim population who continued to live in India.

Decolonization was not a movement made accessible to the people of Jammu and Kashmir or Alsace-Lorraine, because both regions were (and, in the case of Kashmir, continue to be) under occupation by the local state that ensconces them.[11] Despite the cultural differences, in terms of religion, language, and ethnicity, between the populations in Alsace-Lorraine and France, and between Jammu and Kashmir and both India and Pakistan, neither region was ever truly given the choice to become independent. The choice for the people of these regions was simply to assimilate to the nation-state they found themselves living within, or to migrate, if they had the means and ability to do so, to the nation-state in which they felt they belonged. The people of French India hoped that their fate would be different: that they would be allowed to vote on their future.

## Familial Democracy

As chapter 2 argued, "friendship" and "family" became the key terms utilized in discourse about the situation of French India, on both the national level in both France and India and locally in French India. The language and imagery of families and friendship were used to encourage a peaceful and amicable debate between the French and the Indian states; diplomats, politicians, and government agents regularly invoked the vocabulary of kinship to describe the situation in French India. The French colonial government used the language of family, specifically *fraternité*, to promote the unity of the French Union. Ideally, *fraternité*, or brotherhood, would gather all the peoples of the French Union, in the colonies and in France itself, into a family united by common ideas of democracy, freedom, and liberty, united by the personification of France,

Marianne. Similarly, Indian nationalism relied on the imagery of Mother India (Bharat Mata) to encourage the many different linguistic, ethnic, and religious communities of India to envision themselves as members of the same nation. Both nation-states engaged in similar gendered language and imagery of needy nationalist mothers and brave citizen brothers, which affected different groups and individuals in different ways. The two governments presented the referendum as a legitimate choice to be made by the people of French India, yet the people were never allowed to vote. Using the language of family, the state as parent never allowed the children to vote, despite the continued insistence that the future lay in their hands.

Although several pro-merger groups associated with anticolonial Indian nationalism emerged in French India before 15 August 1947 and called for the integration of French India into India on the day of independence, the incoming national Indian Congress Party urged those in French India to remain calm and let the central government deal with France once the dust around Partition settled. To placate those in French India who wanted immediate merger into India, a pamphlet with a statement from M. K. Gandhi circulated that read, "After crores of Indian friends have been liberated from the British regime, the people of small French India cannot live in an oppressed condition."[12] While the new Indian government assured French-Indians that the French would not be able to remain much longer in India, other political parties within French India were eager to debate the merits of joining the French Union. The French India Socialist Party (FISP), which was the biggest foe of the Communist Party, led by K. Muthu Pillai, printed a pamphlet early in 1947 outlining its program for the future of French India, which included joining the French Union and petitioning the Indian and French governments to allow for dual citizenship, an idea that was also heavily promoted by the Aurobindo Ashram. A Tamil tract written by K. S. Parassouramin, printed in Yanam on 8 August 1947, called on French-Indians to remember that those living in French India lived under a democratic government, and that only France—and certainly not England—espoused ideals of democratic equality.[13]

The call to vote *oui* on the referendum to join the French Union did not sit well with the incoming Indian Congress Party government: on 7 August 1947, N. V. Rajkumar, a secretary for the Foreign Department in New Delhi, wrote a letter to Pillai expressing his absolute displeasure with the program of the FISP, noting repeatedly what a mistake it would be for any French-Indian political party to go against the wishes of the central Indian government.[14] Denying the touted benefits of the French Union, Rajkumar wrote, "We cannot visualise any part of Mother India, however small it may be, remaining under the alien domination, even if that domination be of a liberal nature. . . . Indians in French India have everything in common with us." Brotherhood, here, is interpreted as a family relation based on blood, not choice, unlike the supposed fraternity of the French Republic. As for the proposal set forth in the FISP pamphlet, Rajkumar wrote, "no amount of verbal quibbling can convince the Congress (and that means Nationalist India) that you should be better off with France as your partner." He ended with the ominous statement: "If you are still thinking in terms of helping your rulers to continue on Indian soil then may God help you and the people of French India."[15] The fact that this letter was written eight days before Indian independence, and over a year before the two governments agreed to hold the referendum in the French Indian territories, tells us that the central government's approach to the continued presence of the French in India was more predetermined than it publicly admitted. Despite an agreement to allow the French-Indians to decide their own fate, the Indian central government was not inclined to allow this choice.

Eager to push along the agenda of merging with India, the French India Congress Party convened the French India Peoples' Convention on 25 January 1948. The convention produced a document that demonstrated not only deep support for the Indian state, but a desire to be seen as an organic part of India, sharing a common history and discounting the importance of the French presence in India. Seven resolutions were "unanimously adopted" at the convention, beginning with an homage to "the Father of Nations, Mahatma Gandhi," in which the Peoples' Convention pray "for his long life, so precious to war-torn humanity and the suppressed peoples of the world." The second resolution pays tribute to the "great martyrs of the freedom fight," followed by the third item, which calls for the "immediate and unconditional withdrawal of French sovereignty from all the five French settlements in India" in order to "merge into the Indian Union, with which our people are linked up ethnically, culturally, economically and linguistically." Fourth, "this convention strongly disapproves of the very idea of holding a referendum as it is an insult and a challenge to the moral right of the people to rejoin our own kith and kin." In points five, six, and seven, the convention announces its solidarity with the people of Goa, Kashmir, and Hyderabad, respectively, all kin who are engaged in a similar "fight for freedom."[16] The French India People's Convention spelled out a clear program of Indian unity that saw the French purely as colonizers who had created a wedge between them and their brethren in greater India.

Between 1947 and 1948, there were numerous debates in the French Indian territories about whether it would be right to hold the referendum on the future of French India. The referendum had not been scheduled in any of the territories, despite the insistence by the French government that the referendum was necessary and would take place. On 8 June 1948, a declaration was made in the French National Assembly that outlined the program for the referendum.[17] Known as the "Indo-French agreement," the declaration begins by highlighting the fact that the people of French India, unlike those in formerly British India, were accustomed to the democracy of the French Republic, a continuation of the tendency in India to treat French belonging as a utopian practice. The French acknowledged that the people in French India were in a unique situation, because they had strong ethnic, racial, and cultural ties to India, but also were accustomed to the rights and privileges of French citizenship. Thus, despite the fact that the Indian government had asked the French to cede the territories without referendum, "the French Government solemnly declares that it intends to give to the populations of the French settlements in India the right to decide their fate and future status."[18] The declaration also stated that the five French Indian territories would vote on their futures separately, not together as one administrative unit, which allowed for the possibility of some territories joining the French Union and others merging with India.

Following the declaration, the Indian government grudgingly agreed to hold the referendums, and the reaction to the declaration in the Pondicherry Representative Assembly was positive, although the French India Congress Party continued to issue statements declaring the referendum offensive. As the two governments moved forward to fix the dates of the referendums, which would begin in Chandernagore, discussions turned to how a "free and fair election" could be guaranteed.[19] Police patrols were intensified in Chandernagore leading up to the election, and, according to historian Sailendra Nath Sen, "each party accus[ed] the other of having hired some 100 goondas from Calcutta."[20] With the increased policing by the French and the goonda activity, the French India Congress Party insisted that a fair election was impossible.

On 19 June 1949, just over a year after the declaration for the referendum was issued, the people of Chandernagore, the one-time "hotbed of revolutionary activity," voted by an overwhelming majority to merge with India. Out of 12,184 registered voters (drawn from a population of approximately 44,500), 7,473 voted for merger with India, while a mere 114 votes went toward inclusion in the French Union, leaving about 5,000 votes not cast. For weeks prior, Indian and French-Indian officials, primarily those associated with the Indian Congress Party, spoke out in public and published editorials in newspapers declaring that they doubted the referendum could be held in a *libre et sincère* (free and fair) environment. They pleaded with the French government to hand over Chandernagore without the agreed-upon plebiscite on the grounds that the threat of violence and intimidation by way of pro-French forces meant that the people of Chandernagore could not vote impartially.[21] Security quickly became a pressing issue: the *Times of India* reported on 14 June 1949 that in anticipation of numerous clashes on voting day, "strong police pickets" had been set up along the "Chandernagore-West Bengal border, and all vehicles entering the French possession are being searched . . . to prevent the entry of arms and ammunition."[22] The Madras-based English-language newspaper the *Hindu* noted on 17 June 1949 that "all approaches to Chandernagore are being guarded to prevent undesirable people from infiltrating in the town."[23] Still, on that same night, an act of arson prompted Deban Das, president of Chandernagore's Administrative Council and Municipal Assembly, to send a telegram to the commissioner of French India at Pondicherry stating, "Miscreants have burnt a voting bureau on the hospital ground last night. Police failed in preventing it. Insist on immediate arrangement to prevent chaos."[24]

Perhaps it comes as no surprise that people resident in India, especially in West Bengal, would associate decolonization with chaos and violence, given the devastating massacres that occurred in Chandernagore's neighboring city of Calcutta beginning in 1946. As a British Consular report from 1947 noted, Chandernagore had become home for an "influx of refugees" following the Partition.[25] Maintaining peace and the semblance of democracy in India had become an international concern by this point: in preparation for the Chandernagore referendum, the International Court of Justice, under the umbrella of the United Nations, sent two neutral observers—Holger Anderson of Denmark and Rodolfo Baron Castro of El Salvador—to India in order to ensure the election ran smoothly. Anderson and Castro reported after the referendum that save for a few small irregularities that were corrected early in the day, the vote took place without the anticipated violence and disorder.[26] One reason for the calm, they wrote, was because the police in Chandernagore had isolated and guarded the "men sent from Pondicherry for the day."[27] The threat of violence was determined to be external and thus containable, though Anderson and Castro were less sure that the same order could be maintained in the four French establishments in the south, partially because the borders that divided Indian territory from French territory were numerous, often undefined, and thus extremely difficult to govern.

Violence erupted in Pondicherry just eight days following the Chandernagore referendum, on the occasion of "Chandernagore Day." The *Times of India* reported that "unruly elements" had attacked a public gathering of nationalists, chanting "anti-Indian slogans," throwing rocks, and attempting to "pull down the Indian Union flag." The newspaper named the agitators as "outsiders," though it gave no indication of where they had come from or who they represented, and explicitly blamed the French-Indian police for allowing the violence to occur. Zeevarathnam, president of the Pondicherry Town Congress, issued a statement saying, "All this happened under the very noses of the police who failed to take any preventative measures." Despite the peaceful polling in Chandernagore, the movement toward holding the same referendum in the southern French possessions was already a violent affair.[28]

The pro-merger groups quickly jumped into action following the Chandernagore vote, demanding immediate integration into India. R. L. L. Purushothaman, president of the French India National Congress, issued a statement on 19 October 1949 denouncing the French colonial political machinery and declaring, "Referendum or no referendum, French India is wedded and longing to throw away the alien yoke and to merge unconditionally into the motherland. . . . French India does not like her freedom to be put in auction between Paris and Delhi by a handful of local mercenaries performing a dilatory gamble under the disguise of finding out the higher bidder for the benefit of the people."[29] Statements like this one from Purushothaman were common in pro-merger circles in French India at this moment: those supporting the merger blamed the colonial machine and its strong men for the lack of democracy in French India and demanded the end to the planned referendum, the logic being that merger with no referendum would be a quicker path to democracy under the Indian government than continued association with France.

The leaders of the new Indian government had been targets of British colonial policing, many of them serving lengthy jail sentences for their political activity. Yet, once the sovereignty of India was in question, the state apparatus sprang into action. Indian police carefully patrolled the many borders between French India and India, while the government began to make appeals to the French for the rights of Indians who had sought refuge from French India in India. Historian David Arnold writes, "To the colonial regime crime and politics were almost inseparable: serious crime was an implicit defiance of state authority and a possible prelude to rebellion; political resistance as a 'crime' or the likely occasion for it."[30] In other words, it was not only colonial regimes that approached crime and politics as inseparable, as the Indian state used the same tactics as the colonial regime had in order to preserve territorial sovereignty. These tactics, which included terrorism by way of arson, bombs, and personal physical attacks, brought terror into the lives of the French-Indians who were attempting to define what decolonization would look like in French India.

## The Goonda Raj

Once it became clear to the Indian government that France would not quickly agree to leave India without the referendum, the two countries began to apply pressure on each other. The years between the referendum in Chandernagore in 1949 and the French agreement to leave its Indian possessions in 1954 were marked by violent encounters at the many borders that separated French from Indian territory. Throughout these years, Indian and French government official reports, local politicians (French, French-Indian, and Indian), and the national Indian media used a variety of words, including "terrorist," "goonda," "hooligan," "rowdy," and "criminal," to explain who was inciting an enormous amount of unrest in the French Indian colonies, and, perhaps more important, thwarting the efforts of the two governments to hold the referendum. The Goonda Raj made it utterly impossible for democracy to function—a thesis that

N. V. Rajkumar argues at length in his book on the situation, *The Problem of French India*.[31] According to Rajkumar, there was no possibility of a fair election in French India. "It is a well-known fact that there has never been a fair election in the history of French India," he writes, because "might was right, and a handful of political bosses with their *goonda* followers, aided by the liberal use of money and liquor, could win them easily for themselves."[32] Rajkumar's provocative statements often describe the French tactics in regard to their Indian territories as "Hitlerian," and he notes that the "Indian people" in the French possessions were "infuriated by the unfair election tactics of the French Indian authorities," causing them to rise "in revolt and [make] a supreme effort to shake off the fetters of slavery."[33] Although Rajkumar had directly witnessed the vote in Chandernagore, he tried relentlessly to prevent the same in the south.

The Indian Government Press Information Service in October 1952 released a report to the press titled "Dark Record of Goonda Raj." The "intermingling" of "French Indian territory" and "Indian Union territory" was, according to the report, a major cause of the success of the goonda in sowing terror into the lives of the people living in both territories. The report notes that due to how intertwined the territories were, "the victims of the goondas frequently run for protection into the Indian Union territory but are sometimes chased and there have been many cases of goondas crossing the border."[34] The territorial divisions were thus a primary instigator of "over 350 major cases of assault, arson and hooliganism" in the French establishments in India since 1947, proof that the French were allowing the "reign of goondas" on what should rightfully be Indian soil.[35] According to this report, at least 1,051 families from Pondicherry had taken refuge in Indian territory, fleeing rampant goondaism. Alarmingly, the "goondas now form a recognised profession in the French Settlements"—one could easily recognize them because they "frequently carry the French Flag."[36] The Indian press quickly picked up on the report: the headline of the *Times of India* dated 27 October 1952 read, "Organised Terrorism in French India" and was followed by the subheadings "Over 350 Major Cases Since August, 1947," "Freedom of Action for "Goondas," and, in slightly smaller text, "Delhi Publishes Complete Dossier of Misdeeds." Over the next two years, the Indian press continued along these lines, painting a picture of Pondicherry as a completely lawless space, overrun with goondas waving the French flag. The emphasis on the misdeeds of the goonda instead of on a specific political party or on the

French state itself is telling here. The goondas enacting violence and chaos were not Europeans, not white men, but brown men (presumably Indian, though their origin is not always made clear in police records). They carried the French flag as a tool of intimidation, not as a symbol of patriotism, an act that could be interpreted as particularly heinous by those loyal to either the Indian or the French state.

The men publicly accused of goondaism in the press and in Indian state propaganda were not charged under any specific goonda laws, but were often stopped and arrested for vandalism, assault, arson, smuggling, or, in a few cases, murder. Most often these men were accused in the press of trespassing, or violating the India/French India border, and of agitation and assault. Because of the many and discontinuous borders in Pondicherry, most people crossed multiple borders every day, often unknowingly, rendering everyone a possible "outside element." The "Dark Record of Goonda Raj" notes that the goondas in French India, while not themselves politically motivated, were hired by political interests to enter the "houses and shops of political opponents" and "molest" the wives of pro-merger people.[37] Their "headquarters" were "taverns and tea-stalls in Pondicherry."[38] The characterization of the French India goonda contain undertones of a toxic masculinity familiar in colonial law: men biologically prone toward violence and sexual assault, signs of the primitive or barbaric individual. This was coupled with a disregard for law and order: the goonda was a man who did not respect women and harassed them sexually, drank alcohol and did drugs, and cared for money above all else, largely because they are "recruited from the working classes."[39] The goonda would target any person for abuse, be it man, woman, or child—a signal that the goonda figure did not respect the boundaries of law, the state, or social norms. An image that appeared in the 1953 Indian National Congress publication *Problem of French India* includes images of people in Pondicherry gathering rather innocuously, even posing for photographs (see fig. 3.1). Although there are no obvious signs of distress on the faces of the people pictured, the captions insist that "ignorant voters" were being pressured to vote for French interests by "bullies." This is one of many examples of the widespread propaganda that promoted the idea that French-Indians would never be allowed to vote freely or fairly under the conditions of French rule.

After India's independence in 1947, the goonda in and around French India became the antithesis of the good Indian and the good Frenchman

The three on the right are Socialist Party men. They see that voters vote the 'right way'.

Polling scene. Ignorant voters being herded by local bullies before being taken to the polling booth.

*Figure 3.1* Illustrations from *The Problem of French India* by N. V. Rajkumar (1953).

at the same time, both of whom would be devoted to order and democracy. He was uninterested in reproducing for the good of the nation, committed only to the fulfillment of his desires for material possessions and sexual gratification. Alternately, the "victims" of these shadowy and nefarious figures were named refugees and/or citizens, indicating their status as people who did legitimately belong to a territory, but, in the case of the refugee, had been forcibly exiled from their homes, in this case by the goondas hired by antimerger politicians looking to exploit their colonial relationship with France. The citizen, national, and refugee all strove to be active participants in the nation, by respecting laws and tradition. The goonda actively sought to destroy the national fabric. The goonda was the "other" of democracy.

But who were these goondas, and where were they coming from? Records show that the Indian and French embassies frequently traded memos between 1949 and 1954 accusing the other of *allowing* goondas to utilize violence against French and Indian citizens, respectively. While the Indian government accused the French officials of instigating an attack on Sellane Naicker, a French-Indian and president of the Comité de Pondichéry pour le Rattachement, the French insisted the Indian government was behind the violence perpetuated by Dadala at the borders throughout 1952.[40] In the case of Naicker, who was shot in the thigh on 29 August 1952, it was suggested that police and government repression in French India was so severe that Naicker was forced to travel to the General Hospital in Madras to have his wounds treated, as he feared that greater harm would come to him if he stayed in Pondicherry.[41] In fact, it was not just Naicker who was forced to seek medical attention outside of French India: according to the Indian embassy, many injured French-Indians were being treated at the border-town hospital in Cuddalore, "as they were told that they could not be rendered any medical aid in French Indian hospitals."[42]

The Indian embassy noted that the people of India were fed up with the goondaism in French India and had recently gathered into large protests to try to stop the violence. The embassy enclosed a picture of a large gathering of "pro-mergerites" who were "stopped by the authorities" before crossing into French India. The picture had run in the *Hindu* on 21 September 1952. It shows a crowd so large that viewers cannot tell where it ends, holding large sticks and other weapons. There is a man in the front of the crowd carrying an Indian flag; a group of four or five French-Indian policemen are attempting to hold the crowd back.

The French ambassador in India, Stanislas Ostrorog, received a copy of the Goonda report on 27 October 1952, the same day as did Indian journalists across the subcontinent. Upon reading the report, Ostrorog sent a telegram to the Ministry of Foreign Affairs, noting that all the major Indian newspapers ran the text of the report immediately after receiving it.[43] The *Hindustan Times* preceded the report with the comment: "The criminals and goondas, with the complicity of the French police, have a free hand in the French Establishments against people who, by natural sentiment, after the reign of the British was finished in India, desire union with the "mere-patrie."[44] At a later date, Ostrorog stated that the great majority of the accusations leveled by the Indian government were fabricated, and that on the whole Pondicherry was a peaceful city wherein the general public were not overly concerned with political issues.[45] A day after the report appeared, on 28 October, Ostrorog wrote a telegram expressing his concern that the Indian government's tactic of labeling the French as dictatorial imperialists was working on the Indian public: he reported that ten thousand people had gathered in Cuddalore to adopt a resolution that the people of India would not tolerate the "atrocities committed by French imperialism on national territory."[46]

According to the Indian government, many of the goondas were French-Indian police officers (who were almost exclusively local residents, not Europeans). While the "Dark Record of Goonda Raj" states that the "leading figures" among the goondas were "well-known by name," the report never actually names any of them. On the other side of the border, in French India, French police reports and government memos do name the accused goondas—including Raphael Ramanayya Dadala, a former member of the French-Indian gendarmerie in the French territory of Yanam who left to become a pro-merger freedom fighter; V. Subbiah, the Communist leader; and eventually Edouard Goubert, the Franco-Indian créole man and leader of the French India Socialist Party who had once supported the antimerger movement but switched sides and began to espouse anti-French, anticolonial positions in 1953.

The ambiguity of national identities and the shifting borders between British India, French India, and, after 15 August 1947, India, led to significant amounts of anxiety for colonial subjects resident in French India. The residents who had the most to lose by the direct merger of French India into India were the various French-Indian communities who had constructed their identities around the existence of a French India, such as the créoles and the low-caste people who had converted to Christianity since the Portuguese had first arrived in India in the late fifteenth century.[47] Some, like the French-Indian politician Edouard Goubert, feared they would lose their political and social power if French India disappeared; others, like the people living in the Sri Aurobindo Ashram, were concerned that the Indian state would not allow them to stay in Pondicherry as foreigners, and still others, such as the descendants of the renonçants, the people who renounced their civil status to take on French citizenship, were concerned that the Indian state would deprive them of resources and opportunities if they continued to live as French citizens on Indian land.

Between 1949 and 1954, people resident in and near French India lived on the edge of empire, both geographically and temporally, as the borders that demarcated an imperial territory from a postcolonial state fluctuated in front of, behind, and down the middle of their homes and villages. The increase in violence on these borders during this period became the foundation for fears about what decolonization might bring for the territories. Many of the concerns about the future of French India were displaced through both the Indian and French states' constant blaming of all the ills of French India on the goonda and through the tensions tied up in the border fences. Because of the borders separating the two territories, those who were not referred to as goondas were often labeled refugees: it was very difficult to distinguish who belonged where. The incident at Suramangalam, one of many border conflicts, will make it clear that the existence of these borders forced everyone into a constant politics of migration and criminality.

## Impossible Borders: The Incident at Suramangalam

On the afternoon of 21 February 1953, Sri Raphael Ramanayya Dadala led a group of people to the border village of Suramangalam in French India to participate in a rally denouncing French imperialism. According to French-Indian police reports, Dadala and his men (who numbered somewhere around fifteen) rode their bullock cart along the border shouting slogans such as "A bas l'impérialisme français!" (Down with French imperialism!), "A bas le gouvernement français!" (Down with the French government!), and "Les chiens de Français doivent quitter l'Inde française sous peu!" (The French dogs must leave French India immediately!). It was forbidden at this point to hold political rallies against the French administration within French Indian territory, so it became a common practice for men like Dadala to gather along the border while on Indian territory and shout into French India, where large crowds gathered on the border. They called for French-Indian nationals to come and listen to their program, which, according to the gendarmerie, consisted entirely of anti-French propaganda.[48] During the course of the afternoon, two notable events took place: first, the French-Indian police arrested a man named Thulasingham, who was wanted by the French-Indian government for the murder of a municipal counselor the previous June.[49] After he was apprehended, the gendarmes put him into a police car and sent him to Pondicherry. People began to scatter and run through the streets and a riot ensued. During the course of this melee, a French-Indian police officer named Ganése, a thirty-nine-year-old man, was shot.[50] He died in the car on the way to the hospital in Pondicherry.

The border between the French Indian village of Suramangalam and the Indian commune of Kottampacom itself was made of rocks, lined up in front of various structures, often in front people's homes. A series of pictures filed by the gendarmerie with the details of the Suramangalam incident show a police officer standing in the middle of a dirt path, indicating the spot where Ganése was killed, on French territory (see fig. 3.2). There are people in the picture standing in Suramangalam, the French territory, watching the investigation play out, while their neighbors across the road in Kottampacom, in Indian territory, engage in the same activity. According to the hand-drawn map included with the gendarme report, Ganése was killed in French territory, approximately two and a half meters from the Indian border.

Two days following the incident, on 23 February 1953, the *Hindu* ran an article with the headline "Clash on French India Border."[51] According to this report, the French-Indian police had entered Indian territory to "kidnap" Thulasingham, a "refugee from French India," who was the secretary of the Merger Volunteers' Dal (committee). "Some pro-merger workers" went "to the rescue of Thulasingham," the article continued, which "resulted in the death of a French constable." While it provided no details of the deceased, the article went on to discuss the injustice in the kidnapping. The author concluded by stating that the people present at the

*Figure 3.2* Photos depicting the border between India and French India, marked by a line of rocks. Image courtesy of the Archives Nationales d'Outre-Mer, Aix-en-Provence, France.

time of the violent border incident held a meeting following the events and "stressed the need for the merger of the French settlements in the Indian Union."[52] This narrative implied that the French were responsible for the death of this French-Indian police officer simply because they had trespassed into India, a location where they did not belong, and that more incidents such as these could be expected if the French continued to hold their colonies in India. Many French-Indian refugees, the article noted, had filed complaints with the government of India in response to the incident, hoping to inspire the release of Thulasingham and push the merger.

The impossibility of strictly adhering to the chaotic and barely visible borders that separated French India and India clearly caused a great deal of tension between the two state powers and, subsequently, between the people who lived on the borders of the territories. While the French officials insisted that the arrest of Thulasingham was entirely legal, they also admitted that it was impossible for the police, both Indian and French-Indian, to avoid crossing the borders that divided the villages. Following this particular incident, the commissioner of the Republic for French India, P. Kresser, wrote a letter to the government of India that admitted how difficult it was to know which land was French and which was Indian, and that on the day that the murder occurred, "like any other day, numerous border crossings on the part of your police as well as ours" had taken place.[53] More important than whether Thulasingham was captured in French or Indian territory, Kresser continued, was the fact that the Indian government had granted asylum to "criminals and fugitives from justice" in the first place.[54] Kresser stated that there had been ninety-two border incidents, including gunfire and beatings, instigated by Dadala and "his gang" as well as by Indian police in the past year. He called for the Indian police to help with the extradition of those responsible for the murder of Ganése, for the sake of the already fragile friendship between France and India. The French-Indian government considered the majority of the refugees who had received asylum across the border in India to be the goondas and terrorists responsible for not only the death of Ganése, but also the numerous other border incidents that had occurred. In a report sent to the Ministry of Foreign Affairs from the Indian embassy on 22 March 1954, a year following the incident, the Indian government reiterated its position that it did not actually matter if Thulasingham was wanted by the police in French India when he was arrested: "The fact remains that he had taken asylum in India and that the action of the French Indian police in kidnapping him from Indian territory is highly improper."[55]

Were the people who attacked Ganése doing so in the spirit of anticolonial agitation? Were they refugees from French India who would stop at nothing to rid India of foreign rule? Were they goondas, hired by political parties to cause chaos and enact violence, simply for the paycheck? The report filed by Capitaine Lagisquet of the Gendarmerie Auxiliaire Indienne includes testimonies from the officers who had been working with Ganése and who testified that while they remained fully in French territory, they were attacked by "gangs armed with sticks" who ran at them from Kottampacom, in Indian territory.[56] The French-Indian administration clearly blamed the violence on these criminal instigators, stripping any idea of legitimacy in their actions. Kresser's use of "criminals" and "fugitives from justice" to describe the people involved in the Suramangalam incident was consistent with the goonda discourse that worked to criminalize any person who could be construed as not belonging (or being disloyal) to a specific territory, to French India or India. Raphael Ramanayya Dadala, the subject of Kresser's anger, was once a loyal member of the French-Indian police force and had only left because of his desire to do what the French revolutionaries had once done—rebel against their leaders in order to gain rights of freedom and democracy.

The Suramangalam incident highlights a primary tension in even contemporary discussions of the state, terrorism, and the struggle for sovereignty: How do we distinguish between the violence legitimated by the state in the form of policing and military aggression and acts of violence undertaken in response to state-based violence? While states depend on depicting certain categories of criminal in order to maintain order and obedience, placing the preservation of the nation-state above the interests of the subjects within the nation-state, the identities of people are more fluid than the state allows. The people who lived on these borders existed in a state of national flux, a situation that was not uncommon for people resident in colonial border zones.[57] The identities that emerged from these border zones were not congruent with the construction of postcolonial nation-states that depended on the unity of nationalism to build strength. Thus, decolonization became a tool to rupture and consequently bury hybrid national identities.

For instance, Dadala had studied French and had great respect for the French Republic, but had chosen to join the freedom struggle to liberate

French India. In his autobiography, Dadala draws heavily on the French history he had learned in school to explain his own decision to leave the gendarmerie and become a freedom fighter for India.[58] He writes that it was from learning about the heroic struggles of "Jeanne d'Arc, Bayard d'Auvergne, the young generals of the French Revolution and the Free French heroes" that "I felt that I should have a motherland for which I must sacrifice my all at its altar."[59] Despite Dadala's claims to historical precedent and his plea reminiscent of a child begging a parent to recognize his maturity and right to autonomy, Kresser saw him as a criminal. The "criminal" was a saboteur of diplomatic relations, the "fugitive from justice" a man who cared more for his own pleasure than the future of democracy, the rogue who betrayed the social contract. If he was no longer for France, he was an enemy of the state.

While Kresser had accused Dadala of being the leader of the goondas, Dadala himself writes in his autobiography that "the Government [of French India] and the police Chief had given carte blanche to the Government candidates and to the goondas to attack me in my station and kill me."[60] Dadala may have brought fear into the minds of the French authorities who were nervous about the possibility of decolonization, but Dadala also professed a fear of the goondas who opposed his anticolonial agitation. In both of these cases, we see the goonda as the unknown enemy: he brought terror into the lives of the residents, citizens, and nationals of French India, whether they were for or against merger with India. The goonda was a criminal and a fugitive and was thus incapable of holding legitimate political concerns. The goonda discourse became an instrument with which both the French and Indian states could discipline their present and future subjects who had been promised democracy.

## The Rising Tide

By the spring of 1954, the Indian government was ready to use every tool available to rid India of foreign rule. The local and national press was in strong agreement and regularly printed articles and editorial cartoons ridiculing the continued presence of the French. A cartoon printed in the *Hindu* depicts the French government as a man dressed in European clothes, napping in a chair. The shore, labeled Pondicherry, is set to be drenched in the rising tide of the "merger movement," a wave that was surely meant to crash into and topple the French government, which was simply sleeping, unaware of its adversary. The cartoon, titled "The New Canute," suggests that the reign of Canute was no match for the unstoppable, divine tide of decolonization.[61]

During this time, the French were deeply entrenched in the war in Indochina. The Battle of Dien Bien Phu was a disaster for the French, and while they were investing massive amounts of resources in trying to defeat Ho Chi Minh and the Viet Minh, sending military into French India was not a high priority. The French government did not want to stage any sort of military action in India, but, according to pro-Indian sources, there were no shortage of hired goondas working against the Indian government *and* Indian people in French India. In his memoir, Raphael Ramanayya Dadala writes extensively about his trouble with goondas; while the word "goonda" appears on practically every page of his fifty-two-page remembrance, he never gives any sort of description of the goondas, nor does he ever make an attempt to find out who they are or seek justice for their offences, even though he insists that they tried to kill him.[62] The goonda is a constant presence in description of his life and his struggle; he believed that they stood in his way in his determination to liberate his "motherland." His duty was to protect the refugees fleeing French India, by housing them and feeding them on Indian land. While Dadala took careful measures to protect "refugees," it is also clear that he understood that, to some people, his own actions were interpreted as goondaism. Dadala was willing to use violence against the French-Indian police (his former employer) and, according to police reports from French India, against civilians. While neither government officially endorsed the use of violence during this period, many inhabitants of the areas advocated for and actively engaged in direct action. The actions of Dadala and his compatriots were closely followed in the French newspapers. Both *Le Figaro* and *Le Monde* reported that French citizens in the comptoirs were regularly molested and abused by both Indian police and "fugitives who had taken shelter in Indian territories."[63] An Indian refugee was easily portrayed in France as a fugitive from French justice.

The violent nature of state interests was not hidden to many people on the ground in French India. A Tamil political tract from 1952, signed by V. Aroumougame, a Tamil French-Indian, accuses the Indian government of allowing violence in direct defiance of Nehru's call for negotiations through peaceful means.[64] Aroumougame distrusted the government in Delhi as well as the French administrators, and directly accused Dadala of perpetuating the violence. He wrote, "It seems that Mr. NEHRU, who is theoretically in charge of 350 million inhabitants, is not being followed by his subjects, because the "peaceful means" at the borders of Pondicherry are shotguns, revolvers, and bats whose victims are frequently the inhabitants of French India, whose occupation has called them into Indian territory."[65] The tract goes on to accuse the Indian government of using violence and fraud to "force the opinion of the people of Pondicherry." The writer charges the Indian government with using the same "peaceful means employed by Hitler" to annex Czechoslovakia and Austria. He makes clear his belief that only those who sided with the Indian state would be protected from the violent actions of the state, in defense of their interests.[66]

Accusations of goondaism and general "lawlessness" led to the cancellation of the referendum. A press release from the government of India issued on 18 November 1952 contained a detailed list of all the "border incidents" that had occurred between July and October 1952. The incidents included an attack on an Indian man for being at the border as he returned from the cinema in Pondicherry, the beating of two Indian women as they walked through French territory to buy food (they were "threatened not to use the French route in the future"), and the detention of an Indian Union postman by the head constable of the French police, who held him at the police station and "forcibly deprived the postman of Rs. 3, the sale proceeds of postcards."[67] One Tamil man, Ponnusamy, identified as a "refugee from French India," had to cross into French Indian territory to "fetch his wife and child." During his attempt to reunite his family under the protection of the Indian Union, he was stopped by "a gang of French Indian rowdies," who assaulted him and knocked out one of his teeth. Despite his pleas to allow him to reach his wife and child, he was "driven back to Indian territory and was told not to enter French limits, as he professed merger of these Settlements with India." His love for his motherland was keeping his family apart.[68]

According to the Indian state, violence tore apart any prospect for democracy in French India. Hoping to maintain friendly relations with each other, the Indian and the French nation-states rarely blamed each other publicly for this violence, but instead faulted an unidentifiable band of outlaws, people with no claim to a legitimate identity within the nation-state.[69] When forced to address the fact that all the goondas, "henchmen," and thugs responsible for sabotaging attempts at the decolonization of French India were in fact *Indians,* nationalists decried the goondas as Indians who exhibited "anti-Indian sentiment."[70] This contradiction is clear in a 1953 nationalist pamphlet printed by Free India Publications in Madras (Chennai), titled "French Pockets in India." The opening paragraph of this twenty-page booklet declares that there has never been anything very French about French India, as not many French people lived there, and there was neither a "racial link nor a religious bond nor even a vitally indissoluble cultural affinity" linking the people of France and India.[71] The pamphlet never mentions the existence of a créole community, insisting that the people in these "pockets" culturally lived the "life of Tamils or Malayalees or Telegus" and *not* of French people. Despite this strict separation of cultural identities, the entire process of merger had been stalled by corrupted Indians, the same cultural "Tamils and Malayalees and Telegus" whom the nationalists wanted to bring into the Indian Union.[72] According to this tract, all the people of French India wanted to merge with India, except for "rich merchants" and "a few Indian nationalists" who continued to profit from smuggling and goondaism.[73]

The question of who the "anti-Indian elements" truly were came to head when, on 2 April 1954, Edouard Goubert led a movement to occupy Nettapakam and Moudoucoure, two French communes in Pondicherry, to proclaim their annexation to India. Of course, up until 1953, Goubert had been the leader of the FISP pro-French lobby in French India. The insurgents took control of the French Indian police stations and constructed a barbed wire barrier that kept French officials from entering the "split sections of Pondicherry."[74] A day later, Goubert and three hundred of his people occupied another seven villages, seized weapons claiming them for the Indian Union, and took two gendarmes as prisoners.[75] Pro-India factions spread throughout the villages, hoisted Indian flags, and painted pro-merger slogans on village walls. The occupations were the latest tactic following years of sanctions on material goods and the creation of travel restrictions and increased border patrolling between India and French India.

An overwhelming feeling of déjà vu must have descended on the residents of Pondicherry as the Indian government responded to the continuation of the French presence by enacting "travel control between India and the settlements of Pondicherry and Karaikal."[76] The wire fence erected decades previously by the British authorities to monitor the smuggling of revolutionaries and contraband across borders had been replaced a year earlier, in March 1953. The Indian government, much like the British Raj before, stated that the fence was meant to "put an end to the contraband which exists on a great scale at the Franco-Indian border."[77] Armed guards staffed the reconstructed border and the Indian government declared, "Any French citizen who wants to visit one of the other parts [of Pondicherry] must now acquire Indian permission,"[78] and that "people resident in India wishing to travel to the settlements would be issued with identity certificates."[79] By 7 April, newspapers reported "processions of men, women, and children filed through the streets shouting at the French, 'Jai Hind.'"[80]

Crossing the fence from French India to India in the struggle for freedom from French India, from a hybrid space to a space under the singular purview of the Indian Union, Goubert declared himself an *Indian*, eschewing his French schooling, position in the French government, and the history of his paternal lineage. Despite the efforts of the Indian government and the numerous Indian political groups devoted to the "freedom struggle," it was the actions of Goubert that turned the tide against the French retaining their colonies in India. The historian Ajit K. Neogy has commented that "deserted by Goubert the chances of survival of France in India disappeared."[81] It took the actions of a prominent member of the créole community to persuade French officials, especially those in the Overseas Ministry. The desertion of Goubert, not only from the French colonies, but also from his French identity, signified the end of an era.

The figure of Edouard Goubert, a man of French name and citizenship and of both French and Indian parentage, who was elected to the French National Assembly and later, after 1962, was elected as the mayor of Pondicherry, provides a powerful representation of the French-Indian créole community in the era of decolonization. At the time of his defection from the pro-French camp in 1953, he was seen as a deserter in the French press, while the *New York Times* called him a "rebel" and a "dismissed Minister in the Government of French India."[82] Various scholars have portrayed Goubert as a self-interested politician who changed his stance on merger for political gain; it is telling that French commentators remember him as a "smiling, unscrupulous, great devil," while the Indian government has memorialized him by naming a street in Pondicherry after him and erecting a statue that is periodically honored by local government officials.[83] Eminent historian of French India Jacques Weber has written that Goubert supported the merger of Pondicherry only once the continuation of French rule "became a threat to his own fortune and political future."[84]

Alternately, Dadala, himself a French-Indian who was low-caste and pro-India, wrote that Goubert was "the only sincere leader in the whole lot."[85] The entry for Goubert in the *Dictionnaire des parlementaires français* emphasizes that Goubert's desire to unite Pondicherry with the Indian Union was due to his Indianness, stating, "Of Indian origin, he took an active and sometimes violent role in the struggle for the merger of Pondicherry to the Indian Union."[86] Statements such as this erase the links, the cultures, and the identities created during the colonial period and highlight the underlying notion that, as decolonization approached, it was not possible to be an ethnic Indian who was loyal to France or an ethnic French person loyal to India. As a politician, Goubert was torn between two political powers, France and India, while his genuine fidelity may have been more toward the people of Pondicherry, who, by 1954, were concerned that their future position in either country would be intermediary, that they would never be fully assimilated to or integrated into either nation.

After months of stalled negotiations between the national governments of France and India, and hundreds of protests, demonstrations, occupations, and riots on the borders of French India and India, France announced in early August 1954 that it would leave India on 14 August. The *New York Times*, drawing on information gleamed from the Indian newspaper the *Statesman* ran a short piece announcing the end of French rule in India, titled "France Is Reported Ready to Quit India."[87] Importantly, while this two-sentence blurb said nothing about the question of French citizenship or referendum in French India, it did end by noting that "the first ship to take departing French families back home would call at Pondicherry on Wednesday." For an international audience, this was perhaps the important piece, detailing what would happen to occupying colonizers. What it left out was the complicated question of *who* was French in French India, a concern that would be of great importance over the coming decade and remains important in these former French territories well into the twenty-first century.

Diplomatic relations between France and India may have survived the struggles of 1947–1954; however, the years of rhetorical and physical violence had taken a toll on the populations of French India—the transition from French India to India was not so smooth or easy in local practice. After centuries of intermarriage, dual-language education, and engagement with French cultural practices, many in the French-Indian community viewed themselves as the hyphen between India and France, a group of people who occupied a physical space that could serve as a bridge or a link between the two nations in the future. The editors of *Le Trait-d'Union* expressed concern that if Pondicherry was incorporated into the Indian Union, the position of Pondicherry, and specifically of Pondichérians, as a *trait-d'union* might vanish. The editors wrote,

> Freed from its concerns in Indochina, and thanks to the disinterested efforts of the Président du Conseil Mendès-France, France will now be able to devote itself urgently to the problem on which its friendship with India depends. In this friendship, some links (*Traits d'Union*) should remain between the inhabitants of these territories, rather than the present situation of indifference which leaves the embittered population asking: "But what do we do in France?"[88]

The people of Pondicherry wondered what role they were to play in the "friendship" between India and France, as well as what would happen to them if they remained in French India, or chose to leave and move to France. The next chapter will explore the decisions that the people of French India had to make as they faced the decolonization of their homeland.

Accusations of terrorism often accompanied newspaper stories and government memos outlining goonda activities in French India. The association of terrorism with border division and state-making, especially in the context of decolonization, is consistent with many anticolonial struggles throughout the twentieth century, including in India. Revolutionary terrorism, an act of personal sacrifice to be made for the good of the national people, was an act to be celebrated in independent India. While Dadala would eventually be recognized in the government of India's 1966 publication *Who's Who of Freedom Fighters (Pondicherry)* for his anticolonial agitation leading to the independence of French India, the goonda discourse did much to delegitimize claims to a political, anticolonial language that would have infused the acts of violence with a nationalist morality.

Partition was a deeply destabilizing event for millions of people in South Asia, an immediate crisis for the new governments of both India and Pakistan in 1947. Stabilizing the population meant tracking populations, and whether this happened through the issuance of passports or the creation of refugee centers, the tools of the postcolonial state—policing, tracking, border violence—continued uninterrupted from the colonial regime. The political theorist Corey Robin argues that at the heart of terrorism lies "political fear," a tool used by both states and groups who oppose a nation-state to generate an affect among a people that the "collective well-being" is in danger.[89] There were significant numbers of both pro- and antimerger advocates in the French Indian territories during this time, and both groups favored a democratic resolution to the merger question—but it was the discourse of terror and the associated fear of instability that effectively stopped the referendum from taking place. The Indian state demanded immediate merger to end the Goonda Raj, but, in doing so, it stripped the colonized subjects of their political expression. Democracy, in both India and France in this moment, imagined itself as nonviolent. The task of imagining other possible futures fell to the colonized subjects, whose efforts were often met with violence.

In opposition to democracy, decolonial movements were by necessity violent affairs, on both sides of the divide. Violence came down from imperial powers and was met with a variety of responses from colonized subjects, which ranged from Gandhi's *satyagraha*, or political resistance, to the armed struggles of the FLN (National Liberation Front) in Algeria. Whether the colonized fought back with boycotts, work stoppages, and peaceful protests, or with suicide bombers and ammunition, the hegemonic power of empire was such that violence—physical and symbolic—was necessary to end its reign. The end of empire brought an enormous threat of destabilization, and with it the fear of losing power, status, and control, to all colonizers throughout the world. Decolonization also brought a deeper threat: the radical idea that the colonized subject may not be interested in democracy as nationalism, an idea that terrorized the prevailing form of the liberal nation-state by suggesting its demise.

It was the radical possibility of a postcolonial world order not based primarily on state borders that was completely submerged by the language of goondaism in French India between the years 1947–1954. Many within the territories saw a possibility in belonging to the French Union and still participating in the cultural life of India, a notion that pushed back against the oft-repeated racial-nationalist phrase "an Indian is an Indian." Despite the explicit violence of decolonization that was occurring daily in the French-Indian possessions during this period, the states that controlled the conversation used the symbolic violence of criminalization to place the blame of violent acts on individuals, ultimately constructing a narrative of the peaceful decolonization of French India.

# PART II
# Unmaking

CHAPTER IV

## Decolonial Crossings

### Settlers, Migrants, Tourists

I hope I shall be allowed to adopt a double nationality, that is to say, to remain French while I become an Indian.
—THE MOTHER (MIRA ALFASSA), 15 AUGUST 1954

Are we Indian, are we French? This is the eternal question that all Pondichérians pose. Sometimes we feel like we are on a desert island, lost, and we don't know what to do, stuck between two situations.
—M. ABEL-CLOVIS, 1964

On est un peu bâtard, on est étranger partout.
(We are sort of like bastards, strangers everywhere.)
—SAM, SIXTY-TWO-YEAR-OLD PONDICHERIAN LIVING IN PARIS, 2008

On 26 November 1954, Jean-Paul Weber, an associate professor of philosophy at the Collège Française de Pondichéry, wrote a letter to the Ministry of Foreign Affairs asking for permission to leave the colony and return to Paris. He had been sent to serve for five years in French India; however, as "there is no longer a French India," he wrote, "my deployment here has ceased to be valid."[1] Since his desire to become a colonial administrator could no longer be realized in India, Professor Weber wished to return to his homeland and marry a woman who lived in Paris.[2] While Professor Weber's situation was particular to only a handful of Europeans employed in the French territories at the time of decolonization, the truth in his statement that "there is no longer a French India" highlighted a problem that troubled tens of thousands of people. When, at 6:45 a.m. on 1 November 1954, Pierre Landy, representing the French Ministry of Foreign Affairs, and Indian consul general Kewal Singh signed an agreement to transfer French India from France to India, French India ceased to exist as a geopolitical entity, and the people of French India found themselves without a homeland.

Once the Treaty of Cession was signed, French India became a place on a map that was now also marked by the bookends of colonial time. As previous chapters have shown, throughout its two-hundred-plus years of existence, French India was a space that served as the foundation for the construction of a multitude of cultures and ethnic and national identities and, often, as an important imperial foil to the British Empire. While anticolonialists and Indian nationalists hoped that the signing of the transfer agreement would erase any traces of French colonial rule in India, it soon became clear that it would not be so easy for the French-Indian people, institutions, or land itself to be free of connections to France. While French India was a series of territories belonging to the French Empire, it was also subject to the dominant politics and culture of the much larger state that surrounded it, including the English language and a very specific strain of anticolonial nationalism that did not take into account the particular circumstances of *being* French-Indian—specifically, the connections brought through the practice of French citizenship. For many French-Indians who had been French citizens since the 1880s, the merger of French India into India signified the loss of an identity without an equal replacement; anticolonial Indian nationalism was based on centuries of struggle against the British, not the French. Instead of "throwing off the yoke of French imperialism," as advocated by the Communist leader V. Subbiah, and melting into greater India, the rupture of decolonization served as a marker for the entrance of French India into a new designation: former French colony, a moniker Pondicherry has never been able to shake. However, although the land remains marked by the allure of French tourist dollars and the mythology that French India was a colony free of colonial oppression, some people in French India have found it difficult, or even impossible, to merge their subjectivities into greater India and continue to exist in a liminal state of belonging neither to France nor to India.

In the previous chapter, I argued that states, in both the European form of an imperial power (France) as well as the postcolonial state (India), employed a discourse of insider and outsider to foment nationalism amongst the general population. The figure of the "goonda," the violent and immoral men allegedly hired by political groups to frighten and intimidate loyal citizens, inundated French India from 1947 to 1954, the period between the independence of India from British control and the transfer of French India to the Indian Union. Remarkably, after 1 November 1954, when the transfer agreement was signed, most discussions of goondas disappeared from the discourse surrounding the former French territories, aided by the pardoning of many crimes by the central Indian government.[3] Once the goonda vanished from the public sphere, he was replaced by a new nebulous outsider: not an individual, but a collective sometimes called the "nowhere people." As the ratification of the transfer of French India from France to India loomed on the horizon, everyone living within the borders of French India was a possible foreigner—that is, any person who did not declare themselves fully French or fully Indian became a potential threat to the stability of the Indian state. As the French and Indian governments entered into discussions about questions of nationality and citizenship, the people in French India and the surrounding areas began to take stock of their situation, weighing the positive and negative elements of French versus Indian citizenship. What would the future hold for those who chose French citizenship but remained in India? Would the Indian government punish those who elected to declare their loyalty to France? Would there be homes, jobs, and cultural acceptance for those who left India to settle in France? While there were hints of answers to some of these questions, based on the previous experiences of French-Indians who had settled outside of French India, the people of the region entered into the merger with many unknowns.

In this chapter, I will show how what I call here the "dual cultures thesis," agreed upon by both the French and Indian governments, conditioned the postcolonial reality of the French-Indian people. I use the phrase "dual cultures thesis" as shorthand to refer to the agreement of the Indian and French governments to promote Indian culture in France and French culture in India. This agreement, laid out in the Treaty of Cession—drafted in 1954, signed in 1956, and ratified in the French National Assembly in 1962—set the groundwork for the postcolonial relationship between France and India.[4] I argue that the discourse of "friendship" and "respect" based on a mutual admiration of culture that dominated public rhetoric surrounding the decolonization of French India was intended to erase the colonial tensions between the two state powers, thus denying the French-Indian people the agency to construct postcolonial identities based on a shared experience of colonial rule. The specific language of decolonization in French India denied the violence of the colonial act, which encouraged the French-Indian diaspora to distance themselves from other colonial subjects of the French Empire. The oft-violent ruptures of decolonization that led to the loss of a homeland and a French-Indian identity for tens of thousands of people were whitewashed by a strategic use of nostalgia that looked to an imagined and idealized past—based on the myth of a centuries-long friendship between France and India—to erase the realities and the violence of the present. This colonial memory, to draw once again on the work of Bancel and Blanchard, has continued to shape the narrative of "good" French colonialism in India.[5] Thus, while this rupture forced French-Indians to seek out spaces where they could continue to perform the identities they had cultivated for centuries, it also opened the former French territory to new types of settlement associated with the Sri Aurobindo Ashram by allowing the Ashram project to acquire land outside the French Indian territories.

The people of French India were eventually, in 1962, given the choice between French and Indian citizenship, during a six-month interval known as the "period of option." The focus of this chapter is to explore what options *actually* existed for the people of French India, and the challenges they faced in making their decisions. While the governments of France and India envisioned a clear choice between the respective nations for their once and future citizens, discussions over the meaning of nationality and citizenship proliferated throughout the period both leading up to and following the period of option. The rupture of decolonization—specifically the loss of a place to call home—ignited a postcolonial migration from India to France, as a certain segment of the population of the former French Indian colonies felt they could no longer live in India, which was the only land many of them had ever known.

In recent years, scholars have begun to discuss the South Asian diaspora, charting the various webs cast out from the subcontinent and tracking the vast networks of South Asians who have settled in various nations throughout the world.[6] While the parameters of the category of "South Asian" would certainly include the people of French India, defined by what may best be described as ethnicity (or perhaps ancestry), this chapter will show that there are some elements of the French-Indian diaspora that set this population apart from the standard understanding of those in the South Asian diaspora. The two primary factors distinguishing this migrant population from the rest are language and nationality. While it is certainly true that the South Asian diaspora in the postwar period was not united by language—South Asia is an intensely polyglot region—the peoples who migrated from French India during the period of decolonization were united by French, a non–South Asian language. This also set this population apart from the massive migrations of South Asians into other European countries, given that the majority of this latter group spoke English, not French. In terms of nationality, the history of citizenship in French India, and the number of non-European-born French-Indians who were French citizens, meant that in the political, and often cultural, field, this population had "imagined" themselves as part of the French nation, not the British or the Indian nation, for over a century. The status of Pondichérians in France as French nationals also sets this population apart from the over seventy thousand Sri Lankan Tamils who sought refuge from the civil war during the 1970s.[7] Grouped together, these groups are referred to as the "Tamil diaspora," although a number of problems exist with this designation as well. Not all French nationals of Indian origin who migrated from the former French colonies are Tamil, although the Tamil designator does represent the majority. The difficulty of categorizing and tracking the French-Indian population as it has dispersed throughout India, France, and the world, I argue, stems from the fractious nature of the French Indian territories under colonialism. Thus, we must look at the moment of decolonization to understand the paths that led from Pondicherry to Paris.

## The Question of Belonging: 1954–1962

On 1 November 1954, as the de facto transfer was becoming a reality, the prime minister of India, Jawaharlal Nehru, was in Beijing and unable to be in Pondicherry to mark the occasion. He did, however, issue a message to be read aloud there as the Indian flag was hoisted above the government building. Nehru insisted that, in addition to English, the message should be translated into French and in Tamil, out of respect for the linguistic plurality that existed in the territories.[8] Nehru began his speech by welcoming the people of the French settlements home to India: "A part of India long separated from the motherland is coming back to us of its own free will. . . . I congratulate the people of what used to be the French enclaves in India and welcome them as nationals of the Republic of India."[9] While Nehru expressed his joy in the decolonizing moment, bringing the nation one step closer to a united India, he also made it clear that he did not hold ill will toward France or, more important, French culture, which he understood was an essential part of life in Pondicherry.

In his message to the crowd, Nehru stated, "I am happy that Pondicherry will continue to be a centre of French language and culture and will be a cultural link between the Republic of India and the Republic of France."[10] He concluded by noting that his only regret was that he could not personally share his message to the people of former French India in French, though it was read aloud in French by a local official. While the message was also relayed in Tamil, Nehru made no explicit mention of its importance to the region.

Nehru's speech and the accompanying ceremony marked the end of the long struggle between the two national powers over the fate of French India. However, it took two more years after the de facto transfer—until 28 May 1956—before the Treaty of Cession was signed. The treaty outlined the terms of the cession, primarily dealing with the details of how economic, juridical, and cultural questions would be addressed during the transfer. All that remained was for the French National Assembly to ratify the treaty, thus allowing the de jure transfer of the territories. It took France another six years to complete this process; the transfer was ratified only after France had agreed to leave Algeria, thus ending its claims to global empire.

The years between 1954 and 1962 were quite tense for the people in the French Indian territories, as they waited to learn what directions their lives would take once the era of French rule had completely ended. The conversation about what to do about the nationality of the people living in French India began in earnest in August 1954, as agents of the French government in Paris and the Indian government in New Delhi negotiated the details of the transfer of French India to the Indian Union. One of the first steps taken by the Ministry of Overseas France was to look back at the cession of Chandernagore for a blueprint for the remaining French Indian territories.[11] A report dated 3 September 1954 noted that when Chandernagore was integrated into the Indian Union, French nationals and citizens of the French Union who were domiciled on the ceded territory would automatically become citizens of India, *unless*, after a period of six months, they opted to preserve their French nationality. Very few people opted for French nationality in Chandernagore, and officials in the Ministry of Overseas France believed this would hold true in the remaining French territories as well.

French ambassador in India Stanislas Ostorog noted in 1955 that the situation in French India was "without precedent in international law," and thus that officials should be careful to follow public opinion in France on the matter.[12] French officials in Paris, at the Ministry of Foreign Affairs as well as the Ministry of Overseas France, asked those on the ground in Pondicherry, particularly Ostorog, to estimate the number of people that may choose French nationality, to determine what provisions would need to be made. Both Ostorog and his colleagues, in particular a man named Armand Gandon, wrote to Paris that it was impossible to calculate what would happen in the future, but they did write of the many problems France might face as plans for the period of option went forward. "It is difficult to penetrate the thoughts of a people who are different from us by race, language, religion, customs and traditions," Ostorog wrote in a 1955 memo. He estimated that of a population of three hundred thousand people, fewer than twenty-five thousand people could be distinguished from the "Tamil peasants."[13] Throughout his extensive correspondence on the question of granting French citizenship to the people of French India, Ostorog highlighted the importance of understanding that outside of a minority of French-Indians who truly showed allegiance to France, mostly by way of mixed racial heritage, the majority of French-Indians were *too different* from *true* French nationals to join their ranks.

Gandon worried about "four-fifths of the population, who are pariahs [who] were so accustomed to the French regime that they forgot that it is the regime that made them like other men."[14] Gandon reiterated the French belief that they were much more sympathetic than the Indian government to the plight of those who were subject to caste oppression, while also suggesting that the French should be quite concerned that the oppressed would come to France seeking to take full advantage of the utopian French republic. After only seven months of Indian rule, Gandon noted, the Brahmins had not delayed in reaffirming their "traditional" superiority, "eclipsing" the centuries of equality brought to the region by the French regime. Likewise, Ostorog observed that except for those who had the financial means and were ready to accept the idea of leaving India for France or another territory in the French Union, those who chose to retain French nationality would have an inferior position in India.[15] They would also find that they would have limits on their professional life due to restrictions placed on foreigners and would not have access to public services. For these reasons, Ostorog wrote, limiting the option of French citizenship to those who already had ties with France would be the "humanitarian" path to take—a paternalist approach to decolonization that continued in the tradition of the French civilizing mission.[16]

While France expected those of mixed race to choose to remain French, it was the population at large, comprised primarily of "ethnic Indians," that gave them concern. In April 1955, Ostorog wrote a report detailing the various groups that were angry with the transfer of French India to India, including the functionaries who believed that their official roles would be diminished under Indian rule; certain young men who had joined and/or fought with the French military and were concerned about their future pensions; the community of old French-Indian families who were "sincerely attached to France"; French nuns and missionaries who remained in India; and a group of people whose language, religion, and education were "closer to the West" than to India, which certainly included a number of people who lived in the Ashram. Another report, written by Gandon, noted that there were three groups of people who were incontestably French citizens: the descendants of Metropolitan French, the mixed ("called here Créole"), and the naturalized and their descendants.[17] For these people, whom Ostorog considered a small minority, he suggested that right of option of nationality should be offered.[18] However, he believed, the French authorities must not forget that the "majority of Tamil peasants, like all the neighboring Indians," voted according to the discretion of public authorities.[19] Ostorog blamed this "voting bloc" of "Tamil peasants" for consistent election fraud in French India. Furthermore, in order to garner favor with the Indian government, French officials would now have to depend on the "same politicians who betrayed us when they left our cause" to advocate for merger with India.[20] Ostorog noted that it would be important to keep an eye on the métis population, as they had betrayed France in the past.[21]

The diplomatic goal was to maintain a "strong friendship" between France and India—two states—while encouraging French-Indians to retain citizenship with their "true homeland." This leads us to a question: How do we define a person's true homeland? French officials agreed that it would be wise to discourage the Tamil peasants from claiming French citizenship, as they were unlikely to ever visit France and only stood to be a drain on French resources. However, Ostorog's greatest concern was that the French-Indian adults who chose to conserve their French nationality would pass it on to their children, who would surely "not retain any ties to the French nation, and quickly integrate with the Indian nation."[22] For Ostorog and many of his supporters in the colonies, nationality ties to France were generational, and if France could manage to limit the option of French citizenship, particularly to the métis who had "French French" ancestors, they could avoid problems in the future. In this way, Ostorog believed that unless a family was likely to move to France, they should be encouraged to become citizens of India, saving their children the "difficulty" of carrying a foreign nationality.

## The Problems of Postcolonial Citizenship

We can see from the correspondence between French intergovernmental agencies as well as between the French and Indian governments that the issue of postcolonial citizenship was tied to the issue of culture and race. The idea to use "culture" to construct strong links between postcolonial India and France preceded the decolonization of British India. As early as 1946, François Baron, the governor-general of Pondicherry, communicated his desire to create multiple French cultural institutions throughout French India that would keep French history, culture, and language alive after colonialism ran its course.[23] The Treaty of Cession was drafted on 21 October 1954 in New Delhi. Among its thirty-five articles detailing the plans for the future citizenship of the people of French India was a clause assuring France the right to continue its cultural projects in India. This was quite explicitly meant to reassure the people of French India that, although they may become Indian citizens, they could still perform and project a French identity. French interests in India, including the Ministry of Foreign Affairs and the Francophone community in French India, were willing to sacrifice the status of the territories in the French Union on the condition that French culture continue to be promoted in the now-former French colonies. This plan was fully endorsed by the government of India; Prime Minister Nehru remarked on numerous occasions that "India has given assurances that it would help to maintain Pondicherry as a centre of French culture and the French language," a move that he believed "has brought India and France even closer to each other than ever before."[24] Nehru stressed the importance of the "peaceful" negotiations that had taken place between France and India in order to come to terms in the Treaty of Cession. However, while both India and France were committed to making sure that French culture remained visible in India, the future of the people of French India was far from clear.

While Nehru welcomed French-Indians into the nation as an act of "free will," there continued to be protests within French-Indian communities by those who were upset that they never got to express their right to vote on their future in a referendum. Despite Nehru's warm welcome, opposition was voiced to the prospect of "joining the Indian family." Take, for example, the following editorial, printed in the Pondichérian newspaper *La Republique Française* on 13 August 1954, in which the author argued, "Though we may well be of the Dravidian race, we take no comfort to be with our Tamil brothers, held in bondage by the master of the Northern capital, which is not ours. Our so-called freedom will only lead to sharing the misery of a nation of our brothers."[25] The lack of enthusiasm for the Congress Party and the central government of India, based in Delhi and culturally, linguistically, and ethnically different than the South, was common throughout South India, and it is not surprising that those living in the French comptoirs had a similar sense of alienation. The French authorities were aware of this, and some of them feared that the North/South division would push many French-Indians to migrate to France rather than "become" Indians. R. Duvauchelle noted in a 1954 memo titled "On the Option for French Nationality" that "many people in the Establishments are very fond of our civilization," and that "the new masters frighten" some people in the French Indian territories and certainly "do not inspire confidence" in the remainder of the population.[26]

The use of "new masters" by Duvauchelle captured the mood among many Pondichérians who feared they would be worse off without the cover of France. This sentiment was a disadvantage to the French Republic, which wanted to keep the number of postcolonial citizens to a minimum. The granting of citizenship to French colonial subjects had been a way for France to promote the supremacy of French language, culture, and power throughout the world; that overseas French citizens might one day migrate to France did not seem to have occurred to the architects of the empire. Duvauchelle worried that without a serious effort by Indian authorities to make the people in the former territories feel as if they would not be swallowed whole by India, people would choose French citizenship and would find themselves foreigners in "their own country," yet another sign that those overseeing the transfer of citizenships did not think French-Indians truly belonged to France. This would lead to this population being subject to all the difficulties that foreigners in India regularly experienced, such as the threat of expulsion and limited ability to travel without prior government approval, among other bureaucratic procedures. Duvauchelle referred to a friend of his who had been a Chandernagorian, living in Calcutta with a French passport. "Proud of his nationality," wrote Duvauchelle, "he lived as an outcaste (*paria*) in his own town."[27] One possible solution to this problem would be to offer people in French India dual nationality—a solution advocated by several groups, including French-Indians who had opposed merger, former soldiers in the French military, and the people who resided in the Ashram.

The movement for dual nationality for the people of French India began in 1947, at the moment of independence. During his early negotiations with the Indian government in Delhi, François Baron had advocated for the option of dual nationality, an idea that was struck down by the French government.[28] Internationally, the idea of dual citizenship was discussed during the interwar period, with most Western countries agreeing that, as stated in the preamble to the Hague Convention of 12 April 1930, "it is in the general interest of the international community to have all its members acknowledge that every individual should possess one nationality and only one."[29] After the conclusion of World War II, as decolonization loomed on the horizon, states around the world agreed that it was best to belong to only one state, that an individual who belonged to multiple states could not foster a sense of belonging or patriotism. Yet, as the prospect of decolonization became a reality, campaigns for dual nationality became increasingly popular, especially in the colonies, in communities that felt they possessed multiple allegiances.

A letter dated 26 October 1954 from the president of the Comité de Défense des Intéréts Français de l'Inde Française, a pro-French group formed in the wake of India's liberation from British rule, made a case for dual nationality, in the interests of the people "of Indian origin" who served France as soldiers and civil servants throughout the colonial period. The letter emphasized the importance of recognizing the long history of French citizenship in India, and the great sense of French nationalism among those French citizens of Indian origin who had fought for France during the two world wars. The writers expressed concern that some would be difficult to live in independent India as French citizens while remaining dependent on their pensions from France that they earned as part of their service. They feared that if they chose French citizenship, they would lose their pensions, but if they chose Indian citizenship, they would lose their "civic rights." Therefore, they argued, "the only equitable solution will be a double nationality, which would be automatically enjoyed by all French citizens by birth or renunciation, natives of the Establishment, that they find in India at the moment of transfer or in some other country." It was not right, they reasoned, to treat anyone who was both French and Indian as a stranger in this land.[30]

The desire for dual nationality had also been expressed in 1947, by the residents of the Sri Aurobindo Ashram, and the campaign increased in intensity after the drafting of the Treaty of Cession. Although Aurobindo had "left his body" in 1950, the Mother continued to run the Ashram and had begun to discuss plans for the construction of an "international township" called Auroville to be built just outside Pondicherry. The Ashram housed hundreds of devotees, many whom were foreigners, originating from nations across Europe, as well as the United States. Many of them had been there for decades and had benefited from the territory's French status, as well as the Mother's relationship with the French colonial administration, thereby avoiding any interaction with the Indian state over issues of visas and passports. Unlike former French military officers of Indian origin or people of mixed French and Indian parentage who were tied to both nations by threads of family and history, the people in the Ashram desired "double nationality" because they believed it was "an inevitable step in the evolution of human unity, a substantial contribution to the onward march of world interaction."[31] While most of the non-Indian residents had no familial or physical ties to French India, they felt that they belonged there, that India was their true *spiritual* home. In a letter sent to Prime Minister Nehru in December 1954, six Ashramites—including one Frenchman, one American, one Briton, and three Indian allies—asked Nehru to consider the possibility of dual nationality. They began their plea by explaining that they were all on the staff of the Sri Aurobindo International University Centre and would very much like to become Indian citizens, but they would also like to retain their primary citizenships. Allowing dual nationality would be a great opportunity for India, they wrote, as they could "make a pioneering advance in this area of international relations."[32]

The Ashram group included with their letter a report that they had compiled with supporting evidence on the benefits of allowing dual nationality. They argued that while double nationality as well as multiple nationalities were facts of modern life, they had been denounced and ignored "in international affairs."[33] The historical moment of "the merger of the French Settlements with the Indian Union provides a natural opportunity for a happy reciprocal agreement at this time by India. There are no doubt a large number of persons who would welcome an opportunity of exercising double nationality in furtherance of Indo-French amity."[34] The final argument of the Ashramites lay in the visions of Sri Aurobindo and the Mother, who "saw dual or multiple citizenship as a substantial not merely a sentimental step towards world integration."[35] They encouraged India to "become all the more, not a 'no-man's land' between hostile blocs in the Cold War, but an 'everyman's land' in the vanguard of world citizenship for a new world order."[36] Fitting with the model of multicultural acceptance that had guided the Ashram's politics since the beginning, the Ashram envisioned decolonization as an opportunity for India to become a leader in the postcolonial world, which could be achieved through cross-cultural collaboration.

In addition to petitioning the Indian and French governments for dual nationality, the Ashramites also sent editorials to French newspapers advocating for the passing of laws that would allow dual citizenship. The Frenchman Bernard Enginger (Satprem), a high-level Ashramite who was very close to the Mother, penned an editorial for the French newspaper *Le Monde* on 2 October 1954, echoing the sentiment that dual nationality was the first step toward the elimination of national antagonism. "It seems that a movement exists," he wrote, "that is attempting to authorize, within certain categories of French nationals or even strangers settled in our Establishments, this claim to a dual nationality. Apart from the idealistic spirit which, very probably, inspires the leadership of the ASHRAM, more material considerations can act equally in favor of a system of dual nationality."[37]

The "international interests" of the people in the Ashram were at odds with the general population in the French Indian colonies. As anticolonial theorist and revolutionary Frantz Fanon writes in the foundational text toward decolonization *The Wretched of the Earth*, the movement for dual citizenship was one example of the "liberal project" of "the intellectual who, for his part, has adopted the abstract, universal values of the colonizer" and is "prepared to fight so that colonist and colonized can live in peace in a new world."[38] Fanon suggests that the dreams of postcolonial unity envisioned in the metropole as well as by Europeans in the colonies was at odds with the interests of both the state and the population that had lived under the colonial system.[39] The multicultural model of interaction proposed by the Ashram, as well as the proponents of the two cultures model, fail to take into consideration the colonial nature of states, subscribing to a belief that national cultures were apolitical and organic, embedded into the bodies of national subjects. The inability to see national cultures for what they were—colonial epistemologies adopted and internalized by the colonized— made decolonization an impossible task.

While India and France both listened to the arguments of those advocating dual citizenship, neither was willing to offer it. Ostrorog had made it clear that he thought dual nationality would only lead to future problems for France and was essentially a bad choice for any state interested in protecting national interests. He argued that dual nationality would be an unfair advantage for those who held it, giving them "the privilege of playing on both tables." The privileges that concerned him the most were the potential for people to apply simultaneously for "administrative careers, to enlist in one or the other army, in short to complain to the Indian about the French and to the French about the Indians." He went on to argue that this would create a new class of people, and used Edouard Goubert as an example for how this had already become a problem. He wrote, "M. GOUBERT, deputy to the French Parliament, who crossed over to abruptly to the opposing camp, is an example of such behaviors. We have an interest in not favoring the support of it." Ostorog made it clear that he believed India and France were on level playing ground and used the "treason" of Goubert in 1953 to illustrate the danger of dual citizenship.[40] Of course, Goubert was in the position he was in *because* he was a product of a colonial system that actively required him to choose between two national interests that were in conflict: that of France and that of India. During the colonial period, it was ordinary to think of the interests of French-Indians, meaning the people who lived in French India, but the tensions of the postcolonial world turned figures like Goubert into traitors.

## Decolonial Rupture: The Period of Option

Despite French and Indian government officials' numerous concerns about offering everyone in French India the option to choose between French and Indian citizenship, by 1956, when the Treaty of Cession was made official, the decision had been made that the treaty could not contain any discriminatory language and must include everyone. Pushing aside his doubts, Ostorog wrote in 1955, "Indeed whatever the nature of the act by which the renouncers have become French citizens, they will not be aware of being placed in a situation different than that of French citizens in full right. They must exercise their right of option if they wish to remain French, even if their families are natives of the metropole. No racial discrimination is conceivable in the matter."[41] The multiculturalism that had already become the norm in many institutions in Pondicherry was augmented by the French Republic's claim to color-blindness—a policy that is still in place today, but that has been widely critiqued.[42] Accordingly, the treaty was written without any reference to race or ethnicity. Articles 4 through 8 outlined the parameters of the option of citizenship that would take effect when the National Assembly in Paris ratified the treaty, placing the greatest emphasis on domicile, or where the potential citizen lived at the time of declaration. French nationals born in the territories of Pondicherry, Karaikal, Yanam, or Mahé *and* domiciled there at the date that the Treaty of Cession took effect would automatically become Indian citizens if they did not formally request French citizenship within six months.[43] Likewise, French nationals born in French India but domiciled on Indian Union territory would automatically become Indian citizens. The only cases in which an individual's citizenship would automatically be French were those born in the French Indian territories who were resident outside of India at the time the treaty took effect. This clause was especially important for the French-Indians living outside of India, primarily in Vietnam.[44]

The treaty, while agreed upon in 1956, was not ratified until 1962, when the Evian Accords, which ended the war in Algeria, was signed. Beginning on 16 August 1962, the people of French India would have six months, until 15 February 1963, to submit the appropriate documentation to receive French citizenship. While the citizenship clauses in the Treaty of Cession were written in a language meant to showcase the commitment of both France and India to the will of the people, many issues faced the populations of French India during the period of option. For those who were born French (of French national parents, many of whom who had one or two parents of Indian origin) but had lived their whole lives in India, if they were to remain in India, they would become foreigners on the only land they had ever known. The only other option for those wishing to remain French was to migrate to France, a decision that would require uprooting entire families, moving halfway across the world, and finding employment, homes, and community in a new country. Needless to say, this was a very difficult decision for most people to make.

Emile Appavou was born in Pondicherry in 1944.[45] His family had been French nationals for several generations, and he grew up attending French schools. In school he was taught about French history, not Indian history, and thus he knew very little about India, despite his Tamil ethnicity. Although he learned Tamil and French, he used French more often. He would remember how he felt, as a child of fourteen, in 1962, when the French prepared to leave India for good. In an oral history conducted in 2009, Appavou spoke of the surprise many in French India felt when the ratification of the Treaty of Cession was announced in 1962. He talked about the confusion and uncertainty about what it would mean to choose one citizenship over the other, and what that choice would mean for the future of education, for job training, and for those who had served France in the the military or civil service. Appavou voiced concern that those who had been raised speaking French as a first or second language would now need to learn English—an issue that had taken hold of the subcontinent as people throughout the country addressed (and protested) the Indian government's language policies.[46]

Appavou opted for French nationality, along with his parents and six of his siblings. He had one sibling who chose Indian citizenship—a brother who decided to stay in Pondicherry as an English teacher and was thus geographically separated from his family when they moved to France. In his narrative, Appavou claimed that everyone who wanted to remain French was forced to leave India and move to France. While this is not technically true, Appavou was not the only migrant who felt that this was the only choice for French nationals. The people in French India who desired French status began to realize the obstacles they would face as they considered remaining in India as juridical foreigners. French-Indians of Indian origin wondered how the Indian government would treat them if they remained in India, especially since many of them had lived under the restrictions of the Indian state placed on Pondicherry to pressure the French to leave.[47]

While the Indian government was not immediately forthcoming with information, there were hints of what life would be like as a French citizen in a postcolonial French India. One glimpse into a future in the region came from the continued travel restrictions and border checks that had made daily life difficult before 1954. In addition, those retaining French citizenship would have to conform to the regulations set by the Indian state for foreigners living in India: they would need to obtain the necessary visas for residence, register with the police, and obtain various permits of residence from the Indian state.[48] There was also widespread anxiety that Pondicherry would be incorporated into the surrounding state of Tamil Nadu and would lose any autonomy that it had gained as an entity separate from the neighboring areas.[49] This was especially troubling for civil servants who spoke neither Hindi nor English, the two official government languages of the Indian state.[50] In addition, there was no guarantee that the Indian government would continue to allow foreigners to remain in India.[51]

The difficulties of migration prevented many people in French India from choosing the French option; they simply could not afford, economically or socially, to be French. Others were excluded from declaring French citizenship by the number of documents required by the French government to prove one's right to declare French citizenship, including, for instance, the birth certificate of one's grandfather.[52] Some Pondichérians have claimed that French officials at the consulate discouraged people from opting for France when they went to declare their French nationality.[53] As Sophie Dassaradanayadou has written, "The negotiations took place without the knowledge of the key stakeholders, and the most humble populations were kept ignorant" of the option.[54] Outside of the center of Pondicherry, people rarely knew that they even had an option.[55] Jacques Weber has noted that neither the French nor the Indian governments did much to advertise the option, as the Indian state did not want to encourage people to leave any more than the French authorities wanted to encourage a wave of migration to France, which was already dealing with the massive influx of *pied-noirs* repatriating to France from Algeria.[56] By the final day of option, 4,944 adults had submitted their written declarations to the French Consulate in Pondicherry; including the children of parents who opted, 7,106 people declared their French citizenship during the six-month period—about 2 percent of the population. The remaining 368,000 residents of French India became Indian nationals, ending their relationship with the French state.[57]

In his book on French India, *Imperial Burdens: Countercolonialism in Former French India*, political scientist William F. S. Miles argues that France has been burdened with the continued citizenship requests of French-Indians, and the incorporation of French-Indians into France, a price paid by France "for her colonial ambivalence," born of the paradoxical idea of equality, the foundation of the French republic, and the practice of colonial rule.[58] Miles's argument suggests that the former colonial subjects of French India have forced France to pay for her colonial sins, as signified by the continued presence of French-Indians in France and the continued requests for citizenship, based on the 1956 Treaty of Cession, into the present day. The flow of postcolonial migrants into France in the postwar period has certainly led to the notion that France has been made to sully a racially homogenous population with the incorporation of nonwhite colonial bodies into the general populace as a result of decolonization. Yet France continues to benefit from its friendly relationship with India. In other words, the two states have continued to be international partners, while both states also cast suspicion on the motives of people of French-Indian origin who make demands on the French government. In the remainder of the chapter, I will examine how decolonization affected the populations and geography of the French Indian territories, by following the French-Indian migrants to Paris; then, in chapter 5, I will examine how Western ideas of global unity and utopian dreams landed in Pondicherry in the aftermath of the decolonial rupture in the form of Auroville.

## Confronting the Color-Blind Republic

Many Pondichérians who migrated to France following the de jure transfer of French India to India in 1962 have commented on the racialization they faced when they reached France. It became clear to many of them that French-Indians were not considered "French French," as their brown skin precluded their inclusion in the white space of metropolitan France.[59] The off-whiteness of their French belonging became painfully clear once they arrived. Emile Appavou, the Pondichérian who moved to France in 1963, noted that, when in Pondicherry, he felt French, and all his friends were French. He writes that he "hardly knew any Indians."[60] However, once he joined the French Air Force, his fellow airmen would often ask, "Where are you from, and what are you doing here?"[61] While Appavou would quickly respond, "I am French! I am from Pondicherry, which was once part of France!," the others would not understand how he could be

French. He said, "Most people like me, who also came from Pondicherry, had a very hard time." Eventually Appavou and his wife, who was also from Pondicherry, moved to the village of Sarcelles, in the northern suburbs of Paris, where other people from Pondicherry had settled.[62] According to Appavou, in Sarcelles they were able to make other French-Indian friends who understood their French identity, although he was disappointed to live so far from the center of Paris.[63]

Appavou's remembrances echo a sort of existential homelessness felt by many in postcolonial diasporic communities.[64] It was common, in the period of migration following the option, for French-Indian migrants in France to express their dismay at being seen as not-French, despite their belief, when they left India, that French society would accept them more readily than Indian society, having been taught the myth of French Republican color-blindness. While the racialized discourses of the nation that "constructed people of African and Asian descent as being outside the 'nation'" were quite common in postcolonial England, France claimed to be color-blind, a notion that was promoted in the colonies through the granting of citizenship rights to colonial subjects in India.[65] In order to look closely at the history of French-Indians migrating to France, we must first ask ourselves how race and ethnicity were understood in this particular time and in these particular places. While it is easy to see the many differences between the French and Indian governments when it came to managing racial categories and ethnic divisions because of their geographic locations and recent histories, the two republics shared an important ideology during this period: both nation-states endorsed a color-blind approach to governance, the color often blinded by a discourse of secular liberalism.

One of the foundational beliefs of the republic, that all citizens should be equal before the state, means that the state has to engage in actively managing and policing citizens to ensure that equality among the people is maintained. When the state refuses to recognize "race" as a policy of color-blind governance, there is a divide between how the state defines difference within the population and how the public sphere, separate from the government, understands these same differences. As an imperial power, France had gained millions of nonwhite subjects throughout the world, many of whom found their way to France at some point during the colonial era. The number of nonwhite laborers in France dramatically increased during the interwar years, a moment that, as Tyler Stovall argues, redefined notions of whiteness and French identity in the metropole.[66] As many scholars have noted in the case of France, avoiding the use of racial categories never eliminated racism in France, but has instead led to the racialization of certain populations, such as immigrants, laborers, linguistic groups, and religions.[67]

India came into being as a republic when the constitution was put into effect on 26 January 1950, a day that is still celebrated as Republic Day. The Republic of India was established as a secular and a democratic state, ready to show its former colonizers that India was more than capable of self-rule and modernization. While the newly born Indian republic faced deep issues as it sought to bring together dozens of linguistic groups, ethnic identities, caste divisions, religious groups, and cultural communities in the name of the national cause, race remained, in the minds of most Indians, an issue tied to colonialism. As the historian Dipesh Chakrabarty has written, as the Indian government went about creating special voting rights and political seat reservations for low-caste groups and expressing concern over continued "communal violence," the question of racism was relegated to the past, to a colonial practice that pitted the white colonizer against the brown colonized subject.[68] Unlike the racism of colonialism, perpetuated by outside sources foreign to South Asia, "what Indians do to one another is variously described as *communalism*, *regionalism*, and *casteism*, but never as *racism*."[69]

Despite the efforts of the French and Indian governments to circumvent discussions of race in their official discourses, Pondicherry remained divided into ville blanche and ville noire, a linguistic marker of the history of racial segregation. The lack of a strong white European community in Pondicherry elevated the importance of the mixed population of French India, as the French colonial administration well understood. As discussions about the future of the people of French India progressed in the post-1954 period, it seemed obvious to French officials that the mixed population would chose to leave India and settle in France, a situation they felt they would be able to deal with, as the majority of the métis understood the French language and culture. The real problem for French authorities was the possibility of the migration of the nonmixed French-Indians, most of whom they believed would not be able to assimilate and would thus become a burden on the French state and the French people. It was imperative to convince the people of French India that each person should chose to belong to their "true homeland." While the French were willing, in this case, to adopt the mixed people whom they admitted may have felt more comfortable in France than in independent India, French-Indians who were not mixed-race belonged in India.

## From Tourist to Migrant

Until the twentieth century, there were few South Asians who had settled in France permanently. Under the ancien regime, South Asians in France were classified as *gens de couleur* (people of color), a designation that makes it difficult to distinguish them from the much-larger population that had come to France from Africa. Some of these early migrants came as domestic servants, travelling with *colon* families that were returning from the French Indian comptoirs, while others were sailors, merchants, or *grands bourgeois*.[70] Outside of these small populations of South Asians living in France, upper-class South Asians were not strangers to travel in Europe by the turn of the twentieth century; in fact, many who studied and traveled in Europe wrote travel memoirs and guidebooks about major European cities, most often London and Paris, detailing their observations of European culture, society, and "civilization."[71] The writing of travel memoirs was so common by the end of the nineteenth century that one author, Romesh Chunder Dutt, who had penned *Three Years in Europe, 1868 to 1871*, suggested to his editor that there was no need for a new edition of his book, as "it is an old story now . . . many of my countrymen have travelled in Europe, and know all about Europe."[72] Perhaps understanding the economic appeal of publishing travel stories, the Calcutta-based editor replied, "It may be an old story, but none the less interesting to us."[73]

Dutt and his companions arrived in Paris on 15 August 1871, during the period immediately following the end of the Franco-Prussian War and, perhaps more significantly to Dutt, the siege of Paris and the fall of the Paris Commune. Dutt remarks that it was a shame that the "rising of the communists have caused a great deal of injury to the town," destroying many symbols of the grandeur of Paris, such as the hôtel de ville.[74] After several days of seeing the Louvre and the Arc de Triomphe and imbibing many cups of coffee and "glasses of liquor," Dutt was surprised when a police officer approached him at the train station in Versailles and asked to see his passport. Instead of simply examining it and letting him go, the officer asked Dutt and his companions to follow him to the "guard house" for further questioning. "I believe our foreign costume had aroused his suspicions!" exclaimed Dutt by way of explanation, suggesting that the police officer "took [them] for communists!"[75] The guards arrested the men on the basis of being "strangers without proper papers," despite the fact that they carried passports with the appropriate visa from the French consulate. Dutt wrote that the guard "treated the passport with contempt and peremptorily demanded proof of our identity!" Despite their papers, and over many objections, the travelers were kept there for twelve hours, "locked up for the night in a miserable cell."[76] After being released, the men spent some amount of time attempting to report their improper detention to the authorities, with little success. Dutt finally commented, "We were fortunate that we were not tried and shot on mere suspicion, as many an innocent man has been in these dark days!"[77]

Dutt's "unfortunate adventure," nestled between descriptions of the gardens at Versailles and the landscape of Belgium, served as a cautionary tale about the dangers associated with travel. As a South Asian, one could, with the right credentials and sufficient wealth, see the wonders of Europe. However, being South Asian meant looking different than those around you, because of both skin tone and dress, and put you in danger of imprisonment, or, as Dutt noted, even death. Dutt was a tourist, economically well off, with the skills and the money and to spend several years touring Europe. Yet he was treated as a potential criminal by the French authorities. While Dutt's temporary status as a tourist sets him apart from the migrant, both groups shared the common experience of being the subjects of xenophobic policies and societal norms.

What separates a tourist from a migrant? Perhaps the most obvious distinguishing marker is the length of time spent in the location that is not home: tourists are temporary visitors, whereas migrants are long-term, potentially permanent, residents. As a tourist, one is usually considered a foreigner, as someone who is outside the nation, but will soon depart and thus does not pose a threat to that nation itself. Today, tourists are often welcomed, in most cases with open arms, by local residents eager to accept the tourist's money. Visitors, or outsiders, who arrive without money and with no intention to leave quickly, are, on the other hand, treated as threats to the safety and the livelihood of the people who live in the particular space entered by the migrant. Tourism is, of course, a modern phenomenon, the idea of "mass tourism" arising in the mid-nineteenth century with the creation of agencies such as Thomas Cook in London that arranged group and package tours, largely for a growing middle class. Postcolonial migration, on the other hand, was not an industry invented for a leisure class, but is instead a foundational element of human life, elevated for colonial subjects who became the primary laborers sent to fill guest work programs when the needs of European industry could not be met with local populations.

Romesh Chunder Dutt, who saw himself as a "legitimate" tourist, with the proper papers and economic means to travel for several years without working, found that he was not always treated in the way that he thought his background should afford him while in Europe. At first, Dutt's experience stands out as an anomaly of the South Asian experience in France. As Catherine Servan-Schreiber and Vasoodeven Vuddamalay have written, in nineteenth- and twentieth-century France, India evoked positive reactions from the population at large, as Orientalist art and literature had created an appreciation for the "old civilizations of India" as well as the embodiment of spirituality.[78] For centuries, French intellectuals, philosophes, journalists, writers, artists, and travelers spoke and wrote of an enchanted land, rich with history, philosophy, myth, and material luxuries ready to be exported. While the fascination with South Asia was certainly not free of value judgments in comparison to Western civilization, India held an admirable place in the hierarchy of foreign cultures and peoples.[79] By the late nineteenth century, it was not uncommon for upper-class Indians to travel to France as tourists and as students, and many of them found a warm welcome from the metropolitan French, albeit one that was contingent on a continuous performance of South Asian identity.[80] In return, tourists and students who traveled to France with the overt objective of studying the greatness of French culture and civilization shared their knowledge of Indian culture and civilization, and they promised eventually to return to the place from which they came were generally rewarded with a friendly and curious, if paternalistic, reception in France. However, if these tourists and students stepped outside the boundaries of their perceived identity, they were treated with suspicion and threatened with deportation.

As the twentieth century progressed and increasing numbers of colonial migrants (mostly North African) made their way to France as laborers, the image and place of South Asians in France began to shift. The role of South Asians in France transitioned from tourists to immigrants, as the end of empire and the period of decolonization caused attitudes toward nonwhite visitors to the metropole to change. The postwar period had brought tens of thousands of North African laborers to France, and by 1962, as the war in Algeria was coming to an end, hundreds of thousands of pied-noirs or European-Algerians fled Algeria and settled in France. Both groups of migrants originating from the former colonies, whether of North African background or pied-noirs, were unwelcome in many sectors of French society. While South Asians were generally not seen as a threat to the fabric of French society, the rising level of xenophobia in France in the postwar period created an atmosphere of uncertainty in French-Indian migrant communities. In the remainder of this section, I will show how South Asian migrants from the former colonies adopted "traditional" Indian identities in France in order to capitalize on the French fascination with India, especially in the 1960s, when Western popular culture began to fetishize "Hindu practices" such as yoga, and South Asian music and fashion were incorporated into "hippie culture."

French-Indians who traveled to Europe were often confronted with the most common stereotypes and representations of India familiar to the local populations. A Pondichérian who called himself Belvis traveled to Europe in 1954 and reported in *Le Trait-d'Union* that in Italy, everyone remarked to him that they thought all Indians had a large beard and a turban, and in Spain, people told him that they were under the impression that Pondicherry was an island. It was in France, however, that the author came face to face with the reality that the people with whom he shared a national identity thought of him as an exotic artifact from the colonies. He wrote,

> In Paris, at a show, in the metro, as soon as someone learns that the person speaking is a gentleman from Pondicherry, there's great amazement. *Pondicherry! India!* Then, like music, the reciting begins. *Pondicherry, Karaikal, Mahé and Yanaon.* The gentleman from Pondicherry does not know how to answer this litany. *You know a bit about our territory. You have perhaps read something. . . . No sir, but it's a memory from primary school.*
>
> Then a woman to add: *Pondicherry, India! The land of yogis and fakirs, of tigers and serpents, of temples and palm trees!* And point-blank, a student who will earn his degree in July asks me: "*You must be an astrologer. Tell me if I will pass my exam this time*" I try to dodge: "*I don't have everything necessary for this study, but I can tell you that you have good luck.*"[81]

Unlike in the other countries this young Pondichérian visited, people in France generally knew that Pondicherry was related to France through the empire. However, throughout his travels Belvis also found that he was confronted with a laundry list of stereotypes of India, from snakes to yogis to coconuts. The popular notions of India in the French imagination were not of their fellow citizens living in the colonies, but instead repetitions of Orientalist images common throughout Western culture.

Migrants from the French Indian territories found themselves migrating to France amid a storm of anti-immigrant sentiment, the racialization of migrant communities, and the continued whitewashing of French citizenship. Although a South Asian community existed in France prior to the cession of the French territories in India, the first wave of migration from the comptoirs came in 1956, after the Treaty of Cession became official.[82] The majority of French-Indians came to Paris in 1962, after the treaty was ratified and decisions about citizenship were made.[83] Today, it is difficult to know how many French-Indians live in France, because the French census (Recensement général de la population) only recognizes ethnic distinctions based on the country of origin of non-French nationals: because migrants from the former colonies were French nationals, often from birth, they are counted as part of the nonmigrant population. Still, researchers have estimated that out of a population of over one hundred thousand South Asians living in France, almost fifty thousand have connections to the former colonies.[84]

The reception of migrants from the French Indian colonies in France was conditioned by the presence of a small but visible Indian community in Paris. Prior to 1940, there were about three hundred Indians living in France; while some were involved in the jewel trade, many were Indian nationalists, refugees from British India. The majority of the Indians in France left in 1940, after the French government surrendered to Germany.[85] Following the war and the liberation of France, the Indian community emerged once more, although in even smaller numbers. The first association formed by the Indian community in postwar France was the Association de l'Inde en France (AIF), presided over by Gopaljee Samboo, founded in 1946.[86] Samboo, who was born in Uttar Pradesh (India), was a medical doctor who had received his medical degree in France and a prolific writer who published seven books on topics ranging from Indian medicine to his own experiences living as an Indian in France.[87] Georges Paillet, the vice president of the Comité France-Inde in February of 1950, spoke of the goals of both organizations, stating that they would "endeavor to inform French opinion, through publications, conferences and meetings, and cinema." Paillet went on to say that he was "confident that the Hindu intellectuals who come to study in France" would maintain in their country the friendship that many of their compatriots had already experienced.[88]

In May 1954, Samboo wrote an essay, published in the AIF newsletter *France-Inde,* that provided details of the Indian community in France. Samboo estimated that there were about 100 Indians living permanently in France.[89] He added to that number another 120 students—80 in Paris, 30 in Montpellier, and a handful in Bordeaux—as well as a "floating population" of tourists, who did not really interact with the Indian community in France. The small number of Indians in France at this time allowed Samboo to gather them all together and engage in community-building activities, which included regular meetings and dinners; receptions for high-ranking government figures such as Jawaharlal Nehru, ambassadors, and UN officials; cultural programs of Indian dance performances; and lectures by Indologists on topics such as contemporary Indian literature, the life and philosophy of M. K. Gandhi, the works of Romain Rolland, and the art of Rabindranath Tagore.[90] One of the primary goals of the AIF was to create relationships between Indians in France and French people who were interested in India, in order to "form links to restore the long Franco-Indian chain" that had been "momentarily broken."[91] Samboo insisted that the group be composed of sincere anticolonialists, both French and Indian, who desired a solution to the problem of French colonies in India that would be favorable to both countries.[92] In fact, the Comité France-Inde did include many non-Indian French nationals, including Jean Rous, at one time secretary general of the Congrès des Peuples contre l'Impérialisme (Congress of People Against Imperialism); Jules Bloch, professor and member of the Institut de Civilisation indienne (housed at the Sorbonne); Krishnan Menon, high commissioner in London; and an assortment of other professors and intellectuals affiliated with the Musée Guimet, a museum that showcased Asian art and artifacts.[93]

Samboo and the members of the Comité France-Inde believed that while the colonial power held by France in India was outdated and should end, it would be easy for France and India to separate the history of colonialism from their postcolonial relationship.[94] In 1955, after the de facto transfer had been set into motion (though before the Treaty of Cession had been accepted), Samboo wrote in *Le Trait-d'Union* that the friendship between France and India in the process of decolonization would be "remembered by history."[95] Samboo argued that while the discussion of colonialism may bring forth memories of racism, Indians had always been welcome in France, as French laws protected all people in France from the social ills of racism and xenophobia.[96] He noted that France had served as a refuge for Indian nationalists wanted by the British government, a sort of distorted truth encouraged by the French state to improve its image against the imperial atrocities of the British.[97] The literature of the AIF stressed the great importance of the friendship between France and India, which, Samboo made clear, would be necessary for Indians to prosper in France. The mission of the AIF, regularly printed in the *France-Inde* newsletter, was to "better understand India in France and France in India," because while "France is a country of liberal and universalist tradition; India is the source of spiritual unity." The AIF believed that France and India were complementary, that when they worked together, the "two civilizations are complete," a mission statement that reinforced the Orientalist/colonialist bifurcation between ancient and modern civilizations.[98] The mission of the AIF, to bring together the universal republicanism of France with the ancient spirituality of (Hindu) India, was of course a familiar trope, popular in the media and the academy, which separated the logical, modern West from the spiritual, ancient East. The AIF and the Comité France-Inde fully embraced the dual cultures thesis promoted by the French and Indian governments, and the associations were rewarded for their support with visits from dignitaries, including Prime Minister Nehru, as well as many visiting ambassadors and intellectuals.

The existence of French-Indian cultural associations became increasingly important to the Pondichérian population in France throughout the 1970s and 1980s, as the population of South Asians in France rapidly increased and diversified. The appearance in France of a growing numbers of Pakistanis, Indo-Mauritians, and somewhere between ten thousand and eighty thousand Tamil Sri Lankans fleeing the civil war displaced Pondicherians as the primary group of South Asians in France.[99] Sri Lankan Tamils have become the most visible working-class group of South Asians, while the growing population has led to the creation of a multitude of new associations for Indians in France, including the IPA (Indian Professional Association), the GOPIO (Global Organization for People of Indian Origin), and the EIEBIG (Euro-India Economic and

Business Group), populated by a thriving South Asian business class.[100] A recent report on South Asians in France notes that for the most part, South Asians are considered a "model minority," and, notably, in comparison to South Asian immigration to neighboring England, "invisible."[101] Just as historian Vijay Prashad has argued, that South Asians in America have been used as a model minority by the state to "show up rebellious blacks for their attempts to redress power relations," the model minority status of South Asians in France stands in strong opposition to the image of North African, particularly Muslim, migrants who are viewed as a danger to the stability of the French state.[102] The Indian cultural associations, run by French-Indians with links to the former colonies, helped promote the interests of the Indian and French states—interests based on the idealization and friendship of two "classic civilizations" that buried the history of French colonial interests in South Asia while also distinguishing French-Indians from other postcolonial migrants in France, which has earned French-Indians, as well as other South Asians, a privileged model-minority status within French society.

## Embodied Nationalism, Embodied Colonialism

The primary frustration expressed by Pondichérian migrants in Paris was, and remains, that the French do not understand that the migrants, too, are French. The concept of extending citizenship to colonized populations did not translate into acceptance once the empire was dissolved and the subjects "came home." In fact, the decision made by people of Indian origin to retain or adopt French citizenship made people both in France and in India extremely uncomfortable and has resulted in the widespread construction of this population as somehow laying outside either nation. Since the final merger of French India into India in 1962, there has been a notable amount of hostility, in both France and India, directed toward the Pondichérian community in Paris and Pondicherry. The population of French nationals of Indian origin in Pondicherry today, which numbers around six thousand, has been consistently constructed and stereotyped as lazy, materialistic, opportunistic, and, perhaps at the root, generally out of tune with the general population, vestiges of the colonial past.[103] The media and numerous academic studies claim that no one particularly respects the choice to choose France over India; it is seen as an act of desperation, of greed, or of both.

In 1989, the Calcutta-based newspaper *Sunday* ran a story that referred to the Pondichérian population as "The Nowhere People."[104] The author of the article, a cynical onlooker from the Bengali north, begins by stating that "the Tamils in Pondicherry who opted for French citizenship now find they belong neither to France nor to India."[105] Assumedly speaking for India, this journalist, Monideepa Banerjie, denies the Pondichérians entry into the Indian community on the basis of their French nationality and their inability to speak English, while at the same time ridiculing them for not being *really* French: "They may have never visited France, may speak at best a pidgin French and imbibe Bordeaux wines with the same gusto as *rasam* and *sambhar,* but address them in English, leave alone Hindi, and the shrug of the shoulders is so eloquent, it would put a white Frenchman to shame."[106] Banerjie creates a connection with the white French population by claiming that despite the great desire of the Pondichérians (whom she calls "French Tamils") to be French, "neither the sizable white French population living in Pondicherry nor the Indians think" that they are. In addition, she suggests that white French people were uninterested in the Pondichérians because they were not *real Indians.* Toward the end of the article, Banerjie goes so far as to suggest that the remaining Pondichérians were simply what remained of "the white man's burden" to the French.[107]

Whether or not the Pondichérian people thought of themselves as existing in a state of cultural liminality, the people who encountered them have been suspicious of their membership in either state. The idea that persons of Indian origin would choose to align themselves with France, a foreign nation, even though that alliance had come about under the system of colonial rule, destabilizes the strongly held belief that national consciousness is fostered through common traits such as race and ethnicity. Pondichérians in France in the 1960s and 1970s were not able to escape the South Asian identity carried in their bodies, projected to a non–South Asian society as the reflection of a national (usually mainstream Indian) identity. However, while South Asians in France without connections to the former colonies are perceived as the embodiment of the Indian nation, Pondichérians, who are explicitly connected to the comptoirs, are considered to belong outside the Indian nation, by choice, and the French nation, by race, and thus continue to represent the embodiment of colonialism, straddling the two states. While India and France are both republics, founded on the principles of democracy and government for the people, there is of course an important global divide between France, a Western power that once held a vast empire, and India, a postcolonial democracy built on a foundation of anticolonial nationalism. As nation-states entrenched in the same system of global capitalism—although at different levels and in different positions of power—they share the need to deny the legitimacy of persons who do not submit fully to one nationalism. After all, how can a person be loyal to the potentially competing interests of two separate and distinct states?

I opened this chapter with three quotes, two from French-Indians, and one from the Mother, a woman of French origin who spent more than half of her life resident in French India/India. M. Abel-Clovis, a well-known Pondichérian who was active in Pondicherry Francophone culture and politics, noted when asked by a French film crew in 1964 that being a French-Indian was like being "on a desert island," "lost," "stuck between two situations." Some Pondichérians sought to remedy this situation by migrating to France, where they felt they would have greater freedom to perform their dual identities. As shown by the 2008 quote from Sam, a sixty-two-year-old Pondicherian in Paris, the sense of estrangement continued for many of those who settled in France.

Contrasting these sentiments, I turn to a quote from a speech made by the Mother of the Sri Aurobindo Ashram on 15 August 1954 that represents here the position of the noncolonized subject at the time of decolonization. Standing on a balcony constructed on the second floor of the Ashram to allow her to speak to her followers below, the Mother spoke of the now-inevitable decolonization of French India, explaining to her audience that from the moment she arrived in India in 1914, she knew that India was her "true country, the country of my soul and spirit."[108] She noted that she was French by both birth and education, but believed that spiritually and affectively she was Indian. Launching into what would be the official stance of the Ashram, she said, "I hope I shall be allowed to adopt a double nationality, that is to say, to remain French while I become an Indian."[109]

What would it mean for the Mother to become Indian? As we can see through the Mother's writings, she understood "Indian" to be a word that implied a spiritualism and philosophy, based on a belief system attributed in this space and time to ancient Hindu writings. This India was Hindu, not Muslim or Sikh or Christian, and casteist. Her reading of India as a spiritual space is informed by Orientalist epistemologies, which she attributed to the land of India itself. For the Mother, becoming Indian would mean being able to call India "home," while retaining her preference to speak French and associate with French disciples.[110] Becoming Indian would not mean being racialized when traveling in international spaces; it would not carry any connotations of ethnicity, caste, or religious identity; and it would not limit her freedom to travel freely throughout the world—all issues faced by South Asians as the colonial world transformed into a postcolonial system.

The privileges of embodied French nationality, expressed through physical appearance, language, and life experience, would always bar people like the Mother from "becoming Indian" in any physical way. As we have seen throughout this chapter, the Mother was not the only individual to desire the recognition of possessing two national characters. Many French-Indians desired some type of dual recognition, but were pushed to migrate to France to express this dualism, as it was not, at the time, allowed in independent India. On the contrary, for Westerners in India, like the Mother, decolonization meant instability only insofar as not knowing if independent India would allow the same sort of foreign presence as the colonial regime had permitted. The Mother was, of course, Sri Aurobindo's closest companion before he passed away in 1950. While followers and admirers of Aurobindo did not universally trust the Mother, she was closely associated with him. Because Aurobindo had once been a deeply influential and important Indian nationalist and continues to be remembered as one of the greatest champions of anticolonial nationalism, Indian politicians and dignitaries took the Mother quite seriously as a cultural force in Pondicherry. This association with a revered anticolonial nationalist infused the Mother with the social capital to continue her projects in India unabated, a privilege not afforded to the majority of people affected by decolonization.

Since its beginning, the Ashram was always a foreign presence in Pondicherry, often out of sync with the local populations, full of European and nonlocal Indian devotees and global tourists. National and international attention paid to Pondicherry often focused on the Ashram, and specifically Sri Aurobindo's role as an anti-British nationalist. As French India became India, the Mother and the Ashram focused on retaining the power they had in Pondicherry, a power based primarily on the legitimacy granted to the project by both the French and the Indian national governments.

Utopianism is the idea that one can experience true peace in what is literally translated to a "nowhere" place. However, when utopian theory was put into practice in this particular time and space marked by the process of decolonization, we see that the "nowhere people" of French India have been treated with suspicion, as potential grifters looking to take advantage of the colonial generosity of France while distancing themselves from what was perceived to be the "true" identity attached to the idea of being Indian, of potential traitors to the race and nation. Meanwhile, utopian dreamers, primarily from the UK and Europe, who sought to build new lives in India, have been celebrated for their ability to create a "new" society that is both modern and deeply spiritual.

In the following, and final, chapter, we will look at the construction of Auroville, a utopia envisioned by the Mother as the answer to colonial divisions. Founded in 1968 just eight kilometers outside the city center of Pondicherry, Auroville was meant to be a "universal city" where people could become "global citizens." By examining the foundations of Auroville and the history of its creation, we will be able to follow a parallel migration to the one examined in this chapter: that of spiritual tourists, who descended on India from Western countries in search of something the West could not provide. Despite the long and rich history of Pondicherry, the people who came to Auroville treated the land as a "nowhere place," erasing the culture and history of the people whose land they acquired and settled, all while depending on local, Tamil labor for the creation of Auroville. It is within this gulf of difference that we move to unsettle utopian narratives of postcolonial global citizenship in the spiritual settlement of Auroville.

CHAPTER V

## From the Ashram to Auroville

*Utopia as Settlement*

Returning now to Pondicherry, 1964, and the French television documentary "Les trois mondes de Pondichéry" that began this book, it is clear that the demarcation of Pondicherry into three distinct worlds—French Pondicherry (located in the ville blanche), Tamil Pondicherry (located in the ville noire), and the Aurobindo Ashram—is consistent with French thinking about what decolonization had meant for France.[1] The end of the empire may have arrived, but that did not mean the end of global French power. For the Paris-based film crew, the question driving the project, "What is left of France in Pondicherry?," was built on the assumption that once France released its hold on colonial territories, the people who lived in these territories would simply "revert" to some sort of primordial nationalism rooted in the land that had been occupied—a notion that the previous chapters of this book challenge. A deep skepticism underlies the short film, one that casts doubt on the possibility of an Indian becoming French. The narration focuses on the remnants of French life that continued in Pondicherry, in particular the French planning that made "straight streets" and "cut everything into right angles," streets that continued to carry the names of the French traders, governors, and religious orders commonly credited in French history with Pondicherry's founding. As the camera zooms in on a brown-skinned man wearing a police uniform, including the kepi hat often associated with the French military and police, the narrator notes, "The police officers look *almost* familiar to us." The warning to the audience seems clear: the streets of Pondicherry may mimic the streets of France, and the people you meet may even speak French and hold French citizenship, but if you look closely, behind the police uniform and kepi hat, you find Indians putting on a French costume.

The uneasiness lurking underneath the narration continues as the film crew moves across the sewage canal that has separated the ville blanche from the ville noire since the eighteenth century. Though still technically set in Pondicherry, the images begin to look more familiar to those accustomed to tropes of India as a tragic mass of humanity, a putrid example of the poverty of the third world, decaying because of an inability to overcome millennia of spiritual mysticism and superstition, or so the Orientalist scholars have told us. The viewer sees scenes of busy streets teeming with people alongside the requisite close-ups of children and older folks staring straight into the camera, wide-eyed. The film then moves to the Immaculate Conception Cathedral, which crowds of people are exiting after a mass. "At the Cathedral of Pondicherry," the narrator observes, "the masses at the exit of Mass show the profound implantation of Christianity here," before a quick cut to a Hindu shrine. As men women, and children play music and socialize in the streets, a sadhu with thick black dreadlocks and a painted face makes his way through the crowd. The narrator continues, "Yet, several hundred meters away, we can see that they have never ceased the rites of the Hindu gods." Much like the French-Indian police officers, the French-Indian Catholics *almost* look familiar, until one looks over to see the unarguably Indian scene nearby, which the narrator implies is incompatible with a *true* Catholic life. Beyond the performance of Frenchness lurks a world incomprehensible to the French viewer.

There is, however, a space in Pondicherry that feels truly familiar to the film crew, and that is the Ashram. The crew spends time interviewing two French-origin inhabitants of the Ashram, Philippe Saint-Hilaire (Pavitra) and woman named Barbara P. The interviews center around the individuals' devotion to the Mother, their contentment to live in her presence and under her spiritual guidance. Unlike the dark-skinned, voiceless people shown in the streets of Pondicherry, these white French Ashram inhabitants had found enlightenment; they were able to balance rational thought with spiritual belief, setting them apart from the Indians who were inhibited by their backward customs. The film closes with a scene of the Mother appearing on the Ashram balcony to greet her followers, who are gathered below her, as the narrator concludes, "Here is the Mother. For forty years, the Ashram lives just through her, and just for her. She is eighty-six years old. She is French." Having spent the previous twenty minutes seeking the remnants of France in Pondicherry, the final scene suggests that the most French part of Pondicherry was the Mother. Unlike the thousands of ethnically Tamil-French citizens in Pondicherry, it was the Mother who truly embodied the French Republic.

Perhaps it is not surprising that the Mother emerges in this film as the most French part of Pondicherry after 1962. However, it also seems likely that she would have disagreed with this conclusion. As previously mentioned, the Mother had stated publicly that while she was French by birth, she hoped to *become* Indian. This stands in stark contrast to the French-Indians who were legally French, but had to constantly assert their Frenchness in order to be seen as French. While the Indian government had already decided that dual citizenship would not be allowed for Indian citizens—a decision that upset many inhabitants of the Ashram—the Mother continued to work toward the creation of a "universal town ... where men and women of all countries are able to live in peace and progressive harmony, above all creeds, all politics and all nationalities."[2] Called Auroville (a name that invokes Aurobindo as well as carries the meaning of "dawn," from *aurore*), the Mother proposed a utopian experiment in living that would be *above* nations, concerned not with sovereignty or passports, but with the "evolution of man on Earth."[3] Whether or not she could become Indian in a legal sense, she had no intention of leaving the Ashram. In fact, with the creation of Auroville, the Mother fomented a new migration of people, mostly Europeans, Australians, and North Americans, into this area of South India, just as thousands of French Indians questioned their own desire, or ability, to stay.

Conceptualized as a project separate from the Ashram, Auroville became a new horizon of possibility for people who, like the Mother, felt abandoned due to the rupture of global decolonization. Auroville also appealed to the Indian government, which saw an opportunity to promote "East/West" friendship. High-level state officials including V. V. Giri (president of India, 1969–1974) and Indira Gandhi (prime minister of India, 1966–1977) visited Auroville and supported the project. On the international scale, the United Nations Educational, Scientific, and Cultural Organization (UNESCO) recognized Auroville beginning in 1966, approving a resolution that lauded the Sri Aurobindo Society, in conjunction with the Government of India (through the Indian National Commission for UNESCO), for its plans to "set up a cultural township known as Auroville where people of different countries will live together in harmony in one community."[4]

It is significant that, despite widespread excitement about the potential of Auroville to be space of "global harmony," the population of French-Indians who felt unsure about whether or not to stay in India after 1962 were not involved with the Ashram or with the planning of Auroville. The envisioning of Auroville was a global affair that lacked local participation. The conception and promotion of Auroville was instigated by people associated with the Ashram in Pondicherry as well as in Sri Aurobindo Society (SAS) centers both throughout India and around the world.[5] The Sri Aurobindo Society, founded in Calcutta in 1960, worked to promote the philosophy and teachings of Aurobindo's Integral Yoga through study groups, ashrams, and schools based on the Mother's teachings on education. Historian Peter Heehs has suggested that the creation of the SAS was related to the expansion of the Ashram, and that by 1965 the SAS had become the main fundraising source for Auroville.[6] The SAS produced a significant amount of promotional materials about Auroville and sent representatives from SAS, including SAS chairman Navajata (Keshav Dev Poddar), to Sri Aurobindo Centers in North America and Europe.[7] These global outreach efforts were instrumental in raising the funds needed to purchase land from small-scale landowners in Tamil Nadu.

Auroville is a project of spiritual settlement. The arrival and settlement practices begun by Aurobindo Ghose and Mira Alfassa in the minor French territory of Pondicherry have proven to hold significant global appeal to those seeking spaces to inhabit that break from the normative structures of twentieth-century capitalist-liberal democracies. In this chapter, I argue that using the theoretical lens of settler colonialism provides new insight into the maintenance of colonial space past what some people see as the *time* of colonialism, through an examination of how religious and spiritual seekers from around the globe came to settle in this geographic space.

In the introductory essay to the journal *settler colonial studies*, founding editor Lorenzo Veracini writes that the relationship between colonialism and settler colonialism is distinct and dialectical, that the colonial encounter is "mirrored" by what he has called the "settler colonial non-encounter, a circumstance fundamentally shaped by a recurring need to disavow the presence of indigenous 'others.'"[8] Important work on white settlement throughout both the British and French Empires, including in the Americas, Australia, Aotearoa/New Zealand, South Africa, Algeria, and contemporary Israel/Palestine shows how the structures of colonial settlement disregard the presence of local and indigenous populations, choosing to ignore and eventually eliminate Indigenous people to see instead vacant land.[9] Building on this work, alongside Eve Tuck and K. Wayne Yang's provocation that decolonization is not a metaphor, but a movement to "repatriate Indigenous land and life," this chapter works to center the issue of land and settlement in order to unsettle the idea that French India is a decolonized space.[10] Auroville is not a French space per se, but it came into existence through French colonial institutions. The reason it appears as a postcolonial and not a colonial space is because of the success France has had in depicting French India as a space of positive colonial existence.

While India was not a settler colony, it was a site of colonial settlement, the kind of settlement that worked/works to disavow the culture, language, and lives of local populations while simultaneously making claims to belong to the land. In and near Pondicherry, the Aurobindo Ashram and Auroville serve as examples of how liberal discourse rooted in multiculturalism, spirituality, equality, and utopianism has displaced local Tamil populations from land and history, time and space. While the Ashram occupies a major part of the ville blanche in the Union Territory of Pondicherry, Auroville is technically outside of Pondicherry, on land that was under British, not French, occupation. However, the extension of the Ashram beyond the colonial borders that previously separated the territories has extended the French influence onto neighboring Tamil land—one important difference being that the people who have been displaced by Auroville were never given a chance at French citizenship.

Decolonization may have come to French India in the 1950s, but colonialism continues into the present day in the form of spiritual settlement. I turn here to the founding years of Auroville, from its beginning in 1968 to the passing of the Mother in 1973, to examine the ways in which the self-described "pioneers" who came to participate in this supposedly postcolonial project reinscribed colonial hierarchies and reinstituted the occupation that had supposedly come to an end with the departure of the colonial powers. This was realized, I argue, by separating the Tamil people from the land and ascribing spiritual value to land while simultaneously viewing the local population as too ignorant, too steeped in Hindu tradition, to understand the enlightened project of Auroville, which led to their systematic exclusion from the utopia built on their homeland.

## European Dreams, Tamil Land

> From the spiritual point of view, India is the foremost country in the world. Her mission is to set the example of spirituality. Sri Aurobindo came on earth to teach this to the world. This fact is so obvious that a simple and ignorant peasant here is, in his heart, closer to the divine than the intellectuals of Europe. All those who want to become Aurovilians must know this and behave accordingly; otherwise they are unworthy of Auroville.
>
> —THE MOTHER, 8 FEBRUARY 1972

The year was 1968, the place, Auroville, a yet-to-be-built city on a stretch of land often described in promotional materials as "barren," but, in reality, dotted by Tamil villages, just a few miles outside the borders of the Union Territory of Pondicherry.[11] On a sunny morning, 28 February, the road from the Ashram to Auroville was filled with buses of people arriving to witness its inaugural ceremony and ground-breaking. The buses carried a variety of passengers, including European and American spiritual tourists who had heard about the construction of this utopian experiment while blazing the hippie trail through India; residents of the Aurobindo Ashram; and UNESCO officials who traveled to the south of India to give this new "international township" their bureaucratic blessing. An air of internationalism pervaded the ceremony as delegations from around the world arrived carrying the soil of 124 different nations, specially flown to Madras courtesy of Air France.[12] While participants made a circle around a container holding the imported earth, the Charter of Auroville was read in 16 different languages and broadcast over speakers to reach the burgeoning crowd, beginning with French and English, followed by Tamil (the language of the local population), Sanskrit, Arabic, Chinese, Dutch, German, Greek, Hebrew, Italian, Japanese, Norwegian, Russian, Spanish, Swedish, and Tibetan. The program handed out at the ceremony read, "Greetings from Auroville to all men of good will. Are invited to Auroville all those who thirst for progress and aspire to a higher life."[13]

The ceremony that marked the founding of Auroville was centered around young children carrying the dirt from 124 nations and depositing it into a large container. The children, often dressed in the "traditional costumes" of the countries they represented, brought the earth packets to the urn, the girl carrying the sign with the name of the country, the boy handling the packet of earth.[14] The significance of removing soil from other nations and combining them into a giant vessel to rest at Auroville's center gives some indication that the architects of the ceremony understood how important land was to settlement, to covering the indigenous soil with the beginnings of a new history, to begin the process of the erasure of the native.

While most of the people in attendance had traveled from afar to witness this inauguration, one Western Aurovilian remembered that "a section had been reserved for the people from the nearby villages, and although it was a large enclosure already you could see it was going to be inadequate. You could see people coming from every direction across the fields."[15] As Europeans and Indians from the north descended on this Tamil land to embark on a self-proclaimed utopian experiment that espoused a new age mixture of socialism, biological evolutionism, and spirituality, the people who lived on the land were kept together behind a barrier, welcome to witness the ceremony as long as they stayed in their designated space, distant from the international participants. This spatial segregation was just the beginning of the ways that Auroville would change the space and time of this area.

The initial plans for Auroville, designed primarily by the French architect Roger Anger (1923–2008) in consultation with the Mother, called for facilities to eventually accommodate 50,000 people. Auroville quickly took on "otherworldly" qualities, with the village taking the shape of a galaxy.[16] The city was planned to be divided into four sectors, one to house a significant industrial zone, another devoted to cultural institutions, another to residential areas, and, lastly, an international zone, dedicated to pavilions representing the different nations of the world.[17] When the first stone was laid in 1968, there were approximately 150 people working on Auroville's construction—a project that is still in progress today, maintaining a steady population of between 1800 and 2000 residents. Unlike many intentional communities constructed in the 1960s and

1970s, Auroville remains a functioning, and expanding, project. Over the past fifty years, Aurovilians have created schools, communal kitchens and dining rooms, health care centers, libraries, and dozens of small businesses producing incense, jewelry, clothes, art, and books, among other goods, for export. Thousands of tourists visit Auroville every year, staying in the many guesthouses run by Aurovilians and participating in the life of the community in various capacities. The many sectors of Auroville are today a success story of small business and tourism, cottage industries run primarily by people who have come from far away and employ local Tamil laborers, serving as a shining example of what successful postcolonial development could look like.

Auroville sought to foster social equality through spiritual transformation, "to be the cradle of a better humanity, united by a common effort towards perfection."[18] Following in many ways the model of socialist communal living put into practice by the kibbutz settlement movement in Israel, working toward social equality for a community meant defining who was a member of that community.[19] The Mother considered India, and Indians, to be spiritually evolved, the only physical location and population in the world that could support the "evolution of a new man." A "simple and ignorant [Indian] peasant" was, according to the Mother, "closer to the divine than the intellectuals of Europe."[20] Yet the self-described "pioneers" who arrived to settle the land found it difficult to cooperate with, and not simply extract land and labor from, the local Tamil population. As the utopian dreams became a lived reality, the tensions between the local population and the Aurovilians escalated. Despite official proclamations that the "Tamils are the original Aurovilians," the Tamil population was largely excluded from Auroville based on its lack of material resources *and* a perceived spiritual incompatibility with the project.[21] The exclusion of the Tamil population has been an undesirable outcome for the visionaries and architects behind the city, as well as for the people who came to take part in the utopian experiment and believed that Auroville could be a "global community" wherein every person would be a "citizen of the world." Instead of an international utopia free from the colonial past, Auroville quickly became a settlement of foreigners who faced challenges of assimilation and integration—they often expressed how difficult it was to learn Tamil, for example, and felt threatened by the local Tamil population that did not approve of Auroville—similar to those faced by European colonizers throughout the previous centuries of expansion.

Echoing the process of change that occurs after all social and political movements, in the supposed aftermath of empire, individuals were forced to reexamine their subjectivities, to rethink their identities and positions in changing communities, nations, and world systems. This was true for those who were colonized, as well as for those who identified with a colonial power. In the case of South India and Auroville, it is telling to see that even when the European colonizers left, their spirit remained, drifting below the surface of a supposedly anticolonial rhetoric heavy with the possibilities of equality and harmony through adherence to a specialized version of the divine, a universal spirituality. When confronted with the reality that the local Tamil population was largely uninspired by this utopian project and viewed the Aurovilians as neocolonizers who had come to take their land and exploit their labor, the Aurovilians believed that if they could convince the Tamils that Auroville's spiritual practices were the *way to the future*, the two groups could live in harmony. However, this emphasis on the future was to the detriment of understandings of the past. Like the colonizers before them, Aurovilians failed to recognize the different subjectivities of the local populations, shaped and reshaped through centuries of struggles with colonizers from all over the world. The Aurovilian insistence on the need to create a "universal city" to espouse a "universal spirituality" failed to recognize the Tamil people as composed of multiple communities distinct from their Western colonizers, their struggles for autonomy throughout their history, and the political realities at the core of their efforts to avoid assimilating into Auroville.

## Divine Unions: The Foundations of Utopia

The foundational texts of Auroville were predicated on the possibility of "unity," and while Auroville rejected formal religion, all Aurovilians were required to subscribe to a particular spiritual worldview that the Mother believed would lead to unity. Robert N. Minor argues that despite the Mother's strict adherence to the necessity of spirituality, the "direct relation to the Divine," her definition of spirituality as different from religion was ambiguous and self-serving.[22] Minor shows that, for the Mother, "'spiritual' teachings are those that agree with the teaching and evolutionary goals of Aurobindo and the Mother . . . if they do not do so, they are defined as 'religious,' not 'spiritual.'"[23] Minor's critique points to one of the foundational paradoxes of the Auroville experiment, one that closely mimics the paradox of the modern liberal nation-state: creating a unified group requires excluding others, producing boundaries that protect the rights and identities of only those who meet the requirements for inclusion.[24]

The idea that "all people are equal" was, of course, fundamental to anticolonial movements that struggled for state-based autonomy. However, as the freedom struggles of anticolonialists like Sri Aurobindo show, the idea that all humans have equal abilities to think and perform actions regardless of biological or racial characteristics does not indicate that they have equal opportunity to exercise these powers. This was a lesson that took Sri Aurobindo the first twenty years of his life to learn and subsequently shaped his political and spiritual philosophies. The psychological effects of colonialism permeated the relationship between Aurobindo and the Mother.[25] Thus, it is important to investigate this union and, perhaps more important, to examine what the figures of Aurobindo and the Mother *represent* individually as well as together. Both figures exhibit the defining features of a particular sort of colonial-era cultural hybridity, a melding of Western thought and Eastern spirituality, though they embody this hybridity in significantly different ways.

Even before she first met Aurobindo, the Mother believed that she was spiritually destined to live and work outside of Europe. She sought her spiritual home away from France at an early age, hoping to transform her identity as a bourgeois white French woman into that of a dedicated Eastern spiritualist, removed from the emptiness of contemporary European life. One could say that Aurobindo spent his adolescence seeking an escape from the very thing Mira desired: the embodied essence of Indian spirituality. Of course, Indian men and women, particularly those immersed in Western circles, had no choice *but* to perform the embodiment of "Indianness," even when they tried to escape it. Institutionalized hierarchies of race and class, constructed throughout centuries of colonialism, reinforced conflations of ethnicity and spirituality, of history and the present.

Aurobindo and the Mother often portrayed their spiritual partnership as a bridge between East and West, as well as a transition from an old world to a new world, a nonlinear evolution to a higher plane of consciousness.

The links drawn between spirituality and science, between meditation and evolution, speak to their attempts not only to combine Western science with Eastern spirituality, but also to move beyond this hybrid spirituality. The Mother argued that a new world was possible—a mantra that has become an important expression of utopian thinking into the twenty-first century—but, for her, the new world would encompass a transformation of "the material world into a divine world."[26] It is perhaps here, in her desire to disengage from the material world, that we can find her inability to see the very real material consequences that accompanied the building of Auroville.

On the one hand, as scholar Leela Gandhi has shown, the Mother spoke as an anti-imperialist, making her an outcast in mainstream Western society as she created strong anticolonial alliances with Aurobindo.[27] Gandhi has argued that the Mother's adherence to a type of "anarcho-socialism" or anticolonial socialism sought to bring spirituality back to a secular politics that was scorned in the West, an attempt at creating an anti-imperialism not based on Western ideas.[28] Gandhi works to show that the Mother was an important type of anti-imperialist, representative of a fin-de-siècle European generation equally interested in socialism and theosophy, in Eastern spirituality and a rejection of Western imperialism. While Gandhi makes an important point, I contend that the anti-imperialism exhibited by the Mother is typical of a certain type of what I have called throughout this book "anticolonial colonialism," which was common in India during this period. The Mother, and other Westerners similar to her, espoused an anticolonialism that denied the key claims of imperial ideology, particularly those to Western superiority and the inability of non-Western nations to practice of self-rule. However, I argue, when the ideology of the Mother was put into practice, particularly in the case of Auroville, we quickly see how colonialism reinserts itself into the anticolonial mission of self-rule and self-determination. In the remainder of this chapter, I will argue that the creation of Auroville exemplifies the phenomenon of anticolonial colonialism, a key concept in understanding neocolonialism in a postcolonial world. While the discourse of anti-imperialism was present, the actions carried out by the Aurovilian pioneers exemplify the construction of a neocolonial space and culture. Western ideas of the Indian other, constructed through centuries of Orientalism, converged with the realities of a postcolonial India to produce racialized divisions of class, labor, and culture, casting the Indigenous Tamil population as an underdeveloped, backward people in need of spiritual and material awakening through Sri Aurobindo's philosophy of Integral Yoga.[29]

## Visions of Utopia: The Universal City of Dawn

Returning to Thomas More's concept of utopia as "no place," it is important to remember that, as a praxis, utopia is hard to enact at home, on known land.[30] Ideally, constructing a utopian society requires a stretch of vacant land, uninhabited by people who possess distinct cultures, languages, and ways of living. The experiments of socialist utopianists in the nineteenth century, such as the Saint-Simonians and Fourierists, who moved throughout the French Empire advocating colonial reforms under the guise of the civilizing mission, sought to create intentional societies, often to the detriment—or at the least exclusion—of Indigenous cultures and peoples in non-Western areas of the world.[31] While the organizing principle of socialist utopianism often set it apart from the capitalism of colonialism, both colonialism and utopianism imagined many non-Western lands as empty and available for their experiments. Lucy Sargisson has argued that the process of estrangement has a "profoundly positive relationship with utopianism," as it permits the members of an intentional community to create a critical distance between the reality of the present time and the future "goodplace" of the utopia.[32] This distancing was critical to Auroville's foundational beliefs. More's utopia took the shape of a newly discovered island somewhere in the new world, while Auroville was conceived of as a "city of the future" on "ancient" land. Imagined utopias take place far from home, often in unimaginable places, in order to provide enough distance from contemporary forms of living to construct a community critical of the present time. This distancing has much different consequences in practice.

The hundreds of pieces of promotional materials about Auroville printed and distributed around the world during the 1960s and 1970s emphasized the concept that Auroville was a physical space wherein individuals could leave both the past and the present behind and head toward the future. Both space and time were used to indicate to people that Auroville was something *new*. The inside cover of the 1971 promotional booklet *Auroville: The Cradle of a New Man* states, "Earth needs a place where men can live away from national rivalries, social conventions, self-contradictory moralities and contending religions, a place where human beings, freed from the slavery of the past, can devote themselves wholly to the discovery and practice of the divine consciousness that is seeking to manifest itself. Auroville wants to be this place and offers itself to all who aspire to live the Truth of tomorrow."[33] The "slavery of the past" here refers not the actual history of enslavement, but instead to people who *felt* enslaved by the history of imperialism. Given the population demographics of Auroville's first five or so years, it is clear that this call appealed not to the formerly colonized, but to those who came from the imperial center, who actually desired to be free of their own complicity in the very recent colonial past.

While a fictional utopia could potentially provide the metaphysical space for an escape from an earth riddled with "national rivalries" and "social conventions," it would be impossible, especially by 1968, to create a space removed from the realities of global capitalism, colonial relationships, and, indeed, the "slavery of the past." Auroville wanted to be free not only from the horrors of history, but also from the reality of the present, failing to recognize that the material conditions of the past were the basis of—and limits of enactment for—their projections of the present into the future. In another promotional pamphlet, the Mother is quoted as saying of Auroville, "At last a place where one will be able to think of the future only."[34] Sargisson views the relationship between utopia and estrangement to be essential in the practice of intentional communities yet paradoxical, as the members of the community struggle with the side effects of estrangement. Estrangement is also essential to the act of colonization and particularly settler colonialism, the key difference between colonialism and utopianism being that colonizers were transparent in their goals to exploit the land and people they were colonizing, while in the case of Auroville, this exploitation was buried beneath a rhetoric of postcolonial equality and color-blindness.

The transformation of a fictional utopia into a utopian experiment—or, in other terms, the translation of ideas into social practices—must confront the realities of locating an area of the world that is secluded from the known (or normative) lives of the future residents. There were two major factors that led to the construction of Auroville in India. First, the West's obsession with India as a breeding ground for spiritual enlightenment and metaphysical experimentation dates back to early days of European exploration and trade in the fifteenth century. Colonial authorities studied the ancient cultures of India, poring over the history and practices of what they called "Hinduism," as well as the caste system. Ancient India was revered as a great, lost civilization that had degenerated into a state of decay. Colonial knowledge production familiarized the West with India's land, food, art, religion, and people. Hundreds of years of colonialism led to, among other things, a well-traveled tourist's path through India, both mental and physical.[35]

Secondly, Auroville was the result of political relationships developed throughout the colonial period, a prime example of anticolonial colonialism. As we have already seen, the Mother came to Pondicherry with her husband, Paul Richard, a French colonial administrator. Of course, the only reason Aurobindo was in Pondicherry was as a result of his involvement with the Indian independence movement, and his need to leave British India. The Ashram always had a significant number of European residents, who had accessed the Mother's writings in French and English while in Europe and had subsequently made pilgrimages to live in the Ashram. While the British, and, in Pondicherry, the French, remained in power, these individuals did not require special permission to stay in India—it was an extension of their rights as British and/or French citizens and subjects. While many of them, like the Mother, sympathized and even supported anticolonial struggles, they depended on their racial privileges inherent in their national belonging to support their lives in India.

The call for people to come to the south of India and participate in the construction of the "universal city" was spread widely through the international press and networks of new age spiritual enthusiasts, yet the Mother and her collaborators tightly controlled the admittance process. Everyone who wanted to come to Auroville was required to submit an application, with a picture of the applicant, which would go directly to the Mother. The initial application had twenty-four questions, beginning with name and nationality and ending with "What can you donate to Auroville?"[36] Potential Aurovilians were asked to explain why they wanted to come to Auroville and questioned as to whether they were familiar with the philosophies of the Mother and Aurobindo. The Mother and the other organizers knew that their goals appealed to a type of person they did *not* desire: those without any money, who showed up lost and poor. They wanted to make sure that the applicants they accepted were not simply drifters or people looking for welfare. M. P. Pandit, the secretary of the Sri Aurobindo Society who oversaw the application process, admitted, "We have a hard time keeping out the hippies. We do not want them, they are not serious about anything."[37]

However, the hippies were already in India, on the beaches of Goa, in the hills of Rishikish, peppering the alleys of Benares (Varanasi). As they continued to seek refuge at Auroville, the rules became stricter. Auroville was to be a place of education and spiritual advancement through meditation, not a place to experiment with psychedelic drugs.[38] In 1971, as more people arrived hoping to join the community, the Mother issued a statement forbidding drug use: "Drugs are prohibited at Auroville. If there are any who take them, they do so deceitfully. The ideal Aurovilian, eager to become conscious of the Divine Consciousness, takes neither tobacco, nor alcohol, nor drugs."[39] A small book of guidelines for the first Aurovilians, which consisted of short statements made by the Mother, includes the following dictate: "Begging is not permitted in Auroville. Persons found begging will be distributed as follows: Children to school, the old to a home, the sick to the hospital, the healthy to work."[40] Everyone who was approved to live in Auroville was meant to have an active role in society. According to the Mother, active labor was essential to spiritual evolution.

What really set apart the Aurovilians from the hippies? At the beginning of the experiment, it was perhaps impossible to tell the difference. Numerous interviews and memoirs from the original Aurovilians confirm that many of them were first attracted to India as a spiritual oasis that would provide them with the space to "discover" themselves. People came to Auroville following stints in the Peace Corps in India; after reading the works of Sri Aurobindo in a number of global cities; and through word of mouth that traveled along the Indian tourist trail.[41] Daniel Roucher, an Aurovilian born in France in 1945, told the *New York Times* that he and his wife "stumbled on" Auroville during their "aimless wanderings in the East."[42] Their daughter was born in Auroville soon after, one of the first children to be born an Aurovilian. Verne, an American Aurovilian, came to Auroville while on a quest "to discover [his] soul" and "unravel the mysteries of life."[43] An American woman he had been involved with in Spain sent him a postcard from Auroville, urging him to come there, with the statement "This is the place I've been searching for my entire life." Paul Pinton, an Aurovilian born in French-occupied Algeria in 1950, was a member of a series of caravans that while destined for Auroville took several months to reach it, traveling overland from Europe.[44] Their caravan consisted of a Mercedes bus and two smaller vans, transporting thirty-four people, "mostly French."[45] Judith, born in 1946 in Manchester, England, took a bus from London to Delhi in 1971, after someone in her local pub told her about Auroville.[46] Lisbeth, a Dutch Aurovilian born in 1948, recalled that, while in Holland, she kept having dreams about India.[47] She and her partner soon set off for India, traveling first to Goa and from there to Pondicherry. Lisbeth remarked that upon arrival at the Ashram "we really looked like hippies. We hadn't worn shoes in a long time and had long hair, bells on my ankles and long skirts." At the Ashram, people said to her, "You really look like pioneers—you should go to Auroville." Once she arrived, she saw that people looked like her, Europeans "dressed in loincloths, smoking their beedies, looking brown and healthy."[48] She felt she had finally arrived at her new home.

Auroville was envisioned as a postcolonial city that would eschew the worst offenses of colonialism, rejecting the constraints of national alliances, global capitalism, racism, and religious strife. The Mother proposed to create this utopia through a combination of innovative architecture, progressive educational programs, and a socialist society that would require everyone to work in equal capacities and operate in a moneyless economy. Labor was seen as one of the primary means to spiritual advancement in Auroville. As the Mother wrote, "Money will be no more the Sovereign Lord."[49] In the final section, I will examine how labor and wealth became the primary point of divergence between the Aurovilians and the Tamils as Auroville attempted to turn utopian dreams into reality.

The support of the international community, especially France, India, and UNESCO, was important to the principal architects of Auroville, for reasons of both economic gain and cultural and social legitimacy. Roger Anger, the chief architect of Auroville, a native Parisian, and the Mother's son-in-law, paid a number of visits to French government officials, including the French ambassador to India, to promote Auroville in the years before it was built.[50] The French diplomatic corps were largely in favor of promoting French culture through the auspices of the Auroville project, especially given their close relationship with the Mother. For the French government, particularly the Department of Foreign Affairs and the cultural ministry, the creation of Auroville presented an opportunity to retain some amount of cultural influence in and around the region of the former French colony. François Baron, the last French governor of Pondicherry, expressed his enthusiasm toward Auroville's creation in a series of letters to government officials. M. Jean Daridan, the French ambassador to India, sent a report to the minister of foreign affairs outlining a meeting he had with Anger in April 1966. Daridan detailed the initial plans for Auroville, including the projections for being able to accommodate fifty thousand residents plus the four zones. He described the cultural zone as a place where numerous national cultures would be represented, a benefit to the spirit of France.[51] Auroville was designed to be an *international* space, expressed through a series of pavilions devoted to the study and performance of a number of national identities.

International recognition was especially important to the people in the Ashram, as the Ashram itself was regularly the target of local populations who saw it as contrary to local interests. Following the transfer of Pondicherry from France to India, the Ashram lost the support of the local government, which had been very friendly to its interests while still in the hands of the French. As the Ashram continued to enjoy the support of the national government—which it emphasized by plastering photos of the Mother with government officials, including Jawaharlal Nehru and his daughter and future prime minister Indira Gandhi, all over its promotional materials—many of the local populations saw the Ashram as representative of both foreign colonial powers and the power of the central Indian government. This opposition was expressed, in one example, on the night of 11 February 1965, when a group of young people thought to be students associated with the anti-Hindi movement first torched the Pondicherry railway station and then set their sights on the Ashram. According to Ashram sources, they showed up in the evening, armed with sticks and stones, while most Ashramites were in meditation. The students allegedly looted and destroyed the Ashram food store, called the Honesty Society, and burned several Ashram residences.[52] Windows were broken in the main Ashram building, and "a stone reached the room of the Divine Mother herself." Eventually, several young men who resided in the Ashram were called to chase of the band of "hooligans," who "retreated against the rush of our boys."[53] The language of the Goonda Raj returned as a useful tool for the interests of the Ashram.

Despite the many claims of the Ashram to be the spiritual and cultural center of Pondicherry, the blessed meeting of East and West, students in Pondicherry who were taking part of the Tamil Nadu-wide protests against Hindi as the national language attacked the Ashram for its promotion of Hindi, English, and French. The Ashram issued a pamphlet following the riots, noting that as a "spiritual institution" it was "above all such issues," but was "nevertheless made a target of the movement."[54] Udar, an Ashramite who wrote the pamphlet, believed that the Ashram *should* be well loved in Pondicherry for several reasons: because it was founded by Sri Aurobindo, a great freedom fighter; "because it has benefitted the town considerably by its example and practice of discipline and hygiene"; because it had brought income and development to the State; and because, the Ashramites believed, it had "done such good work in its housing and departments and projects." He characterized the groups who opposed the Ashram as jealous and petty and blamed the Catholics for not understanding the role of spiritual leaders in India: "The Anti-Hindi agitation was launched by the students and so they must take full responsibility for the accompanying violence. It is an open question, however, whether many of them actually took part in the attacks, which was largely composed of the hooligan element."[55] While the students attacked the Ashram for perpetuating colonial legacies of language instruction and Western practices, the Ashram declared the "hooliganism" of the students to be the problem, the foreign element disturbing a peaceful city, with the Ashram at the spiritual center.

Udar stressed that the Ashram was strictly apolitical: "One of the few fundamental rules that govern the behaviour of members of the Ashram is the interdiction against politics. The Ashram is above all political affiliations or ideas and does not participate in any political movements," a statement that Ashramites had previously issued during the tumultuous years of anticolonial agitation between 1947 and 1954.[56] The Mother also issued her response to the incident and addressed the role of the Ashram in Pondicherry; she began by asking, "How is it that the Ashram exists in this town for so many years and is not liked by the population?" Her response: "The first and immediate answer is that all those in this population who are of a higher standard in culture, intelligence, good will and education not only have welcomed the Ashram but have expressed their sympathy, admiration and good feeling." In plain language, anyone who had sympathies with the colonial regime and considered themselves a part of the French cultural milieu *understood* the importance of the Ashram in a way the local, non-Westernized populations could not. She pointed her finger at four groups who continued to oppose the Ashram: the Catholics ("because they are convinced that whoever is not a Catholic must be an instrument of the devil"), the Communists, the DMK ("who cannot tolerate the presence on their soil of people coming from the North"), and, lastly, "a rather low category of the population who had succeeded in taking advantage of the French rule and are dead against all change and progress."[57] Much like the filmmakers who declared the Mother the most French part of post-1962 French India, the Mother herself distrusted the people of French India, equally convinced that they were greedy individuals who instrumentalized religion, national identity, and global politics for their own gain.

## Constructing Utopia: Barren Lands, Active Laborers

### CONDITIONS FOR LIVING IN AUROVILLE

From the psychological point of view, the required conditions are:

1. To be convinced of the essential unity of mankind and to have the will to collaborate for the material realization of that unity.
2. To have the will to collaborate in all that furthers future realization.

The material conditions will be worked out as the realization proceeds.
—THE MOTHER, 1967

Despite the hassle of obtaining a visa, Europeans, North Americans, and Australians came to Auroville.[58] During the first few years of construction, beginning as early as 1966, newspapers in the West, from France to the United States, published numerous articles lauding the efforts of the Aurovilians. In 1970, the French magazine *Marie-Claire* declared Auroville the new "capital of a spiritual empire,"[59] while one year later the *New York Times* profiled the "utopian town in India built on a dream."[60] The coverage provided by the international press, along with a deluge of promotional materials produced and distributed by over eighty SAS centers scattered throughout the world, encouraged anyone who believed in the possibility of spiritual harmony and the betterment of all humans to come join the effort to construct an "international township" where everyone would be considered "citizens of the world." While the initial plans for

Auroville called for a population of 50,000 people, the actual population during the first five years (1968–1973) fluctuated between 150 and 400 people.[61] The population data for 1972 lists 320 residents, 121 of whom were Indian, and 190 Western. Of the 121 Indian residents, approximately 15 were Tamil, about 4.6 percent of the total population.[62]

After the excitement of the inaugural ceremony settled down, the immense amount of work that lay ahead of the Auroville pioneers began to emerge. While Roger Anger and his team of French architects were busy creating plans for this "city of the future," the caravans of people recruited from around the world began to arrive to the sight of a large stretch of red desert, surrounded by small, desiccated farms. Roy Chyat, a newcomer to Auroville in its early years, would remember, "There was nothing here. No trees. It was like a desert."[63] Bob and Deborah Lawlor, an American couple who were among the first to settle on Aurovilian land, slept outdoors and "felt very isolated."[64] As they had no local source of water, they had to wait for a jeep to deliver milk containers full of water from Pondicherry every few days.[65] "It was a moonscape. Nothing was growing," remembered Francis, another early Aurovilian.[66] These "pioneers" all recalled the challenges that faced them when they arrived in Auroville and consistently remarked that there was nothing to see but red dirt and the Bay of Bengal in the distance. They were faced with constructing an entire city on inhospitable land: dry, infertile, uncultivated, and hot.

A "progress report" on the initial phases of the construction of Auroville, produced in November 1968, stated that the particular land chosen for the construction of Auroville was chosen because "the land is sparsely populated [and] a city can be built with minimum disturbance to the local population. Much of the land is uncultivated."[67] Despite countless allusions to the "deserted" land, there was a sizeable local population that watched curiously as Westerners and north Indians descended on their territory. The local populations greatly outnumbered the initial migration of foreigners. During the first few years of Auroville's existence (at least until 1974), the population did not top four hundred.[68] The surrounding villages, meanwhile, held thousands of people who were somewhat bewildered, and frustrated, by the presence of these new arrivals. When asked about the presence of the Aurovilians in 1974, the local villagers gave a variety of responses, from "I don't know about Auroville. It should not disturb the village people," to "It may be slavery again, as before, because they find us black, ugly and poor," and "Previously the white men were cruel. Now they look nice and quiet."[69] It slowly became clear to the Aurovilians that, despite the "spiritual superiority" of the Tamils, it would take hard work to integrate their project with the lives and interests of the local villagers.

From the beginning, the Mother had insisted that all Indians were spiritually in tune with the ideals of Auroville. Neither she nor any of the planners predicted encountering any resistance from the local Tamil population. Her view was that "Auroville belongs to nobody in particular," but to "humanity as a whole."[70] This meant that all people, including the local population, could choose to become Aurovilians by accepting the spiritual life that it offered. However, this universal ideal did not always manifest itself in material reality. The tensions between the Aurovilians and the local population started before the inauguration, as representatives from Auroville began to purchase the desired land. Dhanapal, a Tamil man born in the neighboring village of Kuilapalayam in 1968, remembered the changes that Auroville brought to the local communities early on: "My family owned large plots of land, and they sold much of it to Auroville. Sharnga [a French-run Auroville guest house] is largely built on land once owned by my father; the land of Prayathna belonged to my Uncle. But the sales did not make us rich."[71] Impoverished local farmers who needed money sold their land to Auroville, only to find themselves unemployed and landless. "I don't know anything about Auroville," remarked an anonymous Tamil villager. "It is a secret. And I don't care much, but I need Rs. 2000 for my marriage so let them buy my one-acre. Then I can marry and get work in Auroville."[72]

Aurovilians were expected to "lose the sense of material possession" and give their belongings to the group, to be distributed to all of Auroville. Once there, they would realize that "work, even manual work, is something indispensable for the inner discovery."[73] The emphasis on the importance of manual labor was repeatedly stressed, largely because the people coming from the West were unaccustomed to working in this capacity. As the planners bought the land for the creation of Auroville, the Aurovilians found themselves in an unfamiliar environment, needing to cultivate the earth and learn about local varieties of plants and foodstuffs, as well as adjusting to the climate and diet of the region. Very few of these pioneers had any experience with farming or manual labor, and while the Mother preached that all must engage in "the yoga of work," most of them quickly realized they could hire the local people as laborers. Roy Chyat recounted, "You couldn't do anything without help from the village people. So everything was basically them. In those days, you would hire a laborer who would work all day for three rupees twenty. Which is really like nothing. Even in those days. Well, the dollar was nine to the rupee then, still, nothing. So you'd have a lot of Tamil people."[74]

Speaking about the building of the Matrimandir, the spiritual orb at the center of Auroville, Francis recalled the mysteriousness of the groups of Tamil laborers that were hired to aid in the construction: "I don't really know where they came from, but they hired themselves out as a full village to dig . . . it was amazing to watch because it was just like ants on the move. You couldn't believe that these little *ammas* (village women) carrying that little bit of soil . . . but it was continuous and down [they] went in the hole."[75] Statements such as these make it clear that many Aurovilians viewed the work of the Tamilians as less valuable than their own. Since the Mother insisted that everyone engage in labor, some of the Aurovilians took to manual labor for the first time. Writing about his work on a dam in 1970, Robert Lawlor describes getting into costume to mimic the native laborer, invoking the idea that this labor was a deed of the past and meant for those of a different race. He writes that to engage in this opportunity to "re-enter the vast ancient region of manual labour," he would dress himself in a "loincloth, bind my head in cloth and with a bun of straw on top and wicker basket in hand, merge myself into the dark-skinned and dust-dressed dance of the ages."[76]

While the "pioneers" took pride in their own labor, believing that they were serving a greater spiritual purpose through their work, they viewed the Tamil laborers as different than themselves: the latter group lived a "traditional," or old, lifestyle, and were not ready for the "progressive" ideas of Auroville. The social and cultural separation, or estrangement, between the Aurovilians and the Tamils made it easier for the Aurovilians to exploit the labor of the Tamilians, never considering them as equals. Both Tamil land and Tamil labor were essential to the building of Auroville, although once the Tamil villagers sold their land, they no longer had any claim to the products of their labor.

The local villagers' loss of land did not appear problematic to the Mother, who conceived of Auroville as a collective, moneyless society. She believed that eventually the Tamilians would understand the Aurovilian project and would thus regain use of the land along with the collective whole. Progress reports on land acquisition noted that while Auroville had not convinced all the villagers to sell their land, it would be better for the villagers if they did sell it, as it would be "given back to all after their and our transformation."[77] The Mother implored the pioneers to "explain to the villagers that we are there to make life better and easier for them and not more difficult. We will like to take them as people of Auroville if they collaborate and are willing for it . . . one has to convince them that we are their benefactors."[78] While the Mother continued to insist that the local population should be integrated into the Aurovilian way of life, the first Aurovilians quickly realized that it was easier to change the landscape than the people.

Despite the Mother's announcement that the Tamil people "are the original Aurovilians," many of the non-Tamil Aurovilians found themselves at odds with the local populations. Deborah Lawlor recalled thinking she was "an object of great curiosity, being the first non-Indian many villagers had seen."[79] Deborah would often ride her bicycle between Auroville and Pondicherry to buy food and other supplies. When she would cycle through the Tamil village of Kottakuppam, "children would tease [her] by throwing stones and calling *vellakari* [white woman]."[80] There were violent incidents in the early years between the Aurovilians and local Tamil villagers who were hired as security guards or manual laborers, when Tamilians were accused of stealing equipment or not fulfilling their duties.[81]

The Mother instructed the Aurovilians to go into the villages and explain their good intentions to the villagers, but few Aurovilians were able to communicate with the people. While some were able to learn Tamil and communicate with the local villagers, most of the first Aurovilians admit that they never were able to learn the language. "People picked up workable Tamil," one pioneer remembered, "but the Tamils are much quicker at picking up English."[82] A 1974 booklet on Auroville-Tamil relations stated, "It takes over three years to learn that difficult Tamil, so hardly anyone knows it yet."[83] While the Aurovilians learned that they could get by with just a few Tamil phrases, those Tamil villagers who hoped to gain employment from their new wealthy neighbors had to become quite fluent in English, a familiar experience for hundreds of thousands of former colonial subjects seeking jobs.

One group of Aurovilians decided to establish their community next to a Tamil village called Kottakarai. In an attempt to integrate themselves with the village, they named their community Kottakarai as well. An article in the Sri Aurobindo Ashram publication *World Union*, penned by an Aurovilian named Ronald Jorgenson, comments on this meeting of cultures and peoples by suggesting that the taking of this Tamil name by a group of Aurovilians showed the "unity between the local Indian villager's ancient past and the international arrival's young present."[84] The Westerners who came to Auroville were generally educated, white, to some degree monetarily secure, and vetted by the Mother. As we have already seen, Westerners comprised about half the population, the other half being people from north India. Like the Westerners, they were often well educated, financially secure, and, notably, much lighter-skinned than the Tamils. The divide between the Tamils and Aurovilians was not limited to Westerners and non-Westerners, but was additionally marked by distinctions of class and race. Within the discourses that created the foundations of the relationships between Aurovilian and non-Aurovilian, these distinctions were often made through a temporal language that saw the Tamil people as "ancient" and the Aurovilians as not only "modern," but the hope for the future. A hierarchy that placed Aurovilian over Tamilian, established through a racialized division of labor and a reliance on the colonial discourses of ancient versus modern during the early years of Auroville, worked to erase the Tamil people from their own land.

## Aurovilian and Non-Aurovilian

> You see, many Tamil Aurovilians feel inferior to the Westerners. We do not have their level of education, we do not master English well enough, and we are not so good in expressing ourselves at meetings. So there has always been a tendency to only stick to one's own work.
> —DHANAPAL, TAMIL VILLAGER AND AUROVILLE EMPLOYEE

By 1974, the year after the Mother "left her body," it was clear to a large portion of Aurovilians that something more had to be done to improve their relations with the Tamil villagers.[85] One Aurovilian wrote in 1974, "There is no trust, really, between 'Us' and 'Them.' 'We' don't know how to behave as 'bosses.' Tend to be overly severe, heavy, threatening—or too 'sweet,' 'wishy-washy' give 'them' the idea 'we' don't really care what 'they' do. We must learn 'their' language or SOME common language must be devised, or what?"[86] Many of the Aurovilians seemed surprised that the

Mother's prediction that the Tamil people would come to believe in their project was not immediately coming to fruition. As they grappled with how to run Auroville without the presence of the Mother, many of them came to accept their cultural and material differences with the local community. While projects geared at "villager integration," largely through education and employment, continued and continue to this day, the early hopes that the Tamil community would organically integrate themselves into the spiritual realm of Auroville had largely dissipated by 1974.

The construction of a subjugated people as ancient, and thus premodern, is a familiar trope in colonial discourses. While Sri Aurobindo and the Mother were ostensibly anticolonialists, their beliefs and practices in "international living" and "progress" translated into an essentialized understanding of national identities that isolated culture from politics. Auroville was envisioned as an international city that would serve as a "bridge" between a series of binaries: East and West, past and future, rich and poor. The Mother and the original Aurovilians envisioned reforesting a land that had been "used, overused, misused, abused, neglected, [and] wasted for thousands of years," for the greater good of all people.[87] They hoped for a redistribution of wealth through a commitment to a collective life governed by a spiritual understanding of the world that replaced material concerns with a common desire to "evolve to the next level." Unlike other experiments in utopia based on Marxist or other socialist ideologies, Auroville always insisted on an understanding of "the divine" for inclusion within its borders. To understand the divine and to be comfortable submitting one's life to the ideals of Auroville, one also had to have an understanding of the self that lay somewhere between the East/West dichotomy that fascinated individuals such as Sri Aurobindo and Mira Alfassa. The construction of the Aurovilian, the modern individual who could work collectively yet still turn inward in hope of personal attainment of a higher consciousness, was exactly the blend of East and West that Westerners (and, to some extent, upper-class or bourgeois "Easterners") were seeking in the secluded spiritual enclaves of "ancient" India. Unfortunately for the local Tamil populations, who were completely immersed in the political present, they did not have the time or means to give their selves to this search for spiritual awakening. Liberal ideologies of universal equality—the basis of the Aurovilian model of utopia—depended on the exclusions of other "nonbelievers" to isolate their community.

## Auroville Today

On 28 February 2016, Auroville celebrated its fiftieth anniversary, an occasion marked by a conference and many cultural programs. Auroville has experienced many changes in the past fifty years. The most significant involved a separation between the SAS—the foundation that took control of the Auroville project following the death of the Mother—and Auroville. A protracted battle over the control of Auroville's assets developed over the course of the late 1970s and ended in the Auroville Emergency Provisions Act in 1980, and eventually the founding of the Auroville Foundation in 1991.[88] This era also saw the end of the belief that Auroville would eventually have 50,000 inhabitants. The original plans for Auroville, which called for the town to take the form of a galaxy, filled with skyscrapers and moving sidewalks, had been abandoned by the mid-1970s, when many Aurovilians recognized how hostile the "modern" extraterrestrial design was toward the local landscape.[89] By the 1980s, one senior Auroville architect "suggested that 10,000 inhabitants was the absolute maximum which could be accommodated."[90] While it is beyond the scope of this chapter to detail the numerous changes in the community, both positive and negative, that Auroville has undergone since the mid-1970s, it is telling that as a society Auroville continues to struggle with the role that Tamil people and culture should play in it. It is not a stretch to say that in Auroville today, the separation between Aurovilian and Tamilian, and the exploitation of Tamil labor for the operation of Auroville, continues to make Auroville a functioning community.

The struggle of the local Tamil communities to resist integration with Auroville and the enclosure of their land has been submerged by Western-style "humanitarian" efforts to bring education to the Tamil children and to provide training for local women to make, for example, incense, soap, and clothes, as well as jewelry and bowls out of recycled trash. A pamphlet put out during Auroville's forty-year anniversary in 2008 boasts of the town's accomplishments in the "creation of employment opportunities for some 4–5,000 local people, some with associated training opportunities," "an active Village Action Group working to improve the life of people in 60 local villages," "5 schools, 2 kindergartens and 2 crèches for Auroville children, plus another 16 outreach schools overseen by Auroville," and, among many more items, "over 140 business business/commercial units under 25 trusts, several exporting to Europe, USA and other parts of the world."[91] Jobs are created for local villagers, largely in the fields of manual labor, craft production, housekeeping, and cooking. The production of Aurovilian handicrafts is extremely profitable, and the over 40 guesthouses, which are staffed almost entirely by Tamil cooks and maids, bring even more revenue into Auroville. The state of Tamil Nadu and the nearby Union Territory of Pondicherry continue to express interest in Auroville's development, particularly because its success brings more tourist money to local merchants and state organizations.[92]

Are the Western residents of Auroville tourists, settlers, or did they, as the Mother suggested in reference to herself, become Indians? In her work on spiritual tourism and "foreign swamis" in India, anthropologist Meena Khandelwal has suggested that, based on her ethnographic work, Westerners who come to India and remain there as members of ashrams and other religious communities are often transmigrants who eschew the language of displacement, as they drop any emotional attachment to their country of origin and refer to India as "home."[93] However, unlike the Westerners that Khandelwal looks at, most of whom renounce their Western citizenship to gain Indian citizenship and fully immerse themselves in the culture of the spiritual groups they join, Auroville was built as a Western utopia on Indian (specifically Tamil) land. The majority of non-Indians who live in Auroville retain their natal citizenships and are actively encouraged to bring their "national culture" into the life of Auroville's global community, as evidenced by the emphasis Auroville places on the operation of national pavilions. The idea of global citizenship allows for a multiplicity of belongings and affiliations, the ability to be French, Indian, British, and American simultaneously. This chapter has shown how the idea of a global citizen worked well for Westerners, who were able, due to the power of their EU and American passports, to live in India *without* becoming Indians. For the local Tamil population, who have been integral to the construction and operation of Auroville, being anything but a Tamil remains mostly impossible, due to the limited power of their passports and their place in the global economic order. Even those Tamils who are French nationals in France are tied to a static identity that separates them from the French population.

Auroville stands on the edge of Pondicherry, just outside the minor borders of colonial and postcolonial rule that have run through and shaped this book. On the surface, Auroville claims to be a space where national cultures can be brought together, regardless of the politics that often keep cultures separate outside this specific space. Just eight kilometers away in Pondicherry, a city constructed by colonial interests and molded by imperial politics, French nationals of Indian origin, who today number over six thousand people, struggle to fit into two different nations, France and India, both of which view them as ghosts of the colonial past. Traveling between these two zones are thousands of Tamil laborers who support the tourist industries, bringing substantial revenue to Pondicherry and Auroville. The meeting of East and West, an idea born of colonial ideology, remains embedded in systems of global capitalism and neocolonialism, undermining the liberatory potential of postcolonial relationships rooted in decolonial ideas.

# Conclusion

*The Messiness of Colonialism*

Walking around the quiet streets of Pondicherry's ville blanche on a summer weekend in 2014, I encountered groups of French tourists, dressed in linen and loose cotton, impressively large cameras hanging around their necks. They walked up and down the beach promenade, settling finally at one of the many cafés that cater to them, sipping cappuccinos and checking their phones, posting photos and tagging them #FranceInde. I turned a corner onto Rue Dumas, bringing the brilliantly pink-hued Église de Notre Dame des Anges into sight. The imposing church, coated in pink plaster thick as frosting, was built in 1858 and is today in great shape, maintained by the French government. Just as I approached the building, a car bearing a French flag came speeding down the street, stopping abruptly in front of the church. An Indian driver and a white man in a dark suit, French consul-general Philippe Janvier-Kamiyama, sweating in the one-hundred-degree midday heat, got out of the government car. The driver handed Janvier-Kamiyama a large flower arrangement as the two approached a small gathering of dark-skinned men who were holding French flags and banners. The group now complete, they marched about two hundred feet around the corner toward a smaller building, the former site of the Église de Notre Dame, where a black banner bearing three crosses hung over the door. The men entered the building, where chairs were arranged in a semicircle facing a large portrait of a man that was surrounded by an impressive collection of flowers.

The procession and memorial service were for Gabriel David, the last surviving French-Indian veteran of World War II, who had recently passed away in Pondicherry at the age of ninety-four. David had served in the Free French Air Force during the war, and later in Indochina, as one of many colonial soldiers sent to defend France against the nationalist uprisings of another colony. David had spent part of his youth in Indochina, where his father, also serving in the French military, was stationed. TamilExpress, a French-language website that shares Tamil news, posted David's obituary, noting that "a page of Franco-Pondicherian history has turned."[1] François Richier, the French ambassador in India, issued a statement that David had made "the courageous choice of fighting for a Free France while she was under Occupation," and that "his life was the epitome of commitment to serving France." The ambassador concluded his condolences by observing that David was "a figure of deep attachment to Indo-French friendship."[2] While David chose to live in Pondicherry over Paris, all his children settled in France, and his body had been sent to be interred at Combs-la-ville, a southeastern suburb of Paris.[3] After spending close to ten years studying the history of Pondicherry and thinking about the ways that people construct, experience, and normalize nationally branded spaces, watching this procession brought to life for me the extreme geographic distance between Pondicherry and France, while simultaneously showing me how the people of French India have managed to navigate these vast divides.

Pondicherry is today, in many ways, alive in a way that it wasn't during the time of direct French rule: the streets of the ville blanche (recently renamed "Heritage Town") remain relatively quiet, while the other 95 percent of Pondicherry explodes with activity. Anna Nagar, the neighborhood I lived in briefly during the summer of David's funeral, is located deep in the "Tamil section"—not really a section at all, but, rather, the majority of the city. About four kilometers from the ville blanche, it was populated with Tamil households, seemingly oblivious to the tourist magnet just beyond their neighborhood. People in Anna Nagar largely spent their days nearby their homes, where it is easy to find fruit and vegetable vendors, tailors, bike repair shops, barbershops, tea stalls, movie houses, and corner temples without the tourists that raise prices and cater to French- and English-speaking desires. Over the first decades of the twenty-first century, there have been more French people coming to Pondicherry to open shops, restaurants, and hotels, and many Europeans and North Americans visit and sometimes settle in Pondicherry or Auroville. While the Ashram, Auroville, and the ville blanche of Pondicherry are undeniably "global" sites, all three spaces remain racially, linguistically, spatially, and economically segregated from the surrounding areas. These lingering borders, which can be seen in both physical and cultural forms, are very effective for the promotion of global capital that enters Pondicherry through tourist money, keeping the laborers who work in the tourist industry as well as in Auroville segregated from consumers. Globalization, in terms of the free trade and free movement of people with capital that was widely celebrated in the 1990s, thrives in this part of former French India today.

At a conference held at Auroville in 2012 commemorating the fifty years since the 1962 Treaty of Cession between France and India, the Aurovilian and writer Claude Arpi welcomed the participants to the colloquium by noting that the French ambassador in India had said to him before his talk, "You should not use the word 'French colonisation.' You should say 'French presence.'" Arpi agreed with the ambassador's suggestion, stating that over the course of the two-day conference, it would become evident that the French territories in India were "rather a mild presence, not a hard colonisation."[4] This is a common statement made in regard to Pondicherry, with people often commenting that the French had failed in colonizing any part of India, evidenced by the small number of people in the former French Indian territories who speak French today. However, against the harsh criticism that the French Republic has faced in the early twenty-first century in regard to the persistent violence engendered by French imperialism, former French India continues to be utilized to elicit good feeling about the great potential of global relationships forged from the colonial past.[5] This idea of a potential for positive colonial relationship proves incredibly useful for furthering the resurgently popular argument that, on the balance sheet of history, colonialism has emerged victorious. Without the age of empire, we would not have the age of globalization—so the argument goes. By exhibiting their friendship and their history of cooperation, India and France can showcase their ability to be simultaneously global and nationalist.

Decolonization as an act of friendship between states exists in direct tension with decolonization as a violent event.[6] The aspiration to decolonize under peaceful and friendly conditions was the desire of nationalist states that planned to participate in the global world system created through imperial expansion and colonial occupation. Today, India continues to operate under the system of law—including several legal codes, such as the sedition laws discussed earlier in this book—brought into existence by the British colonial government. The violence inherent in structures institutionalized by colonizing states does not disappear with the formal withdrawal of the imperial power. The space/time of decolonization as a historic event, then, is a convenient marker for the state's promotion of nationalist unity in the interest of creating an Indian nationalist selfhood, but it does not capture the ways that colonialism continued, and continues, to shape the daily lives of the colonized. Fanon wrote that the colonial world is a world compartmentalized by the colonizer in order to exercise control over the colonized.[7] In French India, the continued presence of those controls persists in the segregation of ville blanche and ville noire, in the winding borders that separated British India from French India. In Auroville, we see compartmentalization in the form of private beaches and other markers that separate Tamil villages from Auroville, and in the pavilions that celebrate national cultures. These separations and segregations that continue to thrive in this supposedly postcolonial space mark the ongoing time of colonialism. The violence that Fanon spoke of as a necessary condition of decolonization was not only physical but also epistemological and ontological. A violent break was the only way, he argued, to abolish the colonial world.

## Toward a Decolonial History

History, as a discipline, contributes to the periodization of decolonization. Establishing timelines and utilizing categories to analyze historical events, actors, and documents is the foundation of historical scholarship, which relies on the researcher's ability to find primary sources and place them in context in a way that makes the past come alive in the present. The discipline and the methods of historical scholarship are products of colonial epistemologies.[8] Decolonization—not as an event, but as a movement, an ongoing struggle for liberation—looks very different than what diplomats and politicians proposed in the 1950s, 1960s, and 1970s, the time when many colonies in Asia and Africa liberated themselves from direct rule by colonial states.[9] By questioning the space/time of decolonization, this book shows the messiness of colonialism and consequently argues that in order to do decolonial history—history that seeks to detach from colonial categories and institutions—it is necessary to dig deep into the mess. The messiness of French India not only questions the accepted argument that colonialism ended with the withdrawal of the French government; it also shifts the process of understanding the making of a national subject away from the nation into the space/time of multiple migrations that transcend national categories. Categories are real in that they are created and employed by states and institutions that desire power over the people and things that are subject to categorization. Thus, historians do need to understand and use categories—a point articulated by many postcolonial historians. However, the use of categories is only useful up to a point, once one recognizes that the unruly mess of history is actually bursting the seams of categorical boxes.

Allowing for messiness as a decolonial method accepts that it is untenable to understand individuals as representations of national selves.[10] It means accepting that questions may not always have answers, or that those answers might not be available in "traditional" forms of historical research (in archives, in documents). It means seeing beyond the colonial binary of success and failure, of colonized and decolonized, because the writing of decolonial histories is still shaping the future.[11] Many of the people discussed in this book exemplify this messiness, since they went through their lives constantly crossing borders, changing passports, and fighting for and against the same national cause—as when flipping from pro-French Union to pro-Indian merger, for example. While people in power often saw the "flip" of a person (as seen in Dadala, Goubert, or Subbiah) against a national interest to be a sign of betrayal, the people of French India were always on the outskirts and margins of national interests. To expect that they would have a strong sense of a national self was more of a hope than a reality, a hope rooted in the interests of creating an "imagined community" of national subjects.[12] While many might read this book as a tale of the failure or tragedy of the people of French India, I invite readers to consider the continued existence of French-Indians, in India, in France, and in the global diaspora, as a success story of how a colonized people have been able to push on racial-ethnic-linguistic definitions of what constitutes a national subject both under colonialism and into the present day.

Every now and then, there is a flurry of news stories and sociological work around the notion that there is a "little India in France," mostly centered around the tenth arrondissement of Paris, home to the most dense concentration in Paris of South Asian restaurants and shops of former Pondichérians, but also a much larger Sri Lankan Tamil community.[13] In fact, the growing visibility of the Tamil population in Paris (the Tamils, who originate from the south of India, are the largest South Asian ethnic group in France) is largely due to the migration of the Sri Lankan Tamils displaced by civil war, leaving the Pondichérians, or the French nationals of Indian origin, in the minority. The presence of the Sri Lankan Tamil immigrant community in France has, in some ways, brought the Pondichérian population in France closer together.[14] L'Association les Comptoirs des Indes, the association dedicated to "conserving the history of *l'Inde française*" and bringing together former residents of the colonies, is one example of a space in metropolitan France where the memory of French India is allowed to flourish, and for the *trait-d'union,* or link, between France and India to be remembered and reproduced.[15] Acknowledging the space of the hyphen, of the in-between, has been important to the preservation of the communities and identities formed in geographic spaces that no longer exist.

Decolonial history likewise asks its authors to acknowledge their own position vis-á-vis their research, acknowledging institutional privileges alongside the conditions that led to their writing, in hopes that this will situate their scholarship in a world beyond the academy and yet linked to it. I came to this research through the study of European history, although my own family history guided me toward work in South Asia. My father, Srinivasan Namakkal, was born in Hyderabad, a Princely State, in 1946, a year before independence. My family is Tamil, though my grandfather had moved to Hyderabad to attend Nizam College and then was hired by a private British company (British Insulated Callender's Cables) and stayed there for many years before returning to Madras. My mother, Carol Sarraillon, was born in Omaha, Nebraska, to second-generation immigrants—her father's side from France. I was born in St. Paul, Minnesota, on occupied Dakota land, the daughter of a Tamil Indian immigrant and a former Catholic-nun white American woman.[16] My Indian family is Tamil and Brahmin, a designation that carries an immense amount of caste privilege in South Asia and throughout the diaspora. Although my own father's education and ability to migrate to the United States was predicated on his caste privilege, because of my biracial parents and geographic distance both from India and from desi communities, my personal relationship to Indian selfhood has always been very marginal, much like the subjects of this book. I share this as part of my work toward writing decolonial history to show how messy identity can be and also to acknowledge the work I am still doing to identify and fight against caste oppression and settler colonialism, through historical scholarship as well as political work beyond the academy.[17]

Just weeks after I arrived in Paris to begin my research on questions of postcolonial identity in France in 2009, the Ministère de l'Immigration, de l'intégration, de l'identité nationale et du développement solidaire, a commission led by former Socialist Party leader Eric Besson, launched a government-funded website on the question of national identity. Although the website has been disabled since 2010, the banner on top of the site read "Grand débat sur l'identité nationale" (The great debate on national identity) and was flanked by the motto of the Republic on the right ("Liberté, Fraternité, Égalité") and the official mark of the French Republic on the left.[18] The question under discussion is "Qu'est-ce qu'être français aujourd'hui?" (What does it mean to be French today?)[19] The site featured testimonies from a variety of people, public officials as well as anonymous citizens, voicing their opinion on the meaning of "French identity." There were statements from the Ministry of Immigration, as well as videos of talks by public intellectuals and a section for reader comments. A series of debates was also organized throughout France to bring the question to a public forum. The launch of this campaign on the question of identity was largely a response to the increasing tensions between Maghrebi communities in France and the "French French," a tension that has been marked by numerous riots throughout the banlieues of major cities, police violence against racialized youth, and debates about the compatibility (or, as many see it, the *incompatibility*) of the practice of Islam with French *laïcité* (commonly translated as "secularism"), marked by the passing of a law in 2010 that outlaws the wearing of burqas (full face veils) in France.[20]

The political urgency of inclusion in mainstream French society is clear for the millions of second- and third- generation French citizens whose ancestors came to France from the colonies, territories, and possessions. The relationships created through hundreds of years of colonization between imperial nation and colonized subject defined and propelled prominent migrations in the space/time of postcolonialism. For example, it seems somewhat obvious to discuss the migrations of South Asians to the United Kingdom after 1947, as well as the migrations of Algerians into France after 1962. The large waves of immigration that followed the end of empire in the case of both France and England were often accompanied by debates about national identity and citizenship, about the right to access the welfare state and about the state's postcolonial obligations to former subjects. However, even as the smaller groups of postcolonial migrants have been overlooked, the minor histories of empire had a significant amount of influence on the system as a whole. The pages of this book are meant as a disruption of ideas, spaces, and temporalities—of the commonly told narratives of colonial and postcolonial history, shedding light on uncommon relationships that also disrupt postcolonial nationalist reliance on the boundedness of race and nation. I offer this disruption in an effort to further the larger project of decolonizing history.

# Appendix

Treaty Establishing De Jure Cession of French Establishments in India

28 May 1956

**TREATY BETWEEN THE REPUBLIC OF FRANCE AND INDIA ESTABLISHING CESSION BY THE FRENCH REPUBLIC TO THE INDIAN UNION OF THE FRENCH ESTABLISHMENTS IN INDIA**

**New Delhi**

Preamble

The President of the French Republic and the President of the Indian Union

CONSIDERING that their Governments, faithful to the common declaration made in 1947 and desirous of strengthening the bonds of friendship, established since then between France and India, have manifested their intention of settling amicably the problem of the French Establishments in India;

CONSIDERING that after the wish of these populations had been expressed by their representatives an agreement was concluded on 21 October 1954, transferring the powers of the Government of the French Republic to the Government of Indian Union;

HAVE DECIDED to conclude a treaty establishing the cession by the French Republic to the Indian Union of the French Establishments of Pondicherry,

Karikal, Mahe and Yanam and to settle the problems stemming therefrom and have designated thereto as their plenipotentiaries

THE PRESIDENT OF THE FRENCH REPUBLIC

H. E. MR. STANISLAS OSTROROG,

Ambassador Extraordinary and Plenipotentiary of France in India.

THE PRESIDENT OF INDIA:

JAWAHARLAL NEHRU, Minister for External Affairs

who, after exchanging their credentials, which having been found in legal form have agreed as follows:

## Article 1

France cedes to India in full sovereignty the territory of the Establishments of Pondicherry, Karikal, Mahe, and Yanam.

## Article 2

The Establishments will keep the benefit of the special administrative status which was in force prior to 1 November 1954. Any constitutional changes in this status that may be made subsequently shall be made after ascertaining the wishes of the people.

## Article 3

The Government of India shall succeed to the rights and obligations resulting from such acts of the French administrations as are binding on these Establishments.

## Article 4

French Nationals born in the territory of the Establishments and domiciled therein at the date of the entry into force of the Treaty of Cession shall become nationals and citizens of the Indian Union, with the exceptions enumerated under Article 5 hereafter.

## Article 5

The persons referred to in the previous article may, by means of a written declaration drawn up within six months of the entry into force of the Treaty of Cession, choose to retain their nationality. Persons availing themselves of this right shall be deemed never to have acquired Indian nationality. The declaration of the father or, if the latter be deceased, of the mother, and in the event of the decease of both parents, of the legal guardian shall determine the nationality of unmarried children of under eighteen years of age. Such children shall be mentioned in the aforesaid declaration. But married male children of over sixteen years of age shall be entitled to make this choice themselves. Persons having retained French nationality by reason of a decision of their parents, as indicated in the previous paragraph, may make a personal choice with the object of acquiring Indian nationality by means of a declaration signed in the presence of the competent Indian authorities, within six months of attaining their eighteenth birthday. The said choice shall come into force as from the date of signature of the declaration.

The choice of a husband shall not affect the nationality of the spouse. The declarations referred to in the first and second paragraphs of this Article shall be drawn up in two copies, the one in French, the other in English, which shall be transmitted to the competent French authorities. The latter shall immediately transmit to the competent Indian authorities the English copy of the aforesaid declaration.

## Article 6

French nationals born in the territory of the Establishments and domiciled in the territory of the Indian Union on the date of the entry into force of the Treaty of Cession shall become nationals and citizens of the Indian Union. Notwithstanding they and their children shall be entitled to choose as indicated in Article 5 above. They shall make this choice under the conditions and in the manner prescribed in the aforesaid Article.

## Article 7

French nationals born in the territory of the Establishments and domiciled in a country other than the territory of the Indian Union or the territory of the said Establishments on the date of entry into force of the Treaty of Cession shall retain their French nationality, with the exceptions enumerated in Article 8 hereafter.

## Article 8

The persons referred to in the previous Article may, by means of a written declaration signed in the presence of the competent Indian authorities within six months of the entry into force of the Treaty of Cession, choose to acquire Indian nationality. Persons availing themselves of this right shall be deemed to have lost French nationality as from the date of the entry into force of the Treaty of Cession. The declaration of the father, or if the latter be deceased, of the mother, and in the event of the decease of both parents, of the legal guardian shall determine the nationality of unmarried children of under eighteen years of age. Such children shall be mentioned in the aforesaid declaration. But married male children of over sixteen years of age shall be entitled to make this choice themselves. Persons having acquired Indian nationality by reason of a decision of their parents, as indicated in the previous paragraph, may make a personal choice with the object of recovering French nationality by means of a declaration signed in the presence of the competent French authorities within six months of attaining their eighteenth birthday. The said choice shall come into force as from the date of signature of the declaration. The choice of a husband shall not affect the nationality of the spouse. The declarations referred to in the first and second paragraphs of this Article shall be drawn up in two copies, the one in French, the other in English and shall be signed in the presence of the competent Indian authorities who shall immediately transmit to the competent French authorities the French copy of the aforesaid declaration.

## Article 9

With effect from 1 November 1954, the Government of India shall take in their service all the civil servants and employees of the Establishments, other than those belonging to the metropolitan cadre or to the general cadre of the France d'Outre-Ministry. These civil servants and employees including the members of the public forces shall be entitled to receive from the Government of India the same conditions of services, as respects remuneration, leave, and pension and the same right as respects disciplinary matter or the tenure of their posts, or similar rights as changed circumstances may permit, as they were entitled to immediately before 1 November 1954. They shall not be dismissed or their prospects shall not be damaged on account of any action done in the course of duty prior to 1 November 1954. French civil servants, magistrates and military personnel born in the Establishments or keeping their family links shall be permitted to return freely to the Establishments on leave or on retirement.

## Article 10

The Government of France shall assume responsibility for payment of such pensions as are supported by the Metropolitan Budget, even if the beneficiaries have acquired Indian nationality under Articles 4 to 7 above. The Government of India shall assume responsibility for the payment of pensions, allowances and grants supported by the local budget. The system of pension of the various local Retirement Funds shall continue to be in force.

## Article 11

The Government of India shall take the necessary steps to ensure that persons domiciled in the Establishments on 1 November 1954, and at present practicing a learned profession therein shall be permitted to carry on their profession in these Establishments without being required to secure additional qualification, diplomas, or permits or to comply with any new formalities.

## Article 12

The administration's charitable institutions and loans offices shall continue to operate under their present status, and shall not be modified in the future without ascertaining the wishes of the people. The present facilities granted to the private charitable institutions shall be maintained and shall be modified only after ascertaining the wishes of the people.

## Article 13

Properties pertaining to worship or in use for cultural purposes shall be in the ownership of the missions or of the institutions entrusted by the French regulations at present in force with the management of those properties. The Government of India agree to recognise as legal corporate bodies, with all due rights attached to such a qualification, the "Counseils de fabrique," and the administration boards of the missions.

## Article 14

Legal proceedings instituted prior to 1 November 1954, shall be judged in conformity with the basic legislation and procedure in force at that time in the Establishments. To this end, and up to final settlement of such proceedings, the existing courts in the Establishments shall continue to function. Officers of the court shall be law graduates, habitually domiciled in the Establishments, honorably known and selected in accordance with the French regulations governing the designation of temporary judicial officers. The interested parties shall be entitled, if they so decide by common agreement, to transfer to the competent Indian Courts, the said proceedings as well as proceedings that, though already open, are not yet entered with the Registrars of the French Courts, and also proceedings that constitute an ordinary or extraordinary appeal. Judgements, decrees and orders passed by the French Courts, prior to 1 November 1954, which are final or may become so by expiration of the delays of appeal, shall be executed by the competent Indian authorities. Judgments, decrees, and orders passed after 1 November 1954, in conformity with the first paragraph of the present Article shall be executed by the competent Indian authorities, irrespective of the courts which exercised the jurisdiction. Acts or deeds constitutive of rights established prior to 1 November 1954, in conformity with French Law, shall retain the value and validity conferred at that time by the same law. The records of the French Courts shall be preserved in accordance with the rules applicable to them on the date of cession, and communication of their contents shall be given to the duly accredited representatives of the French Government whenever they apply for such communication.

## Article 15

The records of the Registrars' offices up to the date of cession shall be preserved in accordance with the rules applicable to them on that date and copies or extracts of the preceedings shall be issued to the parties or the authorities concerned. The personal judicial records of the Courts Registries up to the date of cession shall be preserved in accordance with the rules applicable to them on that date and copies or extracts of these records shall be issued on request to the French authorities and likewise to the persons concerned in accordance with the legislation in force prior to 1 November 1954. The said requests on the part of the French authorities and likewise the copies addressed to them shall be drawn up in the French language and shall entail no reimbursement of costs. The French and Indian authorities shall mutually inform each other of penal sentences involving registration in the record of convictions of their own territory and pronounced either by French judicatures or by judicatures sitting in territories ceded to India concerning nationals of the other country born in the aforesaid territories.

Such information shall be sent free of charge through diplomatic channels, either in French or together with a translation into French.

## Article 16

The provisions of Article 14 of this treaty shall apply to proceedings that the "Counseil du Contentieux Administratif" is competent to deal with. Temporary magistrates and local civil servants selected in accordance with the principles of the second paragraph of the said Article 14 shall compose this body.

Article 17

Nationals of France and of the French Union, domiciled in the French Establishments on 1 November 1954 shall, subject to the laws and regulations in force for the time being in the Establishments, enjoy in these Establishments the same freedom of residence, movement and trade as the other inhabitants of the Establishments.

Article 18

All persons of French nationality acquired under Articles 4 to 8 or in any other manner and all French corporate bodies shall be permitted to repatriate freely their capital and properties over a period of ten years from 1 November 1954.

Article 19

The Government of India takes the place of the territory, with effect from 1 November 1954, in respect of all credits, debts, and deficits in the care of the local administration. Therefore, the Government of India shall immediately reimburse to the French Government the amount of Treasury loans and various funds placed by the latter at the disposal of the territory, as well as advances made by the Caisse Central de La France d'Outre-Mer, with the exception of sums remitted as grants. In addition the Government of India shall pay the indemnity agreed upon by the two Governments for the purchase of the Pondicherry power station. Simultaneously, the French Government shall reimburse to the Indian Government the equivalent value at par in pound Sterling or in Indian Rupees of the currency withdrawn from circulation from the Establishments before 1 November 1955.

Article 20

The Indian Government agree to the continuation of the French institutions of a scientific or cultural character in existence on 1 November 1954 and by agreement between the two Governments to the granting of facilities for the opening of establishments of the same character.

## Article 21

The College Français de Pondicherry shall be maintained in its present premises as a French educational establishment of the second degree with full rights. The French Government should assume the charge of its functionment as well in respect of the selection and salaries of the staff necessary for management, teaching, and discipline as in respect of the organization of studies, syllabi, and examinations and the charge of its maintenance. The premises shall be the property of the French Government.

## Article 22

Private educational institutions in existence on 1 November 1954 in French Establishments shall be allowed to continue and shall be permitted to preserve the possibility of imparting French education. They shall continue to receive from the local authorities subsidies and other facilities at least equal to those which were being granted on 1 November 1954. They will be permitted to receive without obstruction the aid which the French Government in agreement with the Government of India may desire to give them.

## Article 23

The French Government or French-recognized private organizations shall be allowed to maintain and to create by agreement between the two Governments in the former French Establishments in India establishments or institutions devoted either to higher studies leading to diplomas of French language, culture, and civilization or to scientific research or to the spreading of French culture in the Sciences, Arts, or Fine Arts. The Indian Government shall grant every possible facility, subject to their laws and regulations in force, for entry into and residence in India to members of French

Universities sent by the French Government for a study visit or a teaching mission to India.

## Article 24

The French Institute of Pondicherry, set up by an understanding reached between the two Governments since the 21 October 1954 Agreement and inaugurated on 21 March 1955 shall be maintained as a research and advanced educational establishment. The Indian Government shall provide such suitable facilities to further the development of the activities of the said institute, as agreed upon between the two Governments from time to time.

## Article 25

Equivalences of French diplomas and degrees awarded to persons belonging to the French Establishments—namely, "Baccalaureat," "brevet elementaire," "brevet d'etudes du premier cycle," with diplomas and degrees awarded by Indian Universities—will be accepted by the Indian Government for admission to higher studies and administrative careers. These equivalences will be fixed according to the recommendations of the Joint Educational Committee, nominated by the two Governments in accordance with the agreement of 21 October 1954. This shall apply equally to degrees in law and medicine awarded in the Establishments. Degrees of a purely local character shall be recognized under usual conditions.

## Article 26

The French Government cedes to the Government of India all properties owned by the local administration of the Establishments with the exception of such property as enumerated in Article 8 of the Annexed Protocol. Properties that are at present in possession of all religious authorities shall be retained by them and the Government of India agree, whenever necessary, to convey the titles to them.

## Article 27

The French Government shall keep in their custody the records having an historical interest; the Government of India shall keep in their custody the records required for the administration of the territory. Each Government shall place at the disposal of the other lists of records in its possession and copies of such records as are of interest to the other.

## Article 28

The French language shall remain the official language of the Establishments so long as the elected representatives of the people shall not decide otherwise. All questions pending at the time of the ratification of the Treaty of Cession shall be examined and settled by a French Indian Commission composed of three representatives of the French Government and three representatives of the Indian Government.

## Article 30

Any disagreement in respect of the application or interpretation of the present treaty that cannot be resolved through diplomatic negotiation or arbitration shall be placed before the International Court of Justice at the request of one or other of the High Contracting Parties.

## Article 31

The French and English texts of the present treaty shall be equally authentic. The present treaty shall be entered into force on the day of its ratification by the two Governments concerned. The exchange of instruments of ratification shall take place at New Delhi.

The present treaty shall be deposited in the archives of the Government of India, which shall transmit an attested copy to the Government of the French Republic.

JAWAHARLAL NEHRU

Prime Minister and Ambassador Extraordinary and Minister for External Affairs.

S. OSTROROG

Plenipotentiary of France in India.

PROTOCOL

Article 1

As regards the communes of Nettapacom and Tirubuvane, which are part of the Establishments of Pondicherry, and as regards the Establishments of Yanam and Mahe, the French Government shall not be responsible, particularly in respect of Articles 3, 9, and 14 of the treaty, for any acts done in these communes and Establishments with effect from the date shown against each: for Nettapacom on 31 March 1954; for Trubuvane on 6 April 1954; for Yanam on 13 June 1954; and Mahe on 16 July 1954.

Article 2

The sets of courses of studies at present in force shall be maintained during the appropriate transitional period in a sufficient number of educational institutions so as to ensure to the people concerned a possibility of option for the future. Transitory periods shall be provided for in every course of studies.

Article 3

All pupils and students now engaged in a course of studies are given the assurance that they will be enabled to complete their studies in French according to the curricula and methods in force on 1 November 1954. They shall continue to enjoy the facilities that they enjoyed on that date, especially regarding free education and scholarships granted by local authorities, whether these scholarships be valid in the Establishments or in France.

## Article 4

Regarding the organization of the examinations of the College Français and the French Institute, facilities shall be given to the representatives of the French Government concerning visas and sojourn as well as practical dispositions to be taken for holding the examinations. The French Government retains the authority to select and appoint examination boards.

## Article 5

Scholarships for the completion of studies leading to the Licence en Droit and Doctore en Medicine when begun before 1 November 1954 shall be granted on request to the students of the former Law College and of the former Medical College. If they so prefer, medical students shall have the possibility to be admitted into Indian medical colleges for completion of their studies, after being given due credits for their previous medical studies.

## Article 6

The Government of India will reimburse to the personnel of education and cultural establishments whose salaries are paid by the French Government, an amount equal to the Indian income tax paid by them unless it is covered by Double Income Tax Avoidance Agreement between India and France.

## Article 7

If French books, publications, and periodicals, as well as educational and teaching equipment and other cultural material intended for use in French Institute and College Francais, are subject to import duty or other taxes, an amount equivalent to the sum so paid shall be reimbursed by the Government of India to the institutions concerned.

## Article 8

The Government of India recognize as being in the ownership of the French Government the following properties: (1) property located in rue de la Marine (for the installation of the French Consulate); (2) properties located on the rue Victor Simonel that are occupied by the College Francais de Pondicherry; (3) the War Memorial; (4) Property No. 13, located at Karikal so called Maison Lazare (for the installation of a branch of the French Consulate); and (5) property located on the rue Saint-Louis (for the Institute).

## Article 9

No one shall be prosecuted on account of political offences committed prior to 1 November 1954 and against whom no prosecution has been instituted on the said date.

# Notes

## Introduction

1. I have chosen to hyphenate the compound identity of French-Indian throughout the book because of the significance of the hyphen (in French, *trait d'union*) as a productive space of in-between among French-Indians.
2. Beginning in the late seventeenth century, the area known today as Puducherry/Pondicherry/Pondichéry was primarily governed and ruled over by France (with brief moments of departure in the eighteenth and nineteenth centuries as French and British interests fought for control of South Asian territories, ports, and resources). Although France had agreed to cede the territories to India in 1954, France did not ratify the agreement until the signing of the Evian Accords in 1962. See chronology for relevant dates of French engagement in South Asia.
3. *Cinq colonnes à la une*, "Les trois mondes de Pondichéry," Office national de radiodiffusion television française, aired on 4 September 1964, on Channel 1.
4. Historian Jyoti Mohan has argued that popular global images of India as chaotic, poor, and undeveloped stem from French Indology of the nineteenth century. See Jyoti Mohan, *Claiming India: French Scholars and the Preoccupation with India in the Nineteenth Century* (Delhi: SAGE/Yoda, 2018).
5. The Ashram was established in 1926 under the direction of Sri Aurobindo Ghose and Mira Alfassa. Sri Aurobindo passed away in 1950, fourteen years prior to the making of this documentary.

6. Blanche Rachel Mira Alfassa was born in Paris in 1878. She was of Sephardic Jewish heritage, though Alfassa considered herself nonreligious. Her father, Moïse Maurice Alfassa, came from the Jewish community in Constantinople, and her mother, Mathilde Ismalun, from Egypt. The family moved to Paris a year before Mira was born. Peter Heehs, *The Lives of Sri Aurobindo* (New York: Columbia University Press, 2008), 445.
7. For more on the place of the Ashram in Pondicherry, see Andrew Davies, *Geographies of Anticolonialism: Political Networks Across and Beyond South Asia, c. 1900–1930* (Oxford: Royal Geographical Society/Wiley, 2020).
8. According to various collected letters and remembrances of the Mother and Aurobindo, the Mother first had the idea of creating a universal city in 1930, though at the time she was thinking about building it on a hill near Hyderabad. *The Auroville Experience: Selections from 202 Issues of Auroville Today, November 1988–November 2005* (Tamil Nadu: Auroville Today, 2006), 6–7.
9. Julie Medlock, "Auroville Takes Shape: An Experiment in Human Unity," *Sunday Standard Magazine*, 28 June 1970, n.p.
10. The founders of Auroville worked very diligently to get UNESCO to recognize Auroville before they laid the first stone, which resulted in UNESCO passing a series of resolutions in 1966, two years prior to Auroville's founding ceremony in 1968. See *UNESCO Resolutions on Auroville* (Paris: UNESCO, 1966).
11. The term "settler utopianism" has been invoked before to signal the tradition of settlement in search of utopia. See Karl Hardy, "Unsettling Hope: Contemporary Indigenous Politics, Settler-Colonialism, and Utopianism," *Spaces of Utopia: An Electronic Journal* 2, no. 1 (2012): 123–36. The sociologist Krishnan Kumar has also written about utopianism being a Western project linked to Christian societies. See Kumar, *Utopia and Anti-Utopia in Modern Times* (Oxford: Basil Blackwell, 1987); and *Utopianism* (Minneapolis: University of Minnesota Press, 1991).
12. *Follow This*, season 3, episode 5, "India's Utopia," directed by Rega Jha, aired on November 1, 2018, on Netflix.
13. On the dominance of British history in global understanding of the history of empire as well as the discipline of history itself, see Priya Satia, *Time's Monster: How History Makes History* (Cambridge, MA: Harvard University Press, 2020). Important recent work on the history of French India and the relationship between France and India includes Danna Agmon, *A Colonial Affair: Commerce, Conversion, and Scandal in French India* (Ithaca, NY: Cornell University Press, 2017); Kate Marsh, *Fictions of 1947: Representations of Indian Decolonization, 1919–1962* (Bern: Peter Lang, 2007); Blake Smith, "Myths of Stasis: South Asia, Global Commerce, and Economic Orientalism in Late Eighteenth-Century France" (PhD diss., Northwestern University, 2017); Jyoti Mohan,

*Claiming India: French Scholars and the Preoccupation with India in the Nineteenth Century* (Delhi: SAGE/Yoda, 2018); and Akhila Yechury, "Imagining India, Decolonizing l'Inde Française, c. 1947–1954," *Historical Journal* 58, no. 4 (2015): 1141–65.

14. "Colonial memory" is a term formulated by historians Nicolas Bancel and Pascal Blanchard. Although the pair have written extensively on this concept, I draw here on "The Pitfalls of Colonial Memory," in *The Colonial Legacy in France: Fracture, Rupture, and Apartheid*, ed. Nicolas Bancel, Pascal Blanchard, and Dominic Thomas, trans. Alexis Pernsteiner (Bloomington: Indiana University Press, 2017), 153–64, 154.

15. For example, the 2001 novel *Life of Pi* by French Canadian author Yann Martel is set in Pondicherry. The novel won the 2002 Man Booker Prize and was adapted into a 2012 film directed by Ang Lee that won four Academy Awards, including Best Director. The novel and film were both extremely popular and brought new attention to Pondicherry as a quaint, idyllic, sleepy French colony in the south of India.

16. Sumathi Ramaswamy, *Passions of the Tongue: Language Devotion in Tamil India, 1891–1970* (Berkeley: University of California Press, 1997).

17. See, for example, Decolonize This Place (DTP), which describes itself as "an action-oriented movement and decolonial formation based in New York City and beyond. DTP consists of over 30 collaborators . . . that seek to resist, unsettle, and reclaim the city. The groups claim solidarity with Indigenous insurgence, black liberation, free Palestine, free Puerto Rico, the struggles of workers and debtors, de-gentrification, migrant justice, dismantling patriarchy, and more." https://decolonizethisplace.org/faxxx-1 (accessed November 25, 2020).

18. For more on these recent movements, see Rhodes Must Fall Oxford Movement, *Rhodes Must Fall: The Struggle to Decolonise the Racist Heart of Empire*, ed. Roseanne Chantiluke, Brian Kwoba, and Athinangamso Nkopo (London: Zed, 2018); and Gurminder K. Bhambra, Kerem Nisancioglu, Dalia Gebrial, eds., *Decolonising the University* (London: Pluto, 2018).

19. Gary Okihiro, *Third World Studies: Theorizing Liberation* (Durham, NC: Duke University Press, 2016).

20. Issac A. Kamola, *Making the World Global: U.S. Universities and the Production of the Global Imaginary* (Durham, NC: Duke University Press, 2019).

21. Nick Estes, *Our History Is the Future: Standing Rock Versus the Dakota Access Pipeline, and the Long Tradition of Indigenous Resistance* (New York: Verso, 2019).

22. Aníbal Quijano, "Coloniality and Modernity/Rationality," *Cultural Studies* 21, no. 2 (2007): 168–78; María Lugones, "Heterosexualism and the Colonial/Modern Gender System," *Hypatia* 22, no. 1 (2007): 186–209; Walter Mignolo, *The Darker Side of Western Modernity: Global Futures, Decolonial Options* (Durham, NC: Duke University Press, 2011).

23. K. Wayne Yang and Eve Tuck, "Decolonization Is Not a Metaphor," *Decolonization: Indigeneity, Education & Society* 1, no. 1 (2012): 1.
24. Jean-Jacques Hemardinquer, "Décolonisation," *Le Monde*, 1 December 1972, n.p. On the etymology and the intellectual history of the word "decolonization," see Stuart Ward, "The European Provenance of Decolonization," *Past & Present* 230, no. 1 (2016): 227–60.
25. Frantz Fanon, *The Wretched of the Earth* (New York: Grove, [1961] 2007).
26. Adom Getachew, *Worldmaking After Empire: The Rise and Fall of Self-Determination* (Princeton, NJ: Princeton University Press, 2019).
27. Michel Foucault, "Of Other Spaces: Utopias and Heterotopias," *Architecture/Mouvement/Continuité* 5 (1984): 46–49, trans. Jay Miskowiec in *Diacritics* 16 (1986): 22–27.
28. Patrick Wolfe, "Settler Colonialism and the Elimination of the Native," *Journal of Genocide Research* 8, no. 4 (2006): 388.
29. Sir Thomas More, *Utopia* (Cambridge: Cambridge University Press, [1516] 1989), xi.
30. On the failures of twentieth-century utopian projects, see Samuel Moyn, *The Last Utopia: Human Rights in History* (Cambridge, MA: Harvard University Press, 2012).
31. Osama W. Abi-Mershed, *Apostles of Modernity: Saint-Simonians and the Civilizing Mission in Algeria* (Stanford, CA: Stanford University Press, 2010), 8.
32. Lucy Sargisson, "Strange Places: Estrangement, Utopianism, and Intentional Communities," *Utopian Studies* 18, no. 3 (2007): 393–424, 393.
33. As Durba Ghosh has written for the case of British India, colonial institutions identified "who was a British subject and who was putatively an 'Indian' before a formal conception of India existed," and the same can be said of French Indian territory. See Ghosh, *Sex and the Family in Colonial India: The Making of Empire* (Cambridge: Cambridge University Press, 2006), 3.
34. Martineau was a founding member of the Société de l'histoire de l'Inde Française, as well as the Société française d'histoire d'Outre-Mer and the Académie des sciences coloniales, and as such contributed greatly to the body of scholarship and research on the history the French colonies in India.
35. Jacques Weber, *Les établissements français en Inde au XIXe siècle, 1816–1914* (Paris: La librairie d'Inde, 1988); Jacques Weber, *Pondichéry et les Comptoirs de l'Inde après Dupleix: La démocratie au pays des castes* (Paris: Denoël, 1996).
36. In addition to S. P. Sen, see Gauri Parasher, "State Building in a Transcultural Context: The Case of the French in India During the Early Eighteenth Century," *Transcultural Research: Heidelberg Studies on Asia and Europe in a Global Context* 3 (2012): 243–49; see also G. B. Malleson, *History of the French in India: From the Founding of Pondicherry in 1674 to the Capture of the Place in 1761* (London: W. H. Allen, 1893).

37. Parasher, "State Building," 245.
38. S. Chandni Bi, *Urban Centers of Pondicherry* (New Delhi: Icon, 2006), 150.
39. Bi, *Urban Centers*, 151.
40. Kévin Le Doudic, "Encounters Around the Material Object: French and Indian Consumers in Eighteenth-Century Pondicherry," in *The Global Lives of Things: The Material Culture of Connections in the Early Modern World*, ed. Anne Gerritsen and Giorgio Rielle (New York: Routledge, 2016), 162–80.
41. There are quite a few works on Dupleix, many written in the nineteenth century by Pondichérians. Some of the more well-known works include Alfred Martineau, *Dupleix et l'Inde Française, 1722--1754* (Paris: Champion, 1920); L. Luceney, *Dupleix, conquérant des Indes fabuleuses* (Paris: Zimmerman, 1946); and Léon Moreel, *Dupleix, marquis de fortune et conquérant des Indes, 1697–1763 (*Rosendaël: Editions le Port de Dunkerque, 1963).
42. For more on what the loss of India meant to the French, see the essays collected in Kate Marsh and Nicola Firth, eds., *France's Lost Empires: Fragmentation, Nostalgia, and la fracture coloniale* (Boulder, CO: Lexington, 2011).
43. Sailendra Nath Sen, *Chandernagore: From Bondage to Freedom, 1900–55* (Delhi: Primus, 2012), 1–2.
44. William F. S. Miles, *Imperial Burdens: Countercolonialism in Former French India* (Boulder, CO: Lynne Rienner, 1995): 3.
45. Sen, *Chandernagore*, 3.
46. Barbara Harlow, "Tipu Sultan: Oriental Despot or National Hero," in *Archives of Empire, Volume I: From the East India Company to the Suez Canal*, ed. Barbara Harlow and Mia Carter (Durham, NC: Duke University Press, 2003), 171–72.
47. Kate Marsh, *India in the French Imagination: Peripheral Voices, 1754–1815* (London: Pickering & Chatto, 2009), 32–34.
48. Miles, *Imperial Burdens*, 5.
49. Prasenjit Duara, "History and Globalization in China's Long Twentieth Century," *Modern China* 34, no. 1 (2008): 152–64, 156.
50. Adrian Carton, *Mixed-Race and Modernity in Colonial India: Changing Concepts of Hybridity Across Empires* (New York: Routledge, 2012), 62.
51. Ann Laura Stoler, "Sexual Affronts and Racial Frontiers: European Identities and the Cultural Politics of Exclusion in Colonial Southeast Asia," in *Tensions of Empire: Colonial Cultures in a Bourgeois World*, ed. Ann Laura Stoler and Frederick Cooper (Berkeley: University of California Press, 1997), 198–237.
52. Ajit K. Neogy, *Decolonization of French India: Liberation Movement and Indo-French Relations, 1947–1954* (Pondichéry: Institut Français de Pondichéry, 1997), 1–2.

53. Rajagopalan Radhakrishnan, *Diasporic Meditations: Between Home and Location* (Minneapolis: University of Minnesota Press, 1996), xiii.
54. For a critique of the nationalist approach to the history of the Indian nation-state, see Partha Chatterjee, *The Nation and Its Fragments: Colonial and Postcolonial Histories* (Princeton, NJ: Princeton University Press, 1993).
55. Todd Shepard, *The Invention of Decolonization: The Algerian War and the Remaking of France* (Ithaca, NY: Cornell University Press, 2006), 2.
56. Barbara N. Ramusack has shown that in the years leading up to independence (1930–1947), it was not a foregone conclusion that the Princely States would be integrated into independent India, though most had agreed to merge with India or Pakistan by 1948 (with the important exception of Jammu and Kashmir, which remains contested territory to this day). See Ramusack, *The Indian Prices and Their States* (Cambridge: Cambridge University Press, 2004), especially chapter 8, "Federation or Integration?"
57. Vazira Fazila-Yacoobali Zamindar, *The Long Partition and the Making of Modern South Asia: Refugees, Boundaries, Histories* (New York: Columbia University Press, 2010).
58. Jason Cons, *Sensitive Spaces: Fragmented Territory at the India-Bangladesh Border* (Seattle: University of Washington Press, 2016).
59. Radhika Mongia, *Indian Migration and Empire: Genealogy of the Modern State* (Durham, NC: Duke University Press, 2018), 127.
60. Todd Shepard discusses the move from "archiving the state" to "archiving the nation" in what he calls the "post-decolonization" era. See Shepard, "'Of Sovereignty': Disputed Archives, 'Wholly Modern' Archives, and the Post-Decolonization French and Algerian Republics, 1962–2012," *American Historical Review* 120, no. 3 (2015): 869–83.
61. Ann Laura Stoler, *Against the Archival Grain: Thinking Through Colonial Ontologies* (Princeton, NJ: Princeton University Press, 2009), 1. On the limits of the archive, see also Saidiya Hartman, *Wayward Lives, Beautiful Experiments: Intimate Histories of Social Upheaval* (New York: W. W. Norton, 2019); and Durba Mitra, *Indian Sex Life: Sexuality and the Colonial Origins of Modern Social Thought* (Princeton, NJ: Princeton University Press, 2020).
62. Mignolo, *Darker Side of Western Modernity*.
63. Stoler, "Against the Archival Grain," 7.
64. Cindi Katz, "Towards Minor Theory," *Environment and Planning D: Society and Space* 14 (1996): 487–99, 489.
65. Dipesh Chakrabarty, *Provincializing Europe: Postcolonial Thought and Historical Difference* (Princeton, NJ: Princeton University Press, 2001).
66. I draw here on the work of Nicholas Thoburn, especially his idea of a minor politics. See Thoburn, *Deleuze, Marx, and Politics* (London: Routledge, 2003), 7.
67. Katz, "Towards Minor Theory," 491.

68. "French Packing Vital Records," *Indian Express*, 7 June 1952, n.p.
69. Eric T. Jennings, *Vichy in the Tropics: Pétain's National Revolution in Madagascar, Guadeloupe, and Indochina, 1940–1944* (Stanford, CA: Stanford University Press, 2001), 1.
70. Partha Chatterjee, "Empires, Nations, Peoples: The Imperial Prerogative and Colonial Exceptions," *Thesis Eleven* 139, no. 1 (2017): 84–96, 93.
71. Shepard, *Invention of Decolonization*.
72. Zamindar, *Long Partition*, 2.
73. Two recent works that think through the politics of the French Union include Frederick Cooper, *Citizenship Between Empire and Nation: Remaking France and French Africa, 1945–1960* (Princeton, NJ: Princeton University Press, 2014); and Gary Wilder, *Freedom Time: Negritude, Decolonization, and the Future of the World* (Durham, NC: Duke University Press, 2015).
74. Gary Wilder, *The French Imperial Nation-State: Negritude and Colonial Humanism Between the Two World Wars* (Chicago: University of Chicago Press, 2005), 205.
75. Neogy, *Decolonization of French India*; Sen, *Chandernagore*; Miles, *Imperial*; A. Ramasamy, *A History of Pondicherry* (New Delhi: Sterling, 1987).
76. Zamindar, *Long Partition*.
77. Danna Agmon, *A Colonial Affair: Commerce, Conversion, and Scandal in French India* (Ithaca, NY: Cornell University Press, 2017).
78. Many historians working in the field of global history have moved to destabilize the importance of national borders in the framing of history, especially those histories focused on transnational movements, mobility, and anticolonial and anti-imperial activity. See, for example, Cemil Aydin, *The Politics of Anti-Westernism in Asia: Visions of World Order in Pan-Islamic and Pan-Asian Thought* (New York: Columbia University Press, 2007); Maia Ramnath, *Haj to Utopia: How the Ghadar Movement Charted Global Radicalism and Attempted to Overthrow the British Empire* (Berkeley: University of California Press, 2011); and Wilder, *French Imperial Nation-State*.

# 1. Carceral Borders

Epigraph: His Majesty's consul general in the French establishments to secretary to the governor of India in external affairs, Simla, 19 April 1937, L/PS/12/4454, India Office Records, British Library (IOR).

1. "French India: Reports on the General Situation," extract from official report between British India and Pondicherry with barbed wire, 14 February 1939, 851–52, L/PS/12/4456, IOR.

2. "French India: Reports on the General Situation."
3. "French India: Reports on the General Situation."
4. "French India: Reports on the General Situation."
5. "French India: Reports on the General Situation," July 1939, L/PS/12/4456, IOR.
6. "A Disquieting Balance Sheet," *Dessobagari*, February 11, 1939, L/PS/12/4456, IOR.
7. Article 11, Treaty of Paris, February 10, 1763, Avalon Project, Yale Law School, https://avalon.law.yale.edu/18th_century/paris763.asp (accessed November 11, 2020).
8. Article 12, Treaty of Paris, May 30, 1814, Napoleon Series, https://www.napoleon-series.org/research/government/diplomatic/c_paris1.html (accessed November 11, 2020). For more on the importance of these two treaties to France's imaging of India, see Ian H. Magedera, "Arrested Development: The Shape of 'French India' After the Treaties of Paris of 1763 and 1814," *Interventions: International Journal of Postcolonial Studies* 12, no. 3 (2010): 331–43.
9. Pondicherry rests on the Bay of Bengal, an important, nonterritorialized space of entry for some people who sought refuge in Pondicherry.
10. Stuart Elden, *Terror and Territory: The Spatial Extent of Sovereignty* (Minneapolis: University of Minnesota Press, 2009).
11. Willem van Schendel and Erik de Maaker, "Asian Borderlands: Introducing their Permeability, Strategic Uses, and Meanings," *Journal of Borderlands Studies* 29, no. 1 (2014): 3–9.
12. Scott defines "Zomia" as all the lands at elevations above three hundred meters, stretching from Vietnam to northeastern India. James C. Scott, *The Art of Not Being Governed: An Anarchist History of Upland Southeast Asia* (New Haven, CT: Yale University Press, 2009).
13. Maia Ramnath, *Decolonizing Anarchism: An Antiauthoritarian History of India's Liberation Struggle* (Oakland, CA: AK, 2011), 46. Although the British freely deployed the term "anarchist" to refer to anyone they considered to be a dangerous anticolonialist, noted Indian anarchist M. P. T. Acharya did spend time in exile in Pondicherry. See Andrew Davies, *Geographies of Anticolonialism: Political Networks Across and Beyond South India, c. 1900–1930* (Oxford: Wiley, 2020); and M. P. T. Acharya, *We Are Anarchists: Essays on Anarchism, Pacifism, and the Indian Independence Movement, 1923–53*, ed. Ole Birk Laursen (Oakland, CA: AK, 2019).
14. Notably, almost all of the organizing by Indians in exile was against British India, not French India or even French colonialism in other parts of the French Empire, until after 1947, when some attention was turned toward Vietnam and Algeria. On Indian revolutionaries in Paris, see Kate Marsh,

"The Only Safe Haven of Refuge in All the World': Paris, Indian 'Revolutionaries,' and Imperial Rivalry, c. 1905–40," *French Cultural Studies* 30, no. 3 (2019): 196–219.

15. HM consul general in French establishments to secretary to the governor of India in external affairs, Simla, 19 April 1937, L/PS/12/4454, IOR.
16. Srilata Ravi, "Border Zones in Colonial Spaces," *Interventions: International Journal of Postcolonial Studies* 12, no. 3 (2010): 383–95.
17. There was a significant French-Indian population in Indochina that played an important role in defining what it meant to be a French-Indian who held French citizenship. See Natasha Pairaudeau, *Mobile Citizens: French Indians in Indochina, 1858–1954* (Copenhagen: Nordic Institute of Asian Studies, 2016).
18. "Indian Desiderata for Peace Settlement," 4 December 1918, L/PS/12/4429/D.238, IOR.
19. "Indian Desiderata for Peace Settlement."
20. "Indian Desiderata for Peace Settlement."
21. "Indian Desiderata for Peace Settlement."
22. Andrew Davies, *Geographies of Anticolonialism: Political Networks Across and Beyond South Asia, c. 1900–1930* (Oxford: Royal Geographical Society/Wiley, 2020), 104.
23. Jason Cons, *Sensitive Spaces: Fragmented Territory at the India-Bangladesh Border* (Seattle: University of Washington Press, 2016), 56.
24. Sumit Sarkar, *The Swadeshi Movement in Bengal, 1903–1908* (New Delhi: People's Publishing House, 1973).
25. Peter Heehs, "Foreign Influences on Bengali Revolutionary Terrorism, 1902–1908," *Modern Asian Studies* 28 (1994): 533–56.
26. Unsigned letter from group of "Bengali swadeshis" addressed to Joseph François, April 1906, carton 333, Affaires politique, Archives Nationales d'Outre-Mer, Aix-en-Provence (FRANOM).
27. "Hutchinson's Report," in *Terrorism in Bengal*, ed. A. K. Samanta (Calcutta: Government of West Bengal, 1995), 338.
28. Political Department memorandum on French possessions in India, 1933, L/PS/12/4430, IOR.
29. "Indian Desiderata for Peace Settlement," 4 December 1918, L/PS/12/4429/D.238, IOR. Interestingly, in the same memo, which is largely devoted to French India, there is a brief mention of the Portuguese possessions in India (Goa, Diu, and Daman), which the British see as fairly benign compared to the French possessions: "The elimination of the Portuguese territorial rights would be an administrative convenience; but it can hardly be put higher."
30. Peter Heehs, *Nationalism, Terrorism, Communalism: Essays in Modern Indian History* (New York: Oxford University Press, 1998), 25.

31. A. K. Samanta, ed., *Terrorism in Bengal*, vol. 3 (Calcutta: Government of West Bengal, 1995), 276.
32. Nigel Stirk, "Arresting Ambiguity: The Shifting Geographies of a London Debtors' Sanctuary in the Eighteenth Century," *Social History* 25, no. 3 (2000): 316–29.
33. Dominique Moran, Jennifer Turner, and Anna K. Schliehe, "Conceptualizing the Carceral in Carceral Geography," *Progress in Human Geography* 42, no. 5 (2017): 666–86.
34. On the complex relationship between anticolonial activity and the image of French India as a site of refuge, see Penny Edwards, "A Strategic Sanctuary: Reading *l'Inde Française* Through the Colonial Archive," *Interventions: International Journal of Postcolonial Studies* 12 (2010): 356–67.
35. Andrew Davies, "Exile in the Homeland? Anti-Colonialism, Subaltern Geographies, and the Politics of Friendship in Early Twentieth-Century Pondicherry, India," *Environment and Planning D: Society and Space* 35, no. 3 (2017): 457–74.
36. Revolutionary activity was not confined to France, as Indian revolutionaries used contacts in Germany, Switzerland, Italy, the United States, Russia, and other countries. See Maia Ramnath, *Haj to Utopia: How the Ghadar Movement Charted Global Radicalism and Attempted to Overthrow the British Empire* (Berkeley: University of California Press, 2011); and Kris Manjapra, *The Age of Entanglement: German and Indian Intellectuals Across Empire* (Cambridge, MA: Harvard University Press, 2014). However, I will concentrate here on how important the French Indian connection was to the circulation of Indian revolutionaries during the struggle for independence.
37. Sri Aurobindo, *Autobiographical Notes: and Other Writings of Historical Interest* (Pondicherry: Sri Aurobindo Ashram, 2006).
38. Peter Heehs, *The Lives of Sri Aurobindo* (New York: Columbia University Press, 2008).
39. Significantly, Aurobindo did not speak any Indian languages until he returned to India in 1893, despite his spending the first seven years of his life there. His father had always insisted on the superiority of English.
40. Heehs, *Lives of Aurobindo*, 30.
41. Heehs, *Lives of Aurobindo*, 29–35.
42. Heehs, *Lives of Aurobindo*, 36.
43. Heehs, *Lives of Aurobindo*, 36.
44. Heehs, *Lives of Aurobindo*, 102.
45. The initial act in 1870 also set the precedent for related regulations that were continuously produced in attempt to stymie the growth of independence movements. The Seditious Meeting Act (1908) and the Indian Press Act (1910) are just two examples of many.

46. IPC 124A is still on the books in India and has been used with increased frequency to target leftist students at JNU in recent years. On the history of the sedition laws, see Aravind Ganachari, "Combatting Terror of Law in Colonial India: The Law of Sedition and the Nationalist Response," in *Engaging Terror: A Critical and Multidisciplinary Approach*, ed. Marianne Vardalos (Boca Raton, FL: Brown Walker, 2009), 93–110; Siddharth Narrain, " 'Disaffection' and the Law: The Chilling Effect of Sedition Laws in India," *Economic and Political Weekly* 46, no. 8 (2011): 33–37; and Chitranshul Sinha, *The Great Repression: The Story of Sedition in India* (Delhi: Penguin India, 2019).
47. Viceroy Lord Minto to secretary of state Lord Morley, 14 April 1910, reprinted in Sri Aurobindo, *Autobiographical Notes*, 260.
48. Sri Aurobindo, *Tales of Prison Life* (Pondicherry: Sri Aurobindo Ashram Trust, 1974), 1–2. Originally published as *Karakahini* in the Bengali journal *Suprabhat* in 1909–1910.
49. Aurobindo, *Tales of Prison Life*, 2.
50. Viceroy Lord Minto to secretary of state Lord Morley, 14 April 1910.
51. Andrew Davies has written about the "Pondicherry Gang," a loosely affiliated group of anticolonial Indian men who spent time in Pondicherry, much to the consternation of the British colonial government. See Davies, *Geographies of Anticolonialism*.
52. "Prosecution, Under Section 124-A, Indian Penal Code, of the Editor and Printer of the Karmayogin Newspaper," extracts from Government of India, Home Department, Political-A, Proceedings, December 1910, nos. 14–42, http://www.sriaurobindoashram.org/research/ (accessed 13 October 2017).
53. Statement by C. R. Cleveland, 12 November 1910, http://www.sriaurobindoashram.org/research/ (accessed 13 October 2017).
54. Sri Aurobindo, letter to the editor of the *Hindu*, 7 November 1910, reprinted in Sri Aurobindo, *Autobiographical Notes*, 264.
55. "Archival Notes: Sri Aurobindo and the Mother, 1914–1920," *Sri Aurobindo Archives and Research* 18, no. 2 (1994): 243.
56. General police reports, Foreign and Political Department, 1914, conf. B., no. 2, 1–3, 12–13, IOR.
57. Ashe is believed to be the last British official assassinated during the freedom movement in south India. A. R. Venkatachalapathy, "In Search of Ashe," *Economic and Political Weekly* 45, no. 2 (2010): 37–44.
58. R. A. Padamanabhan, "A CID Policeman's Pocket Diary," *Indian Review*, May 1976, 29–40.
59. Edward Said, "Reflections on Exile," *Granta* 13 (1984): 173–86.
60. Avtar Brah, *Cartographies of Diaspora: Contesting Identities* (New York: Routledge, 1996).
61. Davies, "Exile in the Homeland?"

62. Ashis Nandy, *The Intimate Enemy: Loss and Recovery of Self Under Colonialism* (Delhi: Oxford University Press, 1983): 85.
63. Barindra Kumar Ghose, *The Tale of My Exile: Twelve Years in the Andamans*, edited by Sachidananda Mohanty (Pondicherry: Sri Aurobindo Ashram, [1922] 2011). The British began using the Andaman Islands to house political prisoners beginning in the wake of the 1857 rebellion, though the Cellular Jail, made famous both for the people imprisoned there as well as the extensive use of solitary confinement, was not built until the early 1900s.
64. Barindra's sentence was commuted to life in prison/exile in the Andaman Islands, though he was released with other political prisoners in 1920. See Sachidananda Mohanty, "Introduction," in Ghose, *Tale of My Exile*, xxxii.
65. Ghose, *Tale of My Exile*, 48–49.
66. Max Théon was also known as Aia Aziz. Madame Théon, who at various times went by the names Una and Alma, did not use a first name, but only Madame, while she associated with Le Mouvement Cosmique. See Boaz Huss, "Madame Théon, Alta Una, Mother Superior: The Life and Personas of Mary Ware (1839–1908)," *Aries: Journal for the Study of Western Esotericism* 15 (2015): 210–46.
67. Matéo Alfassa would later serve as the governor-general of French Congo and French Equatorial Africa.
68. Michel Paul Richard, *Without Passport: The Life and Work of Paul Richard* (New York: Peter Lang, 1987), 60.
69. The French edition was called the *Revue de la Grande Synthèse*. The journal was published between the years 1914–1921. The majority of the articles were written by Aurobindo and were eventually compiled into several volumes that are considered the foundation of Aurobindo's philosophy, including *The Life Divine*, *The Synthesis of Yoga*, *The Secret of the Veda*, *The Foundations of Indian Culture*, and *The Ideal of Humanity*.
70. Richard, *Without Passport*, 72. They returned to France from India in 1915 and soon thereafter sailed to Japan for the duration of the war.
71. Although the Mother and her followers never discuss the relationship between Paul and Mira, Paul wrote about their growing estrangement leading up to her permanent move to India, including his fathering a child with another woman. See Richard, *Without Passport*.
72. Shyam Kumari notes that while there was some grumbling among Aurobindo's followers about the amount of power held by the Mother, Aurobindo continued to reassure them that she truly was the "Divine Mother." Kumari, *How They Came to Sri Aurobindo and the Mother: Twenty-Nine True Stories of Sadhaks and Devotees* (Bombay: Mother Publishing House, 1990), 33.
73. The Frenchman Philippe Barbier Saint-Hilaire is a good example of the type of European who came to live in the Ashram. Saint-Hilaire became

interested in theosophy and traveled to Japan and Africa before landing in Pondicherry and joining the Ashram in 1926. See Saint-Hilaire, *Itinéraire d'un enfant du siècle: Correspondance de Pavitra avec son père, 1918–1954* (Paris: Buset/Chastel, 2001).

74. Nolini Kanta Gupta, *Reminiscences* (Pondicherry: Sri Aurobindo Ashram, 1969), 44–45.
75. Gupta, *Reminiscences*, 45.
76. Bhikaji Cama, "Letter to the Editor," *Indian Sociologist: An Organ of Freedom, and of Political, Social, and Religious Reform*, November 1907, n.p.
77. Editorial, quoted in Bhikaji Rustom, *Madam Cama: Mother of Indian Revolution* (Calcutta: Manisha, 1975), 14.
78. Rustom, *Madam Cama*, 15.
79. While Varma did move the editorial office of the *Indian Sociologist* to Paris, it continued to be printed in England.
80. T. R. Sareen, *Indian Revolutionary Movement Abroad, 1905–1921* (New Delhi: Sterling, 1979), 38.
81. Sareen, *Indian Revolutionary Movement*, 38.
82. "Révolutionnaires Hindous," dossier pour M. le Directeur de la Sûreté Générale, F7/12900, Archives Nationales, Paris (AN).
83. "Révolutionnaires Hindous," AN.
84. Prabha Chopra and Pran Nath Chopra, eds., *Indian Freedom Fighters Abroad: Secret British Intelligence Report* (New Delhi: Criterion, 1988).
85. "Révolutionnaires Hindous," AN.
86. Shyamji Krishnavarma, "A Rejoinder to a Malignant Attack," *Indian Sociologist*, February 1909, n.p.
87. G. Berthy, "L'Inde aux Hindous," *L'éclair*, 28 December 1908, n.p.
88. For more on the interest of the French press in the treatment of Indian by the British, see Kate Marsh, *Fictions of Decolonization: Representations of Indian Decolonization, 1919–1962* (Oxford: Peter Berg, 2007).
89. Edwards, "Strategic Sanctuary."
90. Varadarajulu Subbiah, *Saga of Freedom in French India* (Madras: New Century, 1990), x.
91. Notebook/general information of the Pondicherry frontier, 1915, 76, L/PS/G84, IOR.
92. "French India: Reports on the General Situation," March 1944, L/PS/12/4456, IOR.
93. When Subbiah ran for election in French India, the French remarked that he had "no knowledge of French," which was a requirement to be elected to the Conseil de la Republique: "French India: Reports on the General Situation," January 1947, L/PS/12/4457, IOR. Jacques Weber has written that, by the 1920s, when Subbiah was a student at the College Calve, very few

*indigenes* were taught French, as English was thought to be a more useful language to learn in India. Weber, *Pondichéry et les Comptoirs de l'Inde après Dupleix: La démocratie au pays des castes* (Paris: Denoël, 1996), 352–53.
94. Subbiah, *Saga of Freedom*, 21.
95. Subbiah, *Saga of Freedom*, 21.
96. Subbiah, *Saga of Freedom*, 96.
97. Weber, *Pondichéry*, 360–62.
98. Subbiah, *Saga of Freedom*, 11.
99. Subbiah, *Saga of Freedom*, 11.
100. Subbiah, *Saga of Freedom*, 195.
101. There was quite a bit of confusion between the French and the British authorities in India as to who was responsible for Subbiah. Later, the French officials in Paris would state that issuing him a French passport had been a mistake. Subbiah, *Saga of Freedom*, 122–28.
102. Subbiah, *Saga of Freedom*, 129.
103. Report of August 1938, L/PS/12/445–6, IOR.
104. "French India: Reports on the General Situation," May–August 1944, /L/PS/12/4456, IOR.
105. "French India: Reports on the General Situation," May–August 1944.
106. "French India: Reports on the General Situation," May–August 1944.
107. "Évolution de la situation politique dans l'Inde Française," 27, Inde/H/23/ Cabinet du commissaire de la république, FRANOM.
108. "French India: Reports on the General Situation," February 1947, L/PS/12/4457, IOR.
109. Notebook/general information of the Pondicherry Frontier, 1915, 6–8, L/PS/G84, IOR.
110. Notebook/general information of the Pondicherry Frontier, 1915, 87.
111. The six chaukis were established at Kandamangalam, Madalapet, Mortandic havadi, Kottakuppam, Tukananbakkam, and Valvudar. Notebook/general information of the Pondicherry Frontier, 1915, 8, L/PS/G84, IOR.
112. Notebook/general information of the Pondicherry Frontier, 1915, 5.
113. Parliamentary notice, 1 December 1908, file 4443, L/PJ/6/907, IOR.
114. A. Ramasamy, *A History of Pondicherry* (New Delhi: Sterling, 1987), 155.
115. James Campbell Ker, *Political Trouble in India, 1907–1917* (Calcutta: Superintendent of Government Printing, 1917). See also Chopra and Chopra, *Secret British Intelligence Report*.
116. Notebook/general information of the Pondicherry Frontier, 1915, 10.
117. Notebook/general information of the Pondicherry Frontier, 1915, 8.
118. John Torpey, *The Invention of the Passport: Surveillance, Citizenship, and the State* (Cambridge: Cambridge University Press, 2000). Torpey starts his study with the question of the passport in the French Revolution, making the invention

of the passport a question of national identity and movement between sovereign nation-states.
119. Radhika Singha, "A 'Proper Passport' for the Colony: Border Crossing in British India, 1882–1920," Yale Agrarian Studies Colloquium Papers, 2006, 2.
120. On Indian labor migration to Canada and the use of passports, see Radhika Viyas Mongia, "Race, Nationality, Mobility: A History of the Passport," *Public Culture* 11 (2003): 527–55.
121. Singha, "Proper Passport."
122. Singha, "Proper Passport," 25.
123. Martin Thomas, Bob Moore, and L. J. Butler, *Empires of Intelligence: Security Services and Colonial Disorder After 1914* (Berkeley: University of California Press, 2008), 249.
124. "Relations Between French and British Local Authorities in Chandernagore and Pondicherry: Revolutionary Activities," file 2315, L/PJ/12/6, IOR.
125. Thomas, Moore, and Butler, *Empires of Intelligence*, 249.
126. "French India: Reports on the General Situation," August 1939, L/PS/12/4456, IOR.
127. "Admission des Français et des étrangers dans les établissements français de l'Inde," *Journal Officiel de la République Française*, 22 November 1936, n.p.
128. "Admission des Français et des étrangers."
129. Letter from Schomberg to undersecretary of the Government of India, external affairs, 21 November 1938, L/PS/12/4454, IOR.
130. Letter from Schomberg to undersecretary of the Government of India, 21 November 1938.
131. "French India: Reports on the General Situation," January 1939, L/PS/12/4456, IOR.
132. Letter from Boag, chief secretary to the Government of Madras, to the Government of India, external affairs, 21 December 1938, L/PS/12/4454, IOR.
133. Letter from Boag to the Government of India, 19 January 1939.
134. Letter from the minister of foreign affairs to the British embassy in Paris, 1938, L/PS/12/4454, IOR.
135. Memo responding to letter from the minister of foreign affairs, 1938, L/PS/12/4454, IOR.
136. Memo from Savidge, secretary to the Government of India, External Affairs, 19 August 1939, L/PS/12/4454.
137. "A Disquieting Balance Sheet," *Dessobagari*, February 11, 1939, L/PS/12/4456, IOR.
138. "Disquieting Balance Sheet."
139. I place "decolonization" in quotes to signify the postcolonial construction of the process of decolonization; when the borders I am referring to were

drawn, it was not necessarily a conscious step towards decolonization, but instead an element of the colonial practice of divide and conquer, or population management.

140. Jawaharlal Nehru, "Foreword," in *What Are the Indian States?* (Allahabad: All-India States' Peoples' Conference, 1939), 5–6.
141. Nehru, "Foreword," 56, emphasis added.

## 2. The Future of French India

1. Clement Attlee, speech to the House of Commons, 15 March 1946, in Attlee, *Parliamentary Debates*, Commons, 5th ser., vol. 420, cols. 1419–25.
2. Attlee, *Parliamentary Debates*, 15 March 1946.
3. Attlee, *Parliamentary Debates*, 15 March 1946.
4. Saroja Sundararajan, *Pondicherry: A Profile* (Pondicherry: Directorate of Art and Culture, Government of Pondicherry, 1995), 95.
5. Sundararajan, *Pondicherry*, 95.
6. Ajit K. Neogy, *Decolonization of French India: Liberation Movement and Indo-French Relations, 1947–1954* (Pondicherry: French Institute of Pondicherry, 1997), 275.
7. Rohit De, "Between Midnight and Republic: Theory and Practice of India's Dominion Status," *I*CON* 17, no. 4 (2019): 1213–34.
8. Frederick Cooper, *Citizenship Between Empire and Nation: Remaking France and French Africa, 1945–1960* (Princeton, NJ: Princeton University Press, 2014), 27.
9. Cooper, *Citizenship Between Empire and Nation*, 31.
10. Anita Inder Singh, "Keeping India in the Commonwealth: British Political and Military Aims, 1947–49," *Journal of Contemporary History* 20, vol. 3 (1985): 469–81.
11. Singh, "Keeping India in the Commonwealth," 470.
12. "Évolution de la situation politique dans l'Inde française," 1947, 3, Inde/H/23/Cabinet du commissaire de la République, Archives Nationales d'Outre-Mer, Aix-en-Provence (FRANOM).
13. "Étude sur les possessions Français dans l'Inde," 24 June 1947, 11, Inde/H/23/Cabinet du commissaire de la République, FRANOM.
14. "La décision Britannique de donner à l'Inde son indépendance ne peut avoir aucun effet sur les possessions françaises des Indes. Les deux questions sont absolument sans rapport. Les possessions françaises aux Indes font partie intégrante de l'Union française" ("Étude sur les possessions Français dans l'Inde," 19).
15. Attlee to the British Parliament, 20 February 1947, in Attlee, *Parliamentary Debates*, Commons, 5th ser., vol. 435, cols. 1395–98.

16. "Étude sur les possessions Français dans l'Inde," 19.
17. "Évolution de la situation politique," 9.
18. Pamila Gupta, "Gandhi and the Goa Question," *Public Culture* 23, no. 2 (2011): 321–30.
19. "Évolution de la situation politique," 10.
20. The Portuguese possessions (which comprised Goa and the much smaller seaside towns of Diu and Daman, located in Gujarat) remained Portuguese until 1961, when the Indian military forcibly took control and ended Portuguese rule in India. See Pamila Gupta, "The Disquieting of History: Portuguese (De)Colonization and Goan Migration in the Indian Ocean," *Journal of Asian and African Studies* 44, no. 1 (2009): 19–47.
21. "Évolution de la situation politique," 10.
22. "Évolution de la situation politique," 2.
23. A report written by the British Consular in French India following Governor Baron's speech about the French Union on 6 April 1946 includes a handwritten note stapled to the front that reads, "The French are making desperate attempts by means of cultural propaganda to check the movement advocating the inclusion of French India in an independent India, but apparently have little hope of success." "Reports on General Situation," 6 April 1946, L/PS/12/4457, India Office Records, British Library (IOR).
24. "Évolution de la situation politique," 4.
25. "Évolution de la situation politique," 4.
26. Adrian Carton, "Shades of Fraternity: 'Créolization' and the Making of Citizenship in French India, 1790–92," *French Historical Studies* 31 (2008): 581–607.
27. "Comme Français, nos droits ont plus d'une fois été écrits en caractères de sang dans les plaines du Carnatic et c'est sur les ossements de nos pères et de nos frères, morts pour le soutien de la Gloire et l'Honneur du nom française, que sont élevés les remparts de Pondichéry." Quoted in Michel Gaudart, *Généalogie des familles de l'Inde Française, XVIe—XXe siècle* (Pondichéry: Société de l'Histoire de l'Inde Française, 1976), 10.
28. Carton, "Shades of Fraternity," 583.
29. The classic work on French assimilation theory is Raymond F. Betts, *Assimilation and Association in French Colonial Theory, 1890–1914* (New York: Columbia University Press, 1961).
30. On French political clubs of the nineteenth century in India, see Henri-Louis Castonnet des Fosses, *La Révolution et les clubs dans l'Inde française* (Nantes: Forest et Grimaud, 1885).
31. These titles represent only a small sample of the over one hundred French-Indian periodicals held at the Bibliotheque Nationale de France. Each of the five comptoirs produced a variety of daily newspapers and monthly journals,

some in regional languages (largely Tamil and Bengali), some in dual- or tri-language format, and some exclusively in French.

32. Nicholas B. Dirks, *Castes of Mind: Colonialism and the Making of Modern India* (Princeton, NJ: Princeton University Press, 2001).
33. Jean-Antoine Dubois, *Mœurs, institutions, et cérémonies des peuples de l'Inde* (Paris: Imprimerie royale, 1825). The historian Sylvia Murr has argued that Dubois's text was based on a text written several decades earlier by another French missionary, Père Coeurdoux. See Murr, "Nicolas Desvaulx (1745–1823) veritable auteur de oeuvres, institutions et ceremonies des peoples de l'Inde, de l'abbé Dubois," *Purusartha* 3 (1977): 245–58.
34. Dirks, *Castes of Mind*, 24–25.
35. Jacques Weber, "Chanemougam, 'King of French India': Social and Political Foundations of an Absolute Power Under the Third Republic," *Economic and Political Weekly* 26 (1991): 291–302.
36. Jacques Weber, *Pondichéry et les comptoirs de l'Inde après Dupleix: la démocratie au pays des castes* (Paris: Denoël, 1996).
37. Animesh Rai, *The Legacy of French Rule in India (1674–1954): An Investigation of a Process of Creolization* (Pondicherry: French Institute of Pondicherry, 2008), 77.
38. Weber, *Pondichéry et les Comptoirs*.
39. Similar legislation had been introduced to Algerian Jews in 1870, and for Annamites in Indochine in 1881.
40. Weber, "Chanemougam," 295.
41. M. D. Moracchini, *Les Indigènes de l'Inde française et le suffrage universel* (Paris: Blot, 1889).
42. Weber, "Chanemougam," 297.
43. Weber, "Chanemougam," 302.
44. Weber, "Chanemougam," 303.
45. Weber, *Pondichéry et les Comptoirs*, 332. The Harijana Seva Sangh was an organization started by Gandhi, initially as the "All India anti-Untouchability League" in 1930. Gandhi used the word *Harijan*, meaning "people of god," instead of the more commonly used "pariah," which is a pejorative word meaning "outcast" or "outsider."
46. M. K. Gandhi, quoted in V. Subbiah, *Saga of Freedom in French India* (Madras: New Century, 1990), 32–33.
47. Subbiah, *Saga of Freedom*, 33.
48. Claude Blanckaert, "Of Monstrous Métis? Hybridity, Fear of Miscegenation, and Patriotism from Buffon to Paul Broca," in *The Color of Liberty: Histories of Race in France*, ed. Tyler Stovall and Sue Peabody (Durham, NC: Duke University Press, 2003), 42–70.

49. N. Hulliet, *Hygiène des blancs, des mixtes, et des indiens à Pondichéry* (Pondichéry: Imprimeur du Governement, 1867), 12.
50. Hulliet, *Hygiène des blancs*, 12.
51. Hulliet, *Hygiène des blancs*, 16–17.
52. Francis Cyril Antony, ed., *Gazetteer, Union Territory of Pondicherry* (Pondicherry: Government Press, 1982), 301.
53. Antony, *Gazetteer*. In 1849 the form changed the categories of Indians and Muslims to Hindus and Muslims, classifying both as "natives."
54. See, for example, Edouard Glissant, *Caribbean Discourse: Selected Essays* (Charlottesville: University of Virginia Press, 2009); and Celia M. Britton, *Edouard Glissant and Postcolonial Theory* (Charlottesville: University of Virginia Press, 2009).
55. This unique usage in French India, to refer to métis and people of French parents born in the colonies, is noted by many people who lived in French India. See, for example, Michel Gaudart de Soulages and Phillippe Randa, *Les dernières années de l'Inde française* (Paris: Dualpha, 2005), 210–12. For more on historical uses of "métis" throughout the French Empire, see Saliha Belmessous, "Assimilation and Racialism in Seventeenth- and Eighteenth-Century French Colonial Policy," *American Historical Review* 110 (2005): 322–49; and Jennifer M. Spear, "Colonial Intimacies: Legislating Sex in French Louisiana," *William and Mary Quarterly* 60, no. 1 (2003): 75–98.
56. Rai, *Legacy of French Rule in India*. Although race-mixing and culture-mixing do go hand in hand, Rai argues that in French India, the two dominant cultures, French and Tamil, never morphed into a hybrid—or métis—culture like those of the West Indies or in Louisiana.
57. Lourdes Tirouvanziam Louis, "Les 'Créoles' ou descendants d'Européens à Pondichéry," PhD diss., Pondicherry University, 1994, 4–5.
58. Louis, "Créole," 7.
59. Tzvetan Todorov, *On Human Diversity: Nationalism, Racism, and Exoticism in French Thought*, trans. Catherine Porter (Cambridge, MA: Harvard University Press, 1993).
60. Adrian Carton, *Mixed-Race and Modernity in Colonial India: Changing Concepts of Hybridity Across Empires* (New York: Routledge, 2012), 13. Most of the local women who married Portuguese and eventually other European men came from marginal social groups and married to improve their social standing.
61. Adrian Carton notes that in the sixteenth and seventeenth centuries in India, the phrase "les filles portugaises" could refer to mixed-race women *or* Christian free women of color, depending on the source. Carton, *Mixed-Race and Modernity*, 19.

62. Very little is said in my sources about the marriage patterns of métis women or métis men. Adrian Carton has suggested that many of them married within the métis community, while a small number traveled to other French colonies and found partners there (*Mixed-Race and Modernity*, 74–75).
63. Isidore Guët, *Origines de l'Inde française, Jân Begum (Mme Dupleix, 1706–1756)* (Paris: Baudoin, 1892).
64. Louis, "Créole," 28.
65. Ananda Ranga Pillai, *The Private Diary of Ananda Ranga Pillai: A Record of Matters Political, Historical, Social, and Personal, from 1736 to 1761.*, trans. Sir J. Frederick Price (Madras: Government Press, 1904). "Dubash" is a word of Hindi origin that translates to "interpreter," or "man of two languages"—most European men in India had a dubash from the local community who would act as a guide and middleman, translating and facilitating alliances between the European and the Indigenous leaders and/or merchants.
66. Pillai, *Private Diary*, 54–57.
67. Pillai often recorded his conversations with Mme Dupleix and would note in his text that she spoke to him in Tamil, a language her husband did not understand.
68. Guët, *Origines de l'Inde française*; Yvonne Robert Gaebelé, *Métis et Grande Dame, Joanna Bégum, Marquise Dupleix, 1706–1756* (Pondicherry: Bibliothèque Coloniale, 1934); Rose Vincent, *Les temps d'un royaume: Jeanne Dupleix* (Paris: Éditions du Seuil, 1982).
69. Gaebelé, *Métis et Grande Dame*.
70. "Étude sur les possessions," 14.
71. Peter Heehs, *The Lives of Sri Aurobindo* (New York: Columbia University Press, 2008), 370.
72. The Ashram school was founded in 1943–1944, as the population of the Ashram had increased and included many children. The Mother devoted herself to questions of education, producing a monthly publication, the *Bulletin d'Education Physique*, which contains articles written by the Mother as well as many pictures of Ashram students engaged in physical education, including posing like Greek deities.
73. The Mother, "Message for the Inauguration of a French Institute at Pondicherry, 4 April 1955," in *Words of the Mother* (Pondicherry: Sri Aurobindo Ashram, 1980), 379.
74. Winthrop Sargeant, "Holy Man: Sri Ramana Maharshi has India's Answer to Most of Man's Problems," *Life*, 30 May 1949, 92–104.
75. Jessica Namakkal, "Decolonizing Marriage and the Family: The Lives and Letters of Ida, Benoy, and Indira Sarkar," *Journal of Women's History* 31, no. 2 (2019): 124–47.
76. Heehs, *Lives of Sri Aurobindo*, 254, 332.

77. Alfassa quoted in Heehs, *Lives of Aurobindo*, 254. Alfassa did have a son, André Morriset (1898–1982). Morriset was born during Alfassa's first marriage, to Henri Morisset. While Morriset was largely estranged from Alfassa for a long period of his adolescence and early adulthood, he met her at the Ashram in 1949 and subsequently started a branch of the Sri Aurobindo Study Centre and worked closely with Alfassa on the founding of Auroville. Morriset, "Remembrances," Overman Foundation, http://overmanfoundation.org/three-talks-by-andre-morisset-the-mothers-son/ (accessed 15 June 2020).

78. Aurobindo's wife, Mrinalini Ghose (née Bose), had not followed Aurobindo to Pondicherry when he fled British India in 1910, at Aurobindo's insistence. She lived with her father in Shillong, waiting for her husband's return to Bengal. Aurobindo never left Pondicherry once he arrived and eventually stopped communicating with his wife at all. She died in 1918, after seventeen years of marriage, although they only lived together until 1908. They had no children. Heehs, *Lives of Aurobindo*, 317–18.

79. The only speculation on the possibility of the two having a physical relationship came in Peter Heehs's biography. The mention of the idea that someone may have once witnessed the Mother and Aurobindo holding hands—the mere hint they may have had a sexual interest in one another—set off a firestorm in India when the book was released, in 2008. The intense controversy over the book speaks to the importance of Aurobindo and the Mother's renunciation of sexual activity to their followers, an importance that seems to have grown over the years since their respective deaths.

80. The Mother, "A Declaration, 1 April 1946," in *Words of the Mother*, 122.

81. Nirodbaran, *Twelve Years with Sri Aurobindo* (Pondicherry: Sri Aurobindo Ashram, 1972), 128.

82. Antoine Mariadassou, "Histoire du combat pour la liberté: du Students Congress de l'Inde Française," *CIDIF* 20 (1998): 16.

83. Mariadassou, "Histoire du combat." Enginger published over a dozen books under the name Satprem, some autobiographical, the others devoted to the lives and thought of Sri Aurobindo and the Mother.

84. Marsland, honorary British vice consul in the French establishments, to Masterman, 9 December 1947, L/PS/12/4434, IOR.

85. Heehs, *Lives of Aurobindo*.

86. "French India: Reports on the General Situation," January 1946, L/PS/12/4457, IOR.

87. François Baron and Surendra Mohan Ghose, "Two Documents of Historical Importance," *Mother India* 28 (1976): 648–49.

88. Baron and Ghose, "Two Documents," 649.

89. Subbiah, *Saga of Freedom*, 261–62.

90. Subbiah, *Saga of Freedom*, 262.

91. Anticolonial movements in India played an important role in the development of the Communist Party platforms during the Second Congress of the Communist International, held in Moscow and Petrograd during the summer of 1920. Manabendranath (MN) Roy, a Bengali who lived in global exile for decades before being imprisoned in India in 1931, presented the Second Congress with two reports "On the National and Colonial Question" at a time when the Communist Party had not taken a strong stance on the issue of the colonies. For more, see Kris Manjapra, *M. N. Roy: Marxism and Colonial Cosmopolitanism* (New Delhi: Routledge, 2010); and John Riddell, Vijay Prashad, Nazeef Mollah, eds., *Liberate the Colonies! Communism and Colonial Freedom, 1917–1924* (New Delhi: Leftword, 2019).
92. Neogy, *Decolonization of French India*, 5.
93. Neogy, *Decolonization of French India*, 6.
94. Subbiah, *Saga of Freedom*, 262–63.
95. Neogy, *Decolonization of French India*, 46.
96. Subbiah, *Saga of Freedom*, 67.
97. Subbiah, *Saga of Freedom*, 67–68.
98. Neogy, *Decolonization of French India*, 50–51.
99. Neogy, *Decolonization of French India*, 59.
100. Subbiah, *Saga of Freedom*, 273.
101. B. Krishnamurthy, *Jawaharlal Nehru and Freedom Movement in French India* (Pondicherry: Centre for Nehru Studies, Pondicherry University, 2007), 57–58.
102. Krishnamurthy, *Jawaharlal Nehru*.
103. "Reds in French India," *New York Times*, 17 April 1954, 12.
104. "Reds in French India."
105. Natasha Pairaudeau, *Mobile Citizens: French Indians in Indochina, 1858–1954* (Copenhagen: Nordic Institute of Asian Studies, 2016).
106. Purushottam to Nehru, 5 May 1947, Reddiar Papers, Puducherry Record Centre, National Archives of India, Puducherry (NAI-P).
107. Sri Raphael Ramanayya Dadala, *My Struggle for the Freedom of French India: An Autobiography* (Kakinada: n.p., 1985). 1. "Scheduled caste" is the administrative designation given to low-caste (previously referred to as "untouchable") people whom the state recognized as socially disadvantaged. The term "scheduled caste" originates with the British government in India, but was kept in use post-1947 in the independent Indian state. I use the term "Dalit" throughout the text to refer to Dadala's position in relationship to caste in recognition of the group's preferred nomenclature.
108. Dadala, *My Struggle*, 1.
109. Dadala, *My Struggle*, preface.
110. Dadala, *My Struggle*, i.

111. Dadala, *My Struggle.*, ii.
112. "Jai Hind" translates to "Hail India" or "Victory to India."
113. Pairaudeau, *Mobile Citizens*, 29.
114. Arthur Annasse, *Les Comptoirs Français de l'Inde (1664–1954): Trois siècles de présence française* (Paris: Le pensée universelle: 1975).
115. Annasse, *Comptoirs*, 115–20.
116. Annasse, *Comptoirs*, 134.
117. Annasse, *Comptoirs*, 187.
118. Annasse, *Comptoirs*, 163.
119. Claude Arpi, *Il y a 50 ans . . . Pondichéry: L'intégration des établissements français en Inde Perspectives historiques et culturelles* (Auroville, India: Auroville, 2004), 27.
120. Dadala, *My Struggle*, 25.
121. The letter from Goubert to the National Assembly is reproduced in *Dictionnaire des parlementaires français, 1940–1958*, vol. 4 (Paris: La documentation française, 2001), 213–14.
122. "Autant j'aime le peuple français qui n'est pas sorti de la France, autant je me vois bien contraint de détester les Français qui se trouvent en fonction dans les territoires d'outre-mer, à part, bien entendu, quelques rares exceptions." *Dictionnaire*, 214.
123. "Étude sur les possessions," 6.
124. "Étude sur les possessions," 6.
125. "Étude sur les possessions," 6.
126. Subbiah, *Saga of Freedom*, 252.
127. "French India: Reports on the General Situation," January 1946, L/PS/12/4457, IOR.
128. Mariadassou gave a lecture recounting his involvement in the Students Congress of French India at a conference held at Pondicherry University in 1998. His speech was printed in its entirety in the Centre d'Information et de documentation de l'Inde francophone (CIDIF) newsletter. Mariadassou, "Histoire du combat."
129. French India National Congress to Nehru and Gandhi, 1947, Reddiar Papers, NAI-P.
130. Mariadassou, "Histoire du combat," 16.
131. Brochure written by the Congress of Students, 1947, Inde/H/23/Rapports de police/agitation politique, Archives Nationales d'Outre-Mer, Aix-en-Provence (FRANOM).
132. Neogy, *Decolonization of French India*, 53.
133. Neogy, *Decolonization of French India*, 53.
134. French India National Congress to Nehru and Gandhi, 1947, Reddiar Papers, NAI-P.

135. Antoine Mariadassaou, "Démocratie?," *Le Trait-d'Union*, August 1947, 2.
136. Mariadassaou, "Démocratie?"
137. "Alors, qu'il n'y a plus qu'une grande famille de citoyens hindous, il est difficile d'admettre des expulsions où nos frères sont traités en étrangers" (Mariadassaou, "Démocratie?").
138. Mohammad Houssaine, "Atmosphère d'indépendance," *Le Trait-d'Union*, August 1947, 1.
139. "L'esclavage a peut être été aboli mais la servitude est restée." Houssaine, "Atmosphère d'indépendance," 1.
140. Neogy, *Decolonization of French India*, 53.
141. As reported in the *Le Trait-d'Union*, 15 August 1947, 7.
142. Neogy, *Decolonization of French India*, 54.
143. Neogy, *Decolonization of French India*, 55.
144. "French India: Reports on the General Situation," January 1946, L/PS/12/4457, IOR.
145. "Mr. Purani called on H. M. Consul-General on New Year's Day and brought him a Christmas card from the Ashram. An article has appeared in the local vernacular press complaining that the Ashram are buying up too many houses. They have, in fact, now about 100 houses . . . the permanent inmates are not believed to number about 370" ("French India: Reports on the General Situation").
146. Ashram secretary to the *Statesman* (Calcutta), 20 August 1947, Reddiar Papers, NAI-P.
147. Ashram secretary to the statesman, 20 August 1947.
148. Nirodbaran, *Twelve Years with Sri Aurobindo*, 161.
149. Nirodbaran, *Twelve Years with Sri Aurobindo*, 161.
150. Sri Chinmoy, "An Ashram Jewel: Mulshankar," Sri Chinmoy: Reflections, http://www.srichinmoy-reflections.com/mulshankar (accessed 3 May 2012).
151. Heehs, *Lives of Aurobindo*, 396.
152. Emmanuelle Pouchepadass, "Lettre à mon pays: de quoi s'agit-il?," *Le Trait-d'Union*, October 1947, 2–3.
153. Pouchepadass, "Lettre à mon pays," 3.
154. Stuart Ward, "The European Provenance of Decolonization," *Past & Present* 230, no. 1 (2016): 227–60.
155. R. Ramasrinivasan, *Karaikal in Freedom Struggle (Commemoration of the "Golden Jubilee Celebrations of the Independence of India")* (Pondicherry: Qualité Offset, 1998), 11.
156. Speech of Subbiah, reprinted in Ramasrinivasan, *Karaikal in Freedom Struggle*, 165. Originally appeared in *Swathanthiram*, a Communist weekly printed in Pondicherry.

157. David Annoussamy, "The Merger of French India," in *French in India and Indian Nationalism: (1700–1963)*, ed. K. S. Mathew (Delhi: BR, 1999), 67.

## 3. Making the Postcolonial Subject

1. The scholarship on Partition is vast, but some key texts that pay close attention to both violence and territory include Yasmin Khan, *The Great Partition: The Making of India and Pakistan* (New Haven, CT: Yale University Press, 2007); Vazira Fazila-Yacoobali Zamindar, *The Long Partition and the Making of Modern South Asia: Refugees, Boundaries, Histories* (New York: Columbia University Press, 2007); Gyanendra Pandey, *Remembering Partition* (Cambridge: Cambridge University Press, 2001); and Urvashi Butali, *The Other Side of Silence* (New Delhi: Penguin, 1998).
2. Stuart Elden, *Terror and Territory: The Spatial Extent of Sovereignty* (Minneapolis: University of Minnesota Press, 2009), 171.
3. In February 1947, the British consul in Pondicherry did include a note in his monthly report that "there has been an infiltration of Indians from Bengal and Bombay ostensibly to join the Ashram." While it is not explicitly clear that this was because of the violence that was starting to ramp up in the north, it is possible the Ashram served as a refuge for some who were fleeing partition violence. L/PS/12/4457, India Office Records, British Library (IOR).
4. On the history of the idea of citizenship in India, see Niraja Gopal Jayal, *Citizenship and Its Discontents: An Indian History* (Cambridge, MA: Harvard University Press, 2013).
5. Durba Mitra, *Indian Sex Life: Sexuality and the Colonial Origins of Modern Social Thought* (Princeton, NJ: Princeton University Press, 2020), 4.
6. The "Goonda Raj" was a term used in hundreds of Indian government reports to describe the French rule in India by the early 1950s. The term was widely circulated in the public with the release of a 1952 report: "Dark Record of Goonda Raj in French Settlements in India," 26 October 1952, New Delhi, Asie Océanie/Inde Française/Maintien de l'ordre incidents policiers, Ministère des Affaires Étrangères Archives, La Courneuve, France (MAE).
7. Zamindar, *Long Partition*, 2.
8. Laird Boswell, "From Liberation to Purge Trials in the 'Mythic Provinces': Recasting French Identities in Alsace and Lorraine, 1918–1920," *French Historical Studies* 23 (2000): 129–162.
9. Boswell, "From Liberation to Purge Trials," 131.
10. Nitasha Kaul, "India's Obsession with Kashmir: Democracy, Gender, (Anti)-Nationalism," *Feminist Review* 119 (2018): 126–43.

11. People both within and outside of academia have begun to talk about decolonizing Kashmir. See, for example, Suvir Kaul, "Indian Empire (and the Case of Kashmir)," *Economic and Political Weekly* 46, no. 13 (2011): 66–75.
12. M. K. Gandhi, 11 November 1947, statement printed in Tamil and distributed widely in the French Indian territories, Archives Nationales d'Outre-Mer, Aix-en-Provence (FRANOM); transliteration: "British aatchiyilirunthu kodikannakkaana inthiya sagodararkal viduthalai pettra piragu icciriya french inthiya-vil ulla makkal adimaikalaaka vaazha mudiyathu" (translated from the Tamil by Anusha Hariharan).
13. Tamil political tract (French translation), 13 August 1947, Inde/Series H, FRANOM.
14. Rajkumar to Pillai, 7 August 1947, folder 8, Reddiar Papers, National Archives of India, Puducherry (NAI-P).
15. Rajkumar to Pillai, 7 August 1947.
16. "French India Peoples' Convention," folder 9, document 22, Reddiar Papers, NAI-P.
17. "Declaration Gouvernementale," folder 9, document 114, Reddiar Papers, NAI-P.
18. "Le Gouvernement français declare solennellement qu'il entend laisser aux populations des Etablissements français dans l'Inde le droit de prononcer sur leur sort et leur statut future" ("Declaration Gouvernementale").
19. Sailendra Nath Sen, *Chandernagore: From Bondage to Freedom, 1900–1955* (New Delhi: Primus, 2012). 100.
20. Sen, *Chandernagore*, 101.
21. "Give Chandernagore Without Plebiscite: French India Leader's Call to France," *Times of India*, 6 June 1949, 1.
22. "Chandernagore Plebiscite: Plans for Polling Day," *Times of India*, 14 June 1949, 9.
23. "Chandernagore Referendum: Polling Today," *Hindu*, 17 June 1949, n.p.
24. "Chandernagore Merger," *Hindu*, June 20, 1949, n.p.
25. "Situation at Chandernagore," 26 November 1947, L/PS/12/4434, IOR.
26. Holger Anderson and Rudolfo Baron Castro, "Report on Chandernagore Vote," 6 August 1949, 61COL2269, FRANOM.
27. Anderson and Castro, "Report on Chandernagore Vote."
28. "Nationalist Meeting at Pondicherry Attacked: Pro-French Rowdies Disturb "Chandernagore Day," *Times of India*, 28 June 1949, n.p.
29. R. L. L. Purushothaman, press release, 19 October 1949, folder 8, Reddiar Papers, NAI-P.
30. David Arnold, *Police Power and Colonial Rule: Madras, 1859–1947* (Oxford: Oxford University Press, 1986), 3.

31. N. V. Rajkumar, *The Problem of French India* (New Delhi: Department of Foreign Relations, Indian National Congress, 1951).
32. Rajkumar, *Problem of French India*, 4–5.
33. Rajkumar, *Problem of French India*, 56.
34. "Dark Record of Goonda Raj in French Settlements in India," New Delhi, 26 October 1952, Asie Océanie/Inde Française/Maintien de l'ordre incidents policiers, 1, MAE.
35. "Dark Record of Goonda Raj."
36. "Dark Record of Goonda Raj," 2.
37. "Dark Record of Goonda Raj," 2.
38. "Dark Record of Goonda Raj," 2.
39. "Dark Record of Goonda Raj," 1.
40. Asie Océanie/Inde Française/Maintien de l'ordre incidents policiers, 75–81, MAE.
41. Embassy of India to the Ministry of Foreign Affairs, 13 October 1953, Asie Océanie/Inde Française/Maintien de l'ordre incidents policiers, 82, MAE.
42. Embassy of India to the Ministry of Foreign Affairs, 13 October 1953.
43. Ostorog to the Ministry of Foreign Affairs, 27 October 1952, Asie Océanie/Inde Française/Maintien de l'ordre incidents policiers, 96–97, MAE.
44. Ostrorog to the Ministry of Foreign Affairs, 27 October 1952.
45. Ajit K. Neogy, *Decolonization of French India: Liberation Movement and Indo-French Relations, 1947–1954* (Pondicherry: French Institute of Pondicherry, 1997), 206.
46. Ostrorog to the Ministry of Foreign Affairs, 27 October 1952.
47. Jacques Weber, *Pondichéry et les Comptoirs de l'Inde après Dupleix: La démocratie au pays des castes* (Paris: Denoël, 1996).
48. Appavou to the commandant of the Gendarmerie Auxiliaire Indienne, 21 February 1953, Asie Océanie/Inde Française/Maintien de l'ordre incidents policiers, MAE.
49. Details of Thulasingham's crimes were recorded in a police report. The French spell his name Tolassingame. See report of Captain Lagisquet, commandant of the Gendarmerie Auxiliaire Indienne, 24 February 1953, Asie Océanie/Inde Française/Maintien de l'ordre incidents policiers, MAE.
50. Tandon, consul general of India in Pondicherry, to Kresser, the commissioner of the Republic for the French establishments in India, 26 February 1953, Asie Océanie/Inde Française/Maintien de l'ordre incidents policiers, MAE.
51. "Clash on French India Border," *Hindu*, 23 February 1953, n.p.
52. "Clash on French India Border," *Hindu*, 23 February 1953, n.p.
53. Kresser to Tandon, consul general of India in Pondicherry, 6 March 1953, Asie Océanie/Inde Française/Maintien de l'ordre incidents policiers, MAE.

The title of Commissioner of the Republic for French India replaced the title of Governor of French India in 1947.

54. Response from the commissioner of the Republic to Tandon, 6 March 1953, Asie Océanie/Inde Française/Maintien de l'ordre incidents policiers, MAE.
55. Embassy of India to Ministry of Foreign Affairs, 22 March 1954, dossier 6, 61COL2273, FRANOM.
56. Report of Captain Lagisquet, 24 February 1953.
57. Adam McKeown, *Melancholy Order: Asian Migration and the Globalization of Borders* (New York: Columbia University Press, 2011); Willem van Schendel and Erik de Maaker, "Asian Borderlands: Introducing their Permeability, Strategic Uses, and Meanings," *Journal of Borderlands Studies* 29, no. 1 (2014): 3–9; David Gellner, ed., *Borderland Lives in Northern South Asia* (Durham, NC: Duke University Press, 2013); James C. Scott, *The Art of Not Being Governed: An Anarchist History of Upland Southeast Asia* (New Haven, CT: Yale University Press, 2010).
58. Sri Raphael Ramanayya Dadala, *My Struggle for the Freedom of French India: An Autobiography* (Kakinada: n.p., 1985).
59. Dadala, *My Struggle*, 8.
60. Dadala, *My Struggle*, 13.
61. The popular legend told about King Canute (Cnut), the ruler of England, Denmark, and Norway in the eleventh century, details how the king tested his alleged divine powers against the forces of nature and lost. The story, which historians date to a twelfth-century chronicle written by Henry, Archdeacon of Huntingdon, tells of King Canute taking his men to the seashore, placing his chair near the water's edge, and commanding the rising tide to retreat. The tide rose as it always did and soaked his feet and shins. It is said that Canute took this to mean that the divine power of kings was in reality empty, and the only true power laid with God. It is said that, after this moment, Canute continued to rule, but refused to wear his gold crown, choosing instead to hang it on a statue of the crucifixion, acknowledging his powers were inferior to those of the divine.
62. "The Government and the police Chief had given Carte blanche to the Government candidates and to the goondas to attack me in my station and kill me." Dadala, *My Struggle*, 13.
63. Neogy, *Decolonization of French India*, 204.
64. V. Aroumougame, Tamil political tract, 1952, Asie Océanie/Inde Française/Maintien de l'ordre incidents policiers, 74, MAE.
65. V. Aroumougame, Tamil political tract.
66. V. Aroumougame, Tamil political tract.
67. "Border Incidents by French India Partisans: Acts of Goondaism Detailed," report issued on behalf of the House of the People, distributed by the

Press Information Bureau, Government of India, 18 November 1952, Asie Océanie/Inde Française/Maintien de l'ordre incidents policiers, 111–13, MAE.
68. "Border Incidents."
69. Internally, both France and India blamed each other for the violence on the borders.
70. *French Pockets in India* (Madras: Free India, 1953), 12.
71. *French Pockets in India*, 1.
72. *French Pockets in India*.
73. *French Pockets in India*, 3.
74. "Paris Complains to Envoy," *New York Times*, 3 April 1954, 4.
75. "Approach to Chaos in Pondicherry, Puzzle of Indian Policy," *Times of India*, 5 April 1954, 7.
76. "Border Incident at Pondicherry," *Times of India*, 3 April 1954, 6.
77. Statement given by A. K. Chanda, vice-minister for foreign affairs in India, 6 August 1953, Inde/H/23/Rapports des fonctionnaires/Mahé, FRANOM.
78. "Approach to Chaos in Pondicherry, Puzzle of Indian Policy," *Times of India*, 5 April 1954, 7.
79. "Border Incident at Pondicherry," *Times of India*, 3 April 1954, 6.
80. "Demonstrations in Mannadipet," *Times of India*, 7 April 1954, 8.
81. Neogy, *Decolonization of French India*, 277.
82. "New Delhi Pushes Drive on Colonies," *New York Times*, 6 April 1954, 7.
83. Miles, *Imperial Burdens*, 65–66.
84. Jacques Weber, in foreword to Neogy, *Decolonization of French India*, xix.
85. Dadala, *My Struggle*, 24.
86. "D'origine indienne, il prend une part active et parfois violente dans la lutte pour le rattachement de Pondichéry à l'Union indienne." "Goubert, Edouard," in Frédéric Barbier, *Dictionnaire des parlementaires français: notices biographiques sur les parlementaires français de 1940–1958* (Paris: Documentation française), 213–14.
87. "France Is Reported Ready to Quit India," *New York Times*, 3 August 1954, 5.
88. "Mais que fait-on en France?" The Editors, "L'Inde Française," *Le Trait d'Union*, July 1954, 1. Note that, in the text, "Trait d'Union" is capitalized, emphasizing the importance of the publication *Le Trait d'Union* as a voice for the Franco-Indian Pondichérian community.
89. Corey Robin, *Fear: The History of a Political Idea* (Oxford: Oxford University Press, 2004), 2.

# 4. Decolonial Crossings

Epigraphs: The Mother, "15 August 1954," in *Words of the Mother* (Pondicherry: Sri Aurobindo Ashram, 1980), 43; *Cinq colonnes à la une*, "Les trois mondes de Pondichéry," Office national de radiodiffusion television française, aired on 4 September 1964, on Channel 1; quoted in Sophie Lakshmi Dassaradanayadou, "Tamouls indiens: de Pondichéry à la France," *Hommes & Migrations* 1268–69 (2007): 73.

1. Weber to Ministry of Overseas France, 26 November 1954, Asie Océanie/Inde Française/Questions culturelles, Ministère des Affaires Étrangères Archives, La Courneuve, France (MAE).
2. The French Indian newspaper *Le Trait-d'Union* reported that Professor Weber left Pondicherry in May 1955.
3. Nehru and the Lok Sabha chose to drop all charges against people involved in any way in the struggle in and around French India leading to the signing of the Treaty of Cession. 16 December 1954, *Lok Sabha Debates*, extracted in Jawarhalal Nehru, *Selected Works of Jawarhalal Nehru*, vol. 27 (New Delhi: Oxford University Press, 1984–2010), 224–31. Two years later, when the Treaty of Cession was signed by both France and India, Article 9 of the protocol stated, "No one shall be prosecuted on account of political offences committed prior to 1 November 1954 and against whom no prosecution has been instituted on the said date." See the appendix for the full text of the Treaty of Cession.
4. See the appendix for full text of the Treaty of Cession.
5. Nicolas Bancel and Pascal Blanchard, "The Pitfalls of Colonial Memory," in *The Colonial Legacy in France: Fracture, Rupture, and Apartheid*, ed. Nicolas Bancel, Pascal Blanchard, and Dominic Thomas, trans. Alexis Pernsteiner (Bloomington: Indiana University Press, 2017), 153–64.
6. Susan Koshy and R. Radhakrishnan, *Transnational South Asians: The Making of a Neo-Diaspora* (New Delhi: Oxford University Press, 2008).
7. Anthony Goreau-Ponceaud, "La diaspora tamoule en France: entre visibilité et politisation," EchoGéo, accessed 18 October 2012, http://echogeo.revues.org/11157.
8. Nehru, *Selected Works*, vol. 27, 221n1.
9. Nehru, *Selected Works*, vol. 27, 221.
10. Nehru, *Selected Works*, vol. 27, 221.
11. Ministry of Overseas France to the French Ministry of Foreign Affairs, August 1954, Asie Océanie/Inde Française/Questions judiciaires, MAE.
12. Ostrorog to Faure, président du conseil, 14 April 1955, Asie Océanie/Inde Française/Questions judiciaires, MAE.
13. Ostrorog to Faure, 14 April 1955.
14. A. Gandon, "Note sur les options de nationalité à Pondichéry," 4 June 1955, Asie Océanie/Inde Française/Questions judiciaires, MAE.
15. Ostrorog to the Minister of Foreign Affairs, 22 June 1955, Asie Océanie/Inde Française/Questions judiciaires, MAE.

16. Ostrorog to the Minister of Foreign Affairs, 22 June 1955.
17. Gandon, "Note sur les options."
18. Ostrorog to Faure, 7 April 1955, Asie Océanie/Inde Française/Questions judiciaires, MAE.
19. Ostrorog to Faure, 7 April 1955.
20. Ostrorog to Faure, 7 April 1955 .
21. Edouard Goubert, the former National Assembly member who "betrayed" France to fight for merger and is the object of Ostrorog's scorn, did choose Indian citizenship, although the remainder of his family retained French citizenship, creating a great divide in the Goubert family. Jacques Weber, *Pondichéry et la comptoirs de l'Inde après Dupleix: La démocratie au pays des castes* (Paris: Editions Denoël, 1996), 404.
22. Ministry of Overseas France to the French Ministry of Foreign Affairs, 3 September 1954, Asie Océanie/Inde Française/Nationalité et Options, MAE.
23. Baron's plans were recorded in a note written by the Ministry of Overseas France in 1946: "Établissements français de l'Inde," 17 September 1946, Asie Océanie/Inde Française/Questions culturelles, MAE.
24. Remarks made in a press conference to Radio France on 31 October 1954 in Saigon. Jawaharlal Nehru, *Selected Works of Jawarhalal Nehru*, vol. 27 (New Delhi: Oxford University Press, 2000), 99.
25. *La République Française*, 13 August 1954, reprinted in Alain Coret, *La Cession de l'Inde Française* (Paris: Librairie Générale de Droit et de Jurisprudence, 1955).
26. R. Duvauchelle, "Sur les options de nationalité française," 21 December 1954, 2, Asie Océanie/Inde Française/Questions judiciaires, MAE.
27. Duvauchelle, "Sur les options," 2.
28. Ajit K. Neogy, *Decolonization of French India: Liberation Movement and Indo-French Relations, 1947–1954* (Pondicherry: French Institute of Pondicherry, 1997), 51.
29. Géraud de la Pradelle, "Dual Nationality and the French Citizenship Tradition," in *Dual Nationality, Social Rights and Federal Citizenship in the U.S. and Europe: The Reinvention of Citizenship*, ed. Randall Hansen and Patrick Weil (New York: Berghahn, 2002), 192.
30. Comité de Défense des Intérêts Français de l'Inde Française to the Ministry of Overseas France, 26 October 1954, Asie Océanie/Inde Française/Questions judiciaires, MAE.
31. Sri Aurobindo Ashram to Nehru, 22 December 1954, Asie Océanie/Inde Française/Questions judiciaires, MAE. The letter was signed by Barbier Saint-Hilaire (Pavitra), Norman Dowsett, Jay Holmes Smith, Nolini Kanta Gupta, Indra Sen, and K. D. Sethna.
32. Sri Aurobindo Ashram to Nehru, 22 December 1954.
33. Sri Aurobindo Ashram to Nehru, 22 December 1954, 2.

34. Sri Aurobindo Ashram to Nehru, 22 December 1954, 3.
35. Sri Aurobindo Ashram to Nehru, 22 December 1954, 3.
36. Sri Aurobindo Ashram to Nehru, 22 December 1954, 4.
37. "Ils semble donc qu'il existe un mouvement tendant à accréditer chez certaines catégories de nationaux français ou même étrangers fixés dans nos Établissements cette revendication d'une double nationalité. En dehors de l'esprit idéaliste qui, très vraisemblablement, inspire les dirigeants de L'ASHRAM, des considérations plus matérielles peuvent agir également en faveur du système de la double nationalité." "Nationalité: Établissements Français de L'Inde," report prepared by the Minister of Overseas France for the Minister of Foreign Affairs, 23 February 1955, Asie Océanie/Inde Française/Questions judiciaires, MAE.
38. Frantz Fanon, *The Wretched of the Earth* (New York: Grove, [1961] 2007), 9–10.
39. In the following chapter, I will show how the desire for "global citizenship," illustrated here by the people in the Aurobindo Ashram, became a call for Westerners to migrate to India, a place they believed they could experiment with new forms of citizenship, community, and belonging.
40. Ostrorog to Mayer, president of the Commission of Foreign Affairs, 18 January 1955, Asie Océanie/Inde Française/Questions judiciaires, MAE.
41. Ostrorog to Gandon, French representative, 18 March 1955, Asie Océanie/Inde Française/Questions judiciaires, MAE.
42. See, for example, the edited volume from Sue Peabody and Tyler Stovall eds., *The Color of Liberty: Histories of Race in France* (Durham, NC: Duke University Press, 2003).
43. See the appendix for full text of the Treaty of Cession.
44. On the French-Indian diaspora in Indochina/Vietnam, see Natasha Pairaudeau, *Mobile Citizens: French Indians in Indochina, 1858–1954* (Copenhagen: Nordic Institute of Asian Studies, 2016).
45. Emile Appavou, "Pondicherry, en 1962, on n'imaginait pas que d'un seul coup, Pondichéry serait abandonné et cédé à l'Union Indienne," oral history collected by Frederic Praud, https://parolesdhommesetdefemmes.fr/pondichery-en-1962-on-n-imaginait-pas-que-d-un-seul-coup-pondichery-serait (accessed 10 September 2012).
46. On the language question in Tamil Naidu, see Sumathi Ramaswamy, *Passions of the Tongue: Language Devotion in Tamil India, 1891–1970* (Berkeley: University of California Press, 1997).
47. William F. S. Miles, *Imperial Burdens: Countercolonialism in Former French India* (Boulder, CO: Lynne Rienner, 1995), 45.
48. Matthews, secretary general of the Cabinet of the High Commissioner, Pondicherry, to Gandon, 12 February 1955, Asie Océanie/Inde Française/Questions judiciaires, MAE.

49. Weber, *Pondichéry et la comptoirs*, 404.
50. Nehru assured the people in Pondicherry that French would remain the primary language in government until the people decided otherwise. By 1965, the Legislative Assembly of Pondicherry had decided that English, Tamil, Malayalam (in Karaikal and Mahé), and Telegu (in Yanam) would be official languages. French was hardly spoken by government workers by this time. David Annoussamy, "The Merger of French India," in *French in India and Indian Nationalism: 1700–1963*, ed. K. S. Mathew (Delhi: BR, 1999), 580–81.
51. The government of India did eventually grant the French nationals of Indian origin who resided in the Union Territory of Pondicherry the right to live as Indian citizens, removing the need to follow the regulations placed on resident foreigners; this was not known at the time of option.
52. Dassaradanayadou, "Tamouls indiens," 71.
53. Miles, *Imperial Burdens*, 45.
54. Dassaradanayadou, "Tamouls indiens," 71.
55. Miles, *Imperial Burdens*, 45.
56. Weber, *Pondichéry et la comptoirs*, 404.
57. Weber, *Pondichéry et la comptoirs*, 404.
58. Miles, *Imperial Burdens*, 54.
59. Miles, *Imperial Burdens*, 54.
60. Appavou, "Pondicherry."
61. Appavou, "Pondicherry."
62. Sarcelles was also a primary spot of residence for the pied-noirs who came to France after the end of the war in Algeria in 1962.
63. Appavou, "Pondicherry."
64. Andrea L. Smith, *Colonial Memory and Postcolonial Europe: Maltese Settlers in Algeria and France* (Bloomington: Indiana University Press, 2006).
65. Avtar Brah, *Cartographies of Diaspora: Contesting Identities* (New York: Routledge, 1996), 3.
66. Tyler Stovall, "National Identity and Shifting Imperial Frontiers: Whiteness and the Exclusion of Colonial Labor After World War I," *Representations* 84 (2003): 52–72.
67. On the topic of of race in France, see Peabody and Stovall, *Color of Liberty*.
68. Dipesh Chakrabarty, "Governmental Roots of Modern Ethnicity," in *Habitations of Modernity: Essays in the Wake of Subaltern Studies* (Chicago: University of Chicago Press, 2002), 80–100.
69. Chakrabarty, "Governmental Roots," 82.
70. Catherine Sevran-Schreiber and Vasoodeven Vuddamalay, "Les étapes de la présence indienne en France," *Hommes & Migrations* 1268 (2007): 10–11.

71. On South Asian travel writing on Europe in the late nineteenth century, see Antoinette Burton, "Making a Spectacle of Empire: Indian Travelers in Fin-de-Siècle London," *History Workshop Journal* 42 (1996): 126–46.
72. R. C. Dutt, *Three Years in Europe, 1868 to 1871, with an Account of Subsequent Visits to Europe in 1886 and 1893* (Calcutta: S. K. Lahiri, 1896), iv.
73. Dutt, *Three Years in Europe*, iv.
74. Dutt, *Three Years in Europe*, 82.
75. Dutt, *Three Years in Europe*, 85.
76. Dutt, *Three Years in Europe*, 86.
77. Dutt, *Three Years in Europe*, 87.
78. Servan-Schreiber and Vuddamalay, "Étapes," 9.
79. Kate Marsh, *India in the French Imagination: Peripheral Voices, 1754–1815* (London: Pickering & Chatto, 2009); Jackie Assayag, *L'Inde fabuleuse: le charme discret de l'exotisme français (xviie—xxe siècle)* (Paris: Editions Kimé, 1999).
80. While students and tourists represent distinct groups, in this time period, they were the two groups that experienced Europe as temporary residents. More often than not, South Asian students in France spent a significant time traveling throughout Europe as a part of their wider studies, creating a similar experience to the nonstudent South Asian tourist.
81. Belvis, "Pondichéry?," *Le Trait-d'Union*, May 1955, 1.
82. According to an article in the *Hindustan Times,* there were about fifty Indians living in France in 1947. Reprinted in Gopaljee Samboo, *Les Comptoirs Français dans l'Inde Nouvelle (de la compagnie des Indes a nos jours)* (Paris: Fasquelle Editeurs, 1950), 171.
83. Dassaradanayadou, "Tamouls indiens," 69.
84. See Dassaradanayadou, "Tamouls indiens"; and Christine Moliner, "Indian Migrants in France: Country Report," CARIM-India RR2012/11, Robert Schuman Centre for Advanced Studies, San Domenico di Fiesole (FI), European University Institute, 2012.
85. Samboo, *Comptoirs*, 150. Samboo also claims that all the British Indians who were present in France in 1940 were sent to "German concentration camps." Samboo does not provide any evidence for this, but it is an interesting proposition.
86. Samboo, *Comptoirs*, 148–49. Earlier in the century, in 1920, the small community of Indians in Paris had founded the Association Sociale et Commerciale Hindou, which served as a sort of refuge and meeting place for the many political figures who traveled through Europe during the interwar years. The inauguration of the Association de l'Inde en France took place on 12 December 1946—a month later, on 16 January 1947, la Comité France-Inde was also established.

87. See Gopaljee Samboo, *Un Indien à Paris* (Paris: Éditions du scorpion, 1966); and *La médecine de l'Inde autrefois et aujord'hui* (Paris: Éditions du scorpion, 1963
88. Extract of speech given by Georges Paillet at the Palais de Chaillot on 4 February 1950, quoted in Samboo, *Comptoirs*, 153.
89. Gopaljee Samboo, "La communauté Indienne en France," *France-Inde*, 6 May 1954, 6–7.
90. For a complete list of activities sponsored by the AFI and the Comité France-Inde from 1946 to 1950, see Samboo, *Comptoirs*, 172–77.
91. Samboo, *Comptoirs*, 143.
92. Samboo, *Comptoirs*, 143.
93. Samboo, *Comptoirs*, 151, 169.
94. Gopaljee Samboo, "Le message tolerance de l'Inde," *Trait d'Union*, November 1955, 5.
95. Samboo, "Message tolerance de l'Inde," 5.
96. Samboo, *Comptoirs*, 148.
97. Samboo, *Comptoirs*, 148.
98. This was a message that often appeared in *France-Inde* throughout its publication run between 1951 and 1975.
99. Servan-Schreiber and Vuddamalya, "Étapes," 17.
100. Servan-Schreiber and Vuddamalya, "Étapes," 17.
101. Christine Moliner, "Invisible et modèle? Première approche de l'immigration sud-asiatique en France," Rapport d'étude pour la Direction de l'Accueil, de l'Intégration et de la Citoyenneté, MIINDS, Septembre 2009.
102. Vijay Prashad, *The Karma of Brown Folk* (Minneapolis: University of Minnesota Press, 2000), 7.
103. Servan-Schreiber and Vuddamalay, "Étapes," 16. See also the film *Two Flags*, directed by Pankaj Kumar, Kumar Talkies, 2019.
104. Monideepa Banerjie, "The Nowhere People," *Sunday Review* (Calcutta), 4 April 1989, 78–79.
105. Banerjie, "Nowhere People."
106. Banerjie, "Nowhere People."
107. Banerjie, "Nowhere People."
108. The Mother, "15 August 1954," in *Words of the Mother*, vol. 13 (Pondicherry: Sri Aurobindo Ashram Press, 1980), 43. This statement originally appeared in *Mother India*, August 1954, n.p.
109. The Mother, "15 August 1954."
110. A document prepared by the French Consulate in Pondicherry in May 1969 noted that Mother chose to surround herself with Frenchmen in the Ashram. Beginning in the 1920s, her second in command was a Frenchman named Philippe Barbier Saint-Hilaire, also known as Pavitra. Following his death in 1969, her companion was Bernard Enginger, known as Satprem, who

had served in the French colonial government under the last governor of Pondicherry, François Baron, who was also a devoted follower of the Mother. French consulate in Pondicherry to the French ambassador in India, 19 May 1969, Asie Océanie/Inde Française/Auroville, MAE.

## 5. From the Ashram to Auroville

1. *Cinq colonnes à la une*, "Les trois mondes de Pondichéry," Office national de radiodiffusion television française, aired on 4 September 1964, on Channel 1.
2. The Mother (1965), quoted in *Auroville: The City of Universal Culture* (Pondicherry: Sri Aurobindo Society, 1967), 1, Auroville Archives, India (AA).
3. Robert N. Minor, *The Religious, The Spiritual, and the Secular: Auroville and Secular India* (Albany: State University of New York Press, 1999), 106.
4. *UNESCO Resolutions on Auroville* (Paris: UNESCO, 1966).
5. Religious studies scholar Robert N. Minor writes, "Just as Sri Aurobindo was a world figure, Auroville was a world city." Minor, *Auroville and Secular India*, 1.
6. The Sri Aurobindo Society (SAS) was founded in Calcutta in 1960 by "ten local businessmen and lawyers interested in Aurobindo's teachings." Peter Heehs, "Sri Aurobindo and His Ashram, 1910–2010: An Unfinished History," *Nova Religio: The Journal of Alternative and Emergent Religions* (19) 2015: 65–86, 73.
7. Minor, *Auroville and Secular India*, 97.
8. Lorenzo Veracini, "Introducing *settler colonial studies*," *settler colonial studies* 1 (2011): 1–12, 2.
9. There is an entire field of scholarship on settler colonialism. Good introductory texts with a global focus include Patrick Wolfe, *Traces of History: Elementary Structures of Race* (New York: Verso, 2016); *The Routledge Handbook of the History of Settler Colonialism*, ed. Edward Cavanagh and Lorenzo Veracini (New York: Routledge, 2016); and the journal *settler colonial studies* (Taylor & Francis).
10. Eve Tuck and K.Wayne Yang, "Decolonization Is Not a Metaphor," *Decolonization: Indigeneity, Education & Society* 1 (2012): 1–40.
11. The Mother dictated the message quoted in the epigraph to Ashramite and Auroville advisor Shyam Sundar in response to rising tensions between Europeans and Tamils at the Auroville Health Centre. Shyam Sundar Jhunjhunwala, *Down Memory Lane* (Pondicherry: Sri Aurobindo's Action, 1996), 123.
12. Air France advertisement in *Equals One: The Quarterly Journal of Auroville* 3, no. 1 (1968), n.p.

13. "Auroville: 28 February 1968," program from the opening ceremony/dedication, AA.
14. Navoditte (Norman Thomas), "The Day the Balloon Went Up," in *Auroville: Dream and Reality, An Anthology*, ed. Akash Kapur (Gurgaon: Penguin India, 2018), 12–13.
15. *The Auroville Experience: Selections from 202 Issues of Auroville Today, November 1988 to November 2005* (Auroville: Auroville Today, 2006), 4.
16. Anger actually proposed several designs, starting in 1965, based on more traditional city designs, but the Mother rejected all of them until the "galaxy" model was developed in 1968, just in time for the inauguration ceremony. See "Towards a Township," in *Auroville Experience*, 44.
17. The plans for Auroville were laid out in detail in many promotional brochures, including this one from 1969 titled *Auroville* (see 4–10), AA.
18. "Information on Auroville, 1966–1974," in *Note of Information* (1969), AA.
19. For more on Kibbutzim, see Melford E. Spiro, "Utopia and Its Discontents: The Kibbutz and Its Historical Vicissitudes," *American Anthropologist* 106 (3): 556–68.
20. The Mother, quote recorded by her devotee, Shyam Sundar Jhunjhunwala, and printed in his *Down Memory Lane*, 123.
21. The Mother (1972) reprinted in Jhunjhunwala, *Down Memory Lane*, 123.
22. Minor, *Auroville and Secular India*, 45.
23. Minor, *Auroville and Secular India*, 45.
24. Minor's work also traces the transformation of Auroville from an experimental "world city," inhabited and operated by its members, to a project overseen by the Indian "secular" state in the 1980s. On the paradoxes of the modern nation-state, see also Uday S. Mehta, "Liberal Strategies of Exclusion," in *Tensions of Empire: Colonial Culture in a Bourgeois World*, ed. Ann Stoler and Frederick Cooper (Berkeley: University of California Press, 1997), 59–86.
25. On the psychology of colonialism, it is impossible not to cite the importance of the work of Frantz Fanon, especially *Black Skin, White Masks* (1967).
26. The Mother, quoted in Huta D. Hindocha, *The Spirit of Auroville* (Pondicherry: Havyavahana Trust, [1974] 2002), 1.
27. See Leela Gandhi, *Affective Communities: Anticolonial Thought, Fin-de-Siècle Radicalism, and the Politics of Friendship* (Durham, NC: Duke University Press, 2006), especially chapter 5, "Mysticism and Radicalism at the End of the Nineteenth Century."
28. Gandhi, *Affective Communities*, 124. The attempt to merge Eastern spiritualism and philosophy with Western secular politics did not originate with the Mother, but is often associated with theosophy and Annie Besant, the Irish woman who moved to India in the name of anti-imperialism and theosophy

and eventually became a member, and then president, of the Indian Congress Party. On the life and work of Annie Besant, see Joy Dixon, *Divine Feminine: Theosophy and Feminism in India* (Baltimore, MD: John Hopkins University Press, 2001).

29. Sri Aurobindo published a prolific amount of work on Integral Yoga. In 1997, the Sri Aurobindo Ashram began to publish the *Complete Works of Sri Aurobindo* in a library edition. Twenty-six volumes have been issued thus far; upon completion, there will be thirty-seven. His principal works on yoga are *The Synthesis of Yoga, I–II*, written between 1914 and 1921.
30. Sir Thomas More, *Utopia* (Cambridge: Cambridge University Press, [1516] 1989), xi.
31. Osama W. Abi-Mershed, *Apostles of Modernity: Saint-Simonians and the Civilizing Mission in Algeria* (Stanford, CA: Stanford University Press, 2010).
32. Lucy Sargisson, "Strange Places: Estrangement, Utopianism, and Intentional Communities," *Utopian Studies* 18, no. 3 (2007), 393–424, 393.
33. *Auroville: The Cradle of a New Man* (Pondicherry: Sri Aurobindo Society, 1971), 1, AA.
34. The Mother, January 1967, quoted in *Auroville* (1969), AA.
35. See, for example, Jeffery Paine, *Father India: Westerners Under the Spell of an Ancient Culture* (New York: Harper Collins, 1999); and Gita Mehta, *Karma Cola: Marketing the Mystic East* (New York: Simon & Schuster, 1979).
36. Auroville application, n.d., AA.
37. Kasturi Rangan, "Utopian Town in India Built on a Dream," *New York Times*, 16 October 1971, 8.
38. Goa, the former Portuguese colony, has long been a favorite spot for hippies and later international tourists to hang out on the beach, party, and take drugs. See Arun Saldanha, *Psychedelic White: Goa Trance and the Viscosity of Race* (Minneapolis: University of Minnesota Press, 2007).
39. The Mother, February 1971, reprinted in *Auroville Guidelines*, AA.
40. The Mother, *Auroville* (1969), 12, AA.
41. There are a collection of short biographies of a select number of Aurovillians in the edited collection *Auroville: Dream and Reality*, ed. Akash Kapur (Gurgaon: Penguin India, 2018).
42. Rangan, "Utopian Town in India."
43. The following oral histories were collected by Kripa Borg and Toby Butler, mostly in 1999. They have been transcribed and are now kept in the Auroville Archives for researchers to access. For this reason, I treat them here as written texts and not as live interviews. Verne, April 1999, transcription from audio recording.
44. Paul Pinton and Laura Reddy interview, March 1999, AA.
45. Paul Pinton and Laura Reddy interview, March 1999, AA.

46. Judith interview, March 1999, AA.
47. Lisbeth interview, March 1999, AA.
48. Lisbeth interview, March 1999, AA.
49. *Auroville: The Cradle of a New Man* (Pondicherry: Sri Aurobindo Society, 1971), 17, AA.
50. Daridan to Murville, 7 April 1966, Ministère des Affaires Étrangères Archives, La Courneuve, France (MAE).
51. Daridan to Murville, 7 April 1966.
52. Udar, "The Impact of the Anti-Hindi Movement on the Sri Aurobindo Ashram." Included as a supplement to *Mother India* 17 (1965).
53. Udar, "Impact of the Anti-Hindi Movement."
54. Udar, "Impact of the Anti-Hindi Movement."
55. Udar, "Impact of the Anti-Hindi Movement."
56. Udar, "Impact of the Anti-Hindi Movement."
57. The Mother, "A Declaration," 16 February 1965, in *More Answers of the Mother*, vol. 17 (Pondicherry: Sri Aurobindo Ashram, 2004), 251–52. The Dravida Munnetra Kazhagam (DMK) is the primary Tamil political party, still prominent in both Pondicherry and Tamil Nadu.
58. The Mother, *Auroville Guidelines*, 1967, AA.
59. "Auroville," *Marie-Claire*, June 1970, 102.
60. Rangan, "Utopian Town in India."
61. "Auroville Population and List of Aurovilians," 1971–1974, AA.
62. "Auroville Population and List of Aurovilians," 1971–1974, AA.
63. Roy Chyat interview, October 1999, AA.
64. "There Was a Kind of Magic," in *Auroville Experience*, 8.
65. "There Was a Kind of Magic," in *Auroville Experience*, 8.
66. "Looking Forward, Looking Back," in *Auroville Experience*, 10.
67. "Auroville International Township Progress Report," 1 November 1968, AA.
68. "Auroville Population and List of Aurovilians," 1971–1974, AA.
69. *Auroville: January, 1974*, 9, AA.
70. Auroville charter, 28 February 1968, reprinted in *Auroville Guidelines*, 1, AA.
71. "Constructing the City: A Portrait of Dhanapal," in *Auroville Experience*, 200.
72. *Auroville: January, 1974*, 8–9, AA.
73. The relationship to material possessions and the importance of labor for spiritual discovery are numbers three and four in the list. "To Be a True Aurovilian" (1970), in *Auroville Guidelines*.
74. Roy Chyat interview, October 1999, AA.
75. "Looking Forward, Looking Back," in *Auroville Experience*, 12.
76. Robert Lawlor, "Early Letters," in Kapur, *Auroville: Dream and Reality*, 17.
77. *Auroville: The City of the Future*, 1974, 19, AA.
78. Jhunjhuwala, *Down Memory Lane*, 121.

79. "There Was a Kind of Magic," in *Auroville Experience*, 8. However, it seems unlikely that after two hundred years of colonial rule by Europeans, the villagers had never seen a white person.
80. "There Was a Kind of Magic," in *Auroville Experience*, 8.
81. *Auroville Voice*, 1970–1974, AA.
82. Shyama interview, March 1999, AA.
83. *Auroville: January, 1974*, AA.
84. Ronald Jorgenson, "'In Auroville': The Community That Lost Its Name," *World Union* 14, no. 4 (1974): 46.
85. Quote in epigraph from "Constructing the City: A Portrait of Dhanapal," in *Auroville Experience*, 200.
86. *Auroville: January, 1974*, 23–24, AA.
87. *Auroville Voice*, 1978, 16, AA.
88. Between 1980 and 1991, the government of India acted as the official manager of all Auroville's assets.
89. "Towards a Township," in *Auroville Experience*, 45.
90. "Towards a Township" in *Auroville Experience*, 45.
91. Aurelec-Prayogashala, "Auroville Celebrates 40 Years," 2008, PRISMA.
92. *Auroville Land Fund Newsletter* 41 (January–March 2008), AA.
93. Meena Khandelwal, "Foreign Swamis at Home in India: Transmigration to the Birthplace of Spirituality," *Identities: Global Studies in Culture and Power* 14 (2007): 313–40.

## Conclusion

1. "Disparition de Gabriel David," TamilExpress, 18 July 2014, http://tamilexpress.fr/disparition-de-gabriel-david/.
2. "Ambassador Richier Conveys His Condolences on the Demise of World War II Veteran," 18 July 2014, French Embassy in New Delhi, https://in.ambafrance.org/Ambassador-Richier-conveys-his.
3. Annie Philip, "Adieu, Last Veteran of World War II," *Hindu*, 17 July 2014, http://www.thehindu.com/news/cities/puducherry/adieu-last-veteran-of-world-war-ii/article6220589.ece.
4. Claude Arpi, "Welcome Address," *Treaty of Cession, 1962: Fifty Years Later, Pondicherry and France* (Auroville: Pavillon de France à Auroville, 2012).
5. Emile Chabal, "From the *banlieue* to the Burkini: The Many Lives of French Republicanism," *Modern & Contemporary France* 25, no. 1 (2017): 68–74.
6. "National liberation, national reawakening, restoration of the nation to the people or the commonwealth, whatever the name used, whatever the latest

expression, decolonization is always a violent event." Frantz Fanon, *The Wretched of the Earth* (New York: Grove, [1961] 2007), 1.
7. Fanon, *Wretched of the Earth*, 5.
8. This is a widely acknowledged argument by this point in time, though of course there would be many who would disagree and argue that history is a neutral social science. On the colonial structure of history, see Dipesh Chakrabarty, *Provincializing Europe: Postcolonial Thought and Historical Difference* (Princeton, NJ: Princeton University Press, 2001); and Bernard Cohn, *Colonialism and Its Forms of Knowledge* (Princeton, NJ: Princeton University Press, 1996). An editorial letter in a recent edition of the *American Historical Review* acknowledges the role historians, and the journals and publishing gatekeepers of the discipline, have had in continuing and promoting structures of colonial power. "Decolonizing the *AHR*," *American Historical Review* 123, no. 1 (February 2018): xiv–xvii.
9. On the many ways in which the decolonization in Africa was envisioned during this time, see Adom Getachew, *World Making After Empire: The Rise and Fall of Self-Determination* (Princeton, NJ: Princeton University Press, 2019).
10. Although messiness as a method is my own formulation, for more on decolonizing methodology, see Linda Tuhiwai Smith, *Decolonizing Methodologies: Research and Indigenous Peoples* (London: Zed, 1999).
11. Nick Estes, *Our History Is the Future: Standing Rock Versus the Dakota Access Pipeline, and the Long Tradition of Indigenous Resistance* (New York: Verso, 2019).
12. Benedict Anderson, *Imagined Communities: Reflections on the Origin and Spread of Nationalism* (New York: Verso, 1983).
13. Vasoodeen Vuddamalay, Paul White, and Deborah Sporton, "The Evolution of the Goutte d'Or as an Ethnic Minority District of Paris," *New Community* 17, no. 2 (1991): 245–58; on the Sri Lankan migration to France, see Anthony Goreau-Ponceaud, ed., special issue, "Diasporas sri lankaises: entre guerre et paix," *Hommes & Migrations* 1291 (May–June 2011).
14. Sophie Lakshmi Dassaradanayadou, "Tamouls indiens: de Pondichéry à la France," *Hommes & Migrations* 1268–69 (2007): 69–70.
15. There are many associations in France dedicated to the preservation of various colonial cultures. My thinking throughout this work on questions of postcolonial identity in France has been greatly influenced by the anthropologist Andrea L. Smith and her book *Colonial Memory and Postcolonial Europe* (Bloomington: Indiana University Press, 2006).
16. I have written about family history elsewhere. See Jessica Namakkal, "Peanut Butter Dosas: Becoming Desi in the Midwest," *Tides Magazine*, April 18, 2017, https://www.saada.org/tides/article/peanut-butter-dosas.

17. On Indians as settlers in the United States, see Sonia Thomas, "Cowboys and Indians: Indian Priests in Rural Montana," *Women's Studies Quarterly* 47 (2019): 110–31.
18. http://www.debatidentitenationale.fr (accessed November 19, 2020). The site was launched on 2 October 2009 by the Ministry of Immigration and Integration. See also "Un outil collaboratif pour débattre de l'identité nationale," *Le Monde*, 2 October 2009, https://www.lemonde.fr/societe/article/2009/11/02/un-outil-collaboratif-pour-debattre-de-l-identite-nationale_1261764_3224.html.
19. http://www.debatidentitenationale.fr.
20. The "burqa ban" passed the French Senate in 2010 by an overwhelming majority. "Burqa: la France prend-elle un risque? (Burqa: Is France taking a risk?)" *Le Monde*, 5 May 2010, http://www.lemonde.fr/a-la-une/article/2010/05/05/burqa-la-france-prend-elle-un-risque_1347074_3208.html. See also Joan Wallach Scott, *The Politics of the Veil* (Princeton, NJ: Princeton University Press, 2010); and Laurent Dubois, "La republique metissee: Citizenship, Colonialism, and the Borders of French History," *Cultural Studies* 14 (2010): 15–34.

# Bibliography

## Archival Sources

AA        Auroville Archives
          Auroville, India

AN        Archives Nationales
          Paris, France

FRANOM    Archives Nationales d'Outre-Mer
          Aix-en-Provence, France

IOR       British Library
          Asian and African Studies Collection
          India Office Records
          London, England

MAE       Ministère des Affaires Étrangères Archives
          La Courneuve, France

NAI-P     National Archives of India—Puducherry Division
          Union Territory of Puducherry, India

## Periodicals

*=1* (Auroville)
*Bulletin d'Éducation Physique* (Aurobindo Ashram)
*Centre d'information et de documentation de l'Inde Francophone Bulletin* (Paris)
*Dessogabari* (Tamil and French publication, Pondicherry)
*France-Inde* (Paris)
*L'Éclair*
*L'Express*
*Le Figaro*
*Le Monde*
*Le Trait-d'Union* (Pondicherry)
*Life*
*Matrouboumy* (Malayalam and French publication, Mahé)
*Marie-Claire*
*Mother India* (Pondicherry)
*New Indian Express*
*Sri Aurobindo's Action*
*Hindu*
*Indian Sociologist: An Organ of Freedom, and of Political, Social, and Religious Reform*
*New Indian Express*
*Times of India*
*Times of London*
*New York Times*
*New Yorker*
*Statesman* (Calcutta)
*Sunday Standard*
*World Union* (Pondicherry)

## Memoirs, Testimonies, Autobiographies

Annasse, Arthur. *Les Comptoirs Français de l'Inde (1664–1954): Trois siècles de présence française.* Paris: Le pensée universelle, 1975.

Appavou, Emile. "PONDICHÉRY, En 1962, on n'imaginait pas que d'un seul coup, Pondichéry serait abandonné et cédé à l'Union Indienne." Oral history collected by Frederic Praud. Accessed December 22, 2020. http://www.parolesdhommesetdefemmes.fr/pondichery-en-1962-on-n-imaginait-pas-que-d-un-seul-coup-pondichery-serait.

Aurobindo, Sri. *Autobiographical Notes: And Other Writings of Historical Interest*. Pondicherry: Sri Aurobindo Ashram, 2006.

———. *Tales of Prison Life*. Pondicherry: Sri Aurobindo Ashram, 1974.

Cortés, Sebastian. *Pondicherry Heritage: From Perception to Action*. New Delhi: Lustre, 2012.

Cotton, Julian James. "Pondicherry." *Macmillan's Magazine* 87 (1905): 125–35.

Dadala, Sri Raphael Ramanayya. *My Struggle for the Freedom of French India: An Autobiography*. Kakinada: n.p, n.d.

Dubois, Jean-Antoine. *Mœurs, institutions, et cérémonies des peuples de l'Inde*. Paris: Imprimerie royale, 1825.

Dutt, R. C. *Three Years in Europe, 1868 to 1871, with an Account of Subsequent Visits to Europe in 1886 and 1893*. Calcutta: S. K. Lahiri, 1896.

Gaudart, Michel. *Généalogie des familles de l'Inde Française, XVIe–XXe siècle*. Pondichéry: Société de l'Histoire de l'Inde Française, 1976.

Gaudart, Michel, and Philippe Randa. *Les dernières années de l'Inde française*. Paris: Dualpha, 2005.

Ghose, Barindra Kumar. *The Tale of My Exile: Twelve Years in the Andamans*. Edited by Sachidananda Mohanty. Pondicherry: Sri Aurobindo Ashram, [1922] 2011.

Gupta, Nolini Kanta. *Reminiscences*. Pondicherry: Sri Aurobindo Ashram, 1969.

Hindocha, Huta D. *The Spirit of Auroville*. Pondicherry: Havyavahana Trust, [1974] 2002.

Hulliet, N. *Hygiène des blancs, des mixtes, et des indiens à Pondichéry*. Pondichéry: Imprimeur du Gouvernement, 1867.

Jhunjhunwala, Shyam Sundar. *Down Memory Lane*. Pondicherry: Sri Aurobindo's Action, 1996.

Kumari, Shyam. *How They Came to Sri Aurobindo and the Mother: Twenty-Nine True Stories of Sadhaks and Devotees*. Bombay: Mother Publishing House, 1990.

Leary, Timothy. *Flashbacks: An Autobiography*. Los Angeles: J. P. Tracher, 1983.

Moracchini, M. D. *Les Indigènes de l'Inde française et le suffrage universel*. Paris: Blot, 1889.

Morriset, Andre. "Remembrances." Overman Foundation. Accessed 15 June 2020. http://overmanfoundation.org/three-talks-by-andre-morisset-the-mothers-son/.

Maufroid, A. *Sous le soleil de l'Inde*. Paris: Librairie Plon, 1911.

The Mother. *More Answers of the Mother*. Vol. 17. Pondicherry: Sri Aurobindo Ashram, 2004.

———. *Words of the Mother*. Pondicherry: Sri Aurobindo Ashram, 1980.

Nehru, Jawaharlal. *The Collected Works of Jawaharlal Nehru*. 42 vols. New Delhi: Oxford University Press, 1984–2010.

———. *Selected Works of Jawarhalal Nehru*. Vol. 27. New Delhi: Oxford University Press, 2000.

———. *What Are the Indian States?* Allahabad: All-India States' Peoples' Conference, 1939.

Nirodbaran. *Twelve Years with Sri Aurobindo.* Pondicherry: Sri Aurobindo Ashram, 1972.

Pillai, Ananda Ranga. *The Private Diary of Ananda Ranga Pillai: A Record of Matters Political, Historical, Social, and Personal, from 1736 to 1761.* Translated by Sir J. Frederick Price. Madras: Government Press, 1904.

Ramasrinivasan, R. *Karaikal in Freedom Struggle (Commemoration of the "Golden Jubilee Celebrations of the Independence of India").* Pondicherry: Qualité Offset, 1998.

Richard, Michel Paul. *Without Passport: The Life and Work of Paul Richard.* New York: Peter Lang, 1987.

Saint-Hilaire, Philippe Barbier. *Itinéraire d'un enfant du siècle: Correspondance de Pavitra avec son père (1918–1954).* Paris: Buset/Chastel, 2001.

Samboo, Gopaljee. *Les Comptoirs Français dans l'Inde Nouvelle (de la compagnie des Indes a nos jours).* Paris: Fasquelle Éditeurs, 1950.

———. *La médecine de l'Inde autrefois et aujord'hui.* Paris: Éditions du scorpion, 1963.

———. *Un Indien à Paris.* Paris: Éditions du scorpion, 1966.

Subbiah, V. *Saga of Freedom in French India.* Madras: New Century, 1990.

## Pamphlets and Government Reports

Antony, Francis Cyril, ed. *Gazetteer, Union Territory of Pondicherry.* Pondicherry: Government Press, 1982.

*The Auroville Experience: Selections from 202 Issues of Auroville Today, November 1988 to November 2005.* Tamil Nadu : Auroville Today, 2006.

"Border Incidents by French India Partisans: Acts of Goondaism Detailed." 18 November 1952. Report issued on behalf of the House of the People. Distributed by the Press Information Bureau, Government of India.

Chopra, Prabha, and P. N. Chopra, eds. *Secret British Intelligence Report: Indian Freedom Fighters Abroad.* New Delhi: Criterion, 1988.

Coret, Alain. *La Cession de l'Inde Française.* Paris: Librairie Générale de Droit et de Jurisprudence, 1955.

"Dark Record of Goonda Raj in French Settlements in India." 26 October 1952. Report issued on behalf of the House of the People. Distributed by the Press Information Bureau, Government of India.

Deloche, Jean. *Le papier terrier de la ville blanche de Pondichéry 1777.* Pondichéry: Institut Français de Pondichéry, 2002.

*Dictionnaire des parlementaires français, 1940–1958.* Paris: La documentation française, 2001.

Duquesne, Jacques. *Les 16–24 ans: Une Enquête de l'Institut Français d'Opinion Publique*. Paris: Éditions du Centurion, 1963.
*French Pockets in India*. Madras: Free India, 1953.
Giroud, Françoise. *La nouvelle vague: portraits de la jeunesse*. Paris: Gallimard, 1958.
*Parliamentary Debates*. House of Commons Official report. First session of the Thirty-Eighth Parliament of the United Kingdom of Great Britain and Northern Ireland. No. 420, 5th series. London: His Majesty's Stationery Office, 1946.
Rajkumar, N. V. *The Problem of French India*. New Delhi: Department of Foreign Relations, Indian National Congress, 1954.
Samanta, A. K. *Terrorism in Bengal*. Calcutta: Government of West Bengal, 1995.
*UNESCO Resolutions on Auroville*. Paris: UNESCO, 1966.

## Articles and Books

Abi-Mershed, Osama W. *Apostles of Modernity: Saint-Simonians and the Civilizing Mission in Algeria*. Stanford, CA: Stanford University Press, 2010.
Acharya, M. P. T. *We Are Anarchists: Essays on Anarchism, Pacifism, and the Indian Independence Movement, 1923–53*. Edited by Ole Birk Laursen. Oakland, CA: AK, 2019.
Agmon, Danna. *A Colonial Affair: Commerce, Conversion, and Scandal in French India*. Ithaca, NY: Cornell University Press, 2017.
Anderson, Benedict. *Imagined Communities: Reflections on the Origin and Spread of Nationalism*. New York: Verso, 1983.
Andreas, Peter, and Thomas J. Biersteker, eds. *The Rebordering of North America: Integration and Exclusion in a New Security Context*. New York: Routledge, 2003.
Annoussamy, David. "The Merger of French India." In *French in India and Indian Nationalism: (1700–1963)*, edited by K. S. Mathew, 569–84. Delhi: BR, 1999.
Arnold, David. *Police Power and Colonial Rule: Madras, 1859–1947*. Oxford: Oxford University Press, 1986.
Arpi, Claude. *Il y a 50 ans . . . Pondichéry: L'intégration des établissements français en Inde Perspectives historiques et culturelles*. Auroville: Auroville, 2004.
———. *Treaty of Cession, 1962: Fifty Years Later, Pondicherry and France*. Auroville: Pavillon de France à Auroville, 2012.
Assayag, Jackie. *L'Inde fabuleuse: Le charme discret de l'exotisme français (XVII$^e$–XX$^e$)*. Paris: Éditions Kimé, 2000.
Aydin, Cemil. *The Politics of Anti-Westernism in Asia: Visions of World Order in Pan-Islamic and Pan-Asian Thought*. New York: Columbia University Press, 2007.
Ballantyne, Tony. *Orientalism and Race: Aryanism in the British Empire*. New York: Palgrave Macmillan, 2001.

Bancel, Nicolas, and Pascal Blanchard. "The Pitfalls of Colonial Memory." In *The Colonial Legacy in France: Fracture, Rupture, and Apartheid*, edited by Nicolas Bancel, Pascal Blanchard, and Dominic Thomas, translated by Alexis Pernsteiner, 153–64. Bloomington: Indiana University Press, 2017.

Bancel, Nicolas, Pascal Blanchard, Dominic Thomas, eds. *The Colonial Legacy in France: Fracture, Rupture, and Apartheid*. Translated by Alexis Pernsteiner. Bloomington: Indiana University Press, 2017.

Baron, François, and Surendra Mohan Ghose. "Two Documents of Historical Importance." *Mother India* 28 (1976): 648–49.

Belmessous, Saliha. "Assimilation and Racialism in Seventeenth- and Eighteenth-Century French Colonial Policy," *American Historical Review* 110 (2005): 322–49.

Berezin, Mable, and Martin Schain, eds. *Europe Without Borders: Remapping Territory, Citizenship and Identity in a Transnational Age*. Baltimore, MD: Johns Hopkins University Press, 2003.

Berthy, G. "L'Inde aux Hindous." *L'éclair*, 28 December 1908, n.p.

Betts, Raymond. *Assimilation and Association in French Colonial Theory, 1890–1914*. Lincoln: University of Nebraska Press, 2005.

Bhabha, Homi K. *The Location of Culture*. New York: Routledge, 1994.

Bhambra, Gurminder K., Kerem Nisancioglu, and Dalia Gebrial, eds. *Decolonising the University*. London: Pluto, 2018.

Bi, S. Chandni. *Urban Centers of Pondicherry*. New Delhi: Icon, 2006.

Blanchard, Pascal, Gilles Boëtsch, Sandrine Lemaire, and Nicolas Bancel, eds. *Culture coloniale en France: De la Révolution française à nos jours*. Paris: Broché, 2008.

Blanckaert, Claude. "Of Monstrous Métis? Hybridity, Fear of Miscegenation, and Patriotism from Buffon to Paul Broca." In *The Color of Liberty: Histories of Race in France*, edited by Tyler Stovall and Sue Peabody, 42–70. Durham, NC: Duke University Press, 2003.

Boswell, Laird. "From Liberation to Purge Trials in the 'Mythic Provinces': The Reconfiguration of Identities in Alsace and Lorraine, 1918–1920." *French Historical Studies* 23 (2000): 129–62.

Brah, Avtar. *Cartographies of Diaspora: Contesting Identities*. New York: Routledge, 1996.

Britton, Celia M. *Edouard Glissant and Postcolonial Theory*. Charlottesville: University of Virginia Press, 2009.

Brown, Callum G. *The Death of Christian Britain: Understanding Secularisation, 1800–2000*. New York: Routledge, 2009.

Brubaker, Rogers. *Citizenship and Nationhood in France and Germany*. Cambridge, MA: Harvard University Press, 1992.

Burton, Antoinette, ed., *After the Imperial Turn: Thinking with and Through the Nation*. Durham, NC: Duke University Press, 2003.

———. *Archive Stories: Facts, Fictions, and the Writing of History*. Durham, NC: Duke University Press, 2005.

———. "Making a Spectacle of Empire: Indian Travelers in Fin-de-Siècle London." *History Workshop Journal* 42 (1996): 126–46.

Butali, Urvashi. *The Other Side of Silence.* New Delhi: Penguin, 1998.

Cama, Bhikaji. "Letter to the Editor," *Indian Sociologist: An Organ of Freedom, and of Political, Social, and Religious Reform,* November 1907, n.p.

Casstonet des Fosses, Henri-Louis. *La Révolution et les clubs dans l'Inde française.* Nantes: Forest et Grimaud, 1885.

Carton, Adrian. *Mixed-Race and Modernity in Colonial India: Changing Concepts of Hybridity Across Empires.* New York: Routledge, 2012.

———. "Shades of Fraternity: 'Créolization' and the Making of Citizenship in French India, 1790–92." *French Historical Studies* 31 (2008): 581–607.

Chabal, Emile. "From the *banlieue* to the Burkini: The Many Lives of French Republicanism." *Modern & Contemporary France* 25, no. 1 (2017): 68–74.

Chafer, Tony. *The End of Empire in French West Africa: France's Successful Decolonization?* Oxford: Berg, 2002.

Chakrabarty, Dipesh. *Habitations of Modernity: Essays in the Wake of Subaltern Studies.* Chicago: University of Chicago Press, 2004.

———. "Postcoloniality and the Artifice of History: Who Speaks for 'Indian' Pasts?" *Representations* 37 (1992): 1–23.

———. *Provincializing Europe: Postcolonial Thought and Historical Difference.* Princeton, NJ: Princeton University Press, 2000.

Chandrababu, B. S. *Social Protest and Its Impact on Tamil Nadu: With Reference to Self Respect Movement, from 1920s to 1940s.* Madras: Emerald, 1993.

Charef, Mehdi. *Le thé au harem d'Archi Ahmed.* Paris: Gallimard, 1983.

Chatterjee, Partha. "Empires, Nations, Peoples: The Imperial Prerogative and Colonial Exceptions." *Thesis Eleven* 139, no. 1 (2017): 84–96.

———. *Nationalist Thought and the Colonial World: A Derivative Discourse?* Minneapolis: University of Minnesota Press, 1986.

———. *The Nation and Its Fragments: Colonial and Postcolonial Histories.* Princeton, NJ: Princeton University Press, 1993.

Clancy-Smith, Julia, and Frances Gouda, eds. *Domesticating the Empire: Race, Gender, and Family Life in French and Dutch Colonialism.* Charlottesville: University of Virginia Press, 1998.

Cohn, Bernard. *Colonialism and Its Forms of Knowledge: The British in India.* Princeton, NJ: Princeton University Press, 1996.

Conklin, Alice. "Boundaries Unbound: Teaching French History as Colonial History and Colonial History as French History." *French Historical Studies* 23 (2000): 215–38.

———. "Colonialism and Human Rights, A Contradiction in Terms? The Case of France and West Africa, 1895–1914." *American Historical Review* 103 (1998): 4–22.

———. *Mission to Civilize: The Republican Idea of Empire in French West Africa, 1895–1930*. Stanford, CA: Stanford University Press, 1997.

Conklin, Alice, and Julia Clancy-Smith. "Introduction: Writing Colonial Histories." *French Historical Studies* 27 (2004): 497–505.

Cons, Jason. *Sensitive Spaces: Fragmented Territory at the India-Bangladesh Border*. Seattle: University of Washington Press, 2016.

Cooper, Frederick. *Citizenship Between Empire and Nation: Remaking France and French Africa, 1945–1960*. Princeton, NJ: Princeton University Press, 2014.

———. *Decolonization and African Society: The Labor Question in French and British Africa*. Cambridge: Cambridge University Press, 1996.

Cooper, Frederick, and Ann Laura Stoler, eds. *Tensions of Empire: Colonial Cultures in a Bourgeois World*. Berkeley: University of California Press, 1997.

Cooper, Nicola. *France in Indochina: Colonial Encounters*. Oxford: Berg, 2001.

Copley, Antony, ed. *Gurus and Their Followers: New Religious Reform Movements in Colonial India*. New Delhi: Oxford University Press, 2000.

Das, S. "British Reactions to the French Bugbear in India: 1763–83." *European History Quarterly* 22 (1982): 39–65.

Dassaradanayadou, Sophie. "Tamouls indiens: de Pondichéry à la France." *Hommes & migrations* 1268 (2007): 68–81.

Davies, Andrew. "Exile in the Homeland? Anti-Colonialism, Subaltern Geographies, and the Politics of Friendship in Early Twentieth-Century Pondicherry, India." *Environment and Planning D: Society and Space* 35, no. 3 (2017): 457–74.

———. *Geographies of Anticolonialism: Political Networks Across and Beyond South Asia, c. 1900–1930*. Oxford: Royal Geographical Society/Wiley, 2020.

"Decolonizing the *AHR*." *American Historical Review* 123, no. 1 (February 2018): xiv–xvii.

de la Pradelle, Géraud. "Dual Nationality and the French Citizenship Tradition." In *Dual Nationality, Social Rights and Federal Citizenship in the U.S. and Europe: The Reinvention of Citizenship*, edited by Randall Hansen and Patrick Weil, 191–212. New York: Berghahn, 2002.

Deloche, Jean. "Old Pondicherry (1673–1824) Revisited." In *Cities in Medieval India*, edited by Yogesh Sharma and Pius Malekandathil, 645–58. Delhi: Primus, 2014.

De, Rohit. "Between Midnight and Republic: Theory and Practice of India's Dominion Status." *I*CON* 17, no. 4 (2019): 1213–34.

Dhareshawar, Vivek, and R. Srivatsan. "Rowdy Sheeters: An Essay on Subalternity and Polities." In *Subaltern Studies IX: Writings on South Asian History and Society*, edited by Shahid Amin and Dipesh Chakrabarty, 201–31. Delhi: Oxford University Press, 1996.

Dirks, Nicholas. *Castes of Mind: Colonialism and the Making of Modern India*. Princeton, NJ: Princeton University Press, 2001.

Dixon, Joy. *Divine Feminine: Theosophy and Feminism in India*. Baltimore, MD: Johns Hopkins University Press, 2001.

Duara, Pressenjit, ed. *Decolonization: Rewriting Histories*. New York: Routledge, 2004.

———. "History and Globalization in China's Long Twentieth Century." *Modern China* 34, no. 1, 2008: 152–64.

Dubois, Laurent. *A Colony of Citizens: Revolution and Slave Emancipation in the French Caribbean, 1787–1804*. Chapel Hill: University of North Carolina Press, 2004.

———. "La republique metisse: Citizenship, Colonialism, and the Borders of French History." *Cultural Studies* 14 (2010): 15–34.

Edwards, Penny. "A Strategic Sanctuary: Reading *l'Inde Française* through the Colonial Archive." *Interventions: International Journal of Postcolonial Studies* 12 (2010): 356–67.

Elden, Stuart. *Terror and Territory: The Spatial Extent of Sovereignty*. Minneapolis: University of Minnesota Press, 2009.

Estes, Nick. *Our History Is the Future: Standing Rock Versus the Dakota Access Pipeline, and the Long Tradition of Indigenous Resistance*. New York: Verso, 2019.

Fabish, Rachael. "The Political Goddess: Aurobindo's Use of Bengali *Sakta* Tantrism to Justify Political Violence in the Indian Anti-Colonial Movement." *South Asia: Journal of South Asian Studies* 30 (2007): 269–89.

Fanon, Frantz. *Black Skin, White Masks*. New York: Grove, 1967.

———. *The Wretched of the Earth*. New York: Grove, [1961] 2007.

Fazila-Yacoobali Zamindar, Vazira. *The Long Partition and the Making of Modern South Asia: Refugees, Boundaries, Histories*. New York: Columbia University Press, 2007.

Fifield, R. H. "The Future of French India." *Far Eastern Survey* 19 (1950): 62–64.

Foucault, Michel. "Of Other Spaces: Utopias and Heterotopias." *Architecture/Mouvement/Continuité* 5 (1984): 46–49. Translated by Jay Miskowiec in *Diacritics* 16 (1986): 22–27.

———. *The Order of Things: An Archaeology of Human Sciences*. Translated by A. M. Sheridan-Smith. New York: Vintage, 1972.

———. *"Society Must Be Defended": Lectures at the Collège de France, 1975–76*. Translated by David Macey. New York: Picador, 2003.

Frader, Laura, and Herrick Chapman, eds. *Race in France: Interdisciplinary Perspectives on the Politics of Difference*. New York: Berghahn, 2004.

Gaebelé, Yvonne Robert. *Créole et Grande Dame, Joanna Bégum, Marquise Dupleix, 1706–1756*. Pondichéry: Bibliothèque Coloniale, 1956.

Ganachari, Aravind. "Combatting Terror of Law in Colonial India: The Law of Sedition and the Nationalist Response." In *Engaging Terror: A Critical and Multidisciplinary Approach*, edited by Marianne Vardalos, 93–110. Boca Raton, FL: Brown Walker, 2009.

Gandhi, Leela. *Affective Communities: Anticolonial Thought, Fin-de-Siècle Radicalism, and the Politics of Friendship*. Durham, NC: Duke University Press, 2006.

Gaudart de Soulages, Michel, and Phillippe Randa. *Les dernières années de l'Inde française*. Paris: Dualpha, 2005.

Gellner, David, ed. *Borderland Lives in Northern South Asia*. Durham, NC: Duke University Press, 2013.

Getachew, Adom. *Worldmaking After Empire: The Rise and Fall of Self-Determination*. Princeton, NJ: Princeton University Press, 2019.

Ghosh, Durba. *Sex and the Family in Colonial India: The Making of Empire*. Cambridge: Cambridge University Press, 2006.

Glissant, Edouard. *Caribbean Discourse: Selected Essays*. Charlottesville: University of Virginia Press, 2009.

Goreau-Ponceaud, Anthony. " La diaspora tamoule en France: entre visibilité et politisation." EchoGéo. Accessed November 19, 2020. http://echogeo.revues.org/11157.

Goreau-Ponceaud, Anthony, ed. "Diasporas sri lankaises: entre guerre et paix." Special issue, *Hommes & Migrations* 1291 (May–June 2011).

Gorman, Daniel. "Wider and Wider Still? Racial Politics, Intra-Imperial Immigrations, and the Absence of an Imperial Citizenship in the British Empire." *Journal of Colonialism and Colonial History* 3, no. 3 (2002): 1–24.

Green, Nancy L. "The Politics of Exit: Reversing the Immigration Paradigm." *Journal of Modern History* 77 (2005): 263–89.

Green, Nancy L., and François Weil, eds. *Citizenship and Those Who Leave: The Politics of Emigration and Expatriation*. Champaign-Urbana: University of Illinois Press, 2007.

Gregory, Derek. *The Colonial Present: Afghanistan, Palestine, Iraq*. Malden, MA: Blackwell, 2004.

Gressieux, Douglas. *Les comptoirs de l'Inde: Pondichéry, Karikal, Mahé, Yanaon, et Chandernagor*. Saint-Cyr-sur-Loire: Éditions Alan Sutton, 2004.

———. *Les troupes indiennes en France: 1914–1918*. Saint-Cyr-sur-Loire: Éditions Alan Sutton, 2007.

Groupe de Réflexion Franco-Indien. *A Guide to Living in France*. Vieux Moulin, France: n.p., 1997.

Guéhenno, Jean-Marie. *The End of the Nation-State*. Translated by Victoria Elliot. Minneapolis: University of Minnesota Press, 1995.

Guët, Isidore. *Origines de l'Inde française, Jân Begum (Mme Dupleix, 1706–1756)*. Paris: Baudoin, 1892.

Guha, Ramachandra. *India After Gandhi: The History of the World's Largest Democracy*. New York: HarperCollins, 2007.

Guha, Ranajit, and Gayatri Spivak. *Selected Subaltern Studies*. Delhi: Oxford University Press, 1998.

Gupta, Nolini Kanta. *Reminiscences*. Pondicherry: Sri Aurobindo Ashram, 1969.
Gupta, Pamila. "The Disquieting of History: Portuguese (De)Colonization and Goan Migration in the Indian Ocean." *Journal of Asian and African Studies* 44, no. 1 (2009): 19–47.
———. "Gandhi and the Goa Question." *Public Culture* 23, no. 2 (2011): 321–30.
Hall, Catherine. *Civilizing Subjects: Metropole and Colony in the English Imagination, 1830–1867*. Chicago: University of Chicago Press, 2002.
Hall, C. Michael, and Hazel Tucker. eds. *Tourism and Postcolonialism: Contested Discourses, Identities, and Representations*. New York: Routledge, 2004.
Hansen, Randall, and Patrick Weil, eds. *Dual Nationality, Social Rights, and Federal Citizenship in the U.S. and Europe: The Reinvention of Citizenship*. Oxford: Berghahn, 2002.
Hardy, Karl. "Unsettling Hope: Contemporary Indigenous Politics, Settler-Colonialism, and Utopianism." *Spaces of Utopia: An Electronic Journal* 2, no. 1 (2012): 123–36.
Hargreaves, Alec. *Immigration, "Race," and Ethnicity in Contemporary France*. New York: Routledge, 1995.
Hargreaves, Alec, and Mark McKinney, eds. *Post-Colonial Cultures in France*. New York: Routledge, 1997.
Harlow, Barbara. "Tipu Sultan: Oriental Despot or National Hero." In *Archives of Empire, Volume I: From the East India Company to the Suez Canal*, edited by Barbara Harlow and Mia Carter, 171–72. Durham, NC: Duke University Press, 2003.
Harp, Stephen L. *Learning to Be Loyal: Primary Schooling as Nation Building in Alsace and Lorraine, 1850–1940*. DeKalb: Northern Illinois University Press, 1998.
Hartman, Saidiya. *Wayward Lives, Beautiful Experiments: Intimate Histories of Social Upheaval*. New York: W. W. Norton, 2019.
Heehs, Peter. "Foreign Influences on Bengali Revolutionary Terrorism, 1902–1908." *Modern Asian Studies* 28 (1994): 533–56.
———. *The Lives of Sri Aurobindo*. New York: Columbia University Press, 2008.
———. *Nationalism, Terrorism, Communalism: Essays in Modern Indian History*. Delhi: Oxford University Press, 1998.
Ho, Karen. *Liquidated: An Ethnography of Wall Street*. Durham, NC: Duke University Press, 2009.
Hunt, Lynn. *The Family Romance of the French Revolution*. Berkeley: University of California Press, 1993.
Huss, Boaz. "Madame Théon, Alta Una, Mother Superior: The Life and Personas of Mary Ware (1839–1908)." *Aries: Journal for the Study of Western Esotericism* 15 (2015): 210–46.
Irschik, Eugene F. *Politics and Social Conflict in South India: The Non-Brahman Movement and Tamil Separatism, 1916–1929*. Berkeley: University of California Press, 1969.

James, C. L. R. *Black Jacobins: Toussaint L'Ouverture and the San Domingo Revolution*. New York: Vintage, 1963.
Jayal, Niraja Gopal. *Citizenship and Its Discontents: An Indian History*. Ranikhet: Permanent Black, 2013.
Jennings, Eric. *Vichy in the Tropics: Pétain's National Revolution in Madagascar, Guadeloupe, and Indochina, 1940–44*. Stanford, CA: Stanford University Press, 2004.
Jobs, Richard. *Riding the New Wave: Youth and the Rejuvenation of France After the Second World War*. Stanford, CA: Stanford University Press, 2007.
Johnson, R. M. "Journey to Pondicherry: Margaret Woodrow Wilson and the Aurobindo Ashram." *Indian Journal of American Studies* 21 (1991): 1–7.
Jouhki, Jukka. "Imagining the Other: Orientalism and Occidentalism in Tamil-European Relations in South India." PhD diss., University of Jyväskylä, 2006.
Jorgenson, Ronald. "'In Auroville': The Community That Lost Its Name." *World Union* 14, no. 4 (1974): 46.
Kamola, Isaac A. *Making the World Global: U.S. Universities and the Production of the Global Imaginary*. Durham, NC: Duke University Press, 2019.
Kapur, Akash, ed. *Auroville: Dream & Reality, An Anthology*. Gurgaon: Penguin, 2018.
Katz, Cindi. "Towards Minor Theory," *Environment and Planning D: Society and Space* 14 (1996): 487–99.
Kaul, Nitasha. "India's Obsessesion with Kashmir: Democracy, Gender, (Anti)-Nationalism." *Feminist Review* 119 (2018): 126–43.
Kaul, Suvir. "Indian Empire (and the Case of Kashmir)." *Economic and Political Weekly* 46, no. 13 (2011): 66–75.
Ker, James Campbell. *Political Trouble in India, 1907–1917*. Calcutta: Superintendent of Government Printing, 1917.
Khan, Yasmin. *The Great Partition: The Making of India and Pakistan*. New Haven, CT: Yale University Press, 2007.
Khandelwal, Meena. "Foreign Swamis at Home in India: Transmigration to the Birthplace of Spirituality." *Identities: Global Studies in Culture and Power* 14 (2007): 313–40.
Kastoryano, Riva. "Negotiations Beyond Borders: States and Immigrants in Postcolonial Europe." *Journal of Interdisciplinary History* 41 (2010): 79–95.
Koshy, Susan, and R. Radhakrishnan. *Transnational South Asians: The Making of a Neo-Diaspora*. New Delhi: Oxford University Press, 2008.
Krishnamurthy, B. *Jawaharlal Nehru and Freedom Movement in French India*. Pondicherry: Centre for Nehru Studies, Pondicherry University, 2007.
Krishnavarma, Shyamji. "A Rejoinder to a Malignant Attack." *Indian Sociologist*, February 1909, n.p.
Kumar, Krishnan. *Utopia and Anti-Utopia in Modern Times*. Oxford: Basil Blackwell, 1987.

———. *Utopianism*. Minneapolis: University of Minnesota Press, 1991.
Kumari, Shyam. *How They Came to Sri Aurobindo and the Mother: Twenty-Nine True Stories of Sadhaks and Devotees*. Bombay: Mother Publishing House, 1990.
Le Doudic, Kévin. "Encounters Around the Material Object: French and Indian Consumers in Eighteenth-Century Pondicherry." In *The Global Lives of Things: The Material Culture of Connections in the Early Modern World*, edited by Anne Gerritsen and Giorgio Rielle, 162–80. London: Routledge, 2016.
Lewis, Mary Dewhurst. *The Boundaries of the Republic: Migrant Rights and the Limits of Universalism in France, 1918–1940*. Stanford, CA: Stanford University Press, 2007.
Lorcin, Patricia. *Imperial Identities: Stereotyping, Prejudice, and Race in Colonial Algeria*. London: I. B. Tauris, 1995.
Loti, Pierre. *L'Inde (sans les Anglais)*. Paris: Calmann-Lévy, 1903.
Luceney, L. *Dupleix, conquérant des Indes fabuleuses*. Paris: Zimmerman, 1946.
Lugones, María. "Heterosexualism and the Colonial/Modern Gender System." *Hypatia* 22, no. 1 (2007): 186–209.
MacMaster, Neil. *Colonial Migrants and Racism: Algerians in France, 1900–62*. New York: St. Martin's, 1997.
Magedera, Ian H. "Arrested Development: The Shape of 'French India' After the Treaties of Paris of 1763 and 1814." *Interventions: International Journal of Postcolonial Studies* 12 (2010): 331–43.
———. "France-India-Britain, (Post)Colonial Triangles: Mauritius/India and Canada/India, (Post)Colonial Tangents." *International Journal of Francophone Studies* 5, no. 2 (2002): 64–73.
Malleson, G. B. *History of the French in India: Fom the Founding of Pondicherry in 1674 to the Capture of the Place in 1761*. London: W. H. Allen, 1893.
Manjapra, Kris. *The Age of Entanglement: German and Indian Intellectuals Across Empire*. Cambridge, MA: Harvard University Press, 2014.
———. *M. N. Roy: Marxism and Colonial Cosmopolitanism*. New Delhi: Routledge, 2010.
Marsh, Kate. *Fictions of 1947: Representations of Indian Decolonization, 1919–1962*. Bern: Peter Lang, 2007.
———. "Gandhi and *le gandhisme*: Writing Indian Decolonisation and the Appropriation of Gandhi, 1919–48." *Modern & Contemporary France* 14 (2006): 33–47.
———. *India in the French Imagination: Peripheral Voices, 1754–1815*. London: Pickering & Chatto, 2009.
———. "'The Only Safe Haven of Refuge in All the World': Paris, Indian 'Revolutionaries,' and Imperial Rivalry, c. 1905–40." *French Cultural Studies* 30, no. 3 (2019): 196–219.
———. "Pondichéry: Archive of 'French' India," *Francosphères* 3 (2014): 9–23.
Marsh, Kate, and Nicola Firth. *France's Lost Empires: Fragmentation, Nostalgia, and la fracture coloniale*. Boulder, CO: Lexington, 2011.

Martineau, Alfred. *Dupleix et l'Inde Française, 1722–1754*. Paris: Champion, 1920.

Maskelyne, John Nevil. *The "Fraud" of Modern Theosophy Exposed: A Brief History of the Greatest Imposture Ever Perpetrated Under the Cloak of Religion*. London: George Routledge, 1912.

Mathew, K. S. *French in India and Indian Nationalism (1700–1963)*. Delhi: BR, 1999.

Mathew, K. S., and S. J. Stephens, eds. *Indo-French Relations*. New Delhi: Pragati, 1999.

McKeown, Adam. *Melancholy Order: Asian Migration and the Globalization of Borders*. New York: Columbia University Press, 2008.

Medlock, Julie. "Auroville Takes Shape: An Experiment in Human Unity." *Sunday Standard Magazine*, 28 June 1970, n.p.

Mehta, Gita. *Karma Cola: The Mystic Marketing of the East*. New York: Simon & Schuster, 1979.

Mehta, Uday S. "Liberal Strategies of Exclusion." In *Tensions of Empire: Colonial Culture in a Bourgeois World*, edited by Ann Stoler and Frederick Cooper, 59–86. Berkeley: University of California Press, 1997.

Michalon, Paul. "Des Indes françaises aux Français Indiens ou Comment peut-on être Franco-Pondicherian?" Master's thesis, Université Aix-Marseille I, 1990.

Mignolo, Walter D. *The Darker Side of Western Modernity: Global Futures, Decolonial Options*. Durham, NC: Duke University Press, 2011.

———. "Delinking: The Rhetoric of Modernity, the Logic of Coloniality, and the Grammar of Decoloniality." *Cultural Studies* 21 (2007): 449–514.

Miles, William F. S. *Imperial Burdens: Countercolonialism in Former French India*. Boulder, CO: Lynne Rienner, 1995.

———. *Scars of Partition: Postcolonial Legacies in French and British Borderlands*. Lincoln: University of Nebraska Press, 2014.

Miller, Timothy. *The 60s Communes: Hippies and Beyond*. Syracuse, NY: Syracuse University Press, 1999.

Minor, Robert N. *The Religious, the Spiritual, and the Secular: Auroville and Secular India*. Albany: State University of New York Press, 1999.

Mitra, Durba. *Indian Sex Life: Sexuality and the Colonial Origins of Modern Social Thought*. Princeton, NJ: Princeton University Press, 2020.

Miyoshi, Masao. "A Borderless World? From Colonialism to Transnationalism and the Decline of the Nation-State." *Critical Inquiry* 19 (1993): 726–51.

Mohan, Jyoti. "British and French Ethnographies of India: Dubois and His English Commentators." *French Colonial History* 5 (2004): 229–46.

———. "*La civilization la plus antique*: Voltaire's Images of India." *Journal of World History* 16 (2005): 173–85.

———. *Claiming India: French Scholars and the Preoccupation with India in the Nineteenth Century*. Delhi: SAGE/Yoda, 2018.

Moliner, Christine. "Indian Migrants in France: Country Report." CARIM-India RR2012/11, 2012, Robert Schuman Centre for Advanced Studies, San Domenico di Fiesole (FI). European University Institute.

———. "Invisible et modèle? Première approche de l'immigration sud- asiatique en France." Rapport d'étude pour la Direction de l'Accueil, de l'Intégration et de la Citoyenneté, MIINDS, Septembre 2009.

Mongia, Radhika. *Indian Migration and Empire: Genealogy of the Modern State.* Durham, NC: Duke University Press, 2018.

———. "Race, Nationality, Mobility: A History of the Passport." *Public Culture* 11 (2003): 527–55.

Moran, Dominique, Jennifer Turner, and Anna K. Schliehe. "Conceptualizing the Carceral in Carceral Geography." *Progress in Human Geography* 42, no. 5 (2017): 666–86.

More, Sir Thomas. *Utopia.* Cambridge: Cambridge University Press, [1516] 1989.

Moreel, Léon. *Dupleix, marquis de fortune et conquérant des Indes, 1697–1763.* Rosendaël: Éditions le Port de Dunkerque, 1963.

Murr, Sylvia. "Nicolas Desvaulx (1745–1823) véritable auteur de œuvres, institutions et ceremonies des peoples de l'Inde, de l'abbé Dubois." *Purusartha* 3 (1977): 245–67.

Namakkal, Jessica. "Decolonizing Marriage and the Family: The Lives and Letters of Ida, Benoy, and Indira Sarkar." *Journal of Women's History* 31, no. 2 (2019): 124–47.

———. "Peanut Butter Dosas: Becoming Desi in the Midwest." *Tides Magazine*, April 18, 2017. https://www.saada.org/tides/article/peanut-butter-dosas.

Nambi, A. K. *Tamil Renaissance and Dravidian Nationalism, 1905–44.* Madurai: Koodal, 1980.

Nandi, Sugata. "Constructing the Criminal: Politics of Social Imaginary of the Goonda." *Social Scientist* 38 (2010): 37–54.

Nandy, Ashis. *The Intimate Enemy: Loss and Recovery of Self Under Colonialism.* New Delhi: Oxford University Press, 1983.

Narrain, Siddharth. "'Disaffection' and the Law: The Chilling Effect of Sedition Laws in India." *Economic and Political Weekly* 46, no. 8 (2011): 33–37.

Nemser, Daniel. *Infrastructures of Race: Concentration and Biopolitics in Colonial Mexico.* Austin: University of Texas Press, 2017.

Neogy, Ajit K. *Decolonization of French India: Liberation Movement and Indo-French Relations, 1947–1954.* Pondicherry: French Institute of Pondicherry, 1997.

Nightingale, Carl H. "Before Race Mattered: Geographies of the Color Line in Early Colonial Madras and New York." *American Historical Review* 113 (2008): 48–71.

Noiriel, Gerard. *The French Melting Pot: Immigration, Citizenship, and National Identity.* Translated by Geoffrey de Laforcade. Minneapolis: University of Minnesota Press, 1996.

Okihiro, Gary. *Third World Studies: Theorizing Liberation.* Durham, NC: Duke University Press, 2016.

Ong, Aiwha. *Flexible Citizenship: The Cultural Logics of Transnationality.* Durham, NC: Duke University Press, 1999.

Padamanabhan, R. A. "A CID Policeman's Pocket Diary." *Indian Review,* May 1976, 29–40.

Paine, Jeffery. *Father India: Westerners Under the Spell of an Ancient Culture.* New York: Harper Perennial, 1999.

Pandey, Gyanendra. *Remembering Partition: Violence, Nationalism and History in India.* Cambridge: Cambridge University Press, 2002.

Pandian, M. S. S. *Brahmin and Non-Brahmin: Genealogies of the Tamil Political Present.* Delhi: Permanent Black, 2007.

Pairaudeau, Natasha. *Mobile Citizens: French Indians in Indochina, 1858–1954.* Copenhagen: Nordic Institute of Asian Studies, 2016.

Parasher, Gauri. "State Building in a Transcultural Context: The Case of the French in India During the Early Eighteenth Century." *Transcultural Research: Heidelberg Studies on Asia and Europe in a Global Context* 3 (2012): 243–49.

Peabody, Sue. *"There Are no Slaves in France": The Political Culture of Race and Slavery in the Ancien Régime.* New York: Oxford University Press, 1996.

Peabody, Sue, and Tyler Stovall, eds. *The Color of Liberty: Histories of Race in France.* Durham, NC: Duke University Press, 2003.

Prakash, Gyan. "Subaltern Studies as Postcolonial Criticism." *American Historical Review* 99 (1994): 1475–90.

Prashad, Vijay. *The Karma of Brown Folk.* Minneapolis: University of Minnesota Press, 2000.

Quijano, Aníbal. "Coloniality and Modernity/Rationality." *Cultural Studies* 21, no. 2 (2007): 168–78.

Radakrishnan, Rajagopolan. *Diasporic Meditations: Between Home and Location.* Minneapolis: University of Minnesota Press, 1996.

Raffin, Ann. "Imperial Nationhood and Its Impact on Colonial Cities: Issue of Conflict and Peace in Pondicherry and Vietnam." In *Cities and Sovereignty: Identity Politics in Urban Spaces,* edited by Diane E. Davis and Nora Libertun de Durén, 28–58. Bloomington: Indiana University Press, 2011.

Rai, Animesh. *The Legacy of French Rule in India (1674–1954): An Investigation of a Process of Creolization.* Pondicherry: French Institute of Pondicherry, 2008.

Rajagopal, I. *The Tyranny of Caste: The Non-Brahman Movement and Political Development in South India.* Madras: Vikas, 1985.

Rajendran, N. *The National Movement in Tamil Nadu, 1905–14: Agitational Politics and State Coercion.* Madras: Oxford University Press, 1994.

Ramasamy, A. *History of Pondicherry.* New Delhi: Sterling, 1987.

Ramaswamy, Sumathi. *The Goddess and the Nation: Mapping Mother India*. Durham, NC: Duke University Press, 2010.
———. *Passions of the Tongue: Language Devotion in Tamil India, 1891–1970*. Berkeley: University of California Press, 1997.
Ramnath, Maia. *Decolonizing Anarchism: An Antiauthoritarian History of India's Liberation Struggle*. Oakland, CA: AK, 2011.
———. *Haj to Utopia: How the Ghadar Movement Charted Global Radicalism and Attempted to Overthrow the British Empire*. Berkeley: University of California Press, 2011.
Ramusack, Barbara N. *The Indian Prices and Their States*. Cambridge: Cambridge University Press, 2004.
Rao, Raja. *The Serpent and the Rope*. New York: Pantheon, 1960.
Ravi, Srilata. "Border Zones in Colonial Spaces." *Interventions: International Journal of Postcolonial Studies* 12, no. 3 (2010): 383–95.
Renan, Ernst. "Qu'est-ce qu'une nation?" In *Becoming National: A Reader*, edited by Geoff Eley and Ronald Grigor Suny, 41–55. New York: Oxford University Press, 1996.
Rhodes Must Fall Oxford Movement. *Rhodes Must Fall: The Struggle to Decolonise the Racist Heart of Empire*. Edited by Roseanne Chantiluke, Brian Kwoba, and Athinangamso Nkopo. London: Zed, 2018.
Riddell, John, Vijay Prashad, and Nazeef Mollah, eds. *Liberate the Colonies! Communism and Colonial Freedom, 1917–1924*. New Delhi: Leftword, 2019.
Robin, Corey. *Fear: The History of a Political Idea*. Oxford: Oxford University Press, 2004.
Rosenberg, Clifford. *Policing Paris: The Origins of Modern Immigration Control Between the Wars*. Ithaca, NY: Cornell University Press, 2006.
Rousso, Henry. *The Vichy Syndrome: History and Memory in France Since 1944*. Translated by Arthur Goldhammer. Cambridge, MA: Harvard University Press, 1991.
Rustom, Bhikaji. *Madam Cama: Mother of Indian Revolution*. Calcutta: Manisha, 1975.
Saada, Emanuelle. *Empire's Children: Race, Filiation, and Citizenship in the French Colonies*. Translated by Arthur Goldhammer. Chicago: University of Chicago, 2012.
Said, Edward. *Orientalism*. New York: Vintage, 1979.
———. "Reflections on Exile." *Granta* 13 (1984): 173–86.
Saldanha, Arun. *Psychedelic White: Goa Trance and the Viscosity of Race*. Minneapolis: University of Minnesota Press, 2007.
Sareen, T. R. *Indian Revolutionary Movement Abroad, 1905–1921*. New Delhi: Sterling, 1979.
Sargeant, Winthrop. "Holy Man: Sri Ramana Maharshi Has India's Answer to Most of Man's Problems." *Life*, 30 May 1949, 92–104.

Sargisson, Lucy. "Strange Places: Estrangement, Utopianism, and Intentional Communities." *Utopian Studies* 18 (2007): 393–424.

Sarkar, Sumit. *The Swadeshi Movement in Bengal, 1903–1908.* New Delhi: People's Publishing House, 1973.

Satia, Priya. *Time's Monster: How History Makes History.* Cambridge, MA: Harvard University Press, 2020.

Scott, James C. *The Art of Not Being Governed: An Anarchist History of Upland Southeast Asia.* New Haven, CT: Yale University Press, 2009.

Scott, Joan Wallach. *Only Paradoxes to Offer: French Feminists and the Rights of Man.* Cambridge, MA: Harvard University Press, 1996.

———. *The Politics of the Veil.* Princeton, NJ: Princeton University Press, 2007.

Sen, S. P. *The French in India, 1763–1816.* New Delhi: M. Manoharlal, 1971.

Sen, Sailendra Nath. *Chandernagore: From Bondage to Freedom, 1900–1955.* New Delhi: Primus, 2012.

Senghor, Leopold. "Negritude and Dravidian Culture." *Journal of Tamil Studies* 1 (1974): 1–12.

Sevran-Schreiber, Catherine, and Vasoodeven Vuddamalay. "Les étapes de la présence indienne en France." *Hommes & Migrations* 1268 (2007): 8–23.

Shepard, Todd. "'History Is Past Politics?' Archives, 'Tainted Evidence,' and the Return of the State." *American Historical Review* 115 (2010): 474–83.

———. *The Invention of Decolonization: The Algerian War and the Remaking of France.* Ithaca, NY: Cornell University Press, 2006.

———. "'Of Sovereignty': Disputed Archives, 'Wholly Modern' Archives, and the Post-Decolonization French and Algerian Republics, 1962–2012." *American Historical Review* 120, no. 3 (2015): 869–83.

Shipway, Martin. *Decolonization and Its Impact: A Comparative Approach to the End of the Colonial Empires.* Malden, MA: Blackwell, 2008.

Silverstein, Paul A. *Algeria in France: Transpolitics, Race, and Nation.* Bloomington: Indiana University Press, 2004.

Singh, Anita Inder. "Keeping India in the Commonwealth: British Political and Military Aims, 1947–49." *Journal of Contemporary History* 20, no. 3 (1985): 469–81.

Singha, Radhika. "A 'Proper Passport' for the Colony: Border Crossing in British India, 1882–1920." Yale Agrarian Studies Colloquium Papers, 2006.

Sinha, Chitranshul. *The Great Repression: The Story of Sedition in India.* Delhi: Penguin India, 2019.

Sinha, Mrinalini. *Spectres of Mother India: The Global Restructuring of an Empire.* Durham, NC: Duke University Press, 2006.

———. "The Strange Death of an Imperial Ideal: The Case of *Civis Britannicus*." In *Handbook of Modernity in South Asia: Modern Makeovers*, edited by Saurabh Dube, 29–42. Delhi: Oxford University Press, 2011.

Smith, Andrea L., ed. *Colonial Memory and Postcolonial Europe: Maltese Settlers in Algeria and France*. Bloomington: Indiana University Press, 2006.

———. *Europe's Invisible Migrants*. Amsterdam: Amsterdam University Press, 2003.

Smith, Blake. "Myths of Stasis: South Asia, Gloval Commerce and Economic Orientalism in Late Eighteenth-Century France," PhD diss., Northwestern University, 2017.

Smith, Linda Tuhiwai. *Decolonizing Methodologies: Research and Indigenous Peoples*. London: Zed, 1999.

Spear, Jennifer M. "Colonial Intimacies: Legislating Sex in Louisiana." *William and Mary Quarterly* 60 (2003): 75–98.

Spiro, Melford E. "Utopia and Its Discontents: The Kibbutz and Its Historical Vicissitudes." *American Anthropologist* 106 (3): 556–68.

Spivak, Gayatri. "Can the Subaltern Speak?" In *Marxism and the Interpretation of Culture*, edited by Cary Nelson and Lawrence Grossberg, 271–313. Urbana: University of Illinois Press, 1988.

Stirk, Nigel. "Arresting Ambiguity: The Shifting Geographies of a London Debtors' Sanctuary in the Eighteenth Century." *Social History* 25, no. 3 (2000): 316–29.

Stoler, Ann Laura. *Along the Archival Grain: Epistemic Anxieties and Colonial Common Sense*. Princeton, NJ: Princeton University Press, 2009.

———. *Duress: Imperial Durabilities in Our Times*. Durham, NC: Duke University Press, 2016.

———. "Sexual Affronts and Racial Frontiers: European Identities and the Cultural Politics of Exclusion in Colonial Southeast Asia." In *Tensions of Empire: Colonial Cultures in a Bourgeois World*, edited by Ann Laura Stoler and Frederick Cooper, 198–237. Berkeley: University of California Press, 1997.

Stora, Benjamin. *Ils venaient d'Algérie: L'immigration algérienne en France 1912–1992*. Paris: Fayard, 1992.

Stovall, Tyler. "The Color Line Behind the Lines: Racial Violence in France During the Great War." *American Historical Review* 103 (1998): 737–69.

———. "National Identity and Shifting Imperial Frontiers: Whiteness and the Exclusion of Colonial Labor after World War I." *Representations* 84 (2003): 52–72.

Sundararajan, Saroja. *Pondicherry: A Profile*. Pondicherry: Directorate of Art and Culture, Government of Pondicherry, 1995.

Thoburn, Nicholas. *Deleuze, Marx, and Politics*. London: Routledge, 2003.

Thomas, Martin, Bob Moore, and L. J. Butler. *Crises of Empire: Decolonization and Europe's Imperial States, 1918–1975*. London: Hodder Education, 2008.

———. *Empires of Intelligence: Security Services and Colonial Disorder After 1914*. Berkeley: University of California Press, 2008.

Thomas, Sonia. "Cowboys and Indians: Indian Priests in Rural Montana." *Women's Studies Quarterly* 47 (2019): 110–31.

Tirouvanziam Louis, Lourdes. "Les 'Créoles' ou descendants d'Européens à Pondichéry." PhD diss., Pondicherry University, 1994.

Todorov, Tzvetan. *On Human Diversity: Nationalism, Racism, and Exoticism in French Thought.* Translated by Catherine Porter. Cambridge, MA: Harvard University Press, 1993.

Toombs, Isabelle, and Robert Toombs. *That Sweet Enemy: The French and British from the Sun King to the Present.* New York: Knopf, 2007.

Torpey, John. *The Invention of the Passport: Surveillance, Citizenship, and the State.* Cambridge: Cambridge University Press, 2000.

van der Veer, P. *Imperial Encounters: Religion and Modernity in India and Britain.* Princeton, NJ: Princeton University Press, 2001.

———. *Nation and Migration: The Politics of Space in the South Asian Diaspora.* Philadelphia: University of Pennsylvania Press, 1995.

Van Schendel, Willem, and Erik de Maaker. "Asian Borderlands: Introducing Their Permeability, Strategic Uses, and Meanings." *Journal of Borderlands Studies* 29, no. 1 (2014): 3–9.

Varshney, Ashutosh. "India, Pakistan, and Kashmir: Antinomies of Nationalism." *Asian Survey* 31 (1991): 997–1019.

Venkatachalapathy, A. R. "In Search of Ashe." *Economic and Political Weekly* 45, no. 2 (2010): 37–44.

Vergès, Françoise. *Monsters and Revolutionaries: Colonial Family Romance and Métissage.* Durham, NC: Duke University Press, 1999.

Vincent, Rose. *Les temps d'un royaume: Jeanne Dupleix.* Paris: Éditions du Seuil, 1982.

Vuddamalay, Vasoodeen, Paul White, and Deborah Sporton. "The Evolution of the Goutte d'Or as an Ethnic Minority District of Paris." *New Community* 17, no. 2 (1991): 245–58.

Ward, Stuart. "The European Provenance of Decolonization." *Past & Present* 230, no. 1 (2016): 227–60.

Weber, Eugene. *Peasants into Frenchmen: The Modernization of Rural France, 1870–1914.* Stanford, CA: Stanford University Press, 1976.

Weber, Jacques. "Chanemougam, 'King of French India': Social and Political Foundations of an Absolute Power Under the Third Republic." *Economic and Political Weekly* 26 (1991): 291–302.

———. *Les établissements français en Inde au XIXe siècle (1816–1914).* Paris: La librairie d'Inde: 1988.

———. *Pondichéry et les Comptoirs de l'Inde après Dupleix: la démocratie au pays des castes.* Paris: Denoël, 1996.

Weil, Patrick. *Qu'est-ce qu'un Français? Histoire de la nationalité française depuis la Révolution.* Gallimard: Paris, 2005.

White, Owen. *Children of the French Empire: Miscegenation and Colonial Society in French West Africa, 1895–1960.* Oxford: Oxford University Press, 1999.

Wilder, Gary. *Freedom Time: Negritude, Decolonization, and the Future of the World.* Durham, NC: Duke University Press, 2015.

———. *The French Imperial Nation-State: Negritude and Colonial Humanism Between the Two World Wars.* Chicago: University of Chicago Press, 2005.

Wolfe, Patrick. "Settler Colonialism and the Elimination of the Native." *Journal of Genocide Research* 8, no. 4 (2006): 387–409.

Yang, K. Wayne, and Eve Tuck. "Decolonization Is Not a Metaphor." *Decolonization: Indigeneity, Education & Society* 1, no. 1 (2012): 1.

Yechury, Akhila. "Imagining India, Decolonizing l'Inde Française, c. 1947–1954." *Historical Journal* 58, no. 4 (2015): 1141–65.

Young, Robert J. C. *White Mythologies: Writing History and the West.* New York: Routledge, 1990.

Zamindar, Vazira Fazila-Yacoobali. *The Long Partition and the Making of Modern South Asia: Refugees, Boundaries, Histories.* New York: Columbia University Press, 2010.

# Index

Abdullah, Sheik, 113
Abel-Clovis, M., 159, 170
Aiyer, R. Vanchi, 48
Aiyer, V. V. S., 48, 57
Albert, Jacques-Theodor, 84
Albert, Jeanne (Mme Jeanne Dupleix), 84–85
Alfassa, Matéo, 51, 234n67
Alfassa, Mira (the Mother): anticolonial colonialism, 183; on Ashram's role in Pondicherry, 190; on Auroville, 152, 175, 181–82, 183, 185, 186–87, 188, 193, 194–95, 197; belief in classical education, 86, 90; biographical information, xvi, 2, 224n6, 243n77; cultural cachet, 171; death, 196; marriages, 87, 186, 243n77; media representations, 174–75; named "the Mother," 52; nationality, 141, 170–71, 175; publications, 52; relationship with Sri Aurobindo Ghose, 87–88, 89, 171, 182, 243n79; spirituality, 51, 87, 170–71, 174, 178, 181–83, 193, 197; support of French culture and values, 86, 170–71; view of India and Indians, 180, 190–91
Algeria, 137, 155; decolonization, 10, 26, 146; French colonization of, 51, 106, 146; migration of pieds-noirs to France, 157, 164, 208; resistance to colonization, 137; utopianists in, 13, 51, 234n66
Ali, Haidar (Hyder), 17
All India Scheduled Castes and Tribes Liberation Organisation, 96
All-India States' Peoples' Conference, 65
Alsace-Lorraine, 41, 112–13
Anderson, Holger, 117–18
Anger, Roger, 179, 188, 192
Annasse, Arthur, 95–96
anti-British activity: in Calcutta, 39; in Chandernagore, 39–41; in France, 52–54; French India as haven for, 40, 42, 61; by Sri Aurobindo Ghose, 103, 104, 171

anticolonial activity: association with terrorism, 136; in French India, 37, 38; importance of French territories, 37, 38, 47; in other French colonies, 14, 137; in Paris, 53, 55; and race, 87; surveillance of, 40–41, 42–43, 48, 57. *See also* anti-British activity; anti-French activity; sedition

anticolonial colonialism, 103, 104, 183, 186

anti-French activity, 91; demonstrations, 95, 97, 125–26; in French territories, 55, 57, 88–89, 97–98; in Indochina, 71; in Suramangalam, 125–30

Appavou, Emile, 156, 158, 159

archives: accessibility, 24; of French India, 21, 38; of Pondicherry, 24; privilege and, 24–25; shaping history, 22; of Sri Aurobindo Ashram, 44; through minor lens, 23–24

Arnold, David, 119

Aroumougame, V., 131–32

Arpi, Claude, 203

*Arya: A Philosophical Review*, 51

Ashe, Robert William D'Escourt, 48

Ashram. *See* Sri Aurobindo Ashram

Association de l'Inde en France (AIF), 105, 165–67

Attlee, Clement, 67, 72

Aurobindo, Sri. *See* Ghose, Sri Aurobindo

Aurovilians: citizenship, 199; demographics, 185, 186, 191–92, 196; earliest arrivals, 194; founders' conception of, 197; local attitudes toward, 192–93, 195; personal recollections, 187, 192; racial privilege, 182, 186, 196; relations with Tamil people, 193, 196–97; struggles with Tamil language, 195; treatment of land, 172, 178; views of Tamil people, 194

Auroville, 4f; 177, 178, 179, 180–81, 181, 183–84, 192–93, 194–95, 196, 204, 179; application process, 186–87; architectural vision, 179, 198; children born in, 187; as "city of the future," 184–85; current status, 179–80, 198–99; displacement of Tamil people, 177, 178, 179, 180–81, 181, 183–84, 192–93, 196, 197; drug prohibition, 187; factors leading to construction, 185–86; fiftieth anniversary, 198; founders' vision for, 3, 152, 175, 197; founding of, xvii, 27, 172; French government support of, 188–89; as global community, 199; ground-breaking, 178–79; international recognition, 188, 189; labor as core value, 188, 193–94; lack of local participation, 176, 178, 180–81, 204; local attitudes toward, 176, 180–81, 192–93; media representations, 191; original inhabitants, 3; origin of name, 175; popular association with Pondicherry, 3; as product of colonialism, 14, 177–78, 180–81; promotional materials, 176, 184–85; reliance on Tamil labor, 193–94, 195, 197, 198–99, 200; residents' treatment of land, 178; as settlement, 176; spiritual worldview, 178, 179, 180, 181–82, 187, 188, 191, 193, 194, 197, 261n73; support from Indian government, 175; UNESCO recognition, 3, 175–76, 179, 224n10

Bancel, Nicolas, 5, 6

Banerjie, Monideepa, 169

Baroda, 45

Baron, François, 72, 73, 88, 89, 91, 103, 149, 188–89; promotion of French

culture, 89, 149; relations with Ashram, 88–89, 103; support for Auroville, 188–89; support for dual nationality, 151; support of French Union, 72, 73, 91
Bay of Bengal, 192, 230n9
Bégum, Johanna (Mme Jeanne Dupleix), 84–85
Bengal partition, 39–40, 46
Besant, Annie, 13, 259–60n28. *See also* Theosophy
Besson, Eric, 207
Bharathi, Sri Subramanya, 48, 57, 60
Blanchard, Pascal, 5, 6
Blavatsky, Helena, 13. *See also* Theosophy
Bloch, Jules, 166
Bonaparte, Napoleon, 17
borders: carceralization of, 28, 36, 37; changing during decolonization, 65, 108, 124–25; colonial, in Asia, 34; construction in Pondicherry, 34, 60–61; discontinuous, 20, 61; disputes over, 112; fences to enforce, 33, 43, 61–62, 133–34; identification required to cross, 21, 62, 134, 156–57; making of, 6, 29, 34–35, 64, 109; minor, 22, 42, 199; policing, 11, 21, 34, 43, 60–61, 64, 70, 109, 119, 133, 137; porousness of, 35, 42, 43, 61; securitization and surveillance, 28, 36, 39, 48–49, 55, 119, 133, 137, 156–57; unstable nature of, 20, 29–30; violence at, 28, 40, 109–10, 119, 126–30, 132, 135; workers crossing, 55, 61, 90, 121, 205. *See also* carceral borders
border zones: anti-British organizing in, 41, 42; defining, 41; identities of residents, 18, 105, 129; as illegitimate spaces, 41; surveillance, 37

Bose, Subhas Chandra, 57
Brazzaville Conference, 70–71
British Commonwealth, 67, 71
British imperialism, 5, 11–12, 16–17, 106
British India (British Raj): anticolonialism in, 69, 81; attempts to regain French Indian territory, 38–39; borders with French India, 33, 35, 38, 39, 42, 48–49, 59, 62, 63, 100; customs tariff, 64; decolonization, 68, 149; French presence in, 38; languages of, 78; Pondicherry as refuge from, 49; seditious literature smuggled into, 60
Buzzfeed India, 3

Calcutta, 39, 47, 117–18
Cama, Madame (Bhikaji), 53, 55
Canute, 131, 250n61
capitalism: colonial, 184; global, 91, 170, 185, 188; green, 5
carceral borders, 108; after Indian independence, 108; defined, 42; making of, 5, 64; physical borders becoming, 28, 35, 37, 48–49; purpose of, 62
Carton, Adrian, 18
caste: after decolonization, 147, 160; attempts to subvert, 80; author's family and, 206–7; Brahmins, 79, 147, 206–7; and colonial rule, 78–79, 80, 95, 147–48, 186; Dalits, 95, 244n107; low-caste people, 125, 135, 160; oppression due to, 53, 80–81, 95, 137; "pariahs," 79; treatment of low-caste people, 79, 80, 160; "untouchables," 79, 244n107; upper-caste people, 93, 109
Castro, Rodolfo Baron, 117–18

INDEX [ 289 ]

Catholicism: conversion to, 78–79, 80, 82, 83, 93, 94; in French India, 95; as identity marker, 18; interracial relationships, 83; media portrayals, 1, 2, 174, 190; métis people, 84; in Pondicherry, 1, 2, 174

census, 21, 82, 165

Chakrabarty, Dipesh, 160

Chandernagore, 6, 7f; anti-British organizing in, 37, 39–41, 47, 54, 55, 59; cession, xvii, 146; colonial control of, 17, 35, 146; descriptions by British officials, 40–41; growth, 16; in Partition, 108–9; referendum in, xvii, 68, 107, 116–18; refugees in, 117; working conditions, 90–91

Chatterjee, Partha, 26

chaukis (customs stations), 55, 59, 60, 63

Chinmoy, Sri, 105

Chyat, Roy, 192, 194

*Cinq colonnes à la une* news program, 1

citizenship: in 1950s and early 1960s, 28; choosing between Indian and French, 29, 93, 155–57, 168, 169; of créole people, 148; documentation required to obtain, 157; dual, 104, 114, 151–54, 175; of French-Indians, 1, 27, 29, 76, 77, 93, 142, 143, 146–49, 154–56, 157; global, 14, 199, 254n39; rights to, 37, 77, 159; of Tamil people, 148, 177; of *toyas*, xvi. *See also* nationality

colonialism: after decolonization, 29; "anticolonial colonialism," 103, 104, 183, 186; Auroville as product of, 14; memory of French, 5, 6, 144, 206, 225n14, 52, 72, 98, 144; neocolonialism, 183, 200; opposition to. *See* anti-British activity; anticolonial activity; anti-French activity Pondichériens as embodying, 169; Pondicherry as product of, 14; race and, 160–61, 167; relationship to settler colonialism, 176–77; spiritual settlement as, 177, 182; and utopianism, 13, 184–85, 188

coloniality, 9, 14, 21, 22

colonial memory, 3, 6, 144, 225n14

Comité de Défense des Intérêts Français de l'Inde Française, 151–52

Comité de Pondichéry pour le Rattachement, 123

Comité France-Inde, 165–66, 167

Communist Party of French India (CPFI): conflict with French India National Congress (FINC), 100; French-Indian members, 93; labor organizing, 90–91; opposition to French Union, 91, 92, 97–98, 99; political nature of membership, 93; press criticism of, 92

Congrés des étudiants (French Indian Students' Congress), 97

Congrès des Peuples contre l'Impérialisme (Congress of People Against Imperialism), 166

Congress Party, 91

Cons, Jason, 20, 39

Cooper, Frederick, 70, 71

créole people: French citizenship, 148; in French India, 18, 81, 83, 125, 133, 134; origin and use of term, 27, 83

customs, 59; agents, 33, 34, 35, 64–65; checkpoints, 28, 55, 60, 112; duties, 64; stations (chaukis), 55, 59, 60, 63

Dadala, Raphael Ramanyya, 96, 97, 135; autobiography, 94–95, 129–30; biographical information, 94–95; changing attitudes, 205; education,

94; employment, 94–95; on goondas, 130, 131; media portrayals, 131–32, 136; named as goonda, 123, 124, 131; Suramangalam incident, 125–26
Daridan, M. Jean, 189
"Dark Record of Goonda Raj," 120, 121, 124
Das, Deban, 117
Dassaradanayadou, Sophie, 157
David, Gabriel, 202
De, Rohit, 69
de Castro, Rose, 84
decolonization: academic work on, 8–10; anxieties over, 110, 124–25; changing borders, 65, 124–25; determining end of, 5, 26–27, 68–69, 204–5; failures of, 6; as "friendly" process, 10, 14, 106, 110, 138, 143, 166–67, 203–4; global context, 8–9; of higher education, 8–9; of history, 69, 208; origin of term, 10; state-led, 11; threats to colonizers, 130, 137; utopic vision of, 14; violence of, 5, 117, 136, 137, 138, 143–44, 203–4. *See also* citizenship; merger of French territories with Indian Union
de Maaker, Erik, 34
democracy: France as bearer of, 52, 68, 71, 75, 106, 113–14, 116; goonda as threat to, 110, 117, 119–20, 123, 132; as nationalism, 137; as nonviolent, 137; right to vote, 71
Derrida, Jacques, 22
*Dessobagari* newspaper, 34, 64, 78
diaspora: French-Indian, 93, 95, 143, 155, 231n17, 254n44; South Asian, 144–45; Tamil, 145
*Dinamani*, 92
*Djothy*, 78

Dravida Kazhagam (Dravidian Party), 99
dual cultures thesis, 143, 167
Dubois, Jean-Antoine, 78–79
du Montcel, Tézenas, 73, 74, 75, 76
*Dupleix*, 78
Dupleix, Jeanne (Mme), 84–85
Dupleix, Joseph Francois, xv, 15; biographical information, 16, 84; campaign for French control of south Asia, 16–17; marriage, 84–85; role in French Indian history, 15, 18, 43
Durara, Prasenjit, 18
Dutch control of Pondicherry, 16
Dutt, Romesh Chunder, 161–62, 163
Duvauchelle, R., 150–51

EIEBIG (Euro-India Economic and Business Group), 167–68
Elden, Stuart, 34, 108
Enginger, Bernard (Satprem), 88, 153, 257–58n110
Evian Accords, xvii, 155, 223n2
exile: French India as haven for exiles, 36, 37, 39; scholarship on, 49; spiritual, 50–51; of Tamil people from Auroville, 177, 178, 179, 180–81, 181, 183–84, 192–93, 194–95, 196, 204

Fanon, Frantz, 10, 22, 153–54, 204
fences, 33–34, 59–60, 61–62, 64, 133–34
First Carnatic War, xv
First Treaty of Paris (1763), xv, 17, 34
FLN (National Liberation Front) (Algeria), 137
Fonfrède, Henry, 10
Foucault, Michel, 12, 22
Fourierists, 184
Fourth Republic, 68, 71, 75

France: as bearer of democracy, 5, 52, 68, 71, 106, 113–14, 116; culture and values transmitted to colonies, 77–78; current French-Indian population, 165; French-Indian people migrating to, 156, 160–61, 165; as "friend" or "family" to India, 74, 76, 86–87, 89, 92–93, 106, 113–14, 136, 143, 203–4; glorification in French India, 52–53, 68, 74; as haven for anti-British organizing, 52–54, 57; Indian cultural activity in, 166; Indian population before 1954, 165–66, 256n86; Ministry of Foreign Affairs, 64, 121, 124, 128, 147, 149; national identity, 112; North African population in, 168; popular attitudes toward India, 163; printing of seditious literature in, 45, 53, 59, 60; race in, 158–61, 167; South Asian population in, 161–62, 167–68; treatment of South Asian immigrants, 159, 161–62, 163–64; withdrawal from Indian territories, 135, 141–48

*France-Inde*, 166

François, Joseph, 40

Franco-Prussian War, 161

freedom fighters, 124, 130; French India as haven for, 97; French support of, 78; recognition by Indian government, 25, 44, 115, 136

French Revolution, xvi

French Congo, 51, 70, 234n67

French East India Company, xv, 16

French imperialism, 16–17, 90, 91, 97–98, 99, 100; Ashram as part of, 103; François Baron accused of supporting, 91; in Indochina, 38; and métis people, 81; opposition to, 97–98, 99–100, 111, 125–26; support in French India, 111; violence of, 203

French India: anti-French sentiment in, 85–86; archives of, 21, 38; as a borderland, 19; borders with British India, 33, 38; borders with India, 69, 109, 119; categorizing populations of, 27; defined, 6; existence after decolonization, 7, 29; French depiction of, 177; as haven for anticolonial activity, 37, 38, 42, 47, 61; historical narratives of, 15; involvement in French politics, 76–77; languages of, 20; location of archives, 21, 24; violence on borders, 109, 110–11

French India Congress Party, 91, 115, 116–17

French India National Congress (FINC), 94, 97, 99, 118; conflict with Communist Party of French India (CPFI), 100

French Indian Communist Party. *See* Communist Party of French India (CPFI)

French-Indian people: alienation from North India, 150; citizenship, 77, 93, 142, 144, 146–49, 151–54, 154–56; cultural links to France, 77–78, 86, 87, 93, 133, 136, 142, 145, 149; culture and history, 76, 106; current population in France, 165; definitions of, 29, 93; diaspora, 93, 95, 143, 155; fate after merger, 135–36, 146–48, 149, 160–61; France's attempts to gain votes from, 75; French stereotypes about, 164–65, 169; hyphenation of term, 223n1; involvement in French politics, 76–77; migrating to France, 157, 160–61, 165; nationality of, 58, 114–15, 136, 142, 145, 146–49, 151, 154; as neither French nor Indian,

168, 169–70, 200; racial classification, 77; stereotypes, 168, 172; treatment in France, 159, 161–62, 163, 172; views on joining French Union, 93, 94, 96, 98–99, 150. *See also* Pondichériens

French Indian Students' Congress (Congrés des étudiants), 97, 99

French India Peoples' Convention, 115–16

French India Socialist Party (FISP), 91, 96–97, 100, 114, 124

"French Pockets in India" pamphlet, 133

French Revolution, 38, 53, 76, 77, 78, 81, 93, 129–30, 236–37n118

French Union, 73; codified, 71; France's desire for India to join, 75, 76, 85–86; French depiction of, 113–14; French Indians' views on joining, 27, 69, 72–73, 93–94, 98–100, 114, 115–16; promoted as end of colonialism, 72; Sri Aurobindo Ghose's view on joining, 103–4; term first used, 71; V. Subbiah's view on joining, 106

Gaebelé, Yvonne Robert, 15, 85
Gandhi, Indira, 175, 189
Gandhi, Leela, 183
Gandhi, M. K., 38, 44, 46; admiration for France, 38, 81; on caste, 80–81, 240n45; education, 71; on fate of French India, 114; on French India, 114; on Portuguese India, 74; strategy of political resistance, 137; support from French India Peoples' Convention, 115
Gandon, Armond, 147
Ganése, 126
Gaudart, Edmond, 15
Geneva Agreements, xvii

Germany, 3, 22, 41, 57, 112–13, 165, 232n36, 256n85

Ghose, Barindra Kumar, 50, 234n64

Ghose, Sri Aurobindo: anticolonialism, 45, 66, 182, 197; arrest and trial, 46; arrival in Pondicherry, 13, 47, 57; biographical information, xvi, xvii, 3, 43–45; biographies of, 44; cultural identity, 44–45, 49; death, 152; education, 44, 49; employment, 45; exile of, 27, 49–50; on French Union, 103–4; marriage, 243n78; nationalism, 171; publications, 46, 47; relationship with Mira Alfassa, 87–88, 89, 171, 182, 243n79; retirement, 52; spirituality, 46, 47–48, 50–51, 182–83; support for dual citizenship, 103–4, 152–53; yoga practice, 48, 51, 176, 260n29

Giri, V. V., 175

Goa, 10, 74, 116, 187, 231n29, 239n20, 260n38

Goonda Raj, 110; attempts to end, 137; government report on, 120, 121, 124; language about, 189; and referendum, 110; as threat to democracy, 119–20; use of term, 247n6

goondas: around Chandernagore referendum, 116–17; blamed for border violence, 109–10, 129, 130, 132–33; blamed for referendum cancellation, 110, 119–20, 132–33; characterizations of, 121, 123; confused with refugees, 125; disappearance from public discourse, 143; French state responsibility for, 120, 124; media representations, 120–21; as "others," 110, 129, 130; public opposition to, 123–24; as threat to democracy, 110, 117, 119–20, 123, 132

GOPIO (Global Organization for People of Indian Origin), 167
Goubert, Edouard (E. G. Pillai): activism, 133, 134; biographical information, 25–26, 96–97; changing attitudes, 205; media portrayals, 134; named as goonda, 124; national identity, 134, 154, 253n21; opposition to merger with India, 125, 133; public opinion of, 25–26, 134–35; street named for, 25
Gupta, Nolini, 52

Heehs, Peter, 44, 176
heteronormativity, 87, 88
*Hindu nesan*, 78
*Hindu* newspaper, 117
Hindu religion: in Bengal, 39, 44; and caste system, 78, 80, 84, 93, 95, 109; colonizers' views of, 67, 74, 186; as Indian national identity, 5, 20, 167, 171–72; intermarriage, 83; persecution of, 84; in Pondicherry, 2, 82, 174; at Sri Aurobindo Ashram, 90, 171–72; Western fetishization, 164. *See also* caste
*Hindustan Times*, 124
hippies, 164, 178, 187, 188
Ho, Chi Minh, 71, 131
Houssaine, Mohammad, 101
Huillet, N., 81–82
Hyderabad, 116

immigration detention, 42
Indian Congress Party, 39, 91, 97, 114, 115, 116–17
Indian Constitution, xvii, 69, 160
*India* newspaper, 60
Indian independence from Britain, 65, 67, 68, 69; effects on France, 72–73; observances of, 104–5; violence, 105

Indian National Congress, 65, 66, 121, 122f
Indian Passport Act (1920), 61. *See also* passports
Indian Penal Code (IPC), 45–46
Indian Professional Association (IPA), 167
*Indian Sociologist*, 53, 54
Indian state: and border violence, 109–10; continuation of British policy, 28, 204; French India Peoples' Convention, 115; and Goonda Raj, 110; language policies, 156; postcolonial, 5, 10, 69; push for merger, 96, 137; recognition of freedom fighters, 10, 25, 44, 115, 136; refugee crisis, 109; relationship with Sri Aurobindo Ashram, 152; restrictions on foreigners, 125, 157; violence enacted by, 119, 132
*India's Utopia* documentary, 3
Indigenous people: class, 83; and colonial settlement, 177, 184; in French India, 18, 63; in North America, 13; in Pondicherry, 65, 183–84; renouncing Indigenous status, 80–81; returning land to, 8, 9
Indochina, 131, 231n17; anti-French movement, 71; French at war in, xvii, 131; French colonization, 14, 38–39, 76, 98, 99, 106; French-Indian diaspora in, 93, 96, 231n17, 254n44
Indo-French Agreement, 116
Institut de Civilisation indienne, 166
Integral Yoga, 51, 176, 183–84, 260n29
interracial relationships, 82, 83
Islam, 15, 207. *See also* Muslims
Israel, 177, 180
Iyengar, V. Ramaswamy, 48

Jammu and Kashmir, 10, 21, 112–13, 116
Jani, Mulshankar, 105
Janvier-Kamiyama, Philippe, 201–2
Jha, Rega, 3
Jinnah, M. A., 44, 71
Jorgenson, Ronald, 196

Karaikal, xvii, 6, 7f, 17, 34, 155
Karaikal National Congress, 97
Karaikal Students Congress, 97
Kashmir and Jammu, 10, 21, 112–13, 116
Katz, Cindi, 23
Khan, Ibrahim, xv
Khan, Akbar Ali, 17
Khan, Mahomet Dervich, 17
Khan, Mahomet Ousman, 17
Khandelwal, Meena, 199
Kresser, P., 128
Krishnamurthy, B., 92
Krishnavarma, Shymaji, 53, 54, 66

Labernadie, Margueritte V., 15
labor organizing, 72, 90–91, 100–1
Lagisquet, Capitaine, 129
Landy, Pierre, 141
*La Republique Française*, 150
L'Association les Comptoirs des Indes, 206
Lawlor, Deborah, 192, 195
Lawlor, Robert, 192, 194
*l'Éclair* (newspaper), 54
*Le Figaro* (newspaper), 131
*Le Monde* (newspaper), 131, 153
Le Mouvement Cosmique, 51
*Le Petit Pondichérien/Putuvei vaci*, 78
*Le Progrès de l'Inde française*, 78
"Les trois mondes de Pondichéry" documentary, 1–3, 29, 173–75
*Le Trait-d'Union*, 101, 102f, 136, 164

*L'Hindou*, 78
*loges*, xv, 6, 38–39, 42
Louis, Lourdes Tirouvanziam, 83
Louis XVI, king of France, 17
Lugones, María, 9

Madras, 16–17, 56, 60, 109
Mahé, xvii, 6, 7f, 17, 34, 155, 164
major history: defined, 22; forces that sustain, 23
maps: distances between French Indian territories, 7f; French communes in Pondicherry, 35f; French Indian territories, xviiif
margins, 21–22, 23, 24, 27, 93
Mariadassou, Antoine, 88, 99
*Marie-Claire* magazine, 191
Martin, François, xv, 15; role in French Indian history, 15–16, 18
Martineau, Alfred, 15, 226n34
Matrimandir, 194
memory: colonial memory of French India, 5, 6, 144, 206, 225n14; memorialization, 21–22
Menon, Krishnan, 166
merger of French territories with Indian Union: aftermath for residents, 142–45, 146–49, 156, 160–61; Ashram's position on, 103–4; citizenship, 146–49; French-Indians' concerns about, 106–7, 124–25; French state views on, 116; French withdrawal from territories, 135; Indian state push for, 130–31, 137; media coverage, 130–31, 133; opposition to, 93–94, 125, 133, 148; political parties' views on, 91, 106–7, 114, 115, 118; referendum on. *See* referendum on future of French India support for, 91–92, 103, 118. *See also* French Union

métis people, 149; becoming part of white class, 82; French attitudes toward, 81–82, 148; French citizenship, 77; in French India, 18; origin and use of term, 82, 241n55; in Pondicherry, 84

Mignolo, Walter, 9, 22

migration: of French-Indians to France, 29, 157, 160–61, 165; of Indians to France, before 1954, 165–66; of North Africans to France, 163–64, 168

Miles, William F. S., 157–58

Minh, Ho Chi, 71, 131

Minor, Robert N., 181

minor borders, 22, 42, 199

minor history, 22–23

Mitra, Durba, 109

modernity, 9, 14, 21

Moniga, Radhika, 20

More, Thomas, 12, 184

Morin, Louise, 57

Mother, the. *See* Alfassa, Mira (the Mother)

multiculturalism, 89, 104, 153, 154, 177

Muslims: in Bengal, 39; characterizations of, 67, 109, 112; colonizers' views of, 67; in France, 168; French-Indian, 80, 95; as Indian nationals, 113; intermarriage, 83; in Jammu and Kashmir, 113; opposition to French colonization, 96; in Pondicherry, 82; religion as identifying marker, 18

Naicker, Sellane, 123

Namakkal, Srinivasan, 206

Napoleonic Wars, 34

nationalism: anticolonial, 5, 39, 46, 47, 68, 87, 106, 114, 142, 170; characteristics of national identity, 58, 87; criticism of, 100; democracy as, 137; French, 112, 151; French-Indian views of, 27; growth of Indian, 67, 94; imperial forms, 8; important figures, 44, 48, 57, 171; Indian, 114; linked to terrorism, 47; mainstream movement in India, 74; narratives of, 19–20, 21; publications, 60; secular, 113; unity of, 114, 118, 204; view of goondas, 132–33; and violence, 136

nationality, 144–45; as biologically determined, 87; choosing between French and Indian, 65, 143, 146–47, 150–51, 156; definitions of, 65, 100; difficulties in determining, 27, 55, 56, 58, 63–64, 129; dual, 151–54, 170; French view of, 148–49; and Partition, 111; of Pondichérians, 169; relationship to territory, 111, 112. *See also* citizenship

nations: definitions of, 111; Indigenous, 8, 9, 13; maintenance, 20–21; origin narratives, 18; relations between, 87, 91; relationships to states, 111, 112; in utopian thinking, 175

Nehru, Jawaharlal, xvii, 44, 46, 57, 65, 91, 92, 132; Ashramites' correspondence with, 152–53; education, 71; media portrayals, 131–32; on Portuguese India, 74; as prime minister, 145–46, 149; visiting France, 166

Neogy, Ajit, 69, 134

*New York Times*, 191

Nirodbaran, 88, 104

nostalgia, 6, 29, 144

"nowhere people," 143, 169, 172

Olcott, Henry, 13. *See also* Theosophy

Orientalism, 90, 163, 165, 167, 171, 174, 183

Ostrorog, Stanislas, xvii, 124, 146–47, 154, 155

Paillet, Georges, 165–66
Pakistan, 5; border disputes, 20, 108, 112, 113; creation of, xvii, 105, 137; migrants to France, 167; refugees, 108; violence around creation, 105
Palestine, 61–62
Pandit, M. P., 187
Paquirissamypoulle, Maurice, 98
Parassouramin, K. S., 114
Partition: border disputes during, 112; histories of, 108; and nationality, 111; refugee crisis, 28, 98, 108, 109, 117, 137; violence of, 26, 72, 98, 109–10
passports, 60–61; as evidence of belonging, 37, 58, 65, 112, 161–62; historical roots of, 61, 236–37n118; Indian Passport Act (1920), 61; requirement to show, 43, 62, 64, 156–57, 161–62; used for surveillance, 28, 36, 112, 137
Patriotes de l'Inde française, 96
period of option, 144, 147, 154, 155
Pillai, Ananda Ranga, 15, 242n65; view of Mme Jeanne Dupleix, 84–85
Pillai, E. G.. *See* Goubert, Edouard (E. G. Pillai)
Pillai, K. Muthu, 114
Pinton, Paul, 187–88
police: British, 47, 48–49, 57; in Chandernagore referendum, 116–17, 118; enforcing borders, 34, 35, 48, 108; French, 41, 42, 52, 56, 57, 59, 161–62; French-Indian, 173–74; goondaism by, 124; Indian, 60, 107, 119, 131; killing of, 125–29; laws governing, xvi, 34, 41; violence, 207; violence by, 90, 101, 123, 131
poll tax, 62, 63, 64

Pondichérians: access to archives, 24; attitudes toward Ashram, 48, 89; citizenship, 145, 157; education, 78; as embodying colonialism, 169; in France, 55, 167–68, 206; hostility toward, 168; languages spoken, 78; media portrayals, 169, 173–75; as neither French nor Indian, 136, 141, 169–70, 200; racialization of, 158–59; use of term, 27
Pondicherry, 173–75; archives of, 24; arrival of anticolonial revolutionaries, 60; colonial history, 223n2; construction of borders in, 34, 60–61; current population, 168; Dutch control of, 16; French conceptions of, 164–65; French culture in, 145–46, 149; historiography, 5; maps, 7f, 35f; nationality of residents, 63, 135, 141, 142, 155; popular association with Auroville, 3; as product of colonialism, 14; as refuge from British India, 49, 55; residents as "nowhere people," 143, 169, 172; segregation in, 160; as site of coloniality, 14; as site of global experimentation, 12; as site of modernity, 14; struggle for sovereignty, 10; surveillance in, 48–49, 52; tourism, 201, 203; as trading post, 16
*Pontikseriyen*, 78
Portugal: arrival in India, 125; control of Goa, 10, 16, 74, 260n38; as imperial state, 20; Indian colonies, 20, 69, 74–75, 231n29, 239n20; Indians of Portuguese heritage, 77, 83, 84, 241n60
Pouchepadass, Emanuelle, 105–6
Prashad, Vijay, 168

INDEX [297]

Princely States, 10, 11, 20, 21, 45, 66, 69, 112, 228n56
prisons, 33–34, 42, 46, 47, 50, 75, 162, 234n63
Puducherry. *See* Pondicherry
Purushothaman, R.L.L. (Purushottam, R. L. [Reddiar]), 94, 118

Quijano, Aníbal, 9

race, 29; and anticolonialism, 87; classification of French-Indian people, 77, 158–61; color-blindness, 155, 158–59, 185; connected to religious and economic status, 83; in development of French India, 81; eighteenth-century conceptions of, 83; in France, 158–61; interracial relationships, 82, 83; racial privilege of Aurovilians, 182, 186, 196; state recognition of, 159
racism, 160, 167, 188. *See also* xenophobia
Radhakrishnan, Rajagopalan, 19
Rajkumar, N. V., 36f, 114, 120
Rama, S. R., 55
referendum on future of French India, 71, 72; blame for cancellation, 110; cancellation of popular vote, 114, 132, 137; election observers, 117–18; fairness of vote, 106, 116–17, 120, 121; Indo-French Agreement, 116; opposition to, 91, 115–16, 117; results, 117; support for, 150; violence around, 131, 132. *See also* merger of French territories with Indian Union
refugees: anticolonial Indians as, 52; from British India, in France, 165; confused with goondas, 125; detention of, 42; from goondas, 120;  media portrayals, 131; resulting from Partition, 108, 109, 117, 137
religion: as factor in marriage, 83; as identity marker, 18, 58, 111; Mira Alfassa's views on, 86, 181–82; oppression due to, 53; racialization of, 160
*renonçants*, 79–80, 125
*Republique française*, 78
Rhodes, Cecil, 8
Richard, Paul, xvi, 51, 87, 186, 234n71
Richier, François, 202
Robin, Corey, 137
Roucher, Daniel, 187
Rous, Jean, 166

Said, Edward, 49
Saint-Hilaire, Philippe Barbier (Pavitra), 174, 234–35n73, 257–58n110
Saint-Simonians, 13, 184
Salazar, António de Oliveira, 75
Samboo, Gopaljee, 165–67
Sargisson, Lucy, 13–14, 184, 185
Sarraillon, Carol, 206
Satprem (Bernard Enginger), 88, 153, 257–58n110
Schomburg, Reginald, 33, 37, 62, 63
Scott, James C., 34
Second Treaty of Paris (1815), xvi, 17, 34
sedition: charges against Sri Aurobindo Ghose, 13; laws against, 42, 45–46, 53; printing of seditious literature abroad, 45, 53, 59, 60
Sen, Sailendra Nath, 116
Servan-Schreiber, Catherine, 163
settler colonialism, 5; Auroville as site for, 176; displacement of native people, 9; relationship to colonialism, 176–77; scholarship on, 12, 176–77, 258n9; in utopian

settlements, 12, 185, 224n11; violence of, 9
settler utopianism, 3, 5, 11, 224n11
Seven Years' War, 17, 34
Shepard, Todd, 26
Singh, Bhagat, 46
Singh, Kewal, 141
Singha, Radhika, 61
smuggling, 33, 41, 57, 59–60, 121, 133–34
Social and Democratic Union party, 91
socialism: at Auroville, 179, 180, 183; French, 54; French India Socialist Party (FISP), 91, 96–97, 100, 114, 124; in utopian settlements, 13, 184, 188
Société de l'histoire de l'Inde française (SHIF), 15, 78
Soubramanien, 99
South Asians: diaspora, 144–45; as "model minority," 168; population in France, 161–62, 163–64, 165, 167–68, 169, 206, 256n80
sovereignty, 108
spirituality, 170–71; "alternative," 51; at Ashram, 174, 189–90; in Auroville, 178, 179, 180, 181–82, 187, 188, 191, 193, 194, 197, 261n73; in colonial spaces, 51; "Eastern," 51, 167, 182, 183, 259–60n28; India as source of, 89, 90, 152, 163, 167, 171, 174, 178, 180, 185–86, 197; of Mira Alfassa, 51, 87, 170–71, 174, 178, 181–83, 193, 197; spiritual motherhood, 87; spiritual settlement as colonialism, 176–77; spiritual tourism, 5, 14, 172, 178, 185–86; of Sri Aurobindo Ghose, 46, 50–51, 182–83. *See also* Theosophy
Sri Aurobindo. *See* Ghose, Sri Aurobindo

Sri Aurobindo Ashram: apolitical stance, 88, 103, 189–90; archives of, 44; as asset to French Union, 86–87; emphasis on French language and culture, 86; founding of, xvi; growth under the Mother, 52; local attitudes toward, 88–89, 103, 171, 189, 190–91; media representations, 2, 87, 174–75; population, 2; power in Pondicherry, 171–72; as product of colonialism, 14, 48, 86; promotional materials, 189–90; property, 89, 103, 144, 246n245; relations with French government, 88, 90, 103, 171–72; relations with Indian government, 171–72, 189; relations with local government, 189; residents, 171; residents' motivations for joining, 88; school, 90, 242n72; separation from Sri Aurobindo Society, 198; as site of exile, 28; spiritual worldview, 174, 189–90; support for dual nationality, 151, 152–53; ties to government officials, 2; violence against residents, 105; Western views of, 87
Sri Aurobindo Centers, 176, 191
Sri Aurobindo Society (SAS), 176, 191, 198
states: colonial nature of, 154; decolonization, 68, 203–4; establishing power, 108; imperial, 20, 28; maintenance, 22, 35; postcolonial, 11, 65; Princely States, 10, 11, 20, 21, 45, 66, 69, 112, 228n56; relations between, 87, 91, 113; relationships to nations, 111, 112; violence by, 131–32, 203–4
Stoler, Ann Laura, 22–23
Stovall, Tyler, 159–60
Students Congress of French India, 97, 99

Subbiah, Varadarajulu, 80–81; activism, 56, 66, 90–91; biographical information, 55; changing attitudes, 205; education, 56; expulsion from Pondicherry, 57–58; memoir, 56–57; named as goonda, 124; nationality, 55–56, 58, 236n101; political affiliation, 56, 57, 90; political career, 56; position on French Union, 72, 89, 91–92, 106, 142; statelessness, 90–91, 92; surveillance of, 57
*Sudandiram*, 92
Sultan, Tipu, 15, 17, 40
Sundararajan, Saroja, 68
*Sunday* newspaper, 168
Suramangalam incident, 110–11, 125–30, 127f
surveillance: of anticolonial activists, 40–41, 42–43, 48, 57, 60; at borders, 36, 37, 39, 48–49, 119; in Chandernagore, 40–41; of colonial subjects, 28, 119; in Pondicherry, 48–49, 52
swadeshis, 40

Tamil language, 1, 6, 84, 156, 195; in Auroville, 178, 180, 195; government communication in, 145–46; names, 80, 196; as official language, 255n50; political literature in, 89, 96, 100, 114, 131–32; publications, 78, 92, 239–40n31; spoken by French people, 78
Tamil Nadu state, 6; Auroville, 176, 199; geography, 3, 6; relation to Pondicherry, 6, 157
Tamil people, 148; author's family, 206–7; diaspora, 145; displaced by Auroville, 177, 178, 179, 180–81, 183–84, 192–93, 194–95, 196, 204; in France, 206; French citizenship, 77, 148, 177; participation in Ashram, 2; physical separation from Aurovilians, 5; relations with Aurovilians, 196–97, 198–99; Sri Lankan, 145, 206
taxes, 43, 63, 64, 65
Tegart, Charles, 41, 62
terrorism: Aurobindo Ghose accused of, 46; at borders, 109–10; linked to Indian nationalism, 47, 54, 136; linked to partition of Bengal, 40; media portrayals, 119–20, 136; political groups classified as, 40; by state, 119, 129. *See also* violence
*The Hindu* newspaper, 126, 130–31, 234n64
Théon, Alma, 51, 234n66
Théon, Max, 51, 234n66
Theosophy, 13, 51, 183, 235–36n73, 259–60n28
third Anglo-Mysore War (1790–1791), 17
Thulasingham, 126, 128, 249n49
*Times of India*, 117, 118, 120
*topas* people, xvi, 80, 81–82, 83
tourism, 162–63; in Auroville, 14, 180, 199, 200; in former colonies, 29, 142, 186; in France, 161–62, 166; in Pondicherry, 14, 142, 200, 201, 203; spiritual, 5, 14, 172, 178, 185–86; at Sri Aurobindo Ashram, 171
Treaty of Aix-la-Chapelle (1749), 17
Treaty of Cession (1956), 142, 143, 146, 149, 154–55, 165, 166–67
Treaty of Paris (1763), 17, 34
Tuck, Eve, 9–10, 11, 177
*Twelve Years with Sri Aurobindo*, 88

University of Cape Town, 8
utopianism, 177, 183; and colonialism, 13, 184–85, 188; defined, 172; effects on non-Western people, 184; settler

utopianism, 3, 5, 11; in twenty-first century, 183

utopian settlements, 197; in nineteenth century, 13, 184; in North America, 13; relation to colonialism, 12, 184; socialist, 13, 184; Western, 199. *See also* Auroville

utopias, 184; France as, 53, 98, 103–4; origin of term, 12

van Schendel, Willem, 34

Veracini, Lorenzo, 176

*ville blanche*, 1, 2, 3, 55, 65, 86, 160, 201, 202

*ville noire*, 1, 2, 3, 55, 65, 86, 160

violence: access to medical treatment, 123; against Ashram residents, 105; against protesters, 101; around Chandernagore referendum, 118; around independence from Britain, 105; around Partition, 98; on borders of French India, 28, 109, 132, 135; by French state in colonies, 14; governments placing blame for, 109; incident at Suramangalam, 126–30; by Indian state, 119

Vuddamalay, Vasoodeven, 163

Ward, Stuart, 10

weapons, 37, 40, 41, 54, 59, 117, 123–24, 133

Weber, Jacques, 15, 79, 134–35, 157

Weber, Jean-Paul, 141

Wilder, Gary, 27

Wolfe, Patrick, 12

World War I, 151

World War II, 70, 151, 202

xenophobia, 163–64, 167. *See also* racism

Yanam, xvii, 6, 7f, 17, 34, 155

Yang, K. Wayne, 9–10, 11, 177

yoga, 48, 51, 164, 176, 184, 193

Zamindar, Vazira Fazila-Yacoobali, 20, 26, 111

Zeevarathnam, 118

COLUMBIA STUDIES IN INTERNATIONAL AND GLOBAL HISTORY
Cemil Aydin, Timothy Nunan, and Dominic Sachsenmaier, Series Editors

Cemil Aydin, *The Politics of Anti-Westernism in Asia: Visions of World Order in Pan-Islamic and Pan-Asian Thought*
Adam M. McKeown, *Melancholy Order: Asian Migration and the Globalization of Borders*
Patrick Manning, *The African Diaspora: A History Through Culture*
James Rodger Fleming, *Fixing the Sky: The Checkered History of Weather and Climate Control*
Steven Bryan, *The Gold Standard at the Turn of the Twentieth Century: Rising Powers, Global Money, and the Age of Empire*
Heonik Kwon, *The Other Cold War*
Samuel Moyn and Andrew Sartori, eds., *Global Intellectual History*
Alison Bashford, *Global Population: History, Geopolitics, and Life on Earth*
Adam Clulow, *The Company and the Shogun: The Dutch Encounter with Tokugawa Japan*
Richard W. Bulliet, *The Wheel: Inventions and Reinventions*
Simone M. Müller, *Wiring the World: The Social and Cultural Creation of Global Telegraph Networks*
Will Hanley, *Identifying with Nationality: Europeans, Ottomans, and Egyptians in Alexandria*
Perin E. Gürel, *The Limits of Westernization: A Cultural History of America in Turkey*
Dominic Sachsenmaier, *Global Entanglements of a Man Who Never Traveled: A Seventeenth-Century Chinese Christian and His Conflicted Worlds*
Perrin Selcer, *The UN and the Postwar Origins of the Global Environment: From World Community to Spaceship Earth*
Ulbe Bosma, *The Making of a Periphery: How Island Southeast Asia Became a Mass Exporter of Labor*
Raja Adal, *Beauty in the Age of Empire: Japan, Egypt, and the Global History of Aesthetic Education*
Mona L. Siegel, *Peace on Our Terms: The Global Battle for Women's Rights After the First World War*
Nicole CuUnjieng Aboitiz, *Asian Place, Filipino Nation: A Global Intellectual History of the Philippine Revolution, 1887–1912*
Michael Christopher Low, *Imperial Mecca: Ottoman Arabia and the Indian Ocean Hajj*

GPSR Authorized Representative: Easy Access System Europe, Mustamäe tee
50, 10621 Tallinn, Estonia, gpsr.requests@easproject.com

www.ingramcontent.com/pod-product-compliance
Lightning Source LLC
Chambersburg PA
CBHW021354290426
44108CB00010B/240